T0349727

Librarians on the Internet
Impact on Reference Services

Forthcoming topics in *The Reference Librarian* series:

• Reference Services Planning in the 90s, Number 43

Published:

Librarians
on the Internet

Impact on Reference Services

Robin Kinder
Editor

The Haworth Press, Inc.
New York · London · Norwood (Australia)

Librarians on the Internet: Impact on Reference Services has also been published as *The Reference Librarian*, Numbers 41/42 1994.

The development, preparation, and publication of this work has been undertaken with great care. However, the publisher, employees, editors, and agents of The Haworth Press and all imprints of The Haworth Press, Inc., including The Haworth Medical Press and Pharmaceutical Products Press, are not responsible for any errors contained herein or for consequences that may ensue from use of materials or information contained in this work. Opinions expressed by the author(s) are not necessarily those of The Haworth Press, Inc.

The Haworth Press, Inc., 10 Alice Street, Binghamton, NY 13904-1580 USA

Library of Congress Cataloging-in-Publication Data

Librarians on the Internet: impact on reference services / Robin Kinder, editor.
    p. cm.
    "Has also been published as The reference librarian, volume 19, numbers 41/42, 1994"–T.p. verso.
    Includes bibliographical references and index.
    ISBN 1-56024-672-3 (alk. paper)
    · 1. Reference services (Libraries)–United States–Data processing. 2. Library information networks–United States. 3. Internet (Computer network) I. Kinder, Robin.
Z711.L487 1994   94-18593
025.04–dc20   CIP

INDEXING & ABSTRACTING

Contributions to this publication are selectively indexed or abstracted in print, electronic, online, or CD-ROM version(s) of the reference tools and information services listed below. This list is current as of the copyright date of this publication. See the end of this section for additional notes.

- *Current Awareness Bulletin,* Association for Information Management, Information House, 20-24 Old Street, London EC1V 9AP, England

- *Current Index to Journals in Education,* Syracuse University, 4-194 Center for Science and Technology, Syracuse, NY 13244-4100

- *Educational Administration Abstracts,* Sage Publications, Inc., 2455 Teller Road, Newbury Park, CA 91320

- *Index to Periodical Articles Related to Law,* University of Texas, 727 East 26th Street, Austin, TX 78705

- *Information Science Abstracts,* Plenum Publishing Company, 233 Spring Street, New York, NY 10013-1578

- *INSPEC Information Services,* Institution of Electrical Engineers, Michael Faraday House, Six Hills Way, Stevenage, Herts SG1 2AY, England

- *Library & Information Science Abstracts (LISA),* Bowker-Saur Ltd., Maypole House, Maypole Road, East Grinstead, West Sussex, RH19 1HH England

- *Library Literature,* The H.W. Wilson Company, 950 University Avenue, Bronx, NY 10452

- *Newsletter of Library and Information Services,* China Sci-Tech Book Review, Library of Academia Sinica, 8 Kexueyuan Nanlu, Zhongguancun, Beijing 100080, People's Republic of China

- *OT BibSys,* American Occupational Therapy Foundation, P.O. Box 1725, Rockville, MD 20849-1725

- *Referativnyi Zhurnal (Abstracts Journal of the Institute of Scientific Information of the Republic of Russia),* The Institute of Scientific Information, Baltijskaja ul., 14, Moscow A-219, Republic of Russia

- *Sage Public Administration Abstracts,* Sage Publications, Inc., 2455 Teller Road, Newbury Park, CA 91320

- *The Informed Librarian,* Infosources Publishing, 140 Norma Road, Teaneck, NJ 07666

SPECIAL BIBLIOGRAPHIC NOTES

related to special journal issues (separates)
and indexing/abstracting

☐ indexing/abstracting services in this list will also cover material in the "separate" that is co-published simultaneously with Haworth's special thematic journal issue or DocuSerial. Indexing/abstracting usually covers material at the article/chapter level.

☐ monographic co-editions are intended for either non-subscribers or libraries which intend to purchase a second copy for their circulating collections.

☐ monographic co-editions are reported to all jobbers/wholesalers/approval plans. The source journal is listed as the "series" to assist the prevention of duplicate purchasing in the same manner utilized for books-in-series.

☐ to facilitate user/access services all indexing/abstracting services are encouraged to utilize the co-indexing entry note indicated at the bottom of the first page of each article/chapter/contribution.

☐ this is intended to assist a library user of any reference tool (whether print, electronic, online, or CD-ROM) to locate the monographic version if the library has purchased this version but not a subscription to the source journal.

☐ individual articles/chapters in any Haworth publication are also available through the Haworth Document Delivery Services (HDDS).

Librarians on the Internet: Impact on Reference Services

CONTENTS

ABOUT THE EDITOR

Robin Kinder, MLS, is a reference librarian at William Allan Neilson Library, Smith College, Northhampton, MA. Her subject interests include literature, government documents, law, and women's studies. She is the Associate Editor of *The Reference Librarian* and *The Acquisitions Librarian*.

Introduction–
Librarians on the Internet

In February, 1993, I posted a Call for Articles to several discussion lists on the Internet, including Lib-Ref, PACS-L, and BI-L. The articles would comprise a collection concerning the Internet's impact on library services. Subject areas were very broad: Articles on bibliographic instruction, reference services, gophers, VERONICA, NREN, sources in subject areas, and evaluation of the Internet were listed as possible topics. The only prohibition was a general rule that the introductions to the Internet, its origins and history, remain limited, unless it illuminated an author's particular topic. The reason is the existence of a number of well-known titles on the Internet, literally and figuratively, to assist the reader.

I kept to a general and open-ended framework in order to discover the ways librarians would respond to the request. Where and why and how they were actively involved in the Internet are intriguing questions. Libraries have evolved over so many years and contain traditions of organization. The Internet–disorganized, non-hierarchical (in its beginnings), fluid, mutative–challenges the logic of the librarian. How responsive are librarians to the Internet? What are their interests? What are their projects? What does the Internet mean to their world? Simple questions. These articles answer a few of those questions, but raise more questions, a perpetual state as long as the Internet remains open and free.

In these articles, the contributors discuss gophers, VERONICA, science sources, virtual libraries, electronic text, bibliographic instruction, evaluation, training, and implementation of information

[Haworth co-indexing entry note]: "Introduction–Librarians on the Internet." Kinder, Robin. Co-published simultaneously in *The Reference Librarian* (The Haworth Press, Inc.) No. 41/42, 1994, pp. 1-2; and: *Librarians on the Internet: Impact on Reference Services* (ed: Robin Kinder) The Haworth Press, Inc., 1994, pp. 1-2. Multiple copies of this article/chapter may be purchased from The Haworth Document Delivery Center [1-800-3-HAWORTH; 9:00 a.m. - 5:00 p.m. (EST)].

1

services, to name only a few. These are not representative articles on the Internet, nor are they meant to be. They are representative of librarians confronting a new task–essentially a virtual library–and their work on this task. This collection represents one of the first attempts to publish a volume of articles by librarians on the Internet.

In the final editing process, I received numerous calls and e-mail from contributors making last minute changes, as they had connected to the Internet for a last look and discovered menus and search protocols completely altered. In discussion with authors, we agreed that this book would undoubtedly be dated before it would be published, due to the changing nature of the Internet. It is interesting to publish an historical account of a current phenomenon, but this is the realm of the Internet. This volume is simply a point in time.

It is to be hoped that others will follow. Entire publications can be devoted to the Internet and . . . bibliographic instruction, NREN, reference services, electronic texts, gophers, sources on the Internet, and WAIS . . . Evaluation of the Internet needs to be addressed. Librarians' involvement in campus wide information services is another area requiring negotiation, skill and expertise. So many issues concerning the Internet belong to librarians, and the only limitation appears to be one of time. There is clearly not enough time and staff to devote to the Internet, as library services are expanding and clientele is no longer well-defined and familiar. It is clear, however, that librarians ignoring the Internet are at a distinct disadvantage in the world of information. It is not possible to neglect the Internet for long. These articles attest to that fact.

Robin Kinder

Getting Started on the Net

Karen R. Diaz

SUMMARY. This introductory essay illustrates the opportunities the Internet provides for the reference librarian, provides practical points of entry for experimentation, defines some common Internet terms, and steers the librarian to sources that will help in getting a better handle on the big picture. Tracing a few introductory steps will hopefully give a broader context to the resources that follow in this issue.

All beginnings are hard.

> –Chaim Potok in *The Chosen*

The Internet has become a buzz word of the library world. Nearly every workshop and conference, it seems, has at least one session on the Internet. Every such gathering seems to be packed. There is an intense curiosity on the part of those who have never used it, and

---

Karen R. Diaz is Reference Librarian and Online Coordinator in the Information Services Department at the Ohio State University Library. She belongs to the American Library Association and the Academic Library Association of Ohio.

[Haworth co-indexing entry note]: "Getting Started on the Net." Diaz, Karen R. Co-published simultaneously in *The Reference Librarian* (The Haworth Press, Inc.) No. 41/42, 1994, pp. 3-24; and: *Librarians on the Internet: Impact on Reference Services* (ed: Robin Kinder) The Haworth Press, Inc., 1994, pp. 3-24. Multiple copies of this article/chapter may be purchased from The Haworth Document Delivery Center [1-800-3-HAWORTH; 9:00 a.m. - 5:00 p.m. (EST)].

a desire for more information from those who only know one or two aspects of it. Users know how quickly the Internet grows and are eager to hear of new features and resources.

The rapid growth of the Internet community has made it almost impossible to find librarians who have not participated in its use, much less those who have not heard of it. But this very fact creates a problem for the neophyte. How does one "break in"? How does one begin to ask questions? How does one find a way to grasp the new jargon bandied about? How does one know WHY to learn about the Internet?

The approach taken in this introductory essay is to illustrate some of the opportunities the Internet provides for the reference librarian, to provide practical points of entry for experimentation, to define some common Internet terms, and to steer the librarian to sources that will help in getting a better handle on the big picture. Other articles in this volume will provide insights into specific resources available to the Internet traveler. Tracing a few introductory steps here first will hopefully give a broader context to the resources that follow in this publication.

WHAT'S IN IT FOR YOU?

Techno-Literacy

An initial, if simplistic, reason for reference librarians to be involved in using the Internet is sheer literacy. Just as awareness of current events or knowledge of a particular subject area may be vital to your skills as a reference librarian, so is knowing about the Internet. Whether the setting is academia, a corporation, or the home, the Internet is revolutionizing the way work is done and how information is being shared. Schools at the K-12 level are introducing more classroom use of the Internet for students. Thus, knowledge of Internet resources is becoming as basic as knowledge of an online catalog, an index, or any tool you may use to help your client find information.

A corollary to knowing what resources are available, is knowing what is NOT available. The Internet has not yet replaced, and may never totally replace, some of the resources used in more traditional reference work. The Internet is still a growing entity. While it has always been true that library selection is based on what is available, apparently that is even more true for the Internet. There will always be resources which are more practical to use in hard copy, rather than in an electronic form.

Technical issues must also be considered. Different systems provide different levels of access. For example, some sites allow their users access to the full range of Internet possibilities, while other sites may allow access only through a controlled group of menu options.

E-Mail

A popular point of entry for many Internetters is e-mail, or electronic mail. Each person who uses e-mail receives an e-mail address. Addresses vary from site to site in their appearance. However, e-mail addresses must contain a personal identification unique to the individual, a site address or machine name, and an identification of whether it is a commercial site, an educational site, or an organization. In the address *ksnure@magnus.acs.ohio-state.edu,* the *ksnure* identifies the individual, *magnus.acs* identifies the machine the account is on, and *ohio-state.edu* identifies the domain, or institution where that machine is located.

E-mail can be an excellent way to avoid telephone tag. By sending a message electronically you can pose the question when it is convenient for you, and the recipients can return an answer when it is convenient for them. Many reference departments are turning this into a facility that not only they, but their patrons can also use. E-mail reference allows librarians to check for questions at a time when they can give full attention to the problem, and allows time to find an answer without having a patron wait on the phone or follow the librarian around the reference room.

Listservs

E-mail also provides a platform for sharing information quickly, and on a grand scale by using listservs. Listservs are electronic groups that typically center around a broad topic such as CD-ROMs in libraries or reference services. Every e-mail message sent to the listserv is distributed to all members of that listserv, which is potentially hundreds or thousands of people. It does not cost anything to subscribe to a listserv, but simply requires that the user send an e-mail message to the appropriate address with the message: subscribe [listserv] Firstname Lastname. Each listserv has one address where a user sends requests to subscribe, unsubscribe, search the archives, etc., and another address to send actual questions or responses to the readers of the list. Along with discussion, job announcements and conference announcements are often posted. Appendix A lists several (certainly not all) listservs that may generally be of interest to reference librarians. An example of how to subscribe to such a site is also given there.

Newsgroups

Another Internet service similar to listservs are newsgroups. The difference between the two is that when you join a group, the mail is no longer automatically deposited into your mailbox. You must go to the newsgroup yourself to read it. Some listservs can also be accessed as a newsgroup. A good analogy to a newsgroup is a bulletin board–you go to it, as opposed to having mail delivered to your desk. The benefit is that your mailbox does not get as cluttered (some groups post 5-20 messages per day) and you can more easily regulate how often you read the messages. A drawback is that you have to remember to go out and look for the information.

There are hundreds of newsgroup communities. They center around topics such as computing, news, recreation, social, and "alternative" topics. Each newsgroup name begins with code that identifies the type of newsgroup that it is. For instance:

comp.human-factors	is a newsgroup dealing with the human factors of computing
soc.college.teaching-asst	is a social newsgroup for college teaching assistants
alt.fan.jimmy-buffett	is an alternative newsgroup for fans of Jimmy Buffett
clari.biz.market.otc	a business newsgroup for discussion of the Over The Counter stock market exchange.

There are newsgroups dealing with virtually every topic under the sun (although new groups appear every day). The only problem you may encounter is that it is up to whoever provides your Internet access to determine which newsgroups will be made available on your system. (This is comparable to the problem encountered with basic cable television.) The decision is often based on system capability, but may also be an issue of censorship. Some of the "alt" groups are truly for adult audiences.

Of course, time has a way of speeding by when you are online, and it is certainly true that not all such time is truly benefiting the objective of providing reference service. While listservs, newsgroups and e-mail may provide a link for solving reference problems or learning of new reference resources, it is wise to occasionally take stock of such electronic endeavors and consider what is being gained in terms of professional development, and when the activities are keeping higher priorities from being accomplished.

Remote Login

Another major use of the Internet is to allow users to connect from their system to a remote electronic system. For instance, hundreds of libraries world-wide have their catalogs available over the Internet. Reference librarians are used to dialing in to such services as BRS, Dialog, STN, OCLC and RLIN. With the Internet it is possible to access such services and much more, without a phone call.

Telnet

One service that makes these connections possible is called *telnet* (not to be confused with telenet). Just as each person on the Internet has an e-mail address, or userid, so does each service have an address called an IP address. (IP stands for Internet Protocol.) Most sites will have two IP addresses. One is made up of letters and is somewhat mnemonic in identifying the service and the site. For example, the Dartmouth library catalog's address is *library.dartmouth.edu*. Its numerical equivalent is *129.170.16.11*. If you have trouble connecting with one address, try the other.

The ability to use telnet will vary from site to site. If your Internet site provides menus only with no way to enter commands, you need to determine if your site has options which will connect you to other sites. This may be the case for users whose access is through free-nets. For those whose site allows them to enter commands at a system prompt, the user would connect to the local site and type the command:

telnet 123.45.67.8.

Most sites will require some sort of login, such as "info," or "library" in the case of library catalogs. Some may ask the user to identify terminal emulation (VT100 is perhaps the most common). Commercial sites, such as Dialog or RLIN, will require a password and ID number, such as is required via dial access.

Many sites offer *hytelnet*, a program that allows a user to look through a menu of options by type of system (library catalog, gopher, etc.). Once the user has selected the site, hytelnet provides the telnet address, logon and logoff instructions for the remote site, and in some cases, will automatically connect the user to the site when prompted. If your system does not provide hytelnet, appendix B provides some options for accessing it.

When telnetting to other sites, you must be prepared to read help screens, and experiment. Many librarians have mastery over their local OPAC as well as some commercial services. However, there is no formal mechanism for mastering the ins and outs of the variety of OPACs, information systems, and gophers that exist in the great world of the Internet. Possible failings of OPACs must also be considered: Certain special collections may not be included, material obtained before a certain date may not be included, or level of cataloging quality may vary from site to site, etc.

Fee-Based Services

Many of the fee-based services librarians used to access through dial access services such as Tymnet or Telenet are now becoming available through the Internet. Each service has a telnet address. For instance, Dialog's IP (or telnet) address is *dialog.com*. The services still require a password and ID to access the system, and still charge for use of the databases. The benefit to libraries may be savings in the cost of telecommunication charges. This benefit will vary from library to library depending on fees they are paying for Internet access. Many university libraries are not responsible for any over-head costs in use of the Internet, so this access costs only pennies in telecommunication charges. Another benefit may be a more reliable connection and faster transmission rate. Again, libraries with a di-rect connection to the Internet will benefit more than those who must dial in to the Internet. Appendix C includes a list of some commercial vendors on the Internet.

Bulletin Board Systems

There have been many Electronic Bulletin Board Systems (BBS's) available through dial access for many years. Now, many of those, or BBS's like those, are making an appearance on the Internet–which means users can access them without the need for a long distance phone call. A large number of BBS's are government or community sponsored. They provide a means for the sponsor to issue announcements, distribute software, and communicate per-sonally (electronically) with the user, etc. Appendix D provides the telnet addresses for a few such systems.

Free-Nets

Free-nets are a type of BBS, but are broad in appeal to the community (as in city or metropolitan area). While they are not library systems, some public libraries are using them to help supply a broader range of services to their patrons. Free-nets connect com-munity members with professionals in the community (doctors, lawyers, travel agents, etc.) as well as provide information about community events, available jobs, etc. Free-nets also provide a link for members of the community to just "talk" to each other electron-ically. Free-nets, however, also often provide links to many library catalogs and provide registered users with an e-mail address that links them to the greater Internet. Bryn Geffert provides an inter-esting look at the use of free-nets in public libraries.[1]

For users with expanded Internet access, it is possible to telnet (or hytelnet) to free-nets. However, for those whose access is via a free-net, access to the expanded Internet is limited to e-mail and the options made available via the free-net menu. Appendix D provides information for connecting to a few free-nets and provides a sample main menu of opportunities.

Gopher

Gopher is an Internet system developed at the University of Minnesota (land of the Golden Gophers) which allows a site to create an invisible tunnel from itself to other sites. Once on a go-pher, you can work through a menu system to connect to other gophers that exist in North America and throughout the world. When ultimately connected to another gopher, the menu looks the same as the home, or initial gopher. There is no prompt to logon. Instead, all of the resources available on the remote gopher appear to reside at the point where you began your search.

The resources on a gopher system vary from site to site. Gener-ally gophers include full text documents (such as speeches, refer-ence books, news items, subject bibliographies, campus publica-tions, etc.), campus or institutional information for that location (class schedules, campus events, lists of campus organizations, job postings), access to library resources and databases, and access to systems other than itself. The resources are found by working through the menu system. Some gopher sites even allow the user to retrieve (FTP) documents found at that site in a very easy manner. (See below for explanation of FTP.) Even if your Internet connec-tion is not a gopher site itself, it is possible to telnet to any number of gophers and use that gopher to tunnel to other gophers. See appendix E for information on connecting to a few interesting sites.

FTP

FTP–or File Transfer Protocol–is a means of transferring elec-tronic documents from one site to another. While an e-mail message is a handy way of sending small messages or documents, FTP is a means of allowing for mass distribution of large documents created at various universities, documents held by libraries, software that is free or shareware, maps and satellite photos.

Depending on the type of information you commonly "broker" or use yourself, you may in time become familiar with certain FTP sites. Using FTP can be rather simple, especially for straight text files. However, for items such as postscript documents, software and pictures, FTPing can be rather frustrating if a few key steps are not known. The ins and outs of using FTP are a bit too complex to address in this introductory essay. Ed Krol provides excellent detail in using FTP.[2] A couple of interesting FTP sites are listed in Appendix F, as well as an example of a straightforward FTP session.

FINDING WHAT'S OUT THERE

While it may be good to learn a few resources that exist on the Internet, any good reference librarian knows that it is just as important (if not more so) to know the resources and tools that locate what's out there. Just as libraries have indexes, catalogs, and directories for finding material in the library, so does the Internet have comparable finding aids.

Archie

The number of items available for FTP is too vast to count and vary from site to site. One tool that currently exists for finding FTP' able material is called Archie. (It searches for archived items). To use Archie, connect to an Archie site through telnet. See Appendix F for a list of Archie sites and an example of using Archie.

When using Archie, it is helpful to consider techniques used when searching many electronic systems. Think of synonyms for your keyword. Try it as a plural or a singular term. Try connecting a two word phrase with a hyphen (like political-science or supreme-court), as many files are named this way. For reference librarians used to polished online or CD-ROM search software, Archie may seem somewhat crude. Just remember that Archie is not searching one database. It is searching a world-wide network of databases, all created locally.

Veronica

Since there are more than 1,500 gopher servers worldwide it is often very difficult to find valuable resources. To help users find information, a new search tool called Veronica has been created. This tool searches gopher servers (often referred to as gopher-space). Veronica servers are often highly used and at times it is difficult to get access. Three such servers can be accessed at the following telnet addresses:

futique.scs.unr.edu
veronica.scs.unr.edu
wisteria.cnidr.org

Searches can be either a single keyword, or a string constructed of an unlimited number of ANDs and ORs and keywords; however, parentheses are not yet implemented. Adjacent keywords without an intervening logical operator are treated as though conjoined by an AND. It is also possible to limit a search to a certain portion of a gopher server. For example, one can search for the word "women" as a directory, thus not retrieving items that are actual file names. Further instructions are provided when one connects to the service.

WAIS

WAIS is a system which searches indexed databases. The database could be of the type reference librarians traditionally think of as a database–such as ERIC, or it could be a full text document, a list of names (like a phone directory), etc. To use WAIS, telnet to a WAIS server, or locate WAIS-based resources on a gopher menu. Select the database you want to search, then enter the word or words to have searched when prompted.

Two public WAIS servers are available at the following telnet sites:

quake.think.com
nnsc.nsf.net

In each case, login as *wais*.

World-Wide Web (WWW)

WWW is a search tool for the Internet based on hypertext. The useful aspect of this finding aid is the ability to browse through a list of subject headings to get an idea of just what kinds of materials exist on the Internet in a given area. As with hypertext, the user is given a variety of links from a word in one document to other documents with information related to that term. As with gopher, the user is given a uniform interface when moving from document to document.

A public server for WWW is the following telnet site:

info.cern.ch

In General

As you become familiar with the electronic tools available for finding information, you may find some tools or services suit your needs (or tastes) better than others. Just as some prefer Dialog while others prefer BRS, you may like the interface of one gopher better than another. Thus, you may telnet to the favored gopher, and from there gopher out to other sites. Also, certain documents may be available in a variety of manners. Consider the *CIA World Factbook* which is available via OPACs, to be searched using a particular OPAC's search software; as well as via WAIS; and it even sits as a text document on some gophers. Thus, there are often many options for accomplishing a single task. For the beginner, it may be enough just to find SOMETHING, but the experienced user may grow more concerned with the manner in which the task is accomplished.

READ ALL ABOUT IT

Electronic Internet tools have been mentioned as a way of finding materials on the Internet. Some of the listservs on the Internet have hosted discussion concerning the need for print materials that essentially accomplish the same tasks as these electronic tools. However, for those who want to learn about Internet resources without having full or even partial connection, as well as for those who are just not sure how to proceed, such printed resources are invaluable. The good news for reference librarians is that there are more and more materials available for helping the user in this format we know and love–books. Here are but five that have become quite popular. These (except for perhaps *Threshold)* should be readily available in most bookstores.

Kehoe, Brendan. *ZEN AND THE ART OF THE INTERNET.* New York: Prentice Hall, 1992.

This book originally appeared on the Internet itself as an FTPable document. After much input from the Internet community it was revised and published as a book. (The first edition still sits on the Internet, but it would behoove the reader to buy a copy of the printed version.) It is the first book to give a comprehensive look at the Internet. It provides information on most Internet tools mentioned in this paper, as well as some other Internet terms and concepts you might hear about. It includes a bibliography, a glossary, lots of information on telnet (including some good sites), and lots on usenet news (newgroups).

Krol, Ed. *THE WHOLE INTERNET.* Sebastopol, CA: O'Reilly & Associate, 1992.

Ed Krol and *The Whole Internet* have each taken their places in the Internet community as essential resources. *The Whole Internet* is biblical in terms of showing the reader how to lead the Internet life, providing step-by-step examples of many Internet processes, as well as describing why and how things are the way they are. Perhaps an even more valuable aspect of the book is the catalog, which lists Internet sites and resources by subject. This is a portion the reference librarian will turn to again and again to find and recommend Internet resources for users.

Lane, Elizabeth and Craig Summerhill. *INTERNET PRIMER FOR INFORMATION PROFESSIONALS: A BASIC GUIDE TO NETWORKING TECHNOLOGY.* Westport, CT: Meckler, 1993.

This primer is written by information professionals who truly understand libraries and librarians. An especially useful section is Chapter 5 which lists network resources that reside on the Internet itself, designed to lead users to helpful Internet resources. To think of these resources in more traditional ways, they are in essence "guides to the literature" and "finding aids" for Internet stuff. *The Internet Primer* also provides useful discussion on the history of the Internet, an understanding of who some of the Internet "players" are, and an interesting discussion of how the Internet is impacting on the roles of librarians, computer scientists, and educators.

LaQuey, Tracy. *THE INTERNET COMPANION*. Reading, MA: Addison-Wesley Publishing Co., 1993.

This book provides a fun and easy to read venture into the various components of the Internet. Its value is in readability and usefulness to the true novice. Examples are given which help the non-Internet-literate truly understand the logic of Internet tools and resources. This book covers reasons for learning about the Internet, a basic description of just what the Internet is, and a bit of detail on communicating with people, using finding aids, and a few issues that go beyond the basics. Another valuable part of this book is a description of exactly HOW to gain connection for those who might not be fortunate enough to have it just "come with the territory." LaQuey even gives a list of commercial Internet providers.

Tennant, Roy, John Ober and Anne Lipow. *CROSSING THE INTERNET THRESHOLD: AN INSTRUCTIONAL HANDBOOK*. Berkeley, CA: Library Solutions Press, 1993.

Originally written as a workbook for an extensive Internet workshop, this is a great book for the beginner to work through. Clear descriptions are given of various Internet processes, including e-mail, listservs, telnet and FTP. At the end of these sections are worksheets to practice what has been learned. Of course, this design also serves as a great resource for those who might attempt to provide workshops themselves. Because the Internet changes so quickly, this–as well as all books mentioned here–does not cover the most recent of Internet features such as Veronica.

Marine, April, Susan Kirkpatrick, Vivian Neou and Carol Ward. *THE INTERNET: GETTING STARTED*. Englewood Cliffs, NJ: 1993.

This book emphasizes the concerns of would-be Internetters outside of the library world. There is a lot of information on how to gain access to the Internet, both in terms of becoming an Internet site and in gaining dial access. It includes information on some of the major U.S. networks that help to make up the Internet, as well as information about the Internet in various countries. This publication offers a lot in terms of technical concepts related to security, the Domain Name System (DNS), protocols, etc. It includes an extensive RFC index, which could actually be gotten from the Internet directly. (RFC's–or Requests for Comments–are technical documents which define the Internet.)

CONCLUSION

The Internet has by no means begun to replace all–or even many–of the resources traditionally used by reference librarians. If anything, it has added to the places we need to look! Even so, the challenge has gone out to all librarians that a dramatic change is coming.[3] While some might choose to remain skeptical, it is true that this new electronic link is having a huge impact on the way libraries select, disseminate and find information–thus greatly evolving the nature of what we, as reference librarians, do. Familiarity with this important tool can only enhance our work, and expertise will in time make our services invaluable to users.

REFERENCES

1. Geffert, Bryn. Community Networks in Libraries: A Case Study of the Freenet P.A.T.H. *Public Libraries,* March/April 1993:91-99.

2. Krol, Ed. *The Whole Internet.* Sebastopol, CA: O'Reilly & Associates, Inc. 1992 pp. 59-90.

3. Churbuck, David C. Good-bye, Dewey decimals. *Forbes,* February 15, 1993: 204-5.

Appendix A

Selected List of Listservs for Reference Librarians

To subscribe to a list (using Libref-L as an example):
1. Send an e-mail message to:
listserv@kentvm.bitnet or to **listserv@kentvm.kent.edu.**
(The first address is a bitnet address, the second is an internet address.)
2. Do not fill in any information in the subject line.
3. In the body of the message type: **subscribe libref-l Firstname Lastname** (yours, that is).
4. Then send the message.

To send questions or comments to the list:
1. Send an e-mail message to **libref-l@kentvm.bitnet.** (Note that the address is different than for subscribing.)
2. Now it is good to include a succinct subject in the subject line. It's helpful for all subscribers to be able to scan a subject line to determine if the message is of particular interest to them.
3. Compose your message and send it.
4. Another way to send a message to the listserv is to reply to a message you have received from the list. Most e-mail interfaces have a simple command to reply to messages so that you do not have to reenter the address or subject line of the message to which you are replying. Just remember, if you do this your message is sent to the entire listserv, not just the one person to who's message you are responding. (One can just imagine the possibilities for embarrassment.)

When you subscribe to libref-l, or any other listserv, you will receive notification (via e-mail) that you were added to the list. Many listservs also send a note describing the nature of the discussion, network etiquette, and a list of commands you'll need to search the archives of the listserv, unsubscribe, etc.

<u>Subscription address</u>   <u>Mailing address</u>

AFAS-L
African American Studies and Librarianship
    listserv@kentvm.bitnet   afas-l@kentvm.bitnet
    listserv@kentvm.kent.edu   afas-l@kentvm.kent.edu

ANN-LOTS
Researchers with an interest in finding and sharing 'pointers' to sources of on-line things. More for posting information than for asking questions.
    listserv@NDSUVM1.bitnet   ann-lots@ndsuvm1.bitnet
    listserv@vm1.nodak.edu   ann-lots@vm1.nodak.edu

BI-L
Discussion of bibliographic instruction
    listserv%bingvmb.bitnet   bi-l%bingvmb.bitnet
    listserv@vm1.nodak.edu   bi-l@vm1.nodak.edu

GovDoc-L
Discussion of information dissemination through Federal Depository libraries.
    listserv%PSUVM.BITNET   govdoc-l%psuvm.bitnet
    listserv@vm1.nodak.edu   govdoc-l@vm1.nodak.edu

APPENDIX A (continued)

Subscription address   Mailing address

Info+Ref
Anyone involved or interested in provision of information and referral services; including information and referral services, reference librarians, and other information professionals.

listserv@indyCMS.bitnet   Info+Ref@indyCMS.bitnet
listserv@IndyCMS.IUPUI.edu   Info+Ref@IndyCMS.IUPUI.edu

INT-LAW
Librarians and others interested in exchanging information related to foreign, comparative and international legal materials and issues.

listserv@uminn1.bitnet   int-law@uminn1.bitnet
listserv@vm1.spcs.umn.edu   int-law@vm1.spcs.umn.edu

LIBREF-L
Discussion among Reference Librarians

listserv@kentvm.bitnet   libref-l@kentvm.bitnet
listserv@kentvm.kent.edu   libref-l@kentvm.kent.edu

MEDLIB-L
Librarians in the Health Sciences

listserv@ubvm.bitnet   medlib-l@ubvm.bitnet
listserv@ubvm.cc.buffalo.edu   medlib-l@ubvm.cc.buffalo.edu

MLA-L
Announcements and information of the Music Library Association. Reference inquiries are also OK.

listserv%IUBVM.bitnet   mla-l%IUBVM.bitnet
listserv@vm1.nodak.edu   mla-l@vm1.nodak.edu

PACS-L
All computer systems that libraries make available to their patrons.

listserv%UHUPVM1.bitnet   pacs-l%UHUPVM1.bitnet
listserv@vm1.NODAK.edu   pacs-l@vm1.NODAK.edu

PUBLIB
Use of the Internet in public libraries.

listserv@nysernet.org   publib@nysernet.org

STUMPERS-L
For help with those tough reference questions.

listserv@crf.cuis.edu   stumpers-l@crf.cuis.edu

Appendix B

SELECTED TELNET SITES WITH THE LATEST VERSION OF HYTELNET

sparc-1.law.columbia.edu
log in: lawnet

info.ccit.arizona.edu
log in: hytelnet

hytelnet.cwis.uci.edu
log in: hytelnet

infopath.ucsd.edu
Log in: infopath
(Choose "computing services", then "other Internet services")

du.edu
log in: atdu
(Choose subject: Internet)

Obtaining a Copy of Hytelnet

If you do not have access to hytelnet at your local Internet site, it is also possible to FTP a copy of this software and load it on an IBM-PC or compatible or a Macintosh that is directly hooked to the Internet.

FTP address: **access.usask.ca**
Change directory to: **pub/hytelnet**

When downloading be sure to change the file type to binary. This version was released February 1, 1993 and is written by Peter Scott – scott@sklib.usask.ca

Appendix C

TELNET ADDRESSES FOR COMMERCIAL VENDORS

NOTE: Anyone can telnet to the following addresses, but a subscription is still required to obtain a password to actually search the service.

VENDOR	TELNET ADDRESS
Dialog	dialog.com
OCLC	epic.prod.oclc.org
STN	stnc.cas.org or 192.88.108.112
BRS	brs.com
Orbit	orbit.com
ECHO (European Community database)	echo.lu *
RLIN	rlin.stanford.edu or 36.54.0.18

* The ECHO database is produced by the European communities. Passwords have been issued to EC depository libraries, however, it is currently possible to log in with any of the following passwords: **echotest, guest**, or **echo**.

Appendix D

A Few BBS's and Free-Net Sites

BBS's

NIH Grant Line (DRGLINE Bulletin Board):
TELNET **WYLBUR.CU.NIH.GOV** or **128.231.64.82**
At the Open prompt, type **,gen1** (must include comma)
INITIALS? **bb5**
ACCOUNT? **ccs2**

University of North Carolina BBS
TELNET **BBS.OIT.UNC.EDU** or **152.2.22.80**
Login in with **bbs**

NEWTON: Educational Electronic Bulletin Board System
Argonne National Laboratory
TELNET **NEWTON.DEP.ANL.GOV** or **130.202.92.50**
login: **cocotext**

Free-nets

Cleveland FREE-NET
TELNET **HELA.INS.CWRU.EDU** or **129.22.8.38**
Login: **visitor**

Heartland FREE-NET
Telnet **HEARTLAND.BRADLEY.EDU** or **136.176.5.114**
Login: **bbguest**

Denver FREE-NET
TELNET **FREENET.HSC.COLORADO.EDU** or **140.226.1.8**
login: **guest**

A Sample Free-Net Menu:

```
[[[ HEARTLAND FREE-NET DIRECTORY ]]]
1   Administration   Building
2   Mailboxes  for  Registered  Users
3   Community  Center  (Calendar,  Public  Forum,  Recreation)
4   Social  Services  and  Organizations  Center
5   Business  Center
6   Senior  Center
7   Teen  Center
8   Government  Center  (Peoria  County,  Peoria,  Job  Service)
9   Professional  Building  (Legal,  Medical,  Tax,  Invest/Banking)
10  Education  Center
11  Science  and  Technology  Center
12  Home  and  Garden  Center
13  Library  Center
14  Special  Interest  Groups  Center
```

Appendix E

Some Interesting Gopher Sites

Following are a couple of interesting gopher sites and their addresses.

University of Minnesota
   This is where gopher began.
   Telnet: **consultant.micro.umn.edu** or **134.84.132.4**
   login: **gopher**

University of Michigan Library's Gopher System
   This gopher has many useful reference materials, including the *CIA World Factbook*, State Department Travel Advisories, etc. It also contains an excellent collection of Internet user guides and finding aids.
   Telnet: **una.hh.lib.umich.edu** or **141.211.190.102**
   login: **gopher**

Washington and Lee University
   This has been dubbed by some to be the "greatest Internet site" because of valuable resources and a good user interface.
   Telnet: **liberty.uc.wlu.edu**
   login: **lawlib**

Appendix F

Using FTP

To access an ftp site, issue the following command from the system prompt:
 	
    ftp   ra.msstate.edu
    Login: **anonymous**
    Password: **youruserid@yourhostname.**
    Type **ls** to get a listing of directories.
    type **cd   directoryname** to change into one of these directories
    Once you arrive at the file you are interested in, type **get   filename**.
 	
This will result in the transfer of a copy of the document from the remote site to your local system. Depending on how you have connected to the Internet, your local system will either be your personal computer or the local Internet machine that connects you to the Internet.

A Few Interesting FTP Sites

Project Gutenberg
This is a National Clearinghouse for machine readable texts and is located at FTP site: **mrcnext.cso.uiuc.edu**

The purpose of Project Gutenberg is to encourage the creation and distribution of English language electronic texts. Some of the works to date include the *Koran, Alice in Wonderland, The Federalist Papers*, and much more. The goal of Gutenberg is to provide a collection of **10,000 of the most used books by the year 2001**. So far most electronic text work has been carried out by private, semi-private or incorporated individuals, with several library or college collections being created, but being made mostly from the works entered by individuals on their own time and expense.   To find out more about Project Gutenberg you can subscribe to the GUTNBERG listserver. You can do it by sending the following message to LISTSERV@UIUCVMD.BITNET: SUB GUTNBERG YOUR NAME

Mississippi State University History Archives
Mississippi State University is maintaining an archive of historical texts, predominantly American so far, that are available through the FTP (File Transfer Protocol) procedure. The FTP address is **ra.msstate.edu**. They are in the docs/history directory. The archive is maintained by Professor Don Mabry (djm1@ra.msstate.edu).

The directories include: Canada, General, Latin_America, Software, USA, Women, articles, bibliographies, databases, diaries

University of Wisconsin-Parkside
An interesting site for music enthusiasts. Several gif (graphic) files, and lyrics to many songs. The FTP address is **cs.uwp.edu**.

Appendix G

Archie Sites

TELNET ADDRESS	IP ADDRESS	SITE LOCATION
archie.rutgers.edu	128.6.18.15	(Rutgers University)
archie.unl.edu	129.93.1.14	(University of Nebraska in Lincoln)
archie.ans.net	147.225.1.2	(ANS archie server)
archie.au	139.130.4.6	(Australian server)
archie.funet.fi	128.214.6.100	(European server in Finland)
archie.doc.ic.ac.uk	146.169.11.3	(UK/Europe server)
archie.cs.huji.ac.il	132.65.6.15	(Israel server)
archie.wide.ad.jp	133.4.3.6	(Japanese server)
archie.ncu.edu.tw	140.115.19.24	(Taiwanese server)
archie.sogang.ac.kr	163.239.1.11	(Korean server)
archie.nz	130.195.9.4	(New Zealand server)
archie.kuis.kyoto-u.ac.jp	130.54.20.1	(Japan)
archie.th-darmstadt.de	130.83.128.111	(Germany)
archie.luth.se	130.240.18.4	(Sweden)

Using Archie

When asked to login, type **archie**. Once connected to an archie site, it is a matter of typing a keyword of the type of document you are seeking. For instance, to see what sorts of bibliographies are available: type **prog bibliography**. (In this case prog is the command given to have it search a term.). Be prepared to press the pause key on your keyboard or turn on the capture feature of your communication software, as you may receive a rather lengthy list of items that will quickly scroll by on your screen. Here's what a search for political-science looks like:

```
archie> prog    political-science          [User types]
# matches / % database searched:   6 /100%    [Note: 6 items were found]
```

One of the "records" retrieved:

```
Host sunsite.unc.edu    (152.2.22.81)
Last updated 08:18 25 Apr 1993


Location: /pub/academic
DIRECTORY rwxr-xr-x        512  Apr 20  22:43    political-science
```

To use the information given here, follow the instructions used for anonymous FTP as shown in Appendix F. In this case the site to telnet to would be: sunsite.unc.edu. The directory the user would change to would be /pub/academic/political-science.

Gopher Searching Using VERONICA

Louise McGillis

SUMMARY. VERONICA stands for Very Easy Rodent-Oriented Net-Wide Index to Computerized Archives and is a service that allows users to search all menu levels of gopher sites. The development of such a tool became necessary to enable users to search for resources on the gopher sites without having to go to each site individually and search each menu level. This article will explain how to access the service and perform searches. How to read search results, look for strings in specific documents and download desired documents will also be explained. Examples of potential questions will illustrate these various procedures. While VERONICA can be used effectively by librarians to answer reference questions, many professionals in the field are somewhat daunted by this very powerful and relatively new reference tool. Examining reference questions that can be answered using VERONICA will shed some light on its effectiveness, thus giving librarians a better sense of how VERONICA fits into the overall reference process.

INTRODUCTION

The Internet is quickly becoming an indispensable resource for information professionals. It provides access to electronic books and journals, reference works, government material, statistical data, directories, indexes, university calendars and documents,

Louise McGillis is Reference Librarian, Information Services Division of the Queen Elizabeth II Library, Memorial University of Newfoundland, St. John's, NF, Canada, A1B 3Y1.

[Haworth co-indexing entry note]: "Gopher Searching Using VERONICA." McGillis, Louise. Co-published simultaneously in *The Reference Librarian* (The Haworth Press, Inc.) No. 41/42, 1994, pp. 25-35; and: *Librarians on the Internet: Impact on Reference Services* (ed: Robin Kinder) The Haworth Press, Inc., 1994, pp. 25-35. Multiple copies of this article/chapter may be purchased from The Haworth Document Delivery Center [1-800-3-HAWORTH; 9:00 a.m. - 5:00 p.m. (EST)].

maps, graphic images and library catalogues. A great deal of this information is mounted on the computer systems of universities and government departments using gopher. Simply put, gopher is a software program that organizes Internet resources using a menu based system. To find information, users browse the menus of the various gopher sites. However, this process has become an increasingly labour intensive task due to the number of gophers. At present there are over 1000 gopher sites and the number grows daily. It would be impossible for a librarian working on the reference desk to locate a copy of the *North American Free Trade Agreement* by browsing gopher sites. The only way this question could be answered in a timely fashion would be if the librarian knew the document was available on the Internet and at which site it was located. However, this does not eliminate the problem since it requires the librarian to know everything that is available and where it can be found. The ultimate solution resides in a tool that allows users to search gopher menus and this is why VERONICA was developed.

VERONICA is a software program that indexes the items on all menu levels of gopher sites and provides users with a mechanism to search the sites. It was developed at the University of Nevada by Steve Foster and Fred Barrie in the fall of 1992. The index is updated every two weeks. As of August 1993 there were four VERONICA servers. This service will be distributed across more sites as the number of users continues to increase.

As the date indicates, VERONICA is relatively new. It is important to keep this in mind because changes and enhancements are continually being made to VERONICA, changes that affect how to construct searches. Users can remain informed of variations by reading the updates available on the VERONICA menu. Despite its somewhat experimental state, VERONICA is a very effective tool. Keyword searching eliminates the need to browse a large number of gopher sites for a specific item. Furthermore, it enables users to locate information on a particular topic quickly and easily.

ACCESSING VERONICA

VERONICA is accessed through the gopher software. If your institution has a gopher, check the menu to see if VERONICA is an option on one of the menu levels. If your institution has not yet mounted its own gopher menu, but the software is available on your system, use the software to access VERONICA on another system's gopher menu. Many of the gopher sites provide this service so within minutes of browsing, you should be able to identify a site that offers VERONICA searching. You can also go directly to one of the VERONICA servers by gophering to one of these four sites:[1]

> system prompt>   gopher veronica.scs.unr.edu
>
> system prompt>   gopher wisteria.cnidr.org
>
> system prompt>   gopher nysernet.org
>
> system prompt>   gopher serra.unipi.it

If you connect to the gopher server at UNR (the first on the list above) you will get the latest list of VERONICA sites.

thanks – louise

MAIL>

Esc-chr: ^] help: ^]? port: 1 speed: 9600 parity:none echo:rem VT102

If your system does not have the gopher software you can still access VERONICA by telnetting to one of these public gopher sites:[2]

> system prompt>   telnet consultant.micro.umn.edu
> login: gopher
>
> system prompt>   telnet gopher.uiuc.edu
> login: gopher
>
> system prompt>   telnet panda.uiowa.edu
> login: panda

You are advised to access the site closest to you to limit network traffic. However, it is recommended that instead of telnetting to one of these public sites you have the gopher software mounted on your institution's system.[3] The software is available free at the following Internet ftp site:

system prompt>   ftp boombox.micro.umn.edu
directory path   pub/gopher

Once connected to a gopher site look for a menu option that reads something like "search gopherspace using VERONICA." This menu option may not appear on the main gopher menu. Sometimes you may have to go down a level or two before you find VERONICA.

THE VERONICA MENU

After selecting VERONICA you will be presented with a menu; see Figure 1 following. The first six menu options offer VERONICA searching and the two remaining options provide background information about VERONICA. Menu option eight instructs users in how to construct searches. Option nine provides information about the VERONICA service. When you select VERONICA, the menu presented may differ slightly from the menu shown in Figure 1. This is because the service is still experimental and changes are constantly being made. In the past month alone the searching features have changed, a fourth server has been mounted and new information item have been added to the menu.

FIGURE 1. Veronica Menu at the University of Nevada (August 1993).

Internet Gopher Information Client v1.11

search gopherspace using veronica

1. Search gopherspace using veronica at NYSERNet <?>
2. Search gopherspace using veronica at University of Pisa <?>
3. Search gopherspace using veronica at PSINet <?>
4. Search gopherspace for GOPHER DIRECTORIES (NYSERNet) <?>
5. Search gopherspace for GOPHER DIRECTORIES (U. Pisa) <?>
6. Search gopherspace for GOPHER DIRECTORIES (PSINet) <?>
7.
8. How to compose veronica queries (NEW June 24) READ ME!!.
9. FAQ: Frequently asked questions about veronica (1993/06/24).

SEARCHING VERONICA

All servers index the same information, therefore a search on any server should return the same results. If variations do occur it may be because the servers are updated at different times. The same search performed over a period of time may also generate different results as more gopher sites are indexed. If option one, two or three from the above menu is selected, a search of all menu items on all gopher levels will be performed. If option four, five or six is selected, only gopher items that are directories will be retrieved. A search of directories will retrieve fewer results.

After selecting one of the search options, the user will be prompted for a word or words to search; see Figure 2.

FIGURE 2. Search Screen at the University of Nevada (August 1993).

```
    Search gopherspace using veronica at NYSERNet < ? >

    Words to search for _

                              [Cancel ^G] [Accept - Enter]
```

The keyword searching feature allows users to search a single word or a string. The "and," "or" and "not" Boolean operators can be used. If no operator is placed between two words an "and" operator will be assumed. An unlimited number of operators can be used. Stem searching is possible using the asterisk (*). Parentheses can be used to group synonyms. Searching is not case sensitive.[4]

A new VERONICA feature allows users to limit search results to a specific type of gopher item. All menu items have visual codes that help you identify the item type. These codes appear at the right end of each menu item. A partial list of codes, item type and corresponding search number follows. A complete list can be found in the document *How to Compose VERONICA Queries.* This document is available on the VERONICA menu.

Code	Item Type	Search Number
.	Document	0

/	Directory	1
<CSO>	CSO Name Server	2
<TEL>	Telnet Connection	8
<?>	Search Prompt	7

To limit a search to a specific item, add "-tnumber" to the search statement. The number tells the computer the item type to look for. For example, to limit the search to documents add "-t0" to the search statement. The search statement "environment -t0" will only return gopher items that are documents containing the word environment.

Another new feature allows the user to set a maximum number of returns for a search by adding "-m" to the search statement. The search "education -m10" will return the first ten items found. The search "education -m" will return all items found in gopherspace. If no number is specified the system will return a maximum of two hundred items. For example, the search "education" will return the first two hundred items found.

SEARCHING TIPS

When searching, try a variety of terms. If a search returns no results think of another word that may be used to describe the topic or item being searched. When looking for information on DNA you might include the terms DNA and genetics. Use the asterick (*) to get variations of a term. For example, the user might structure the above search as follows; "(dna or gene*) not (general or generic)." This search will enable the user to pick up the words, gene, genes, genetic and genetics, while at the same time eliminating such unwanted words as general and generic by using the "not" command.

Try both broad and specific terms. If the user is looking for lyrics to John Lennon songs and a search of his name produces no results, the user should broaden the search. In this case it may be wise to search on the words, "music or lyric."

If you think the search will turn up a lot of results, do a directory search first. I was curious to see if there was some kind of film database on the Internet. Searching on the string "movie or film" on all gopher levels returned over 900 items. Restricting the search to directory items reduced the number of items found to under 100. Limiting searches to directory items is a very popular VERONICA feature. It is for this reason there is a separate menu option for this type of searching, "search gopherspace for gopher directories," in addition to the "-t1" feature.

Try your search on all the servers. It is possible that the information you are looking for has recently been indexed and does not yet appear on all the servers.

If a search returns the phrase "nothing available" it is possible that the search halted because the results included some item that the computer could not recognize. This problem is being addressed in the newest release of the gopher software.[5]

If a search returns the phrase "your search returned no results" try the search on another server. It is possible there is information available but the server is not operational at the time of the search.

VERONICA SEARCH RESULTS

A VERONICA search will return a gopher menu composed of items whose title match your search criteria. As with any gopher menu you can access an item by scrolling to the desired item and hitting <return> or typing the line number and <return>. If the search returns a large number of items, you can view results one screen at a time by pressing the space bar. Pressing the letter "b" will take you back one screen. Figure 3 following, shows some results from a search on the string "dna or gene*" and illustrates the type of information a search will retrieve. In this case the results included databases, information about courses and conferences and items from newsgroups. You will also notice that by using the asterisk (*) the search picked up variations of the word, gene, including genes, genetic and genetics.

Since the search has taken items from varying sites and created a specialized gopher menu to match your search request, you do not know where the items are from. To get location information, press the equal sign key = when the cursor is on the item of interest. This will give you an item description which includes the name of the gopher where the item resides and the directory pathway. The pathway tells you which items to select on each gopher menu in

FIGURE 3. Sample Search Results.

```
Internet Gopher Information Client v1.11

Search gopherspace using Veronica at NYSERNet: dna or gene*

        1.  DNA modelling.
        2.  DNA and Protein Sequence Databases/
        3.  Genes/
        4.  DNA-Protein Symposium.
        5.  Biology, Genetics, & Medicine/
        6.  DNA modelling.
        7.  Genetic Programming.
        8.  Re: Displaying Protein with DNA.
        9.  BIOL 918  GENETICS  MWF 0900-0950.
```

order to locate the specific item on the host gopher.[6] To find out which gopher site has the "DNA and Protein Sequence Databases," press the equal sign key when the cursor is on item 2. The computer will respond with the following information:

> Name = DNA Protein and Sequence Databases
> Type = 1
> Port = 70
> Path = 1/med/topics/dna
> Host = micro.ec.hsysyr.edu

You can find the name of the site by going directly to the host name using the gopher command.

> system prompt>   gopher micro.ec.hsysyr.edu

Often you can identify a useful gopher site by doing a VERONI-CA search. The above search led me to the State University of New York, Health Science Centre at Syracuse where I found a list of Internet sources for medicine. When trying to find a music lyric archive using VERONICA, I found a music gopher that included not only a lyric archive but also discographies, press releases and articles and a music newsgroup archive. When using VERONICA to locate the *Rio Declaration* from the Earth Summit in Brazil, I found an entire gopher specializing in environmental information.

You will notice that the same item may appear more than once in the results. In the above menu "DNA Modelling" appears twice. The reason is that at the present time VERONICA does not eliminate duplicate items. As a result, if the same item appears on a number of different gophers all occurrences of the item will appear in your results.

SEARCHING FOR A STRING IN A DOCUMENT

It is possible to search the newly created gopher menu or a specific item from that menu. To do this, hit the slash key/. You will be prompted for a word or string to search. The computer will display the screen that contains the desired word. The computer responds by taking you to the screen where the word appears. It should be noted that the word or string will not be highlighted. You must read through the screen to find the word. To locate the next occurrence of the word, press the letter "n." If the computer does not find the word or string, the response "pattern not found" will appear on the screen. The string must match exactly in case and punctuation. This type of searching only works on machines using the UNIX operating system. This is a useful feature if your search returns a large number of items or you are looking for a particular word or string in a document.[7]

SAVING DOCUMENTS RETRIEVED IN A SEARCH

It is possible to download or mail documents retrieved in a search. When you get to the end of a document a series of options will be presented at the bottom of the screen; see Figure 4 following.

FIGURE 4

Press <RETURN> to continue, <m> to mail, <s> to save, or <p> to print

Pressing the <return> key will bring you back to the previous menu level. If you press the letter "m" you will be prompted for an e-mail address. If you press the letter "s" you will be asked if you want to save the named document. Pressing <return> at this point will save the document in your home directory. Pressing the letter "p" will send the document to the system printer.[8]

It is not necessary to scroll through the whole document in order to mail or save the information. Once you are in a document, press the letter "q" and <return>. At this point the exit, mail, save and print options will be presented at the bottom of the screen.

VERONICA AS A REFERENCE TOOL

The experimental state of VERONICA leaves many reference librarians concerned about its effectiveness as a reference tool. Librarians want to be able to answer questions in a timely fashion using the most appropriate tool. A VERONICA search may take a long time depending on the time of day or it may return hundreds of items. It is also possible that all lines to the servers may be busy or that the servers themselves may be down. Given these limitations, a librarian working on a busy reference desk may be somewhat hesitant to use VERONICA. However, it should be noted that some of these problems are being solved. Over the past few months search time has been reduced considerably and the number of servers has increased, thereby providing a greater number of users simultaneous access.

Another concern for librarians centres on the relative newness of the service. Before being able to use VERONICA on the desk, a librarian must be familiar with all the searching features and the kind of information a search will retrieve in order to determine if using VERONICA is the most effective way to answer a question. While this cannot be done while actually working on the desk, librarians can note specific questions and then, once off the desk, perform VERONICA searches to see if these questions could have been answered. In a more relaxed atmosphere the librarian can determine how long searches take and the type of information being retrieved.

It is important that librarians begin to develop this type of expertise. As more faculty members and students gain access to the Internet, the more they will approach librarians with questions about the type of information sources available on it. If a reference librarian is asked to locate a copy of the *North American Free Trade Agreement* and is unsure of the workings of the Internet, that individual could consult the catalogue to determine if the library owned a copy of the document. However, there may be an increasing number of questions related specifically to the Internet. A patron may want to know if a copy of the *North American Free Trade Agreement* is available on the Internet or simply want to know what biological information is available on the Internet. These types of questions can be addressed quite effectively using VERONICA.

While improvements are continually being made, given the experimental state of VERONICA at present, it may be best to tell patrons you will get back to them if you find more information or ask them to come back when you are off the desk. This type of approach enables librarians to draw on the many Internet resources accessible through VERONICA and at the same time expand their knowledge and command of the service.

REFERENCES

1. Foster, Steve and Fred Barrie. *FAQ: Frequently Asked Questions About Veronica.* June 24, 1993. Question 1.

2. *FAQ: Frequently Asked Questions About Gopher.* 1993. Question 2.

3. Ibid. Question 3.

4. Foster, Steve and Fred Barrie. *How to Compose Veronica Queries.* June 24, 1993.

5. Foster, Steve and Fred Barrie. *FAQ: Frequently Asked Questions About Veronica.* June 24, 1993. Question 9.

6. Ibid. Question 3.

7. *Using Gopher.* Document by Gettysburg College Computing Services. March 1992.

8. Ibid.

How to Use VERONICA
to Find Information
on the Internet

Jackie Mardikian

SUMMARY: As more navigational tools, such as Archie, WAIS, Gopher, World-Wide Web and VERONICA are introduced on the Internet, it is critical that reference librarians understand the function of each one. VERONICA (Very Easy, Rodent-Oriented, Net-Wide Index to Computerized Archives) is the newest, and most powerful tool, and it takes away the mystery of where files are hidden on the Internet. Using specific examples, this article takes the reader through step-by-step guides of menu choices showing how VE-RONICA is accessed through a Gopher client using simple keyword and Boolean searching. In addition, this article discusses the limitations and frustrations encountered when attempting to access information using gopher servers.

INTRODUCTION

The Internet has been compared to a network of super highways or an ocean in which a searcher can literally drown in this vast sea of knowledge. Fortunately, many navigational tools that come to the rescue have been introduced on the Internet. It is critical that refer-

Jackie Mardikian is Medical Librarian, Library of Science and Medicine, Rutgers, the State University of New Jersey, Piscataway, NJ 08855-1029, Mardikian zodiac.rutgers.edu.

[Haworth co-indexing entry note]: "How to Use VERONICA to Find Information on the Internet." Mardikian, Jackie. Co-published simultaneously in *The Reference Librarian* (The Haworth Press, Inc.) No. 41/42, 1994, pp. 37-45; and: *Librarians on the Internet: Impact on Reference Services* (ed: Robin Kinder) The Haworth Press, Inc., 1994, pp. 37-45. Multiple copies of this article/chapter may be purchased from The Haworth Document Delivery Center [1-800-3-HAWORTH; 9:00 a.m. - 5:00 p.m. (EST)].

ence librarians understand the functions of the numerous navigation tools that now exist: Archie (an ARCHIVE server) developed at McGill University as an index of FTP (File Transfer Protocol) servers; Gopher, begun at the University of Minnesota as a menu-driven campus-wide information system; World-Wide Web, a hypertext system developed in Geneva at the Center for Nuclear Energy Research; and WAIS, a Wide Area Information System providing menus with unique search capabilities.[6]

VERONICA (Very Easy Rodent-Oriented Net-wide Index to Computerized Archives) is the newest and one of the most powerful search tools that takes away the mystery of where files are located on the Internet. Presently, there are no clients called VERONICA; it can be accessed through various Gopher sites, and is a choice option on Gopher. When you browse through a Gopher, similar to browsing stacks of shelves in a library, you can learn about Internet resources that you never dreamed existed. With VERONICA, the user can search for documents across all Gopher servers, having a choice of just browsing or searching for specific information.

VERONICA was developed in November 1992 by Steve Foster and Fred Barrie at the University of Nevada in Reno as an experimental service to index titles of Gopher resources available from sites across the Internet. As of November 17, 1992, 258 Gophers were indexed by VERONICA. Eventually, the developers expect to distribute this service to other sites. As of May 7, 1993, there were three publicly-accessible VERONICA servers: UNR, at the University of Nevada in Reno; CNIDR, the Clearinghouse for Networked Information Discovery and Retrieval at the University of Nevada; and NYSERnet, the New York State Education and Research Network.[2] On June 24, 1993, a fourth server was announced called SERRA at the University of Pisa in Italy.[3-5] Just as you think of Archie as a tool to scan directories of FTP sites, think of VERONICA as a tool to scan resources, newsgroup archives and telnet sites of numerous Gophers.

REFERENCE USES FOR VERONICA

One way researchers are notified about new electronic journals, newsgroups, bulletin-boards or databases in their field of interest is through newsgroups or electronic discussion lists for which they subscribe. A personal experience may best illustrate VERONICA's usefulness.

Recently, I saw an announcement on MEDLIB-L, an electronic discussion list for medical librarians, for a new electronic journal called AIDS BOOK REVIEW. The message also gave detailed instructions on editorial and subscription information. In my haste I deleted the message. However, by searching gopherspace using VERONICA, I was able to read the first issue (March 1993). VE-RONICA allowed me to search for the journal title by entering keywords and from a choice on the resulting menu, and retrieved the issue for me to read.

What makes VERONICA powerful is that it has the capability of retrieving resources by subject without needing to be concerned with the location where the information resides. This is specifically why I became interested in examining VERONICA as a possible tool in locating resources on the Internet by subject. During Internet training, one of the most commonly asked questions upon demonstrating Internet services such as telnet and FTP, is "How did you know the existence of such a file, directory, resource, newsgroup?" By demonstrating VERONICA, we can show researchers that this tool is a feasible method for retrieving subject specific resources on the Internet.

In the retrieval lists, some entries end with a marker <TEL> indicating that this is a telnet resource, and some have a suffix <?> indicating that the entry is an indexed directory resource, and this symbol (/) indicates that the source is a Gopher sub-directory or folder. With VERONICA, the user can locate the particular database from the listing, and directly telnet to it without having to know the Internet address (IP) or how to access it.[7] This is a very useful feature when providing reference service. Being able to locate full-text documents on the Internet could be equated with instantaneous document delivery service.

Recently, monthly Internet Hunts have been issued by Rick Gates, Director of Library Automation at the University of California at Santa Barbara, testing users on their proficiency in using the Internet on the Internet/Bitnet Network Trainers listserv. Increasingly, the winners of the Internet Hunt have stated they used VE-

RONICA to search through gopherspace for answers. This is yet another valuable reference use for VERONICA.[8]

EXAMPLES WITH STEP-BY-STEP INSTRUCTIONS

1. Simple Keyword Searching

This is a step-by-step guide of menu choices that I used to access the electronic journal called "Psycoloquy." Diagrams Al-A5 demonstrate the menu driven steps used to retrieve this document. You do not need to know the Internet address to access the journal.

At the $ prompt, type TELNET CONSULTANT.MICRO.-UMN.EDU. At the login: command, type GOPHER. Press enter at VT 100. The main menu of the University of Minnesota's Gopher service will appear. Choose 9 (Other Gopher and Information servers). Select 2 (Search titles in Gopherspace using VERONICA) from the second menu. Select 1 to Search Gopherspace using VE-RONICA at CNIDR, or 3 (Search gopherspace using VERONICA at NYSERNET) or 5 (Search gopherspace using VERONICA at UNR). In the "words to search for" box, type PSYCOLOQUY. "Psycoloquy" is a refereed electronic journal sponsored by the American Psychological Association's Science Directorate and Office of Publication and Communication, and co-edited by Steven Harnad and Perry London at Rutgers University.[1] From the menu of documents displayed, select "Psycoloquy (Journal)" and read the most recent issue.

DIAGRAM A-1

```
$ telnet consultant.micro.umn.edu
Trying... Connected to HAFNHAF.MICRO.UMN.EDU.

AIX telnet (hafnhaf)

Login as "gopher" to use the gopher system

IBM AIX Version 3 for RISC System/6000
(C) Copyrights by IBM and by others 1982, 1991.
login: gopher
TERM = (vt100)
Erase is Ctrl-H
Kill is Ctrl-U
Interrupt is Ctrl-C
I think you're on a vt100 terminal
```

DIAGRAM A-2

```
Internet Gopher+ Information Client v1.2beta3

Root gopher server: gopher2.tc.umn.edu

      1.   Information About Gopher/
      2.   Computer Information/
      3.   Internet file server (ftp) sites/
      4.   Fun & Games/
      5.   Libraries/
      6.   Mailing Lists/
      7.   UofM Campus Information/
      8.   News/
----9.     Other Gopher and Information Servers/
     10.   Phone Books/
     11.   Search lots of places at the U of M <?>
     12.   Search Gopher Titles at the University of Minnesota <?>


Press ? for Help, q to Quit, u to go up a menu         Page 1/1
```

DIAGRAM A-3

```
Internet Gopher+ Information Client v1.2beta3

Other Gopher and Information Servers

      1.   All the Gopher Servers in the World/
----2.     Search titles in Gopherspace using veronica/
      3.   Africa/
      4.   Asia/
      5.   Europe/
      6.   International Organizations/
      7.   Middle East/
      8.   North America/
      9.   Pacific/
     10.   South America/
     11.   Terminal Based Information/
     12.   WAIS Based Information/


Press ? for Help, q to Quit, u to go up a menu         Page 1/1
```

2. Boolean Searching

In another example, Diagram B1-B2, I have demonstrated how to retrieve subject-specific resources on the Internet using Boolean searching. Follow steps one to three exactly as you did in the previous example. When the system prompts you to enter keywords for searching, you can enter titles separated by Boolean operators. If

DIAGRAM A-4

```
          Internet Gopher+ Information Client v1.2beta3

              Search titles in Gopherspace using veronica


     1.   Search gopherspace using veronica at CNIDR <?>
     2.   Search gopherspace for GOPHER DIRECTORIES (CNIDR) <?>
----3.   Search gopherspace using veronica at NYSERNet <?>
     4.   Search gopherspace for GOPHER DIRECTORIES (NYSERNet) <?>
     5.   Search gopherspace using veronica at UNR <?>
     6.   Search gopherspace for GOPHER DIRECTORIES (UNR) <?>
     7.
     8.   How to compose "simple boolean" veronica queries ( NEW May 19 ).
     9.   FAQ: Frequently-Asked Questions about veronica (1993/05/15).
    10.   Setting up a veronica server: new code available .
    11.   NEW_FEATURE:__Search_by_Gopher_type.
    12.   Older_veronica_documentation/


Press ? for Help, q to Quit, u to go up a menu          Page 1/1
```

DIAGRAM A-5

```
          Internet Gopher+ Information Client v1.2beta3

              Search titles in Gopherspace using veronica


     1.   Search gopherspace using veronica at CNIDR <?>
     2.   Search gopherspace for GOPHER DIRECTORIES (CNIDR) <?>
----3.   Search gopherspace using veronica at NYSERNet <?>
     4.   Search gopherspace for GOPHER DIRECTORIES (NYSERNet) <?>
 ┌───────────Search gopherspace using veronica at NYSERNet───────────┐
 │                                                                    │
 │ Words to search for  psycoloquy                                    │
 │                                                                    │
 │                          (Cancel ^G) (Accept - Enter)              │
 │                                                                    │
 └────────────────────────────────────────────────────────────────────┘

    12.   Older_veronica_documentation/

Press ? for Help, q to Quit, u to go up a menu          Page 1/1
```

two words are entered adjacent to one another without a specific operator, the system will assume the terms are combined with an "AND" operator.

To retrieve files on AIDS (Acquired Immunodeficiency Syndrome) and drugs, the VERONICA server returns a Gopher menu of items whose titles match the specified keywords. An unlimited number of ANDs and ORs may be used in a search query. Note that for more complex Boolean searches, the "OR" takes precedence

DIAGRAM B-1

```
Internet Gopher + Information Client v1.2beta3

     Search titles in Gopherspace using veronica

     1. Search gopherspace using veronica at CNIDR <?>
     2. Search gopherspace for GOPHER DIRECTORIES  (CNIDR) <?>
---- 3. Search gopherspace using veronica at NYSERNet <?>
     4. Search gopherspace for GOPHER DIRECTORIES  (NYSERNet) <?>
┌────────Search gopherspace using Veronica at NYSERNet────────┐
│                                                             │
│ Words to search for    aids and drug*                       │
│                                                             │
│                     (Cancel ^G)  (Accept - Enter)           │
│                                                             │
└─────────────────────────────────────────────────────────────┘

    12. Older_veronica_documentation/

Press ? for Help, q to Quit, u to go up a menu        Page 1/1
```

DIAGRAM B-2

```
Internet Gopher+ Information Client v1.2beta3

   Search gopherspace using veronica at NYSERNet: aids and drug*

----1. Fighting AIDS: Scientists seek new drug design route.
    2. NIH-NIAID-DAIDS-93-25 DRUG DEVELOPMENT FOR TOXOPLASMOSIS ASSOC.
    3. R2: NIH-NIAID-DAIDS-93-25 DRUG DEVELOPMENT FOR TOXOPLASMOSIS ASSO.
    4. GM-91-02 STRUCTURAL BIOLOGY AS APPLIED TO THE PROBLEM OF TARGETED..
    5. GM-91-02-FT STRUCTURAL BIOLOGY AS APPLIED TO THE PROBLEM OF TARGE..
    6. R5: GM-91-02 STRUCTURAL BIOLOGY AS APPLIED TO THE PROBLEM OF TA...
    7. R5: GM-91-02-FT STRUCTURAL BIOLOGY AS APPLIED TO THE PROBLEM OF TA.

Press ? for Help, q to Quit, u to go up a menu        Page 1/1
```

over the "AND" operator. The use of parenthesis for more complicated Boolean searching and the "NOT" as a logical operator are two new enhancements introduced in version 0.4. With the new feature of restricting the search to certain Gopher types, the user can, for example, type "-tl" before or after a keyword, allowing the searcher to link exclusively to Gopher directories.[3,4] Terms are not case-sensitive, and the truncation symbol is an asterisk symbol which is used as a wild card for endings of words.

HELPFUL FEATURES

VERONICA searches the titles of almost all Gopher servers on the Internet. Similar to any Gopher menu, one can access the item of interest by double clicking or selecting the numbered item one needs. It is easy to return to a previous menu by typing "U" and "Q" to quit searching. Searching VERONICA is simple and it is easy to move through the Gopher menus.

The help screens describing how to move around gopherspace, and how to create and view bookmarks are very useful. If a researcher finds a particular resource interesting, he/she can save the item in the bookmark list. In addition, the FAQ (Frequently Asked Questions about VERONICA) offer very helpful hints.[2,3] If you select #8 from the "Search Titles in Gopherspace using VERONICA" menu, you can read instructions on conducting a Boolean search. All versions of FAQs are archived and can be read when you search for VERONICA as a single keyword.

LIMITATIONS

In spite of its being easy to use, VERONICA is still in its experimental stage and has certain limitations. Searching for matching titles in gopherspace takes a long time. Once a list of files has been retrieved, and the searcher selects an item from the menu, the wheel spins while the Gopher is fetching the item for an Internet site, and unfortunately, in many cases responds with a "nothing available" message. The problem is that some files contain unrecognized data and non-standard formats that cannot be handled by certain client servers. In addition, when VERONICA searches for items not recognized by the client, the Gopher client "hangs." You may also encounter responses such as "cannot access directory" or "connection refused by host" or "restricted access" that could be frustrating after you have waited for over 15 minutes for a response. During certain times of the day, and especially in the afternoons, Eastern standard time, it is virtually impossible to get connected to some servers. Also, if you decide to cancel a search once the system starts searching, there is no obvious way to stop the process. You may want to try Ctrl C to cancel your connection.

Because indexing is dependent on words of Gopher titles alone, users may end up having to select irrelevant documents just to determine their contents. In addition, the problem of duplication still exists in spite of new software introduced by the developers in December

1992, to collapse the many listings for the same document.[8] It appears that this problem will be addressed if the Internet adopts a Uniform Resource Number scheme. Much work is being done by the Internet Engineering Task Force to investigate the possibility of providing uniform numbers for locating Internet documents and services.

CONCLUSION

The development team is constantly changing and enhancing searching capabilities and updating the database on a weekly or biweekly basis. By the time this article is published, many of the menus described will have changed. Furthermore, many more files and resources continue to be added almost daily. As educators are discovering the wealth of resources on the Internet, they are also finding out that it is virtually impossible to remain proficient in searching techniques. Librarians should continue to play an important role in training users how to search the Internet, in using it for their own research and in providing general and specialized reference service. I see VERONICA as a useful tool for accessing Internet resources by subject, but until faster searching services are available, reference librarians will find it unsatisfactory for providing ready reference.

REFERENCES

1. *Directory of Electronic Journals, Newsletters and Academic Discussion Lists,* edited by Ann Okerson, second edition, Washington, DC, Association of Research Libraries, 1992.

2. *FAQ: Frequently-Asked Questions about Veronica* (1993/05/07).

3. *FAQ: Frequently-Asked Questions about Veronica* (1993/06/24).

4. *How to compose veronica queries* (NEW June 24) READ ME!!

5. Search gopherspace for GOPHER DIRECTORIES (U. Pisa) <?>.

6. Smith, Judy and Updegrove, Daniel " Navigating the Internet" *PENN-PRINTOUT* 9 (4), February 1993 (University of Pennsylvania).

7. *The Whole Internet: User's Guide & Catalog,* edited by Ed Krol, Sebastopol, CA, O'Reilley & Associates, 1992, Chapter 11.

8. Wiggins, Rich, "The University of Minnesota's Internet Gopher System: A Tool for Accessing Network-Based Electronic Information." *The Public-Access Computer Systems Review* 4 (2), 1993: 4-60. To retrieve this file, send the following e-mail messages to LISTSERV@UHUPVM1; Get files: Wiggins 1 and Wiggins 2.

The Internet Gopher:
A Reference Tool

John Joseph Small

SUMMARY. An overview of the Gopher distributed document delivery resource. Internet access through various ports are indicated. Usage, set-up, and reference area ideas; the benefits of the client-server protocol; and Gopher strengths and weaknesses are discussed.

INTRODUCTION

Gopher is one of the most powerful Internet tools yet developed, and it offers advantages and benefits that the reference professional cannot, in good conscience, ignore. The interface is particularly easy to use and requires few computer skills. It has been my experience that even the most computer-phobic librarian can use Gopher to the fullest extent. Gopher was designed as a local document delivery system, and has grown from that point. Gopher itself is a client-server protocol which functions as a worldwide information retrieval system. When you log into a Gopher server you are presented with a menu. Choosing from that menu, the computer can either access a local database or a remote database. Gopher then returns either another menu full of choices, the document requested or a remote database to search. Gopher gives the user a "consistent,

John Joseph Small is Electronic Resources Librarian, Ward Edwards Library, Central Missouri State University, Warrensburg, MO 64093.

[Haworth co-indexing entry note]: "The Internet Gopher: A Reference Tool." Small, John Joseph. Co-published simultaneously in *The Reference Librarian* (The Haworth Press, Inc.) No. 41/42, 1994, pp. 47-54; and: *Librarians on the Internet: Impact on Reference Services* (ed: Robin Kinder) The Haworth Press, Inc., 1994 pp. 47-54. Multiple copies of this article/chapter may be purchased from The Haworth Document Delivery Center [1-800-3-HAWORTH; 9:00 a.m. - 5:00 p.m. (EST)].

simple menu interface and hides the method used to retrieve" the information.[1] It is possible to access information stored half a world away by simply following a menu path until you reach a logical conclusion. "Documents reside on many autonomous servers on the Internet. Users run client software on their desktop systems, connecting to a server and sending the server a selector . . . via a TCP connection at a well known port."[2]

It is important to keep in mind that since Gopher is being constantly updated, continual searching must be done to make sure information is the most current and applicable. Simply identifying a number of sources and habitually checking those will not always guarantee that you are getting the best information.

There are many differing types of information available through Gopher. Much of the information deals, naturally, with computers, but there are many other subject areas covered as well. There are "phone books, recipes, resource indexes, scientific data, weather, library databases, books, government information, local trivia, reference and much more."[3]

GOPHER GENESIS

Gopher was designed by a team of specialists in April 1991 at the University of Minnesota Network Center with the intention of helping University of Minnesota students to answer their computer questions. (E-mail can be sent to the designers at Gopher@Boombox.Micro.UMN.Edu.) The first attempt at designing an in-house CWIS was a "classic design-by-committee monstrosity."[4] The University of Minnesota Gopher team designed a simple interface, and were eventually allowed to proceed with their plans. Gopher development continues, and is available for most platforms with significant upgrades being added or worked on. The Gopher design group wanted to allow University of Minnesota departments to be able to "[publish] information from their desktop machines" and to be able to arrange this information in a simple, logical manner.[5]

Gopher has evolved, in the two and one-half years since its design, into one of the most heavily used Internet tools. The fact that the protocol can be run on so many different systems, and that it can be customized to provide access to many differing types of files and formats is its major strength. The same relatively simple software that was designed to link multiple servers at University of Minnesota now links hundreds of servers across the world, creating a de facto worldwide information system.[6] "The fundamental concepts in Gopher are the menu, the link, the document and the index."[7] The menu is the navigation tool, the link is what allows you to move about within gopherspace, the outside connection is generally a telnet connection, often to a library catalog, and the index is what allows searching.

GOPHER REFERENCE USES

Since Gopher places information hierarchically within the menu structure it is far easier to retrieve than if it were located in a number of disparate sources and/or locations.[8] This structure, reminiscent of a filing cabinet, is one of the major reasons that Gopher functions so intuitively. Since it can be safely assumed that most of the users of a program like Gopher have some experience using a basic document retrieval source like a filing cabinet, the designers created what functions as a giant (even world-sized) virtual filing cabinet.

There are so many different kinds of information contained in Gopher, and so many different locations for the information, that it is possible to have a terminal logged into a Gopher server at the reference desk. When traditional sources cannot find the information sought, Gopher is a logical alternative. Another strength of the Gopher system is the penchant for today's students to prefer electronic information sources to print resources. I have suggested a publicly available Gopher terminal located near all the other terminals at the reference desk for patron use.

One of the reasons Gopher is so useful to the practicing reference librarian is the ability to place "bookmarks" in desired locations, allowing easy recall of specific menus and pieces of information. By placing a bookmark at the main menu of, for example, the on-line version of the *Chronicle of Higher Education,* the librarian can instantly recall that menu, without going through the mental gymnastics required to find the location again.

EXISTING GOPHERS SERVERS

Many of the pieces of information located on Gopher servers are copied in numerous databases around gopherspace. One of the difficulties in accessing information from a Gopher platform is that you can rarely be certain that you have the most current available copy of the work in question. Because of the electronic format, it is possible to update and edit the information placed on a Gopher server with great ease. E-journals are another example. While many Gopher servers simply access a remote database where the most current edition is held, some Gopher administrators try to beat the time lag by loading copies of a journal on their local machine. While this can work out well in some cases, it can also be neglected after the initial load, leading the user to the conclusion that they have copied the most current edition of a journal, when in reality they have only accessed the most current edition available on the machine they were interacting with.

LIBRARY CATALOGS THROUGH GOPHER

Most library catalogs available through Gopher are network telnet connections. Since Gopher cannot yet be truly interactive, built-in telnet links are established to various catalogs so that searching can be accomplished without having to leave the Gopher domain. This is one of the major strengths of the Gopher system, because catalogs can be invoked and searched by a fairly novice Internet/Gopher user without having to learn telnet commands and without learning the actual name of the machine that is to be searched. To telnet to the on-line catalog at Princeton, you need to know the name or logical number of the machine the catalog resides on, but if you're in Gopher all that needs to be done is a VERONICA search on the name, Princeton. This will lead you to a series of menu choices, one of which is the automatic telnet connection to the catalog.

ACCESSING GOPHER

If you have access to the telnet protocols, you have access to limited-use Gophers. While it is infinitely preferable to run your own Gopher client software, there are a number of remote log-ins available for exploration and use. A list of some of the more common and accessible sites follows this article. It is important to note that not all information located on a Gopher server is available through the remote log-in. Local databases, UPI news feeds and other contracted databases are often blocked off unless the user is entering through a locally funded account. A list of sites where Gopher software can be obtained (by the way, it's free) is in the Gopher FAQ located in a number of places both within and without Gopher. The most common place to FTP the software is in the/pub/gopher directory of boombox.micro.umn.edu.[9]

A short list of public Gopher login sites includes:

Hostname:	Login as:
consultant.micro.umn.edu	gopher
gopher.uiuc.edu	gopher
panda.uiowa	panda
gopher.sunet.se	gopher (Europe)
info.anu.edu.au	info (Australia)

It is also possible, albeit more complicated, to develop your own Gopher server, that is, to offer your own information and information structure to all the other Gopher users. Server software is also available for a number of machines, from a number of locations. This software can also be downloaded from a number of locations.

VERONICA/ARCHIE SEARCH ENGINES

Archie is "a network service that allows you to search quickly the contents of anonymous FTP sites all over the Internet. This is the best way to find elusive shareware or freeware."[10]

VERONICA is "a service that maintains an index of titles of Gopher items, and provides keyword searches of those titles."[11] VERONICA is one of the key elements in successfully finding information in Gopher. Limited Boolean searching is available, and enhancements are anticipated.

UNIVERSITY OF ILLINOIS AT CHICAGO GOPHER

The UIC root Gopher format is both logical and intuitive. It sets up its internal hierarchy on concepts that are familiar to all and inherently logical. The initial (root) screen offers basic choices that allow the user to burrow selectively depending on the type of information being sought. It also allows information to be structured without resorting to Dewey or LC breakdowns, an idea many users aren't intimately familiar with and one that the Gopher designers are not in favor of. GOPHER.UIC.EDU looks like this:

<document>	UIC/ADN – INTRODUCTION
<document>	What's New (date)
<Menu>	Search the UIC Campus and Beyond
<Menu>	The Administrator
<Menu>	The Campus
<Menu>	The Classroom
<Menu>	The Community
<Menu>	The Computer
<Menu>	The Library
<Menu>	The Researcher
<Menu>	The World

Once you have navigated a number of Gopher servers you will become intimately aware of the differences and similarities inherent in the structure of the information. Some structures are logical and a joy to use. Others are, charitably, experimental and erratic. Moving from one server to another the user can begin to see some standard formats developing, but there is still time to develop your own vision for Gopher layouts.

Librarians have had an enormous impact on Gopher use and development. In many universities the Gopher client and/or server is under the control of the library. Since we, as librarians, have the requisite knowledge and experience in storing and organizing information, this is as it should be. One of the problems engendered by this situation, however, is the temptation to use formats designed for print sources in this more fluid environment. As one example, many library science articles, such as this one, delve into the field of computer science. A cataloger would likely place these types of information in the library section. With a Gopher, however, you could place pointers in both library and computer science without having to store the information more than one time. This allows us to create as many subject headings as a piece of information warrants without worrying about overloading a MARC record or purchasing multiple copies.

CONCLUSION

"Gopher makes it possible to have one program that everyone knows how to use that allows them access to information from all university departments as well as from outside the university."[12] Since you can access many differing types of information and services using one consistent interface, Gopher is a sound choice for all users, but it is a magnificent tool for beginning Internet users, and further development should allow for simpler net-wide searching abilities.

Gopher functions as a virtual, self-serve reference desk. Many users can navigate Gopher on their own, but it is important for reference librarians to develop their own skills in this area. I have mediated Gopher searches at the reference desk and converted a number of patrons into Gopher users. Much of what is currently available in Gopher is available in other sources, or in other Internet locations. The major difference is that when using Gopher the librarian or patron can locate this information through the use of one technology, with a consistent interface.

REFERENCES

1. University of Illinois. *Information Services Document #100* (ADN Computer Center. consult@uicvm.uic.edu n.d.).

2. Bob Alberti et al., *The Internet Gopher Protocol: A Distributed Document Search and Retrieval Protocol* (University of Minnesota: Microcomputer and Workstation Networks Center, 1992).

3. University of Illinois. ADN Computer Center. *Information Services Document #100* (consult@uicvm.uic.edu, 1993).

4. Prentice Riddle. *GopherCon '93: Internet Gopher Workshop and Internet Gopher Conference* (riddle@is.rice.edu, n.d.).

5. Bob Alberti et al. *The Internet Gopher Protocol* 1992.
6. University of Illinois. "Exploring the Power of the Internet." *UIUCNews 6* (1992): 2-5 ftp cso.uiuc.edu doc/net/uiucnet).
7. Nathan Torkington. *Gopher–The Internet Resource Discoverer* (Nathan. Torkington @VUW.AC.NZ, n.d.).
8. Paul Gibbs. *Gopher at the University of Illinois* (gopher@uiuc.edu, n.d.).
9. Netnews. *Frequently Asked Questions on Internet Gopher* (Netnews/ Usenet Frequently Asked Questions Series, 1993. comp.infosystems.gopher).
10. Joel Cooper. *Campus and Worldwide Information* (University of Notre Dame Information. Notre Dame Document G2690, 1992).
11. University of Illinois at Chicago. *Gophering at UIC Quick Facts for On-line Information Services through Gopher and UICINFO* (ADN Computer Center Document #1001005 consult@uicvm.uic.edu).
12. Gibbs. *Gopher.*

BIBLIOGRAPHY

In keeping with the focus of this issue all the citations and research for this article were taken from various Gopher sources and Veronica searches. Most of the information will come up by searching Veronica with the key word "Gopher." I do, however, suggest that other key words are added to refine your search. In some cases I have been able to identify the author of the works cited. Where possible this information has been included. However, many of the citations are for corporate authors, and it is common for no dates to be made available.

Alberti, Bob et al. 1992. *The Internet Gopher Protocol: A Distributed Document Search and Retrieval Protocol.* University of Minnesota Microcomputer and Workstation Networks Center.

Cooper, Joel. 1992. *Campus and Worldwide Information.* University of Notre Dame Information. Notre Dame Document G2690.

Gibbs, Paul. n.d. *Gopher at the University of Illinois.* gopher@uiuc.edu.

Netnews. 1993. Frequently Asked Questions on Internet Gopher. Netnews/Usenet *Frequently Asked Questions Series.* comp.infosystems.gopher.

Riddle, Prentice. 1993. *GopherCon '93: Internet Gopher Workshop and Internet Gopher Conference.* riddle@is.rice.edu.

Torkington, Nathan. n.d. *Gopher–The Internet Resource Discoverer.* Nathan.Torkington@VUW.AC.NZ.

University of Illinois. 1992. *Exploring the Power of the Internet.* UIUCnet. 6:2-5. ftp.cso.uiuc.edu doc/net/uiucnet.

University of Illinois. ADN Computer Center. 1993. *Information Services Document #100.* consult@uicvm.uic.edu.

University of Illinois at Chicago. 1993. *GOPHERING at UIC. Quick Facts for Online Information Sources through Gopher and UICINFO.* ADN Computer Center Document #1001005. consult@uicvm.uic.edu.

SELECTED SOURCES
ON THE INTERNET

Geoscience Resources on the Internet

Ralph Lee Scott

SUMMARY. This article will describe Geoscience resources available on the Internet, primarily the Weather Underground, the Geographic Name Server at the University of Michigan, and the Weather Machine at the University of Illinois. Instructions for connecting to these three sites will be given, as well as information on two gopher sites that have these systems on their menus. The Weather Underground and the Weather Machine provide real time analysis of North American weather, climate and active geographic phenomena. In addition to current weather analysis the Weather Underground provides current information on active hurricanes, earthquakes, and in the winter, "Current Ski Conditions." A special section covers near-shore and offshore marine forecasts, warnings, and notices to mariners (such as missing or lost vessels).[1] Weather forecasts are avail-

Ralph Lee Scott is Head, Documents/Maps, J.Y. Joyner Library, East Carolina University, Greenville, NC 27858.

His mailing address is B07 Joyner Library, East Carolina University, Greenville, NC 27858. Email: lbscott@ecuvm1.bitnet (Bitnet); ralsco@joyner.library ecu.edu (Internet).

[Haworth co-indexing entry note]: "Geoscience Resources on the Internet." Scott, Ralph Lee. Co-published simultaneously in *The Reference Librarian* (The Haworth Press, Inc.) No. 41/42, 1994, pp. 55-63; and: *Librarians on the Internet: Impact on Reference Services* (ed: Robin Kinder) The Haworth Press, Inc., 1994, pp. 55-63. Multiple copies of this article/chapter may be purchased from The Haworth Document Delivery Center [1-800-3-HAWORTH; 9:00 a.m. - 5:00 p.m. (EST)].

able for most U.S. cities as well as immediate postings of weather warnings and watches. Storm damage reports are also listed, in most cases soon after the event happens. Reports come from the U.S. Weather Bureau central offices (e.g., National Hurricane Center, National Severe Storms Center), local weather offices (e.g., Chicago Weather Bureau), and a nationwide network of individual spotters and law enforcement officials. Reference librarians can use this server to provide clients with real time information on current conditions both locally and continent wide. The Weather Machine also provides additional geoscience information sources to consult as well as many of the services offered by the Weather Underground.

The Geographic Name Server provides a listing of cities and geographic features in the United States. Searches can be done by Zip Code, and Place Name. The server will respond with the city location, time zone, latitude and longitude, Zip Code, Area Code, etc.

INTRODUCTION

Locating geoscience information sources on the Internet can be a difficult experience for the reference librarian. This paper will cover two of the most common types of geographic information found on the Internet: weather information and geographic name information. The Weather Underground at the University of Michigan and the Weather Machine at the University of Illinois provide real time current data and reference information on weather events. These two collections of online Internet reference materials may be accessed by a local gopher/WAIS server or through the nationwide Internet access servers at the University of North Carolina at Chapel Hill (laUNCh) or University of Washington at St. Louis (services).[1] The Weather Underground and the Weather Machine provide current weather observations and forecasts as well as special files unique to each system.

WEATHER UNDERGROUND

The Weather Underground is run by the University of Michigan Department of Atmospheric, Oceanic and Space Sciences with help from the University Corporation for Atmospheric Research in

Boulder, Colorado. The Main Menu of the Weather Underground is divided into eleven sections. The first section provides current United States forecasts and climate data. It is updated whenever a local weather office issues a new forecast. This is usually at least twice a day, with additional forecasts as conditions warrant. To print out a forecast you need to know the three letter city code for the forecast office. This is usually, but not always, the same as the three letter code for you main local airport. (For example, the code for Los Angeles is LAX). When you select the United States forecast section from the Main Menu, you are directed to the City Forecast Menu. Here you may directly type in the three letter code for the forecast (if you know it) or press number 3 for a list of three letter codes for a selection state. If you do not know your state's two letter code (required for step 3) press 4 and you will be shown a list of two letter state codes. If you press 2 from the City Forecast Menu you will be prompted for the three letter code, only this time you will get selected climatic data for the city (usually on a 24-hour basis). The same type of basic forecast information is available from Environment Canada by selecting 2 on the Main menu. You are then shown a list of Canadian provinces to select from for their local forecasts' stations.

Selection 3 on the Weather Underground Main menu provides current real time weather observations for the United States by state. The choices from the Current Weather Menu are either to display current observations by state two letter code or to display a list of two letter state codes. A main feature of the Weather Underground is real time current weather observations, updated once an hour on or about the top of the hour. It is useful for tracking the progress of storms and determining the forecast for your local area between weather station forecasts.

Current ski conditions can be obtained on the Weather Underground from selection 4 on the Main Menu. These appear to be supplied by ski promotion offices in states that have large business interests in ski operations. Updating of the reports varies, but is usually rather current on a daily basis in season. The usual information is supplied: conditions on the slope, amount of recent snow and general pro-skiing propaganda for the area (e.g., it has been raining for two days on 32 inches of packed powder, conditions are poor but expected to improve as soon as you show up with your money).

Section 5 of the Weather Underground provides intermediate and long range forecasts by the United States Weather Service. The Long-Range Forecast Menu, as it is called, provides 1-7 day outlooks; 6-10 day outlooks; 30 day outlooks and 90 day outlooks. The 1-7 day outlook is by region (Eastern, Central, Southwest, Northwest and Canada) and addresses specific areas in terms of specific temperature and humidities. The 6-10 day outlook is by specific area and provides information on the outlook for temperature and humidity. The 30 day and 90 day outlooks are more general in nature due to their more advanced look forward. This reviewer will not comment on the specific accuracy of these forecasts except to say that they are the best your tax dollars can buy at present. The overall accuracy range improves as the time of the forecast gets shorter.

The latest earthquake reports are available on the Weather Underground as main menu option 5. These are worldwide reports from the United States Geological Survey National Earthquake Information Center, and give the strength and location of earthquakes during the past few months. No local damage data is provided other than a general statement about the severity of the quake. Earthquakes are posted within minutes of their detection.

A very important part the weather service provides is up-to-the-minute severe weather announcements. This service is available as main menu option 7 on the Weather Underground. The Severe Weather Menu provides you with the number of current severe watches in effect; severe warnings issued; flood warnings given; storm damage reports (filed by local weather offices from law enforcement officers; weather spotters; pilots and ham radio operators); severe weather statements (actual observations of severe weather as opposed to warnings and watches); winter weather statements (again, actual observations, e.g., "22 inches of snow fell on Donner Pass this morning, travel difficult"; winter weather watches and warnings are given in the watches and warning section); and a special weather statement section (which can cover any special weather event in progress or anticipated soon: fog, smoke, heavy rain, frost, freeze, strong thunderstorms, hail, Emergency Broadcast

Service tests, etc.). This is a very important and potentially life-saving service offered on the Weather Underground. Information comes directly from the National Weather Service Severe Storms Forecast Center and local weather offices. Also on the severe storms menu are a daily log of tornado and severe thunderstorms and monthly tornado statistics.

Selection 8 on the Main Menu is the Hurricane Advisories and Tropical Weather Summaries Menu. These are provided worldwide by oceanographic area: Atlantic; East Pacific; Central Pacific; West Pacific; and Indian Ocean. This menu also offers (prior to the hurricane season) an annual Atlantic Hurricane Season Summary (numbers, severity and frequency of past season storms) and (during hurricane season) an annual Atlantic Hurricane Season Storm Forecast (numbers, severity and frequency of projected storms). Special hurricanes such as Andrew rate a special report selection on the Hurricane summary menu. Current real time statements (warnings and watches for hurricanes and tropical storms) supplied by the National Hurricane Center in Coral Gables, Florida are given for local stations during actual storm events. Again, a real life saving service by the Weather Underground.

A daily National Weather Forecast Summary is posted each day around 4 p.m. Eastern Time (Daylight or Standard as appropriate) by the National Weather Service in Kansas City, Missouri as menu selection 9 on the Weather Underground. These forecasts are rather general in nature ("snowstorm looms for parts of the Rockies and Plains") but do offer insight into what local conditions are forecast for a very broad area. This is the daily general syntoptic (frontal) forecast for the United States provided by the United States Weather Service. Main Menu selection 10 is reserved for a future international real time data and forecasts, should the International Meteorological Organization ever get such a service up and running through the Internet.

Choice 11 on the Weather Underground Main Menu provides marine forecasts and observations. These are grouped by nearshore (1-5 miles) forecasts, offshore (6-25 miles) forecasts, and marine observations (selected deep water observations and forecasts). The latter sometimes contain postings of notices to special marine interests such as missing boats, aircraft, etc. As you can see, these services provided by the Weather Underground are useful from a reference point of view. In fact, at times they can provide patrons with lifesaving information on road conditions, hurricanes, tornados, floods and localized severe weather. The same type of information is also provided by the Weather Machine at the University of Illinois, but with the addition of some special files.

WEATHER MACHINE

The Weather Machine at the University of Illinois is also menu driven. One uses a pointer to select the submenu files one wants to see. The pointer is moved by the keyboard up and down arrow keys. After getting the pointer to the correct position, the user presses the enter or return key and is connected to the submenu selected. To go up to a prior menu, press the u key (no enter or return). The initial menu on the Weather Machines offers choices of: a tour; system update information (called maintenance–similar to a software read.me file); Canadian weather; Caribbean weather; documents on other weather information on the Internet; current nationwide forecast information; Illinois weather; weather maps images (GIF); a miscellaneous section; regional weather information; weather satellite files (GIF); servers; severe weather information; weather state by state; surface weather; and upper atmosphere weather.

Each of these submenus leads the user to additional files online. For example, selecting the Images submenu can lead to: strip charts; an upper air map; a 6-panel surface weather map; infrared satellite images; satellite visible images; water vapor images; and many others. Selecting the satellite visible images leads to yet another submenu, this time giving thirteen GIF images from the visible light satellite depicting the East Coast of the United States at hourly intervals for the previous thirteen hours.

Selecting the Documents submenu gives three pages of further selections of information on other weather reference materials including books, periodicals, and Internet servers. This is sort of like a FAQ section, for those of you familiar with server FAQ files. For example, here you can: search the library book database of the University of Illinois Department of Atmospheric Sciences library; look at a list of weather stations; search a glossary of weather terms;

look for weather pictures or look for additional information sources on the weather (FAQ.WEATHER).

The FAQ.WEATHER section begins with changes in online weather information sources available on the Internet. Recent additions include a Great Blizzard of 1993 ftp information site; a Great Blizzard of 1993 mac ftp site; a server providing NOAA AVHRR information on Western Europe; and another server giving online weather information from Chile. The archive then continues with a chapter on data servers available over the internet; a chapter on weather research data on tape and other media; and a chapter on weather related listservers (or mailings lists) on the Internet. No doubt the recent Midwest floods of 1993 statistics will soon be recorded in FAQ.WEATHER.

Typical weather related servers on the Internet include special files on: GMS-4 images of Australia; Oregon weather forecasts; Chilean weather (in Spanish); information on climatic change; information on Ocean data; Viking, Magellan and Voyager images from CD/ROM; snow cover maps; pictures taken from the Space Shuttle; elevation data; the CIA World Bank 0.5 degree elevation dataset; East Coast Blizzard movie; Hurricane Andrew images; Hurricane Hugo images; images from Europe; datasets from the National Climatic Data Center (Asheville, NC); Advanced Very High Radiation Radiometer (AVHRR) images; and ham radio storm chasers frequencies.

The complete wealth of weather information available here is beyond the scope of this paper; users needing reference information are urged to explore the various submenus for additional clues to sources of information available at the University of Illinois Weather Machine.

GEOGRAPHIC NAME SERVER

The Geographic Name Server is located at the University of Michigan. It can be most easily accessed through the University of North Carolina laUNCH Internet access server.[2] The Geographic Name Server contains a listing of geographic place names in the United States. This includes cities, towns, counties, national parks, geographic features, bodies of water, etc. Searches can be done by zip code, and place name. When the server locates information on the place it will respond with: the location, time zone, latitude and longitude, elevation, county, state, and zip code(s). This server can be very useful to reference librarians needing local information on geographic locales. For long entries, the information retrieved may be more than one screen, all of which flies past the reader in one shot. There is a piping feature that allows the user to view the information one screen at a time (control g). The outputted information is unlabelled, but most information is obvious. There is a help section which is accessed by entering help at the system prompt.

CONCLUSION

Reference librarians can use these three servers to provide real time information on current weather conditions and geographic place name data. The "Weather Underground," the "Weather Machine," and the "Geographic Name Server" are examples of the types of reference information sources available on the Internet. For more detailed information on additional geoscience sources, see the online FAQ section on the Weather Machine.[3] The author hopes you will enjoy your visits to these sites and that you will return to them frequently to assist your patrons with their geoscience reference questions.

REFERENCES

1. The servers are located at the following addresses:

Name of server	Telnet address:	Telnet mnemonic:
laUNCh (UNC)	152.2.22.80	ebb.oit.unc.edu
Univ. of Washington	128.252.120.1	wugate.wustl.edu
Weather Underground	141.212.196.79	madlab.sprl.umich.edu 3000
Weather Machine	128.174.80.10	wx.atmos.uiuc.edu 70

The last two can be ftped from your local site using anonymous as your login and your email address as the password (if requested). However, it is much easier to use either laUNCh or services. LaUNCh at the University of North Carolina at Chapel Hill and Services at the University of Washington at St. Louis, provide nationwide access to the Weather Underground. LaUNCh provides nationwide access to the Weather Machine at the University of Illinois and the Geographic Name Server at the University of Michigan. To reach LaUNCh telnet to the address given, then type "launch." Follow the prompts to register (LaUNCh only requires your name and city to register. Registration and access free). To reach the University of Washington at St. Louis Services telnet to the address given, then type "services" at the system prompt. No registration is required.

2. The Geographic Name Server can be accessed at the University of North Carolina by teleneting to: open 152.2.22.80 or connecting to: lambda.oit.unc.edu.

3. For access see above.

Economic and Statistical Information on the Internet

Keith A. Morgan

SUMMARY. A complex and dynamic economy requires the most timely and comprehensive information. The expansion of the Internet is perfectly suited to the requirements of the economic researcher. Two specific sources of Internet accessible economic information, the Economic Bulletin Board and EconData are described and contrasted. Directions for access are provided and a brief listing of other resources for economic information are listed. Illustrations of the various screen access points are also included.

INTRODUCTION

The study of economics is carried out with text, numerical, and equation-based research. This combination not only makes economics unique in the social sciences, it also makes it the academic discipline perfectly suited to benefit from Internet access and expansion. In a complex and dynamic economy researchers will always have a need for the latest and most comprehensive datasets.

Keith A. Morgan is Assistant Reference Librarian and Economics Subject Specialist, Dewey Library for Management and the Social Sciences, Massachusetts Institute of Technology, Cambridge, MA 02139-4307. Internet: kamorgan@Athena.MIT.EDU.

The author wishes to thank the many librarians, professors, students, researchers, and others who make online research so rewarding.

[Haworth co-indexing entry note]: "Economic and Statistical Information on the Internet." Morgan, Keith A. Co-published simultaneously in *The Reference Librarian* (The Haworth Press, Inc.) No. 41/42, 1994, pp. 65-79; and: *Librarians on the Internet: Impact on Reference Services* (ed: Robin Kinder) The Haworth Press, Inc., 1994, pp. 65-79. Multiple copies of this article/chapter may be purchased from The Haworth Document Delivery Center [1-800-3-HAWORTH; 9:00 a.m. - 5:00 p.m. (EST)].

But how will the existence of these new sources affect librarians at the reference desk? The purpose of this article is to discuss a number of the more important Internet access points for economics, explain both where they are and what they contain, and, finally, to suggest how knowledge of these sources can be incorporated into the reference transaction.

Electronic sources of macroeconomic data have been available for some time but until recently have been accessible only through magnetic tapes which require mounting on mainframe computers. The Inter-university Consortium for Political and Social Research (ICPSR) has, for many years, been an excellent source of comprehensive numerical data. However, some important institutions do not belong to ICPSR. Also, in some academic institutions ICPSR is managed through the campus computer systems department or academic data laboratories. Although librarians are increasingly becoming involved as Official Representatives to the ICPSR or as liaisons between the computer center and the library, librarians are still sometimes unaware of how the datasets may be used. For this reason, librarians are often circumvented in the promotion of ICPSR or other electronic media. With Internet access in the library, it is now possible for librarians to obtain certain economic datasets directly. Of course, it is important to emphasize that what is so far available via the Internet is not in any way as comprehensive or flexible as the raw data available through ICPSR. Nevertheless, there are important sources out on the Internet.[1]

THE ECONOMIC BULLETIN BOARD

The most essential source of online United States Government economic information is the Department of Commerce's Economic Bulletin Board or EBB. The EBB contains 20 separate file areas, with over 2000 daily updated files. A researcher can obtain such current economic and trade information, for example, as economic indicators, U.S. Treasury auction results, unemployment statistics, Federal Reserve Board interest rates, and economic condition summaries.

The EBB has been accessible since 1987 through dial-up modem access directly to Washington. Unfortunately, for libraries and researchers outside the District of Columbia, accessing the EBB incurred long distance connect charges as well as a modest subscription fee. However, in late February 1992, the EBB became available through the Internet. The University of Michigan Libraries downloaded over one-third of the EBB (approximately 700 files) and made them available via FTP and telnet protocols. In July 1992 the University of Michigan Libraries mounted the EBB files on the newly installed "gopher" program.

Since then, the popularity of the gopher software, especially its ability to reproduce the contents of one site at another, has allowed the EBB to become available at hundreds of Internet sites worldwide. Many gopher sites "bundle" diverse economic information resources together so that the EBB can often be found with such other files as, for example, 1990 Census data, various U.S. county profiles, or documents on the North American Free Trade Agreement. Of course, part of the challenge for librarians is discovering the unique sources that might reside on only one specific gopher or FTP site. In my conclusion I will offer suggestions as to the most efficient method of searching out new sources.

The University of Michigan Libraries gopher is accessed by invoking the command: "telnet una.hh.lib.umich.edu." Since the logon procedure cannot be effectively demonstrated within the confines of a textual article, several examples of accessing EBB and other sites are appended. Although local procedures may vary, these examples should substantively reflect individual experience. The University of Michigan gopher, like many systems, presents the user with the option of entering a local password for UPI newsfeed access. Simply pressing return at this point invokes the gopher program (see Figure 1). As the illustrations indicate, moving the cursor to the appropriate number on the screen and pressing return, moves you to the selected area.

The dynamic nature of the Internet means that change occurs rapidly. Hence, a caution that the numbered file areas mentioned here may change as new subject areas are added. The novice gopher searcher will soon encounter "under construction" signs or the comment "nothing available" attached to many file areas in go-

FIGURE 1

```
Internet Gopher Information Client v1.02

             University of Michigan Libraries

     1.  About Using the ULibrary Gopher/
     2.  Contents of the ULibrary Gopher/
     3.  About Univ. Michigan Libraries and Information Resources/
     4.  News Services/
     5.  General Reference Resources/
     6.  Humanities Resources/
     7.  Science Resources/
 --> 8.  Social Sciences Resources/
     9.  Library Catalogs/
    10.  Univ. Michigan Campus Information (GOpherBLUE)/
    11.  Other Gophers/
    12.  What's New & Featured Resources/


Press ? for Help, q to Quit, u to go up a menu            Page: 1/1
```

phers worldwide. Despite these changes essential structures and search procedures will remain the same.

As of this writing the University of Michigan Libraries gopher has 12 main subject access points. Economics information is found within section 8, Social Science Resources (see Figure 2). The Economics area, at this moment, has 10 distinct listings, EBB is number 5 (see Figure 3). Once within EBB, the searcher is presented with 21 specific subject areas (see Figure 4). Each of these areas contains further information, in some cases statistically-based, in others textual, such as the press releases of the U.S. Trade Representative or *International Market Insight Reports.*

The EBB contains 11 essential statistical areas: Current Business Statistics, Economic Indicators, Employment, Energy, Foreign Trade, Industry, Monetary, Price and Productivity, Treasury Auction Results, Regional, and the National Income and Products Accounts. All of these groupings contain further information. Current Business Statistics, for example, has 73 different files; Economic Indicators has 74.

The Foreign Trade area contains such diverse information as the final 1992 Merchandise Trade table, weekly exchange rate tables, and dollar rate against selected benchmark currencies. Many of

FIGURE 2

Internet Gopher Information Client v1.02

Social Sciences Resources

1. 1990 Census (UMich)/
2. Area Studies (under construction)/
3. Diversity Resources/
--> 4. Economics/
5. Education/
6. General Social Sciences Resources/
7. Government and Politics/
8. History/
9. Library Studies/
10. Psychology, Sociology, and Anthropology/

Press ? for Help, q to Quit, u to go up a menu   Page: 1/1

FIGURE 3

Internet Gopher Information Client v1.02

Economics

1. Commerce Business Daily/
2. Directory of Economists (by name)/
3. EGopher archives (Economics Gopher and Information Coordinators)/
4. EconData/
--> 5. Economic Bulletin Board (UMich)/
6. Gross State Product Tables from US Bureau of Econ. Analysis (UMi/
7. Michigan County Profiles (Go M-Link)/
8. North American Free Trade Agreement Documents/
9. President Clinton's Economic Plan/
10. Statistics and Econometrics Collection/
11. UNCED Documents: U.N. Conference on Environment and Development/

Press ? for Help, q to Quit, u to go up a menu   Page: 1/1

these file areas in turn often contain numerous sub-groupings. U.S. Import data, a file on Foreign Trade, has 103 files within its structure. National Income and Products has datasets from 1929-1959, as well as quarterly NIAP data. Industry Statistics contains information of Inventories, Shipments, and Orders from 1958-1992, as well

FIGURE 4

```
Internet Gopher Information Client v1.02

Economic Bulletin Board  (UMich)

  1.  About the Economic Bulletin Board.
  2.  Current Business Statistics/
  3.  Defense Conversion Subcommittee (DCS) Info/
  4.  EBB and Agency Information and misc. files/
  5.  Eastern Europe trade leads/
  6.  Economic Indicators/
  7.  Employment Statistics/
  8.  Energy statistics/
--> 9.  Foreign Trade/
 10.  Industry Statistics/
 11.  International Market Insight (IMI) reports/
 12.  Monetary Statistics/
 13.  National Income and Products Accounts/
 14.  Press releases from the U.S. Trade Representative/
 15.  Price and Productivity Statistics/
 16.  Regional Economic Statistics/
 17.  Special Studies and Reports/
 18.  Summaries of current economic conditions/

Press ? for Help, q to Quit, u to go up a menu                Page: 1/2
```

as the Federal Reserve Board's compilation of Industrial Production and Capacity Data. As a more comprehensive illustration Figure 5 shows the complete screen listing for the Foreign Trade area. This is where a great deal of Import/Export data information is obtainable, as well as merchandise trade information, current-account estimates, and more (Figure 6).

File Transfer Tips

It is of little use to become aware of this data without some understanding of how to download it or to render it into a manageable and understandable format. Much of the information available on the EBB can be obtained through the simple gopher protocol of mailing a copy to yourself. At the end of each file gopher prompts–Press <Return> to continue, <m> to mail. Pressing "m" causes the system to prompt for your e-mail address. Type this information, press return and the selected file will be sent to you. However, many of the files in EBB are presented in an 80 column format and so not

FIGURE 5

```
Internet Gopher Information Client v1.02

Foreign Trade

1.  BEA - U.S. Canadian Current Account Estimates 90-91.
2.  Capital expenditures by majority owned affil. of US firms.
3.  Final 1992 Merchandise Trade tables.
4.  Foreign spending in US to acquire or establish new business.
5.  Key dollar exchange rates from USDOC/ITA/TIA/OTIA.
6.  Merchandise Trade (exhibit 9).
7.  Merchandise trade (complete release).
8.  Merchandise trade (compressed DOS version).
9.  Merchandise trade press release (text only).
10. Merchandise trade, balance of payment bases.
11. Net international investment position of the U.S., 1991.
12. Summary of international transactions, 2nd qtr. 1992.
13. Supplement to merchandise trade release.
14. Textile Summary of Agreements.
15. Textile and apparel imports.  .
16. Textile quotas filled.
-->  17. U.S. Export Data/
18. U.S. Import Data/

Press ? for Help, q to Quit, u to go up a menu          Page: 1/2
```

all of the information is visable on the screen. To overcome this obstacle the Department of Commerce has placed within EBB several software programs either to convert the file data to a widescreen format or alternatively, into a *Lotus 123* format. Finally, many of the larger files are available in a compressed-DOS format which will require the use of such readily available decompression utilities as PKUNZIP or PCZIP.[2]

Two examples of conversion programs on the EBB are peeper.exe or make123m.exe. Peeper can be found in area 4 of the EBB: EBB and Agency Information and misc. files. Notice that you cannot mail a copy of Peeper or any of the other conversion programs to yourself: the system tells you that Peeper is an 81 kb program and must be obtained through FTP. The reason for this is that both Peeper and make123m, as well as all the compressed DOS files and any other executable files, are in binary format. It

FIGURE 6

```
Internet Gopher Information Client v1.02

                   U.S. Export Data

  -->   1.  Exports data, 01-59 (DOS self-extracting archive).
        2.  Exports data, 60-99 (DOS self-extracting archive).
        3.  expcty.txt.
        4.  expde.txt.
        5.  hse1.txt.
        6.  hse10.txt.
        7.  hse11.txt.
        8.  hse12.txt.
        9.  hse13.txt.
       10.  hse14.txt.
       11.  hse15.txt.
       12.  hse16.txt.
       13.  hse17.txt.
       14.  hse18.txt.
       15.  hse19.txt.
       16.  hse2.txt.
       17.  hse20.txt.
       18.  hse21.txt.

Press ? for Help, q to Quit, u to go up a menu           Page: 1/6
```

is important to remember that any file ending with either .exe or .zip is a binary file. It is sometimes possible to download these files through gopher but you will not be able to read them. To obtain these files at your system prompt type: "ftp una.hh.lib.u-mich.edu" Login as "anonymous," give your e-mail address, and at the FTP prompt set the transfer protocol to binary. (See Figures 7, 8, and 9 for illustrations of a typical FTP session for obtaining EBB files.)

Finally, it must be stressed that the EBB files available on the Internet do not represent the complete EBB. The Department of Commerce announced on April 13, 1993 that they would soon be providing Internet access to the entire EBB. As of this writing, Commerce plans to be fully operational by the fall of 1993. This service will continue to be on a subscription basis. For many library patrons, the partial datasets now available will be more than adequate. Libraries with more substantive and longer-term needs might be interested in the subscription option.

FIGURE 7

```
athena% ftp una.hh.lib.umich.edu
Connected to una.hh.lib.umich.edu.
220 una.hh.lib.umich.edu FTP server (ULTRIX Version 4.1 Tue Mar 19
00:38:17 EST 1991) ready.
Name (una.hh.lib.umich.edu:kamorgan): anonymous
331 Guest login ok, send ident as password.
Password:
230 Guest login ok, access restrictions apply.
ftp> ls
200 PORT command successful.
150 Opening data connection for /bin/ls (18.71.0.52,4854) (0 bytes).
.oldstuff
.remote
.veronica
aboutgopher
aboutulib
bin
census
contents
ebb
etc
genref
gophers
gsp
humanities
journals
news
newstuff
science
socsci
yalelibs
226 Transfer complete.
175 bytes received in 0.07 seconds (2.4 Kbytes/s)
```

ECONDATA

The Economic Bulletin Board is an excellent source of economic and statistical information but it is not the only resource available. Professor Clopper Almon and the INFORUM research group of University of Maryland's department of Economics have constructed the EconData system. Through the reproductive miracles of gopher technology EconData can now be found on many other systems throughout the world. Coincidentally, it is available

FIGURE 8

```
ftp> cd ebb
250 CWD command successful.
ftp> ls
200 PORT command successful.
150 Opening data connection for /bin/ls (18.71.0.52,4855) (0 bytes).
.cache
.cap
cbs
defense
ebbhelp
ebbinfo
employment
energy
europe
foreign
imi
indicators
industry
monetary
nipa
price
regional
special
summaries
top
treasury
usda
ustr
226 Transfer complete.
190 bytes received in 0.46 seconds (0.41 Kbytes/s)
```

on the University of Michigan Library gopher in the Economics area.

EconData contains three main directories: USNational, State-Local, and International. The National directory, for example, is the largest containing four subdirectories: Accounts, Labor, Price, and BusInd. Accounts contain compressed files of such data as the Annual National Income and Product Accounts and Flow of Funds Accounts. The Labor subdirectory contains the monthly national employment, hours, earnings and diffusion indices, both seasonally and non-seasonally adjusted. The Price subdirectory has the Producer Price and Consumer Price Indexes and BusInd includes the

FIGURE 9

```
ftp> cd foreign
250 CWD command successful.
ftp> ls
200 PORT command successful.
150 Opening data connection for /bin/ls (18.71.0.52,4862) (0 bytes).
.cache
.cap
cap-exp.bea
exh9.cen
export
exrates.txt
for-spen.bea
for-trd.cen
for-trd.txt
ft900_92.cen
ftrd-sup.cen
import
imports.otx
int-inv.bea
inter.bea
sumagree.otx
texqfill.otx
trade
trade.bea
trd-updt.txt
uscancur.bea
226 Transfer complete.
245 bytes received in 0.1 seconds (2.4 Kbytes/s)
ftp> get for-trd.txt
200 PORT command successful.
150 Opening data connection for for-trd.txt (18.71.0.52,4866) (5494 bytes).
226 Transfer complete.
local: for-trd.txt remote: for-trd.txt
5606 bytes received in 0.2 seconds (27 Kbytes/s)
```

Business Conditions Indicators and the Blue Pages of the *Survey of Current Business,* among other files. Once again, it is critical to note the compressed, binary nature of most of these files. Although EconData is accessible via gopher, binary file download requires FTP access.[3]

EconData is an important resource but it is equally important to understand the differences between it and EBB. As part of my research for this article I posted a question to the Usenet discussion group, sci.econ, asking economics faculty and students to comment on the various Internet economic resources. When EconData was mentioned it was usually praised as superior to EBB or damned for being too difficult to use. Again, it is important to understand the differing mission of EconData.

Although EconData is superficially similar to EBB some of the data is not as current; however, for both archival and statistical manipulation purposes, EconData is superior. The essential difference between the two systems lies in the fact that EconData has taken several hundred thousand time series, all produced by the U.S. Government, and standardized their differing formats in the G Data-Bank Format. G is a regression and model building program; a public-domain version, PDG, is accessible through EconData. It is not PDG's virtue as an econometric package that recommends it for the Internet economics researcher as much as its impressive data storage capabilities.

The researcher's problem with EBB is that EBB contains mainly ASCII files and the Lotus files are usually just the same ASCII files after being imported. This is not an effective method of storing data. The G Data Banks are very efficient for data storage and more efficient file compression means faster network transfers. The crux of the difference is that EBB data often requires editing. Despite these advantages there are good reasons to prefer one system over the other at different times. At the reference desk, particularly, EBB can be accessed quickly and statistical information obtained for the patron needing, for example, the latest merchandise trade balance or today's exchange rates. EconData requires, as one Economist related to me, "a little trip up the learning curve." In the context of teaching methods of accessing economic information on the Internet it is important to discuss EconData's existence and setup; however, quick reference demands are better addressed through EBB. Finally, it is only fair to note that EconData is not a competitor with EBB. The data within EconData has been placed there to meet the needs of the INFORUM research group. Its availability and accessibility through the Internet means that students, faculty, and librarians can always find necessary archival materials.

OTHER ECONOMICS RESOURCES

There are many, many other Internet resources that are important to be aware of. The limitations of space do not allow a comprehensive discussion of all of them so I will simply list some of the more interesting and add a brief description. As with EBB and EconData the gopher protocol means that many of these will be available at other sites.

Gophers

University of Michigan Libraries

The University of Michigan Libraries gopher has many other resources collected together in the Economics area.

1. Commerce Business Daily.
2. Gross State Product Tables for the U.S. from the Bureau of Economic Analysis.
3. North American Free Trade Agreement documents. This file contains the NAFTA draft and a synopsis.
4. President Clinton's Economic Plan. Documents related to White House economic planning.
5. The Statistics and Econometric Collection. This area contains four files: the archives of the discussion lists SAS-L, SPSSX-L, CHANCE, and Graphics; the Journal of Computational Economics gopher server; the StatLib gopher server; and the UIC Stat Archive.

NetEc Gopher

NetEc is a term that unites a number of projects for networking interaction in academic Economics. At the moment, there are two projects called BibEc and WoPEc. BibEc is a start at a bibliographic database for Economics working papers. WoPEc is an attempt to gather Economics working papers in a full-text Internet accessible site. Telnet to "uts.mcc.ac.uk" and login as "gopher."

University of Michigan Department of Economics

Another University of Michigan gopher with some different Internet resources is operated by the Department of Economics. Telnet to "alfred.econ.lsa.umich" and login as "gopher," or from the UMich Library Gopher choose option 11, Other Gophers, then, option 1, Gopher Servers at the University of Michigan, and finally, option 4, Economics Department. This gopher will lead to other Economics Gophers such as that at Sam Houston State University and the Technical University in Berlin. A dataset of Dow-Jones averages, 1885-1985 is one particular highlight here.

Datasets via Anonymous FTP

The Penn World Tables:
ftp nber.harvard.edu   pub/nber/pwt5.asc

The Backus and Kehoe dataset from *American Economic Review* 82:4: ftp uts.mcc.ac.uk   pub/Krichel/DatEc/*.trl

New England Economic Indicators:
ftp neeedc.umesbs.maine.edu [login with "pass"] cd frbb

Regional Economic Information System:
ftp neeedc.umesbs.maine.edu [login with "pass"] cd bea

Survey of Consumer Finances, 1962-63; 1983-86:
ftp nber.harvard.edu   pub/scf6263 [and] pub/scf8386

Datasets via Telnet

Bank of England Quarterly Bulletin Time Series Data:
telnet sun.nsf.ac.uk
login: janet
hostname: uk.ac.swurcc
username: press [SEND]
Which service: PMAC
Select 3 from menu

UK Central Statistical Office Macro-Economic Time Series Data:
telnet sun.nsf.ac.uk
login: janet
hostname: uk.ac.swurcc
username: press [SEND]
Which service: PMAC
Select 1 from menu

CONCLUSION

The information technology explosion of the last few years has placed new burdens on reference librarians. The resources mentioned in this article can be either another burden or a challenging opportunity. There is no doubt that such resources can be used to advantage by researchers; however, the question arises whether simply knowing about them is sufficient. In my experience it is not necessary, for example, to understand completely the complexities of G Data-Bank format, but it is important to be able to delineate the advantages of using one system over another. This is particularly crucial because many library patrons will encounter Internet resources in an unmediated situation. Even if resources are introduced at a reference desk, the patron will often leave the library to use them. A sense of evaluation and any possible followup is therefore lost. On the other hand, despite a growing awareness of these resources amongst students, faculty and other researchers, there are many who can be introduced and taught to use them as an integrated part of the research process. Mastering the basics of accessing such resources as EBB or EconData is essentially the same as mastering the basics of any paper-based statistical source. In the case of Internet resources the rewards are as great as the challenges.

REFERENCES

1. There are a limited number of ICPSR files available for FTP on the Internet. ICPSR is in the process of transferring its holdings from magnetic tape to an optical disk jukebox. This process is expected to take several years to complete.

2. Pkzip and other decompression utilities are available in the "Tools" subdirectory of EconData as well as many other public archive sites.

3. EconData's FTP access is anonymous ftp to info.umd.edu–cd info/Econdata/Instructions–get contents.doc, gbankdoc, and guide.doc. These essential documents are all in ASCII format.

Science Resources on the Internet

John Maxymuk

SUMMARY. This article focuses on resources for science reference available on the Internet. The types of resources covered include: anonymous FTP files and archives; telnet and finger sites; electronic journals and Usenet conferences; and access tools like gophers and WAIS. Examples of these resources are shown for: General Science, Agriculture, Biology, Health Sciences, Environmental Sciences, Physical Sciences and Mathematics. Appendices list network addresses of cited resources as well as additional sources not covered in the text.

INTRODUCTION

As is indicated by the scope of the articles in this volume, the Internet is a vast, rapidly-changing, incompletely mapped terrain. One does not attempt to outline the available resources in this terra "nonfirma" for a topic as broad as the sciences without cautioning the reader in two ways: (1) There are many more resources than can be covered in any one article or volume, and they are increasing steadily. Therefore, the purpose of this article is not to be encyclopedic, but to be introductory. The reader will discover individual favorites while exploring the Internet on his or her own. This article

John Maxymuk is Reference Librarian, responsible for the Sciences, Government Documents and Microcomputers at the Robeson Library, Rutgers University, Camden, NJ 08101.

[Haworth co-indexing entry note]: "Science Resources on the Internet." Maxymuk, John. Co-published simultaneously in *The Reference Librarian* (The Haworth Press, Inc.) No. 41/42, 1994, pp. 81-98; and: *Librarians on the Internet: Impact on Reference Services* (ed: Robin Kinder) The Haworth Press, Inc., 1994, pp. 81-98. Multiple copies of this article/chapter may be purchased from The Haworth Document Delivery Center [1-800-3-HAWORTH; 9:00 a.m. - 5:00 p.m. (EST)].

is intended as a signpost and offers some fruitful directions to travel. (2) The Internet is constantly evolving, and files or sites are moved, updated or dropped each day. While every resource referred to here has been checked and doublechecked, net users must be flexible, adaptable and willing to try different avenues when familiar ones are blocked.

The methodology employed here is to provide an overview of the better examples of four different types of resources. First, file transfer protocol (FTP) resources comprise documents and software programs which can be obtained freely by the user. Also included here are archives of transferable files. Second, telnet or remote login sites feature specialized databases accessible over the nets. Third, communication media such as electronic journals, Usenet electronic conferences and BITNET listservs that serve the same function in an e-mail environment connect users with common interests. Finally, the access tools including gophers, VERONICA and WAIS are the fourth resource type. These tools serve a vital indexing role on the Internet and have made exploring the nets much easier for both novices and experienced users.

Examples of these four kinds of resources are described for 7 different science subtopics–General Science, Agriculture, Biology, Health Sciences, Environmental Sciences, Physical Sciences and Mathematics. Within these disciplines, we'll take a closer look at the best sources. Network addresses and applicable login commands are listed in Appendix A for all sources described in the text. Appendices B and C list additional resources not mentioned in this article.

GENERAL SCIENCE

These are resources which are multidisciplinary in nature. One good example is the Science and Technology Information System (STIS) accessible via telnet. STIS is a database of National Science Foundation (NSF) publications. It includes NSF awards, reports and programs, and the full text of all of these documents is searchable. STIS is a menu-driven system and allows for three types of searches: word, Boolean and topic. "Word" searches for a particular string, and "topic" is essentially a controlled vocabulary subject search. The most useful option is "Boolean." A Boolean search for "diversity and education" retrieved 45 items including the reports "Report on Minority Scientists Workshop" and "America's Academic Future." Search results such as these can be copied from the system. First time users should peruse the "30 Second Users' Guide" to become familiar with the system's commands and eccentricities. This database is useful for anyone with ties to NSF.

Another useful resource is the SIMTEL20 Archives of software. These archives hold public domain and shareware software programs for many different computer operating systems. The programs are available via anonymous FTP. Subdirectories under the MSDOS directory of programs include astronomy, biology, chemistry, engineering, math and more. As an example, files under the chemistry subdirectory include a molecular modeling program and an electronic periodic table of the elements. The SIMTEL20 Archives are mirrored at a number of different network addresses, and its files are checked for known viruses.

The most useful resource in this area is the North Carolina State University (NCSU) Libraries Gopher. Since a gopher is organized as a series of menus, it is easy to travel the following path: select "NCSU's Library Without Walls" and then "Discipline Specific Study Carrels." The next menu is a two screen list of disciplines including biology, chemistry, engineering and math–each of which leads to a catalog of subject-specific telnet sites, readable files and other gophers directly accessible from this gopher. Figure 1 is the first page of the gopher menu for Agriculture and Biology.

AGRICULTURE

An Agriculture researcher would do well to start with "Not Just Cows: A Guide to Internet/Bitnet Resources in Agriculture and Related Sciences," written and compiled by Wilfred Drew of SUNY Morrisville. This guide covers network-accessible libraries with extensive agriculture collections, electronic bulletin boards and conferences related to agriculture as well as a host of miscellaneous services of interest. The publication is available via anonymous FTP.

```
Agriculture and Biology
     1.  Advanced Technology Information Network (ATI-NET) <TEL>
     2.  Arabidopsis Research Companion, Mass Gen Hosp./
     3.  Australian National Botanic Gardens/
     4.  BIO - Directory for Biological Sciences at NSF/
     5.  BIOFTP EMBnet Switzerland/
     6.  Clemson University Forestry and Agric. Network <TEL>
     7.  Duke Botany Dept. Chlamydomonas Genetics Center/
     8.  EcoGopher at the University of Virginia/
     9.  EnviroGopher/
    10.  Finnish EMBnet BioBox
    11.  Fossil software (DOS)/
    12.  ICGEBnet/  ^[[K
    13.  INN, Weizmann Institute of Science (Israel)/
    14.  IUBio Biology Archive, Indiana University (experimental)/
    15.  Images Animals and Plants
    16.  Libraries with Extensive collections in Agriculture/
    17.  Master Gardener Information (from Texas Agr. Extension)/
    18.  Museum of Paleontology Gopher/

                        Page: 1/2
```

FIGURE 1: NCSU GOPHER -- AGRICULTURE AND BIOLOGY CONNECTIONS

One of the sources listed in "Not Just Cows" is the Clemson University Forestry and Agriculture Network (CUFAN). The CUFAN information system is menu-driven and covers the topics of weather, economics, plants, animals, engineering, food, home, education and human resources as they relate to agriculture, particularly of the Southeastern U.S. The system is very simple to use and relies on the use of function keys, but the menus go very deep and require many choices. As an example one would have to make the following nine menu choices to get to an extension page on stink bugs and tomatoes: Plants/Horticultural/Home/Vegetables/T-Z/Tomatoes/Pest Management/Insect/Stink Bugs.

A similar, but better system is PENpages provided by Pennsylvania State University. PENpages is also a menu-driven agricultural database accessible via telnet. However, PENpages offers an "Index–Keyword Search" option on its main menu which allows for access to the complete database without paging through menus. The Index option is a template arrangement and permits the retrieval of multiple records. For example, if we enter "milk" at the screen prompt for keywords, the system will show an alphabetical list of keywords in the "m"s. Since Milk is a keyword, we can select it by number and then type "N" to enter another keyword, "fat" (Figure 2). The resulting list of 14 documents includes "Trouble-Shooting Problem/Milk Fat Test Depression" and "Should Children Drink Milk?" from the Penn State Nutrition Center.

BIOLOGY

Biology is a discipline well served by the nets. The best starting place is "A Biologist's Guide to Internet Resources" by Una R.

```
Enter additional keyword to reduce selection: <*> fat

   1   FAST-FOOD

   2   FASTING

-> 3   FAT

   4   FAT-FEEDING

   5   FAT-FREE-PRODUCT

   6   FAT-INTAKE

   7   FAT-O-MEATER

   8   FAT-SOLUBLE

   9   FAT-SOLUBLE-VITAMIN

-------------------------------------------------------------------

(1-9) Selects Keyword      (N) Next Keywords      (?) Help

(KEYWORD) Another Search   (P) Previous Keywords (@) Exit

-------------------------------------------------------------------

Enter keyword # or choice: <3>

MILK R FAT

14 documents found

-------------------------------------------------------------------
(L) List Titles      (R) Reduce Selection     (S) Search Again
(?) Help             (E) Expand Selection     (D) Display Options
(@) Exit

-------------------------------------------------------------------

Enter choice: <L> L
```

FIGURE 2: PENpages -- INDEX SEARCH FOR MILK AND FAT

Smith from the Biology Department at Yale. This 20 page guide covers various information archives and internet basics for the biology researcher and is available via anonymous FTP.

Also related to file transfer, the IUBio Archive at Indiana University is an excellent repository of biological data and software. A user can access the files either by anonymous FTP or by gopher (see Figure 1: Choice 14). In particular, molecular biology and drosophila research are areas of concentration, but there are files related to chemistry and general science as well. Software for all major computer operating systems is included.

Biologists make good use of a wealth of Usenet conferences arranged under the general heading of BIONET. A list of BIONET conferences is shown in Figure 3. There are also a large group of Bitnet listservers in this field. Furthermore, the area of Behavioral Biology is covered in the pioneering, peer-reviewed, electronic journal *Psycoloquy* sponsored by the American Psychological Association and edited by Stevan Harnad and others. It carries no subscription charge.

Finally, there are many fine biology databases available via remote login. One that is best searched by gopher or WAIS (Wide Area Information Server) is "Prosite: A Dictionary of Protein Sites and Patterns" created by Amos Bairoch of the Medical Biochemistry Department at the Centre Medical Universitaire in Geneva, Switzerland. The WAIS system allows for keyword searching of files. After logging on to WAIS, the user pages through screens of available databases and selects those to search, in this case, Prosite. Then the "w" command calls up the keyword prompt. A search for the term "bacterial" would yield a list of entries including the sample record in Figure 4. BIONET conferences and many other science resources can also be searched via WAIS.

HEALTH SCIENCES

Again, a written guide is a good place to start. The "Internet/ Bitnet Health Sciences Resources" compiled by Lee Hancock of the University of Kansas Medical Center and available via anonymous FTP covers Usenet conferences, electronic newsletters and

bionet.agroforestry	Agroforestry research
bionet.announce	Announcements
bionet.biology.computational	Biol. Comp. and math applications
bionet.biology.n2-fixation	Biological nitrogen fixation
bionet.biology.tropical	Tropical biology and ecology
bionet.general	General discussion
bionet.genome.chrom22	Chromosome 22 of humans
bionet.genome.arabidopsis	Arabidopsis thaliana genome project
bionet.immunology	Research in immunology
bionet.info-theory	Information theory in biol.
bionet.jobs	Job opportunities in biology
bionet.journals.contents	Biological journal TOCs
bionet.journals.note	Publication issues in biology
bionet.molbio.ageing	Cellular and organismal ageing
bionet.molbio.bio-matrix	Searches of biological databases
bionet.molbio.embldatabank	Info on EMBL Nucleic acid database
bionet.molbio.evolution	Evolution, especially molecular
bionet.molbio.gdb	The GDB database
bionet.molbio.genbank	The GenBank nucleic acid database
bionet.molbio.genbank.updates	Sequence data for local updates
bionet.molbio.gene-linkage	Genetic linkage analysis.
bionet.molbio.genome-program	Human Genome Program issues
bionet.molbio.methds-reagnts	Tips on lab techniques and materials
bionet.molbio.hiv	The molecular biology of HIV
bionet.molbio.proteins	Protein database searches
bionet.molbio.rapd	Randomly Amplified Polymorphic DNA
bionet.molbio.yeast	Yeast researchers' discussion
bionet.neuroscience	Research issues in the neurosciences
bionet.photosynthesis	Photosynthesis research
bionet.plants	Plant biology: genetics and ecology
bionet.population-bio	Population biology, especially theory
bionet.sci-resources	Information about funding, etc.
bionet.software	Free/shareware for biology
bionet.software.gcg	Genetics Software Discussion
bionet.software.sources	Software source codes
bionet.users.addresses	Locating biologists who use e-mail
bionet.virology	Research in virology
bionet.women-in-bio	By and about women in biology
bionet.xtallography	Protein crystallography

FIGURE 3: BIONET CONFERENCES

journals, FTP archives and remote login databases related to the Health Sciences.

OCLC and the American Association for the Advancement of Science have collaborated on a full-text with graphics, peer-reviewed electronic journal, *The Online Journal of Current Clinical Trials* which was selected 1992 Product of the Year by the journal *DATABASE*. OCLC is now collaborating with the nursing honor society Sigma Theta Tau to create an electronic nursing journal–*The Online Journal of Knowledge Synthesis for Nursing*. Both of these journals carry subscription charges.

CancerNet is a free service from the National Institute of

```
//

ID    PILT; PATTERN.
AC    PS00662;
DT    JUN-1992 (CREATED); JUN-1992 (DATA UPDATE); JUN-1992 (INFO
UPDATE). DE      Bacterial protein export pilT protein family
signature. PA    L-R-x(2)-P-D-x-[LIVM](3)-G-E-[LIVM]-R-D.
NR    /RELEASE=22,25044;
CC    /TAXO-RANGE=???P?; /MAX-REPEAT=1;
DR      P25953, CMG1_BACSU, T; P22608, PILB_PSEAE, T; P24559,
PILT_PSEAE, T; DR    P15645, PULE_KLEPN, T; P07169, VIBY_AGRT5, T;
P05360, VIBY_AGRT9, T; DO    PDOC00567;
//
A number of bacterial proteins, which are probably involved in a
specialized export  system have been found [1] to be evolutionary
related.  These proteins are listed below.
   - Agrobacterium tumefaciens Ti plasmid virB operon protein 11.
       This protein is required for the transfer of T-DNA to plants.
   - Bacillus subtilis comG operon protein 1 which is required for
       the uptake of DNA by competent Bacillus subtilis cells.
   - Klebsiella pneumoniae pullulanase secretion protein pulE.
   - Pseudomonas aeruginosa protein pilB.
   - Pseudomonas aeruginosa protein twitching mobility protein pilT.
These proteins have from 344 (pilT and virb11) to 566 (pilB) amino
acids, they are probably  cytoplasmically located and, on  the
basis of the presence of a conserved P-loop region, bind ATP. As a
signature pattern we selected a region that overlaps the B motif of
ATP-binding proteins. -Consensus pattern: L-R-x(2)-P-D-x-[LIVM](3)-
G-E-[LIVM]-R-D-Sequences known to belong to this class detected by
the pattern: ALL. Other sequence(s) detected in SWISS-PROT: NONE. -
Last update: June 1992 / First entry. [ 1] Whitchurch C.B., Hobbs
M., Livingston S.P., Krishnapillai V., Mattick J.S. Gene
101:33-44(1991).
//
```

FIGURE 4:   PROSITE RECORD RETRIEVED VIA WAIS

Health. From it, one can obtain treatment guidelines and other National Cancer Institute publications. One can access the network by e-mail and request either a contents list or specific documents. However, a much better way to access CancerNet is via gopher. If accessing CancerNet via the NIH Gopher, one chooses "Health and Clinical Information," and then "CancerNet Info" and finally "Search CancerNet Database <?>." The user is next prompted for a search keyword–"breast" for example. The gopher responds by listing all materials which include the word "breast" in the title. Selecting "Breast cancer_patient" from the list calls to the screen a seven page document from the Institute's Physician Data Query (PDQ) system which describes breast cancer and outlines the treatment options. One could also recall this and other PDQs by selecting "PDQ Diagnosis List for Patients" instead of "Search CancerNet Database <?>." The user would then select from an alphabetical list of types of cancers (see Figure 5). For CancerNet and for much more, the NIH Gopher is an excellent tool for medical research.

ENVIRONMENTAL SCIENCES

This discipline is best approached through a number of very good gophers. Two favorites are EnviroGopher at Carnegie Mellon and Ecogopher at the University of Virginia. EnviroGopher is organized to present material on ENVIRO: Action (what you can do), Info (general facts), Issues (discussion on topics from biodiversity to recycling), Media (publications of all types), Networks (databases, listservers and more), Orgs (organizations for environmental advocacy) and Politics (political documents). EcoGopher provides in-

```
Retrieving Directory...

For Patients

 1.  Adrenocortical Carcinoma . . . . . . . . . .[201198].
 2.  Anal Cancer. . . . . . . . . . . . . . . . .[200022].
 3.  Bladder Cancer . . . . . . . . . . . . . . .[201206].
 4.  Brain Cancer / Adult .. . . . . . . . . . ..[201143].
 5.  Brain Cancer / Childhood .. . . . . . . . ..[200047].
 6.  Breast Cancer . . . . . . . . . . . . . . . [200013].
 7.  Cervical Cancer. . . . . . . . . . . . . .. [200103].
 8.  Colon Cancer . . . . . . . . . . . . . . . [200008].
 9.  Esophageal Cancer. . . . . . . . . . . . . .[200089].
10.  Ewing's Sarcoma. . . . . . . . . . . . . . .[200021].
11.  Extrahepatic Bile Duct Cancer.. . . . . . . .[201191].
12.  Gallbladder Cancer . . . . . . . . . . . . .[201186].
13.  Gastric Cancer . . . . . . . . . . . . . . .[200025].
14.  Gastrointestinal Carcinoid Tumor . . . . . .[201064].
15.  Gestational Trophoblastic Tumor. . . . . . .[201163].
16.  Hypopharyngeal Cancer. . . . . . . . . . . .[201500].
17.  Islet Cell Cancer. . . . . . . . . . . . .[200790].
18.  Laryngeal Cancer . . . . . . . . . . . . ....[2001519].
         Page: 1/5

6

Receiving Information...
CancerNet from the National Cancer Institute's PDQ System
         Information for Patients
Breast cancer
208/00013
```

FIGURE 5:   CANCERNET VIA THE NIH GOPHER

formation on environmental activity at the University of Virginia and also on environmental organizations and actions. Mailing list entries, environmental fact sheets and EcoNet documents are available, and connections to other related gophers and sites are featured. Best of all, one can choose KATIE (Keyword searching of All Text In EcoGopher) to search all materials accessible by EcoGopher.

Samples from *The Green Disk* are accessible via these gophers. *The Green Disk* is a paperless environmental journal, and its issues are available for a subscription charge either on the Internet or on computer diskette (IBM or MAC format). This unique journal includes reports, press releases, action alerts and news summaries from worldwide environmental groups–much of which is generally hard to find. A glance at the contents file (see Figure 6) for an issue of this serial will attest to its value.

Another resource accessible via either of these gophers or by telnet is the Environmental Protection Agency's Online Library System (EPA OLS). This menu-driven system provides keyword search access to several different databases of bibliographic citations. These databases include the EPA's Library and ones on hazardous waste, clean lakes and chemicals. Books, EPA and NTIS reports are included in these files.

PHYSICAL SCIENCES

For the physical sciences, which include astronomy, NASA is a major purveyor of network materials. For example, NASA News Releases are available daily from MIT via the Finger command. In addition, the NASA Langley Technical Report FTP Site contains PostScript files of technical memos, papers and translations produced at NASA's Langley facility since 1991. For each year there is an ASCII abstract file listing available papers. Another FTP archive of note is the National Science Institute (NSI) File Cabinet which includes many general networking files, but also a large supply of picture files–including a host from NASA. There is also a great deal of software available; of special note is a planetarium program for Windows 3.1 called SkyMap which will draw a map of the sky as seen from any place on earth for any date from 4000 B.C. to 8000 A.D.

Vol. 1, No. 4. December 1992 - January 1993.

BCNDEC92.1#4, BCNJAN93.1#4 The complete text of the Smithsonian's Biological Conservation Newsletter, December 1992 and January 1993.

COLLEGES.1#4 University programs in environmental studies, training programs, post-docs, research assistanceships, faculty positions.

ECOLINKN.1#4 An introduction to the world of environmental computer networking, by Ecolinking author Don Rittner.

ECONET.1#4 A detailed description of EcoNet - the environmental computer network for the planet.

ENIDEAS.1#4 Energy Ideas newsletter, Jan. 1993.

ENVBBS.1#4 A comprehensive listing of environmental electronic bulletin board services (BBS's) you can log onto from your computer.

ENVED.1#4 Environmental education resources, materials, projects.

GRNCOMP.1#4 How to practice greener computing by reducing the waste and energy consumption associated with computers.

INTERNET.1#4 An introduction to the Internet and listing of environmental resources available over the Internet.

INTRO.1#4 This document. Always read first when you receive a new issue.

JOBS.1#4 Employment, internships, and other opportunities.

LOOKFOR.COM A shareware program that will allow you to search your current or past issues of The GreenDisk for key words and phrases.

MAGAZINE.1#4 An index to magazines covering all aspects of the environment.

MEETINGS.1#4 A listing of conferences, meetings, rallies, upcoming events.

NEWSLTRS.1#4 An index to the newsletters of environmental groups.

ORDRFORM.1#4 Print, fill out, mail in to subscribe to The GreenDisk.

PRESSRLS.1#4 Press releases and news reports from environmental orgs.

PUBS.1#4 Listings of recent environmental publications and how to order.

SCLUBNNR.1#4 The Sierra Club National News Report, #1, 1993.

TROPINET.1#4 Tropinet, the newsletter of the Association of Tropical Biology.

USINGIT.1#4 A guide to using The GreenDisk with your computer.

FIGURE 6: CONTENTS OF THE GREEN DISK VOL. 1, NO. 4

The Lunar and Planetary Institute (LPI) provides a variety of files for searching on its menu-driven system. The Institute's book and journal catalogs, a bibliography of planetary literature since 1980 and the Gazetteer of Planetary Features prepared by USGS are the major options available from LPI. As seen in Figure 7, the USGS Gazetteer offers extensive data on craters and other attributes of planets. However, the Gazetteer can be difficult to use if the name of the feature to find is not known prior to searching.

The NASA/IPAC Extragalactic Database (NED) contains information on approximately 200,000 extragalactic objects–offering not only positions, names and basic data, but also bibliographic references, abstracts and notes. NED is searched from menus, and one first searches for an object and then obtains literature references to that object. See Figure 8 for basic data and a sample reference for the Andromeda Galaxy.

The databases previously mentioned are also accessible through the Physics Gopher maintained at the University of Chicago. This gopher also avails the user of physics preprints, journal abstracts from leading astrophysical journals, the European particle physics database CERN and more. Another database of interest is Bucky-

```
2 FEATURE ENTRIES FOUND

1.    Copernicus (Crater) Moon
2.    Copernicus (Crater) Mars

[Arrows Ret KP1 KP2 move, expand, remove, CTRL/Z quit]


FEATURE RECORD 1

NAME: Copernicus              TYPE: Crater
No Diacritics                 SIZE: 107
PLANET: Moon                  LATITUDE: 9.7N
SATELLITE:                    LONGITUDE: 20.1W
MAP: LAC                      NUMBER:58

ADDITIONAL INFORMATION
APPROVAL LEVEL: Adopted 1935
CONTINENT: EU                 ETHNIC GROUP: PO
ATTRIBUTION - Nicholas; Polish astronomer (1473-1543).. (Reference
66)

- + prev/next, GOLD KP1/KP2 top/bottom, + see next, - remove,
CTRL/Z quit
```

FIGURE 7:   LPI -- SEARCH ON GAZETTEER OF PLANETARY FEATURES FOR
            COPERNICUS

```
Performing search for object "ANDROMEDA GALAXY*" ...
1 object(s) found.
#  Object Name  Equatorial              Type Dist. No. No.
                (B1950.0 Equinox)            amin  Ref Note
1  NGC 0224     00h40m00.1s, +40d59m43s  G   0.0   891  4

All the names and basic data for Object No.  1.
       Name                    Type
NGC 0224                       G
UGC 00454                      G
CGCG 0040.0+4100               G
MCG +07-02-016                 G
MESSIER 031                    G
Andromeda Galaxy               G
CGCG 535-017                   G
IRAS F00400+4059               IrS
IRAS 00400+4059                IrS
87GB 004002.2+405940           RadioS
87GB[BWE91] 0040+4059          RadioS
1H 0039+408                    XrayS
1ES 0039+409                   XrayS
B3 0040+409                    RadioS


Equatorial (B1950.0)                : 00h40m00.13s  ,+40d59m42.7s

Positional Uncertainty (arcsec)     : 1.25E+00  x 1.25E+00
Source of Position                  : 1992ApJ...390L...9C
Galactic Extinction (B mag)         :  0.10
Diameters (arcmin)                  :  190   x 60
Magnitude                           :  4.36
Morphological Type                  : SA(s)b
Helio. Velocity (km/s), or [Redshift] :  -300

Position reference:
CRANE, P. C., DICKEL, J. R., AND COWAN, J. J.
DETECTION OF AN UNRESOLVED NUCLEAR RADIO SOURCE IN M31
Ap. J.
1992  vol. 390  p. L9-L12


891 reference(s) for object No. 1.


Reference No. 1 of 891:  1993MNRAS.261..445F
M. N. R. A. S.  1993  vol. 261  p. 445-452
FITT, A. J., AND ALEXANDER, P.
MAGNETIC FIELDS ON LATE-TYPE GALAXIES
```

**FIGURE 8:   NED -- DATA AND FIRST OF 891 REFERENCES FOR ANDROMEDA
              GALAXY**

balls accessed through the University of Arizona Library. Bucky-
balls is a bibliography of citations related to fullerenes and related
chemical structures. It employs the easy Innopac interface which
permits keyword, author and title searches. The entire bibliography
on which the database is based is available via anonymous FTP.

Finally, for data on recent earthquake activity, The University of Washington has a Finger site, Quake (See Figure 9).

MATHEMATICS

The American Mathematical Society (AMS) created e-Math as a menu-driven system, and it features an author index to Mathematical Reviews, electronic distribution of the *Bulletin of the AMS* (although the articles are in AMS Tex 2.1 format which does not translate well to ASCII), the Employment Opportunities in Mathematical Sciences file, a document delivery component and more. They have since developed gopher and WAIS interfaces and are moving existing applications onto those platforms which will make e-Math a more useful service. From the e-Math Gopher, one can

```
$ finger quake@geophys.washington.edu  Login name: quake In real
life:  Earthquake  Information    Directory:  /u0/quake   Shell:
/u0/quake/run_quake  Last login Tue May 18 08:44 on ttyi2
New mail received Tue May 18 06:42:34 1993;
   unread since Tue May 18 00:57:17 1993
Plan:
Information about Recent earthquakes are reported here for public
use.   Catalogs    are    available   by    anonymous    ftp   in
geophys.washington.edu:pub/seis-net   DATE-TIME  is  in Universal
Stardard Time which is PST + 8 hours, LAT and LON are in decimal
degrees, DEP is depth in kilometers, N-STA is number of stations
recording event, QUAL is location quality A-good, D-poor, Z-from
automatic system and may be in error.

Recent events reported by the USGS National Earthquake Information
Center
DATE-TIME (UT)  LAT     LON    DEP  MAG  LOCATION AREA
93/05/17 06:06  55.0N  160.4W 33   5.5  ALASKA PENINSULA
93/05/17 16:02   5.2S  151.9E 33   6.4  NEW BRITAIN REGION, P.N.G.
93/05/17 23:20  37.1N  117.8W 10   6.0  CALIFORNIA-NEVADA BORDER
93/05/18 01:38   5.3S  151.5E 33   5.5  NEW BRITAIN REGION, P.N.G.
93/05/18 10:19  19.8N  122.4E 200  6.3  PHILIPPINE ISLANDS REGION

Recent earthquakes in the Northwest located by Univ. of Wash. (Mag
> 2.0)
DATE-TIME (UT)  LAT(N) LON(W)   DEP· MAG N-STA QUAL
93/04/15 06:44  45.00  122.58  18.9  2.1  24   C    25.0 km  SE of
                                                         Woodburn, OR
93/04/16 23:00  46.50  122.33  17.7  2.3  40   A     7.6 km  SW of
                                                         Morton
93/04/19 01:11  48.78  122.15   0.0  3.1  16   C FELT    5.9 km ESE
                                                         of Deming
```

FIGURE 9: EARTHQUAKE INFORMATION FINGER SITE

access the AMS membership list, Math Reviews Subject Classifications, The National Science Foundation Gopher, discussion lists, library catalogs, the Nuclear and High Energy Physics Information Service and the Mathematical Physics Preprint Archive, to name a handful of possibilities. The WAIS platform permits keyword searching of the AMS Catalog of publications.

Preprints play a significant role in mathematics, and there are a number of depositories of these documents accessible on the Internet. Yale's Instant Math Preprints (IMP) menu-driven service is one of the best known of these databases. The file is fully searchable by author, title and abstract words. Included in each abstract is the network address of the complete text of the article, available via anonymous FTP.

A final resource worth noting is the University of South Carolina Department of Mathematics' Gopher specializing in Wavelets research. Available here are Wavelet papers and publications, Wavelet programs, Wavelet Theory description and the *Wavelet Digest*. From the "REFERENCES" path, one can also utilize WAIS indexing of the Wavelet Reference List Database and perform keyword searches on this bibliographic database of wavelet research. Figure 10 shows the results of a WAIS search for the term "transforms."

CONCLUSION

Although the size and permutability of the Internet can be intimidating, the key lesson to be learned is that it offers so much useful material that it cannot be ignored. Furthermore, while exploration of the net has always been enjoyable and challenging, the advent of gophers and VERONICA makes it easier and more addicting than ever.

There are a number of ways to keep up with the frequent changes on the nets. The "SURANET Guide to Selected Internet Resources" is updated monthly and is available via anonymous FTP. It is a good basic guide to Internet resources. Other more specific subject guides like "A Biologist's Guide to Internet Resources" and the "Internet/Bitnet Health Sciences Resources" mentioned previously are also regularly updated and available via anonymous FTP. Subscribing to either appropriate Usenet conferences or Bitnet

```
Wavelet Bibliography Search: transforms

1.   Families of Wavelet Transforms in Connection with Shannon's..

2.   Continuous and Discrete Wavelet Transforms ,  .

3.   Fast Wavelet Transforms and Numerical Algorithms  I   ,  .

4.   Computer 2-D Gabor transforms by neural network for image.

5.   Wavelet transforms: a primer ,  .

6.   Reading and understanding continuous wavelet transforms ,  .

7.   Orthogonal pyramid transforms for image coding ,  .

8.   Transforms associated to square integrable group .

9.   Orthogonal pyramid transforms for image coding ,  .

10.  The wavelet transform, time-frequency localization and sig...

11.  A family of polynomial spline wavelet trasnsform    By Mich...

12.  On the asymptotic convergence of B-spline wavelets to Gabor...

13.  Polynomial Splines and Wavelets--A Signal Processing Persp...

14.  Orthogonal wavelet transforms and filter banks.

15.  Orthogonal wavelet transforms and filter banks.

16.  Video compression using 3D wavelet transforms.

17.  Decomposition of functions into wavelets of constant shape...

18.  Transforms associated to square integrable group representa...

Page: 1/2                    References
```

FIGURE 10: RESULT OF SEARCH FOR TRANSFORMS IN WAVELET BIBLIOGRAPHY VIA WAIS FROM SOUTH CAROLINA MATH DEPT. GOPHER

listservers is another good way to stay current on what's out there. In particular, science librarians may want to subscribe to the electronic journal *Issues in Science and Technology Librarianship* sponsored by the ACRL Science Section. Finally, gopher and VE-RONICA make the Internet so accessible that time spent in cyberspace exploration can reap great rewards.

APPENDIX A
Network Addresses for Internet Resources in Text

FTP FILES AND ARCHIVES

Files:

Name	Address	Directory	Filename
Not Just Cows	FTP.SURA.NET	PUB/NIC	AGRICULTURAL.LIST
Biologist's Guide	RTFM.MIT.EDU	PUB/USENET/ NEWS.ANSWERS/ BIOLOGY	GUIDE
Medical Resources	FTP.SURA.NET	PUB/NIC	MEDICAL.RESOURCES
SkyMap	OAK.OAKLAND.EDU	MSDOS/ASTRONOMY	SKYMAP21.ZIP
Buckyballs Bib.	PHYSICS.ARIZONA. EDU	AFC	BUCKYBIB.ASC
SURANET Guide	FTP.SURA.NET	PUB/NIC	INFOGUIDE.TXT

Archives:

Name	Address		
SIMTEL20	WSMR-SIMTEL20.ARMY.MIL	or mirror site	
	OAK.OAKLAND.EDU	or mirror site	
	WUARCHIVE.WUSTL.EDU		
IUBioArchive	FTP.BIO.INDIANA.EDU		
NASA Langley	TECHREPORTS.LARC.NASA.GOV	PUB/TECHREPORTS/LARC	
NSI File	NIC.NSI.NASA.GOV		

TELNET SITES

Name	Address
STIS	STIS.NSF.GOV (login: PUBLIC)
PENpages	PSUPEN.PSU.EDU (username: 2 letter state postal code)
CUFAN	EUREKA.CLEMSON.EDU (username: public)
WAIS	QUAKE.THINK.COM (login: WAIS)
EPA OLS	EPAIBM.RTPNC.EPA.GOV
LPI	LPI.JSC.NASA.GOV (login: LPI)
NED	NED.IPAC.CALTECH.EDU (login: NED)
Buckyballs	SABIO.ARIZONA.EDU (login: SABIO)
e-Math	E-MATH.AMS.COM (login and password: E-MATH)
Yale's IMP	YALEVM.YCC.YALE.EDU (userid, password & op. id: MATH1)

Finger:

NASA News	NASANEWS@SPACE.MIT.EDU
Earthquake Info	QUAKE@GEOPHYS.WASHINGTON.EDU

ELECTRONIC JOURNALS

Name

Psycoloquy   send subscription message to LISTSERV@PUCC.BITNET
Current Clinical Trials contact: OJC Subscription Dept./PO Box 3000/Denville, NJ 07834-9653
Knowledge Synthesis for Nursing   contact: OCLC
The Green Disk send message to: GREENDISK@IGC.APC.ORG
Issues in Sci. Tech. Librarianship send message to: ACRLSTS@HAL.UNM.EDU

GOPHERS

Name	Set Gopher to this Address
North Carolina State	DEWEY.LIB.NCSU.EDU
NIH	HELIX.NIH.GOV
EnviroGopher	ENVIROLINK.HSS.CMU.EDU
EcoGopher	ECOSYS.DRDR.VIRGINIA.EDU
Physics	GRANTA.UCHICAGO.EDU
South Carolina	BIGCHEESE.MATH.SCAROLINA.EDU

APPENDIX B
Telnet Sites Not Included in Text

Name	Address	Subject
CERN	INFO.CERN.CH	Physics
CHAT	DEBRA.DOC.CA (login: INFO)	AIDS
Einstein Online	EINLINE.HARVARD.EDU (login: EINLINE)	Physics
Global Land Info Sys.	GLIS.CR.USYS.GOV	Geol.
HSLC Healthnet	HSLC.ORG (login: SAL)	Health
Johns Hopkins Genetics	contact: HELP@WELCH.JHU.EDU	Biol.
Math Algorithms Bibs.	RESEARCH.ATT.COM (login: WALK)	Math
Ntl. Space Sci. Data Ctr.	NSSDCA.GSFC.NASA.GOV (login: NODIS)	Astron.
Oceanic Info Ctr.	DELOCN.UDEL.EDU (login: INFO)	Ocean.
QUERRI	ISN.RDNS.IASTATE.EDU (dial: QUERRI)	Agric.

APPENDIX C
Bitnet Listservers of Interest to Science Librarians

CHMINF-L@IUBVM	(Chemistry)
ELDNET-L@UIUCVMD	(Engineering)
GEONET-L@IUBVM	(Geosciences Librarians)
MEDLIB-L@UBVM	(Medical Librarians)
SCIFAQ-L@YALEVM	(Science Frequently Answered Questions Docs from Usenet)
VETLIB-L@VTVM2	(Veterinary Medicine Library Issues)

A Virtual Library for Librarians: JANET's Bulletin Board for Libraries

Jo Kibbee

SUMMARY. The Joint Academic Network (JANET) in the United Kingdom supports electronic communication, access to online library catalogs, and access to fee-based information services, maintaining services and resources targeted specifically at librarians. This paper focuses on one such service, the Bulletin Board for Libraries (BUBL), and the professional development resources it provides for librarians involved with electronic networking. These include current awareness services, full texts of publications related to networking, training materials, and other resources relevant to libraries and the networked world.

INTRODUCTION

Accessible via the Internet, the Joint Academic Network (JANET) in the United Kingdom is unique in targeting librarians as a distinct user group. JANET's administrative team, the Network Executive,

Jo Kibbee is Chair of Central Public Services and Associate Professor of Library Administration, University of Illinois at Urbana-Champaign. She is a member of the Library and Information Technology Association and the Reference and Adult Services Division of the American Library Association, and a member of the advisory committee for the Women, Information Technology, and Scholarship (WITS) group at the University of Illinois.

Support for this project was provided by a grant from the University of Illinois Research Board.

[Haworth co-indexing entry note]: "A Virtual Library for Librarians: JANET's Bulletin Board for Libraries." Kibbee, Jo. Co-published simultaneously in *The Reference Librarian* (The Haworth Press, Inc.) No. 41/42, 1994, pp. 99-107; and: *Librarians on the Internet: Impact on Reference Services* (ed: Robin Kinder) The Haworth Press, Inc., 1994, pp. 99-107. Multiple copies of this article/chapter may be purchased from The Haworth Document Delivery Center [1-800-3-HAWORTH; 9:00 a.m. - 5:00 p.m. (EST)].

maintains a Library Liaison Office which holds responsibility for developing and promoting library services on the network. This office, in turn, works with the JANET User's Group for Libraries to encourage and support the use of the network by librarians. In addition to offering standard network services, such as providing access to online library catalogs and to fee-based vendors (e.g., DIALOG and the British Library's BLAISE-Line), JANET also offers services and resources targeted specifically at professional development for librarians.

This paper highlights one such service, the Bulletin Board for Libraries (BUBL), which constitutes a virtual library for librarians. (Since *virtual* denotes that which is apparent rather than real, a *virtual library* is not an actual physical facility, but a collection of books, articles, and other texts in electronic format, which in essence constitute a library.) BUBL's primary focus is on electronic networking, and included among its resources are full text articles, directories, and reference works about networking. The bulletin board also features current awareness services for librarians, job vacancy listings, and general news and information for librarians. Though some of these resources may also be available through various gopher servers, BUBL is a useful prototype of a "librarian-friendly" network service.

WHAT IS JANET?

Established in the United Kingdom in 1984, JANET is the acronym for the Joint Academic Network. Under the administration of the Department of Education and Science, the network is managed by the Joint Network Team at the Rutherford Appleton Laboratory near Oxford. JANET was instituted to provide telecommunications links among British universities and research institutions, as well as with networks outside the U.K. At present JANET connects over 150 sites, including all British universities and polytechnics, the British Library and the National Libraries of Scotland and Wales, research councils, and selected commercial organizations with links to academic institutions (e.g., Blackwell Booksellers Ltd.).

Analogous to Bitnet, JANET supports electronic mail, conferences, and bulletin boards. Librarians use JANET to access fee-based services, such as the British Library's BLAISE-Line, and other European and North American online vendors. The network provides access to over 75 library OPACs throughout the U.K., as well as to a growing number of Campus Wide Information Systems, non-bibliographic databases, and software and data sets.[1] With its Bath Information and Data Service (BIDS), JANET offers an innovative service to its users: subscribing libraries in the U.K. are provided with fixed-cost, unlimited access to ten years of selected ISI databases such as *Science Citation Index* and *Social Science Citation Index*.[2] Through these and other services, JANET plays an increasingly important role in the information infrastructure of British libraries.

Not least among its services, however, is linking the library community through networking. Librarians worldwide are familiar with electronic conferences such as PACS-L and LIBREF-L, through which subscribing individuals discuss library issues and share information via e-mail. JANET takes a different approach to information sharing, and utilizes the mechanism of an electronic bulletin board, wherein documents, discussions, notices, etc., are posted by the bulletin board managers (largely a volunteer effort) for the library community. Details of this service are provided below.

THE BULLETIN BOARD FOR LIBRARIES

A unique feature of JANET's administration is the focus placed on librarians as network users. The JANET User Group for Libraries (JUGL) was established in 1986 to encourage the use of JANET by libraries. To this end, JUGL serves as a forum for a discussion of networking applications, assists in network development and training, and promotes standards and service objectives. JUGL has representatives from all JANET libraries, with a steering committee of elected members responsible for achieving the goals of the group.[3]

The Bulletin Board for Libraries (BUBL) is one of JUGL's most ambitious initiatives. Run jointly on behalf of JUGL by the universities of Glasgow and Strathclyde, BUBL is designed to host information of interest to JANET-using librarians. The Bulletin

Board's establishment was prompted by concerns that librarians are confused about what resources and services are available through networks, and how to access them. BUBL also functions as a news service to library and information science professionals, offering contents pages of recent journals in library and information science, reporting on the activities and meetings of professional groups, and listing job vacancies and other news of interest to librarians.[4]

BUBL is accessible through JANET, via the Internet. To connect, use the following procedure:

1. At the system prompt, type *telnet sun.nsf.ac.uk* (or if using the numeric address, type *telnet 128.86.8.7*).
2. At the *login* message, type *janet* (lowercase).
3. When asked for the *password*, type *guest* (lowercase).
4. When asked for the *hostname*, type *uk.ac.gla.bubl* to connect to the Bulletin Board for Libraries. (Note: If connecting to another host on JANET, type in the appropriate hostname, e.g., *uk.ac.janet.news* for JANET News, or *uk.ac.humbul* for the Humanities Bulletin Board.)
5. BUBL's on-screen commands provide a *quit* option, which disconnects JANET and returns the user to the system prompt.

JANET's menu is user-friendly and the nested, hierarchical structure is similar to that of gopher servers. Navigation through BUBL is relatively easy. Though the software is not particularly powerful, features such as the keyword search enable the user to maneuver quickly through lengthy texts.

BUBL'S VIRTUAL LIBRARY

After logging onto BUBL, the following menu appears:

BULLETIN BOARD FOR LIBRARIES

--*****MAIN MENU*****--

A–All about BUBL   J–Glossary
B–Information Networking   K–Exercises and Education

C–New titles in LIS
D–Directories
E–Current Contents
F–Mailing lists
H–LIS: Services,
  Education, Surveys, News

L–British Library R&D
N–Latest changes to BUBL
5–Electronic Journals and Texts
V–Library Systems and Software
Z–CTILIS

A quick scan through the various sections reveals a variety of resources and services. Though their boundaries overlap, the contents can be characterized as professional development tools for networking, and current awareness services. The former includes sections on information networking and network-related directories, while the latter involves current contents of journals, and general news and announcements of interest to librarians. Moreover, BUBL includes a full text glossary, and a selection of electronic journals and texts. In essence, logging onto BUBL presents the librarian with a virtual library of reference materials and professional literature.

Information Networking (Section B) contains an extensive collection of full text articles and documents on electronic networking. This section is subdivided into topics such as standards, multimedia, networking tools (e.g., WAIS, WWW, gopher), and resource guides. In addition to being able to read discussions on these topics, the BUBL user can access the full text of bibliographies, reports, and other documents relating to the topics covered. Some of these have been previously published (in print format), while others are available only as electronic documents. Selected files in Section B include:

- Study Report on Electronic Document Delivery
- The Virtual Library: Myth or Reality (Charles Oppenheim, lecture)
- Bibliography of Information Resources to Assist the Network Novice
- Bibliography of Internet Books (Quarterman)
- Short Guide to Internet Resources (Kesselman)
- A Selection of Interesting Internet Services (Yanoff)
- OCLC Internet Cataloguing Experiment–short report
- Network Services Available over JANET

Directories (Section D) provides the full text of networking directories, such as the *Directory of Electronic Conferences*, compiled by Diane Kovacs; Peter Stone's *Directory of OPACs on JANET*; several directories of internet guides to libraries, such as Billy Barron's *Guide to Internet Libraries*; and directories of British university libraries and library schools, among others.

Electronic Journals and Texts (Section S), offers a good introduction to the concept of electronic publications. In addition to a discussion of e-texts and journals, selected electronic text projects, such as the Oxford Text Archive, are described and discussed. Moreover, the full text of recent issues of selected electronic journals are posted, including the following:

- Public Access Computer Systems Review and News
- Issues in Science and Technology Librarianship E-journal
- Newsletter on Serials Pricing Issues
- Information Networking News E-Journal
- ALA Washington Office Electronic Newsletter

Not all of BUBL is concerned with networking: current awareness services for librarians are also an important component of BUBL. *New Titles in LIS* (Section C) contains an annotated bibliography of new books in library science. Descriptive summaries of recently published books on all aspects of librarianship are included. This section also provides access to the latest issue of *Current Cites*, an annotated bibliography of recently published books and articles on library technology, compiled by the Library Technology Watch Program at the University of California, Berkeley.

Current Contents (Section E) offers a posting of current contents from nearly one hundred journals in library and information science (mainly North American and British). An abbreviated sample menu is reproduced below:

Section E: Current Contents

Advances in Librarianship	EA7
American Libraries	EA1
Annual Review of OCLC Research	EA6
ASLIB Information	EA2

| ASLIB Proceedings | EA3 |
| Assistant Librarian | EA4 |

For librarians without access to current library literature, these services serve as inexpensive and convenient current awareness and professional development tools.

An assortment of notices, job vacancy postings, and other news items of interest to librarians are listed in Section H, *LIS: Services, Education, Surveys, News, Organisations*. The job vacancy listings are not extensive, but they may be of interest to librarians seeking positions in the U.K. (The posting also includes selected job vacancies in U.S. libraries.)

For both novice and experienced librarians, understanding the specialized vocabulary of the library and information science profession can be a challenge. To address this problem, BUBL has mounted an online glossary, compiled from several previously published sources. The *Glossary* (Section J) includes definitions of terms in library and information science as well as networking vocabulary. Despite its lengthy size, individual words and phrases can be retrieved using the *search* command.

The above examples represent but a cursory overview of BUBL's contents. Though only selected portions of many files have been cited here, they amply illustrate the range and breadth of BUBL's database. (Additional files, such as *Exercises and Education*, have not been discussed since they fall outside the scope of this paper.)

CAVEAT EMPTOR

While JANET serves as a useful medium for locating information about networking, and for professional development, certain of its limitations should be kept in mind. Since the network is experiencing increasing traffic, several attempts may be necessary before a logon is successful. At this point, accessing BUBL from a Reference Desk to utilize one of the online directories would hardly be the most efficient means of answering a question. Since the software is not particularly sophisticated, navigation through the program can be slightly cumbersome at times.

With regards to BUBL's content, many of the entries are not

dated, and the directories and other guides may not be the latest editions available. Considering that BUBL is largely a volunteer effort, however, the quality of the database is considerable. By its very nature, BUBL is a dynamic, evolving resource, constantly undergoing revision and enhancement, and can best be considered as a "work in progress."

CONCLUSION AND RESOURCES

In summary, BUBL is a librarian-friendly networking application which provides librarians with a virtual library of professional literature, particularly for networking. Librarians who find "surfing the network" to be a daunting experience should be rewarded by the ease with which they can explore BUBL's resources.

For additional information about JANET or BUBL:

Network Executive/Library Liaison Office: The Network Executive is primarily responsible for the operation of the basic bearer network and management of the gateways; the Library Liaison Office was established to develop user services for librarians and coordinate the network's library applications.

Rutherford Appleton Laboratory
Chilton, Didcot, OX11 0QX
e-mail: JANET-Liaison-Desk@JNT.ac.uk

JANET User Group for Libraries: Established to promote the use of the network within the library community, JUGL provides input from librarians into the development of the system, and explores training and current awareness initiatives.

c/o Ms. Frances Krivine, Head
Library and Information Services
Aston University
Birmingham, West Midlands B4 7ET

JUGL Newsletter: the Journal of the JANET User Group for Libraries. No. 1 (summer 1990) -. Also available online, this journal keeps librarians informed about new services and developments on the network.

Stone, Peter. *JANET: A Report on its Use for Libraries.* London: British Library Research and Development Department, 1990 (British Library Research Paper, no. 77).
   This report provides details on JANET's organization and management, information services to network users, use by libraries, training and public awareness initiatives, and future developments.

REFERENCES

1. For a concise overview of JANET's services, see Martin Kesselman, "Beyond Bitnet: Telnetting to the United Kingdom." *C&RL News* 54, no. 3 (March 1993): 134-36.

2. For a specific discussion of this initiative, see Terry Morrow, "BIDS ISI–A National Experiment in End-User Searching." *Electronic Networking* 2, no. 4 (winter 1992): 61-73.

3. For additional information about JUGL, logon to *janet.news* or consult the *JUGL Newsletter.*

4. Section A on BUBL's main menu, *All about BUBL*, provides additional discussion on BUBL's management, purposes and role, and facilities and structure.

Texas Woman's University and White House Communications on the Internet

Joseph A. Natale

SUMMARY. During the course of the 1992 United States Presidential campaign, electronic discussion lists were established on Bitnet which allowed "subscribers" to openly discuss issues relevant to each candidate's campaign. A discussion list was formed for each of the three candidates. In the summer of 1992, the Clinton and Bush campaigns began posting full-text documents (speeches, interviews, platform positions, etc.) to each respective list on Bitnet, making available information that was almost non-existent in any other format to faculty and students at Texas Woman's University. It was soon discovered that these documents were available elsewhere, but only through the Internet, and they were readily accessible for the taking. Organizations such as the federally sponsored Hermes Project and the National Public Telecomputing Network (NPTN) also provided access to these documents. The reference department at TWU soon took advantage of this information, and with the realization that most of the university community was still alien to electronic file transfer and Bitnet discussion lists, decided to make these documents available in a more traditional manner by retrieving them either through the discussion lists or through one of the other organizations providing campaign documents via the Internet. This article documents the reference department as an instrumental part in using the

Joseph A. Natale is Access Services Librarian, Mary Evelyn Blagg-Huey Library, Texas Woman's University, TX, and is a member of both The Internet Society and the Association of Computing Machinery.

[Haworth co-indexing entry note]: "Texas Woman's University and White House Communications on the Internet." Natale, Joseph A. Co-published simultaneously in *The Reference Librarian* (The Haworth Press, Inc.) No. 41/42, 1994, pp. 109-126; and: *Librarians on the Internet: Impact on Reference Services* (ed: Robin Kinder) The Haworth Press, Inc., 1994, pp. 109-126. Multiple copies of this article/chapter may be purchased from The Haworth Document Delivery Center [1-800-3-HAWORTH; 9:00 a.m. - 5:00 p.m. (EST)].

109

Internet in the acquisition of these campaign documents both before and after the November election for use by faculty and students, as well as members of the city of Denton, Texas.

INTRODUCTION

As the Internet continues to evolve and expand, any librarian familiar with it cannot help but be amazed at what it can offer faculty, other librarians or anyone else in terms of access provided to different types of information and communication possibilities. To the average user, the Internet can certainly be a resource of information never before made available, and the speed at which information can be obtained is, in itself, enough to boggle the mind.

Through a librarian's eyes, the Internet can be, and has been, viewed in one of two ways. One way is an avenue of information that is exciting and beneficial to the library community. The other way is as a threatening techo-monster, frighteningly more than just another source with which to become acquainted. But those librarians that have looked to the Internet as a source for information available in a new way have not been disappointed by the opportunities it affords to researchers, students and other, potential network users.

Appreciation of the Internet can be more of a reality when one is an academic librarian. Many public and school libraries, as well as corporate and special libraries, do not have access to the Internet; however, as more and more network organizations that serve commercial users and non-college/university users come into being, even these libraries will be better served. One example of such a network is TENET, the Texas Education Network, sponsored by the University of Texas. Its subscribers are classroom teachers and other educators who are interested in networking with other teachers in Texas and all over the world. TENET serves all those professionals concerned with education from pre-school through graduate school.

Plenty of publications, available in both paper and electronic formats, offer a wealth of information to both the novice and the experienced Internet user. Several books have recently been published, covering the Internet as a tool for information access. Many more publications have been made available in electronic format, located all over the Internet. These electronic texts can be accessed by electronic mail, Telnet, or FTP.

Electronic mail allows a user to send and receive messages to other individuals across the network. Access to electronic discussion lists is one facet of what electronic mail enables the user to do. Commands can be sent to nodes running Listserv software, and certain types of information can be obtained without the traditional human-computer-human interaction needed for traditional electronic mail correspondence.

Telnet allows a user to connect with remote computers and databases of various types. Very popular types of databases to access are those run by Gopher software. Gopher has proven beneficial to users because it allows a quick and non-technical avenue for accessing text files and documents. Telnet also allows a computer terminal to emulate the library catalog of another institution, located several hundred–or thousand–miles away.

FTP (File Transfer Protocol) enables a user to actually access databases at remote locations and retrieve both "binary" and text files. Several hundred FTP site databases currently exist on the Internet. Each site usually houses a variety of information.

The above three methods of accessing information are available to any user with access to the network. Once the discovery is made about each function and its use, the value of the Internet soon becomes apparent.

No longer is the individual student, faculty member, staff member or librarian confined to seeking information within the four walls of the library itself. The Internet network provides something for everyone. One example of this kind of environment is LIBREF-L@KENTVM, a forum for reference librarians to discuss reference issues, moderated by Diane Kovacs at Kent State University. Libref-l is only one of several thousand discussion lists, dedicated to a wide variety of subjects. Other "list" topics include English literature, personal computers, teaching biology in secondary schools, stamp collecting, classical music, and on and on and on. By subscribing to discussion lists, users can surround themselves with other interested individuals, as well as with experts in the field. By posting messages to lists, users put themselves in contact with others who may be able to answer questions, provide advice or help contact other individuals.

In addition to the discussions that can be conducted through the use of electronic mail and discussion lists, countless documents in the forms of bibliographies, dissertations, guides, reports, glossaries, directories, etc., have been made available to users of the network. Finding out what is available is the most difficult step in the process of accessing this type of information. Users will find the discussion list HELP-NET@TEMPLEVM helpful. This discussion list is dedicated to providing network novices and veterans assistance with items related to the network itself. This discussion list has proved very valuable to a number of network novices and is a good place to begin if one has a question about the location of items on the Internet and how to get them.

THE INTERNET
AND TEXAS WOMAN'S UNIVERSITY LIBRARY

During the course of the last year, the TWU library has become more aware of the growing number of sources and services available on the Internet. As a result of this awareness, a decision was made to begin looking at how the library staff could start bridging the gap between electronic sources available and the Texas Woman's University community, made up of a student body and a faculty that do not readily have access to the network due to a number of factors, the most prevalent being a lack of available hardware beyond the library.

This decision to put the university community in touch with the Internet came in the summer of 1992, and as the library's search for the perfect starting point began, the CLINTON, BUSH and PEROT discussion lists were created as a result of the upcoming Presidential election. It was soon discovered that these lists were making available more than just discussions about the respective candidates; it was also providing access to campaign documents in fulltext format. As quickly as it had begun, the search for a place to start putting the university in touch with electronic access was over–a source had been found. It was decided that the library would experiment with campaign information found on the Internet and offer this information to the university community through the library's Reserve Desk. These texts would be printed out and organized in notebooks so that the university community could be provided easy access.

THE PRESIDENTIAL CANDIDATE DISCUSSION LISTS

In August of 1992, three discussion lists were added to the ever-growing number of bulletin boards available electronically. CLINTON, BUSH and PEROT came into existence and were based out of Marist College. Lee Sakkas (urls@marist or urls@vm.marist.edu), originator of the idea to create these lists, wanted to provide the electronic world with a forum that afforded the opportunity for individuals to discuss the political positions of the candidates. To librarians, these lists became much more than simply a forum for citizens to discuss election issues during the summer and fall of 1992; they became avenues of accessing election information, available only in a limited way.

A heavy amount of communication on the three candidates' lists took place over a period of four weeks, two weeks before and two weeks after the November election. At the time of this writing, posting to the PEROT list has come to a near standstill, the BUSH list has been renamed REPUB-L, with posting activity continuing at a moderate rate. The CLINTON list continues to provide subscribers with ongoing discussions about current issues in government, and in addition, White House briefings, press releases, schedules, speeches and presidential activities are made available as well.

Subscribers are able to retrieve log files of each list, containing all postings made to each respective list, including the administrative press releases and other documents distributed through servers at MIT, set up before the election to help distribute campaign texts distributed by both the Bush and Clinton campaigns.

Eric Loeb (loeb@ai.mit.edu) and John Mallery (jcma@reagan.ai.mit.edu) at MIT were responsible for setting up these large servers, and they still continue to maintain the operation of distributing Clinton administration documents.

To access the log files of the CLINTON list, the user should first retrieve the document that lists these log files by name. To get a copy of this list of log files, the user can send the message

GET CLINTON FILELIST F=MAIL

to the address listserv@marist. To obtain the filelists of the other major candidate lists, replace the name CLINTON with BUSH or REPUB-L or PEROT in the above message. The address listserv@marist remains the same for each of the other filelists. The F=MAIL portion of the message above tells the listserv software at Marist College to send the filelist log as a mail message.

When the filelist arrives in the user's mailbox, it looks similar to what appears in Figure 1.

The user can select as many logs as needed by sending a message to listserv@marist that is similar to the following:

GET CLINTON LOG9208 F=MAIL
GET CLINTON LOG9209 F=MAIL
GET CLINTON LOG9210 F=MAIL

Here, the log files for August, September and October of 1992 are requested.

The archived filelist logs of these discussion lists contain the actual messages posted since the inception of each candidate's list since their beginning in August of 1992. In addition to discussions and commentaries are the full-text transcripts of both the Presidential debates and the Vice-Presidential debate, as well as poll results, other transcripts and documents concerning each party's national convention, the election itself, and post-election issues. The PEROT list lacks somewhat in providing an extensive variety of documents in the filelist logs. However, the electronic version of Perot's book *United We Stand* was posted in four parts; but, after the posting of these four segments, subscribers to PEROT were instructed to disregard and destroy the electronic text of the candidate's book (complete with ASCII graphs), as it was discovered that making the book available in electronic format was a violation of copyright.

Using the Listserv at Marist is a great way to retrieve interviews and other documents relevant to the 1992 Presidential election. The CLINTON list itself is very useful for remaining current with what

FIGURE 1

```
                           rec           last - change
 filename filetype   GET PUT -fm lrecl nrecs  date    time   Remarks
 -------- --------   --- --- --- ----- -----  -------- -------- ------
 CLINTON  LOG9208       PRV OWN V    80 46947 92/08/31 22:10:47 Started on
Mon, 10 Aug 1992 03:57:07 EDT
 CLINTON  LOG9209       PRV OWN V    80 73975 92/09/30 23:50:35 Started on
Tue, 1 Sep 1992 01:37:35 -0500
 CLINTON  LOG9210       PRV OWN V    80 07056 92/10/31 23:42:11 Started on
Thu, 1 Oct 1992 00:28:00 EST
 CLINTON  LOG9211       PRV OWN V    80 49439 92/11/30 23:53:32 Started on
Sun, 1 Nov 1992 04:25:46 -0500
 CLINTON  LOG9212       PRV OWN V    80 30927 92/12/31 23:06:17 Started on
Mon, 30 Nov 1992 21:18:57 PST
 CLINTON  LOG9301       PRV OWN V    80 47179 93/01/31 23:10:40 Started on
Fri, 1 Jan 1993 12:09:35 EST
 CLINTON  LOG9302       PRV OWN V    80 94244 93/02/28 23:58:36 Started on
Sun, 31 Jan 1993 22:44:35 -0600
 CLINTON  LOG9303       PRV OWN V   424 97905 93/03/31 23:23:18 Started on
Mon, 1 Mar 1993 08:36:00 ET
 CLINTON  LOG9304       PRV OWN V   105 07615 93/04/30 20:06:25 Started on
Thu, 1 Apr 1993 00:15:00 EST
 CLINTON  LOG9305       PRV OWN V    86 20412 93/05/03 17:21:20 Started on
Sat, 1 May 1993 00:39:52 EDT
```

is happening in Washington, but there exist other ways by which to access these documents.

THE CAMPAIGN INFORMATION SERVICE

The Campaign Information Service, set up by Eric Loeb and John Mallery of the MIT Artificial Intelligence Laboratory, provided many different types of information about the Presidential candidates via e-mail. It is currently possible to subscribe to this service and receive the same full-text documents that are posted to the CLINTON list as they are made available. By subscribing to this service, the subscriber receives only texts, briefings, schedules, etc., produced by the Clinton administration's Electronic Publishing and Public Access E-mail Office.

During the campaign, the Campaign Information Service began offering campaign releases for each candidate over the network to individual subscribers. Through an interactive process, subscribers were able to request specific types of information they wanted to receive, including information about each major candidate's eco-

nomic policy, foreign policy, social policy, speeches, news, or subscribers can request any combination of these.

To obtain more information about subscribing to the Clinton
server, those interested can send a mail message to

clinton-info@campaign92.org

In the subject line, include only the word HELP–there is no need to
write a request message. The interactive server at campaign92.org
will then return, via e-mail, a WELCOME sheet and instructions
about how to receive documents as they are made available in
electronic form.

This is an excellent example of the use of electronic mail as a
method used to access information. As briefings, speeches, and
other documents are made available in electronic format, they are
subsequently sent to subscribers.

TEXAS WOMAN'S UNIVERSITY
AND THE CAMPAIGN TEXTS

As a result of making the decision to provide campaign documents to the students and faculty of Texas Woman's University,
electronic subscriptions to the MIT Campaign92 servers were acquired through the electronic mail account of one of the reference
librarians. Mail in this account was accessed daily by the librarian
and the full-text documents posted to the three major candidates'
MIT servers, as well as the related-documents posted to the CLINTON,
BUSH and PEROT lists, were taken from their original, electronic
form and converted to hard copy.

The telecommunications software used to establish a direct line
interface between the university mainframe and the personal computer used to read this mail was Procomm Plus, produced by Data-
storm Technologies, Inc. This software, as well as many other
brands, allows for ASCII and binary file transmission back and
forth between mainframe environments and personal computers. As
these campaign documents were read as mail and subsequently
extracted to text files, they were separated by candidate. KERMIT,
the file transfer protocol developed at Columbia University, was

used to transmit the text files down from the librarian's electronic mail account to floppy disks on a personal computer. The KERMIT protocol is included in the Procomm Plus software.

WordPerfect 5.1 was then used to clean up the files, add page numbers and update each notebook's table of contents page, one for each candidate's documents. The files were then printed using a Hewlett Packard LaserJet III. As documents were posted to the CLINTON, BUSH and PEROT discussion lists, they were retrieved and added to each candidate's respective notebook twice each week. This was also the case for the documents posted to candidates' lists via the servers at MIT.

Soon after the subscriptions to the three lists and the Campaign Information Service were initiated, it became apparent that there were also other sources of election-related documents housed on databases at various nodes on the Internet. The reference staff discovered that full-text documents concerning biographical information, the National Convention speeches, and party platforms were being made available on the Internet by the National Public Telecommunications Network based in Cleveland. Accessing these already available documents was not as easy as getting electronic mail. It was necessary to go out on the Internet and retrieve them, rather than have them come to an e-mail box automatically. Newcomers to the BUSH and CLINTON discussion lists would ask if the candidates' convention speeches were available and where they could be obtained. Usually, these requests were answers with copies of the speeches themselves, posted to the lists by those who had already retrieved them. In addition to the speeches themselves, several FTP and Gopher site addresses that housed these on the Internet were mentioned, complete with login instructions. One site mentioned was the Gopher Information Client at the University of Maryland or info.umd.edu. The reference staff at TWU soon discovered that not only did this site hold the speeches that were made by several individuals at the Republican and Democratic National Conventions, but it also held the full-text party platforms of the major candidates. This database is now one of several available on the Internet that house Campaign 1992 and White House documents.

At the time of this writing, the variety of information available via Gopher at info.umd.edu had increased substantially since November, but it still houses the same documents of the 1992 Campaign as it did at the time of the 1992 election.

The database at info.umd.edu is accessible by use of the TELNET command. Use of the FTP command will allow access to the database, but it does not allow the Gopher function to be employed. Gopher software, from the perspective of the user, allows one to move around in a database, or between databases at different sites, with the touch of just one or two keys. It also allows the user to retrieve documents easily via electronic mail.

GOPHER AND CAMPAIGN/WHITE HOUSE DOCUMENTS
AT info.umd.edu

To access the Gopher at the University of Maryland, TELNET to info.umd.edu. The user is connected and then presented with a screen illustrated in Figure 2. At the login: prompt, the term 'gopher' is entered to access the database. As a result, the user is presented with information about the University of Maryland Information Service. At the main menu, the user may choose from a number of possibilities. To those unfamiliar with Gopher, the possibilities this software holds for librarians and patrons are endless.

Whenever logging into a new system or database, it is a wise idea to read the information files the user is directed to initially. Choice 1 in Figure 3 offers such information. The bottom of the screen offers a menu with three action options:

Pressing ? will provide a Gopher help screen.
Pressing q allows the user to exit the Gopher.
Pressing u allows the user to backup one menu.

Choosing line 3 and pressing Enter will produce a menu of files available in the database accessible by the Gopher system.

Figure 4 reflects the subjects of the several databases at this site. Item 7 allows the user to see and retrieve campaign documents and White House press releases.

At the screen illustrated in Figure 5, the user should select item 5. By choosing item 5, the user will be led to United States govern-

FIGURE 2

```
At the login: prompt below, enter:
    info      for access to the Information On-line files and programs.
    gopher    for access to the Gopher interface and Internet Resources.
    newmenu   for access to the NEW UMCP Information Service menus.

login: gopher
```

FIGURE 3

```
                Internet Gopher Information Client v1.1

           University of Maryland at College Park (in development)

        1.  About This System (PLEASE READ)/
        2.  Faculty/Staff Phone Book <TEL>
        3.  Info - Gopher Interface/
        4.  Info - UMCP Developed Interface <TEL>
        5.  Victor - Online Library Catalog <TEL>
        6.  Other Systems/

   Press ? for Help, q to Quit, u to go up a menu:           Page 1/1
```

ment items. Documents from the 1992 Presidential election are available via item 6 in Figure 6. White House briefings by President Clinton and his staff members are available via item 13. An added feature includes keyword searching of election documents. After finding a document that is of particular interest, the user may have it mailed to any electronic mail address on the Internet. While viewing a document, the user can use the quit function by pressing q. This brings up a secondary menu, which appears at the bottom of any document screen. The menu looks much the same as that in Figure 7.

If the user presses m, for mail, the document is removed from the screen and the user is bounced back to the previous menu screen where a box, like that in Figure 8, appears in the center of the screen

FIGURE 4

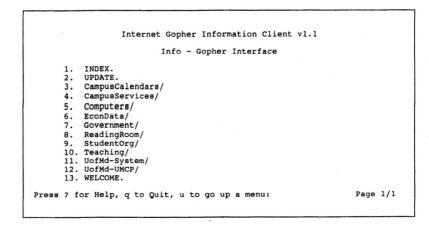

```
            Internet Gopher Information Client v1.1

                    Info - Gopher Interface

     1.   INDEX.
     2.   UPDATE.
     3.   CampusCalendars/
     4.   CampusServices/
     5.   Computers/
     6.   EconData/
     7.   Government/
     8.   ReadingRoom/
     9.   StudentOrg/
    10.   Teaching/
    11.   UofMd-System/
    12.   UofMd-UMCP/
    13.   WELCOME.

Press ? for Help, q to Quit, u to go up a menu:       Page 1/1
```

FIGURE 5

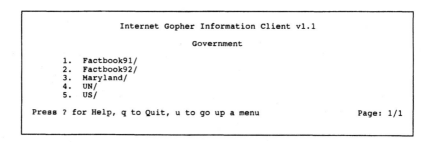

```
            Internet Gopher Information Client v1.1

                          Government

     1.   Factbook91/
     2.   Factbook92/
     3.   Maryland/
     4.   UN/
     5.   US/

Press ? for Help, q to Quit, u to go up a menu         Page: 1/1
```

which prompts the user to input an address to which the user wants the document sent.

Using this exact method of retrieving documents from a remote database using Gopher software, the reference department at the TWU library was able to collect party platforms, biographies, speeches and other full-text information that was initially made available to the Internet public during the late spring and early summer of 1992. These were treated the same as the e-mail documents, in that they were retrieved from the mainframe with Kermit and subsequently formatted and printed with WordPerfect 5.1 and a Hewlett-Packard Laserjet III printer.

FIGURE 6

```
            Internet Gopher Information Client v1.1

                              US

      1.   ADARegulation/
      2.   Budget-93/
      3.   Census-90/
      4.   Congress/
      5.   Constitution/
      6.   Election92/
      7.   GAO/
      8.   Legislation/
      9.   NATO/
      10.  NutrientData/
      11.  SupremeCt/
      12.  Travel/
      13.  WhiteHouse/
      14.  education-goals.
      15.  inaug-address.

Press ? for Help, q to Quit, u to go up a menu          Page: 1/1
```

FIGURE 7

```
        Press <RETURN> to continue, <m> to mail:
```

FIGURE 8

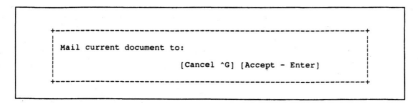

```
    +---------------------------------------------------------+
    |                                                         |
    | Mail current document to:                               |
    |                                                         |
    |                   [Cancel ^G] [Accept - Enter]          |
    |                                                         |
    +---------------------------------------------------------+
```

Documents relevant to each party's National Convention were kept separate from those documents that were being made available after the conventions. This proved helpful to students and faculty members who were interested in each candidate. It was possible to see all speeches made at a party's convention in one section of the candidate's notebook, complete with a table of contents.

THE FTP COMMAND
AND CAMPAIGN/WHITE HOUSE DOCUMENTS
AT *sunsite.unc.edu*

Another method used to retrieve campaign documents for the candidates' notebooks was by FTP. FTP is an initialism for File Transfer Protocol, a method of sending electronic files from one location to another. The library's reference department discovered that relevant campaign and convention documents were accessible also at the University of North Carolina's Office for Information Technology, accessible via FTP.

FTP access is similar to searching for files through DOS directories on a personal computer. Through FTP, files can be retrieved using the "get" command.

To access the database at the University of North Carolina, the user would initiate the FTP command in this way:

ftp sunsite.unc.edu

After connection takes place, the user will then see a prompt that looks like an address. Figure 9 illustrates the login procedure. At the "address-prompt" the user enters (usually in lower-case letters) the login phrase:

user anonymous

When prompted for a password, the user enters his or her own address in the same fashion as it is demonstrated in Figure 9. The password will not be displayed on the screen as it is entered by the user.

After gaining access, the user will need to change directories in order to find campaign and White House documents. Most of the documents are located via directory/pub/academic/political-science. At the SUNSITE.UNC.EDU> prompt at the top of Figure 10, the command to go to this directory is issued (cd–change directories). Subsequently the 'dir' (for directory) command is issued so that the user can view the contents of this directory.

Figure 11 shows the contents of the 'speeches' directory. The lines that begin at the left side of the screen with 'dr' indicate a directory. Seven directories and eight files are included in Figure 11. Each of the major 1992 Presidential candidates has a directory of files.

FIGURE 9

```
<SunSITE is from UNC & Sun.Read DISCLAIMER.readme for our legal disclaimer

SUNSITE.UNC.EDU>user anonymous

<Guest login ok, send e-mail address as password.

Password:s_natale@twu.edu
```

FIGURE 10

```
SUNSITE.UNC.EDU>cd pub/academic/political-science
<CWD command successful.
SUNSITE.UNC.EDU>dir
<Opening ASCII mode data connection for /bin/ls.
total 1522
-rwxr-xr-x  1 root     daemon      172 Mar 18 19:36 .cache
-rw-r--r--  1 root     daemon      367 Apr 13 04:34 README
.
. [A large portion of the directory contents have been edited out]
.
drwxr-xr-x  9 root     daemon      512 Feb 10 19:43 speeches
drwxr-xr-x  3 65       20          512 Mar  1 16:33 whitehouse-papers
<Transfer complete.
SUNSITE.UNC.EDU>
```

It is always a good idea to retrieve the README file from any FTP site before doing anything else. This file usually explains a lot about the database itself and it may include any disclaimers about the use of the material. Figure 12 illustrates how to retrieve the README file by using the 'get' command. Any text file can be retrieved in this fashion. In order to properly initiate the 'get' command, the user must type in the name of the file just at it appears in the database directory, making sure to observe all upper- and lower-case letters (in this instance README). The second filename is what it will be called when it arrives in the user's account (read-me.txt). Exiting the database is done by entering the term 'exit' at the SUNSITE.UNC.EDU> prompt.

FIGURE 11

```
SUNSITE.UNC.EDU>cd speeches
<CWD command successful.
SUNSITE.UNC.EDU>dir
<Opening ASCII mode data connection for /bin/ls.
total 51
-rwxr-xr-x  1 root     daemon      1262 Mar 18 19:36 .cache
-rw-r--r--  1 root     daemon      3616 Aug 26  1992 ABOUT.NPTN.TXT
-rw-r--r--  1 root     daemon      2484 Aug 26  1992 CAMPAIGN.92.TXT
-rw-r--r--  1 root     daemon       613 Jan  4 17:30 INDEX
-r--r--r--  1 root     daemon      5206 Oct 28  1992 INDEX.BUSH
-r--r--r--  1 root     daemon     13177 Nov  2  1992 INDEX.CLINTON
drwxr-xr-x  2 root     daemon       512 Mar  4 18:29 Perot
-rw-r--r--  1 root     daemon       124 Jan  4 17:31 README
drwxr-xr-x  2 root     daemon      3584 Mar 18 14:12 bush.dir
-r--r--r--  1 root     daemon      3003 Oct 19  1992 c199.txt
drwxr-xr-x  2 root     daemon       512 Mar  4 21:21 clinton-positions
drwxr-xr-x  2 root     daemon      9216 Mar  4 21:26 clinton.dir
drwxr-xr-x  2 root     daemon       512 Oct 21  1992 debates
drwxr-xr-x  2 root     daemon       512 Aug 26  1992 demo-conv
drwxr-xr-x  2 root     daemon       512 Mar  4 20:48 kibo-for-prez
<Transfer complete.
SUNSITE.UNC.EDU>
```

FIGURE 12

```
SUNSITE.UNC.EDU>get README readme.txt
```

After reading the README file, the user can return to the FTP site, enter one or more of the candidate or White House document directories and retrieve a number of text files. By following the directions stipulated above for changing directories and using the 'get' command to initiate file transfer, the user will be successful retrieving documents.

MAKING THE CAMPAIGN DOCUMENTS AVAILABLE AT TWU

As the candidate notebooks were readied with respective biographical information, platforms, speeches, etc., the reference department announced the availability of this information in *Update,* the weekly university calendar. In addition, a large sign produced by the library's graphics department was displayed just inside the entrance to the library and placed on an easel. The poster announced that full-text speeches, platforms and other campaign information were available at the Reserve Desk. Material placed at the Reserve Desk circulates, but circulation is restricted to in-building use for up to four hours.

The results of the efforts of this venture were quickly seen as the three notebooks were heavily circulated soon after the poster was set up. Faculty members in the history and government department began requiring their students to look at the campaign documents as assignments given involved extensive use and analysis of the platforms, speeches and debate texts. Updating each candidate's notebook was not as easy as originally anticipated; the most difficult obstacle to overcome was waiting until the notebooks became available so that new documents could be added and the tables of contents could be revised. Even local high school faculty called the library asking for copies of platforms or speeches or texts of the debates. Word did indeed get around.

Because of the amount of information being made available by the Clinton campaign, a second notebook had to be added for the Clinton documents near the end of October. On the other hand, additions to the Bush notebook almost stagnated by the time of the election. After the election, Clinton-related documents became too numerous to collect and make available in paper form to the university community. At this point accessing the White House briefings, the speeches of members of the Clinton administration, and related documents were performed via Gopher software on an as-needed basis. As the November election faded into history, demand for the notebooks dwindled. Even now as the Clinton administration battles health care costs, the situation in Bosnia, and reduction of the national deficit, demand for issue-related documents has waned since November when the craze to know the issues was at its height.

WHAT THE ELECTRONIC FUTURE HOLDS FOR TWU

The availability of public campaign information and Clinton White House communications underscores the pronounced recent change in information access on the Internet. Lee Sakkas' contribution to the Internet with her creation of the CLINTON, BUSH and PEROT lists is evidence enough that it is possible to create forums or arenas that can exist most effectively in electronic form for the simple purpose of sharing ideas and knowledge in a constructive way for the betterment of the academic community.

The Texas Woman's University Library will continue to search for and discover other methods of making the Internet an integral part of reference services. Currently, other Internet-related projects are being planned and implemented.

Internet Resources:
Opportunity Knocks at Our Door

John H. Pollitz

SUMMARY. This article is aimed at the practical applications of information available on the Internet and how it creates a new role for reference librarians as information facilitators. It focuses on the Info.umd.edu database developed by the University of Maryland and how it makes the transfer of files very easy. There are examples of how this database can be used to facilitate librarian and faculty interaction and collegiality, and how it is a resource for answers to specific questions. It contains specific examples of how the database was used in the above situations. One such example is how the author introduced the Women's Studies sections of the database to the Women's Studies faculty. They saw it as a wonderful resource for information as to what other faculty are doing across the country. The database has been used to enhance the image of the library on campus. Within minutes of downloading the text of the Democratic National Platform from Info, the college president's office called thanking the library for making it available to the campus. It presents the idea that the information available on the Internet is still essentially an untapped resource by many faculty and students. Librarians have the skills to become guides and mentors in the exploitation of that resource. Databases like Info.umd.edu and knowledge of them make us a valuable commodity on campus.

John H. Pollitz is Assistant Director, Automated Services, Augustana College Library, Augustana College, Rock Island, IL 61201. ALIJP@AUGUSTA-NA.EDU.

[Haworth co-indexing entry note]: "Internet Resources: Opportunity Knocks at Our Door." Pollitz, John H. Co-published simultaneously in *The Reference Librarian* (The Haworth Press, Inc.) No. 41/42, 1994, pp. 127-137; and: *Librarians on the Internet: Impact on Reference Services* (ed: Robin Kinder) The Haworth Press, Inc., 1994, pp. 127-137. Multiple copies of this article/chapter may be purchased from The Haworth Document Delivery Center [1-800-3-HAWORTH; 9:00 a.m. - 5:00 p.m. (EST)].

INTRODUCTION

On September 1, 1992 the walls of the Augustana College Library collapsed. Yet no books fell off the shelves, and no one was injured. The striking arched glass windows still reflect the pond that wraps around the south and east sides of the building. But even before the foundation of the three-year-old building had been poured, the walls had already started to crumble. Despite this, many brave souls still come in and study here. They check out books, write term papers and meet friends. There are some who have not yet realized that the walls have fallen. On September 1, 1992, our connection to the Internet was activated and an entirely new world of electronic information and communication was opened up to our students and faculty. Walls of libraries across the country have long been falling and librarians have been the ones dismantling them. We have pushed for greater access to the holdings of libraries across the country and around the world. Long before the Internet, OCLC was a type of network of networks.

At Augustana, like many other colleges, we have a campus network that allows faculty and students to search library holdings and do literature searches from anywhere on campus. Faculty can send e-mail requests for copies of articles from journals to which we subscribe or interlibrary loan requests for those to which we do not. Students can verify bibliographic citations from the same computer on which they are typing a term paper. But before the Internet was delivered to their desktops, access to many of the resources beyond the walls of the library still had to be mediated by librarians. Connection to the Internet has meant that access to data, text and even graphic information may not necessitate direct involvement of a librarian. Librarians are concerned that access to the Internet will become so universal that libraries may become superfluous. If patrons can access huge databases of information by pressing keys on their personal computers, if they can find journal articles on services like CARL UnCover and order next day delivery simply by entering their credit card number, then why would patrons go to the library to request an interlibrary loan?

The answers to these concerns remain the same as those librarians had when end-user searching was introduced and it seemed that librarians would lose their place in the database searching field.[1] Although the Internet is becoming easier to negotiate, the breadth of information available calls out for the organizational and service skills of librarians.

Electronic information is merely a new form of information. If we consider libraries as places where people and information are connected, as well as a storehouse of the world's accumulated knowledge, it is easy to conceptualize what the role of the librarian will be in the world of electronic information. Just as there will remain the need to archive the information that the world produces, no matter what format, there will also remain the need for people to help connect others with information, no matter what format it takes.[2] We are experiencing a revolution in how information is distributed and accessed. As the Internet develops, how librarians do business will change but our mission of connecting people with information will remain.

The following represents an attempt to describe one of the examples of excellence in the organization of electronic information as well as to illustrate some of the practical applications of the information available electronically through the Internet. The rich resources available on the Internet are growing at such a rate that it is difficult at best for faculty and students to keep up. By increasing knowledge of electronic information sources, librarians can develop their skills as guides and mentors in the exploration of the resources on the Internet.

While writing this article I came face to face with one of the challenges that the Internet as an information resource presents librarians. Just prior to completion of the final draft, the name and interface for the system that this article describes was radically changed. It was a graphic reminder that the Internet is in the very early stages of development and in a fluid state. Local systems are constantly adding and taking away features. Discussion groups randomly appear and disappear. As information providers this often tests our patience and adaptability. When helping people use Internet resources we need to prepare them for the possibility of change and the stress that comes with change.

INFO.UMD.EDU

The information database at the University of Maryland College Station (*inforM*) is an excellent example of the attempt to simplify access to the information held on the Internet. It is a Campus Wide Information System (CWIS) that is designed to meet some of the information needs of the university's community and since they allow remote login it meets many information needs of the Internet community as well. Topics range from campus schedules and official campus documents to White House press releases.

The *inforM* system is based on the "Gopher" software developed at the University of Minnesota and which is becoming something of a standard for CWIS. One of *inforM's* greatest values is in the unique way it simplifies the transfer of software files. Although the Gopher system allows easy transfer of text files using a mail function, it does not facilitate the transfer of binary files such as computer software. People commonly need to use File Transfer Protocol or FTP in order to move these types of files from a distant computer to their personal computers. This can sometimes be confusing and difficult for those who are not completely comfortable with manipulating different types of computer systems.[3] *inforM* has included a subsystem which simplifies the transfer of software files. By moving to the main menu choice of "Computing Resources," opening that directory, then selecting the "Software – U of MD Interface <Tel>" a special file transfer interface is opened. One can open up directories of information and move deeper into the University of Maryland database without knowing complex Unix commands. The menu bar at the top of every screen is where action choices are highlighted by pressing the arrow keys or the first letter of the item representing a desired action. There are two basic screens: one for moving around directories, and one for movement within actual files. Figure 1 represents the main screen and is a directory level screen.

The first choice, "View," allows the display of a file's text or opening up a highlighted directory. The description column clearly delineates which are files and which are directories. "Return" or the escape key allows one to move backwards to previous screens. By choosing "Select" one can mark files for later transfer. "Go-to"

FIGURE 1

```
VIEW  Return  Select  X-fer  Go-To  Protocol  Quit |        INFO 2.0k
--------------------------------------------------------------------
6 FILES IN /
        Name          Description              protocol = None
--------------------------------------------------------------------
  1     EconData      Directory    20 Aug, 1993 14:58
  2     Macintosh     Directory    12 Aug, 1993 11:08
  3     Novell        Directory    20 Aug, 1993 01:30
  4     OS2           Directory    20 Aug, 1993 01:30
  5     PC            Directory    20 Aug, 1993 01:30
  6     Umail         Directory    28 Jun, 1993 17:03
--------------------------------------------------------------------

Use the up/down arrow keys to select a directory or file, press the first
letter of a menu item to act on the selection. Press ? for help.
* info.umd.edu                                         12:34:18    MOF
```

131

opens a secondary menu with searching and page movement selections. It also allows one to move to known directories or files. "Protocol" sets the default file transfer application and "Quit" is obviously the way one exits *inforM*.

"X-fer" is one of the most useful features of this system's interface. By using this function one can easily download files of information contained in *inforM*. The interface walks the user through the transfer process in the following manner. One can highlight one file if a single transfer is to be attempted or select any number of files to do a multiple file transfer. Once the "X-fer" process is begun, the interface gives a choice of protocols for file transfer. One can choose either Kermit, FTP, or TFTP. After the protocol is selected the software asks for the address where the file is to be sent, the user's name on that system, the password needed, and finally confirms the selected files. It is a very simple process that unlocks the sometimes forbidding world of FTP.

As Figure 1 illustrates, directories are marked and dates of last additions are given so that one can easily see the date when files were added to the system as well as the file's size. When one is accessing a directory containing software files, there is always a text file marked "contents" which explains what each file represents. This facilitates browsing for software and eliminates the need to be looking only for a known item.

HIGHLIGHTS OF INFORM'S FEATURES

The University of Maryland College Park computer center has done an excellent job in gathering information available across the Internet and placing it on their system. It is the breadth of this material that makes this system so useful to the reference librarian.

The "Government" directory which is accessed from the "Educational Resources" section of the main menu can be used for accessing information, data and texts from different political sources. Census information can be found in the "Census90" directory, which includes broad data organized by state. In the legislative subdirectory there are various files that hold information regarding the past election. The final election result percentages for congressional elections are given in one file, while short biographies of

Democratic representatives are included in another. The names and phone numbers of members of the House of Representatives can be found in yet another file. For students and faculty planning overseas trips the "Travel" directory which contains Department of State travel advisories can be helpful.

Information from the Government Accounting Office is also represented in the "Government" directory. The information presented is a result of a GAO project to make their reports available over the Internet. Position papers cover a wide range of topics from the budget, commerce and health care to NASA and national security. There is also a directory that has NATO press releases. These items provide an interesting way to follow the allied military aspect of current developments in the Bosnian region. White House press releases are in the "White House" subdirectory and are divided into Economy, Environment, Foreign, Health Care, and Miscellaneous subdirectories. There is also a "Speeches" subdirectory where entire texts of President Clinton's speeches can be downloaded. All of these text files are easily downloaded to the home computer using the directions provided by the mail option which is presented at the end of the text.

Perhaps one of the most exciting aspects of *inforM* can be found in the "Women's Studies" subdirectory of the "Educational Resources" directory. This directory demonstrates how the Internet can facilitate scholarly communication and cooperation. There are lists of conferences and employment opportunities, information on political issues concerning women, and an archive of postings to the women's studies discussion group. There is even a subdirectory of movie reviews from a feminist perspective. But most exciting is the "Syllabi" subdirectory. Located here are the syllabi of courses from women's studies programs from across the country. Faculty at the University of Maryland, and others who access *inforM* from the Internet can consult these syllabi to see how others are structuring their courses. All files contain the name and directory information of the person who designed the class so that contact between scholars is facilitated. Most syllabi contain bibliographies, some very extensive. These can be very helpful to faculty, when designing a new course. They can also be used by librarians as a collection development tool. Since directory files are listed by course subject, one can find syllabi from courses similar to those offered on campus and compare the bibliographies to library holdings. This spirit of cooperation represents the true potential of Internet communication. Colleagues across the country can exchange ideas that will make their daily duties easier to perform. Everyone benefits from this type of communication, perhaps students most of all.

PRACTICAL APPLICATIONS

The Women's Studies directory first alerted me to the reference potential of the Internet. After hearing about the *inforM* system at the University of Maryland, College Park on the popular listserve Pacs-L, I accessed it to see what it contained. As the women's studies bibliographer here at Augustana, I was immediately drawn to the "Women's Studies" subdirectory. I found an interesting syllabus from a course similar to one taught on our campus. *InforM* made it very easy to download the syllabus to the PC on my desk. Soon afterward, at a small reception attended by many of the faculty who teach courses related to women's studies, I coerced everyone into gathering around the computer and demonstrated downloading syllabi from the *inforM* system. In a scene vaguely reminiscent of singing carols around a piano at an office Christmas party, we investigated the potential of Internet information. Within the week those who had seen the system were connecting to it on their own. They quickly recognized the value of the information that *inforM* provided. One faculty member who previously had used a computer only for word processing now connects to *inforM* and has downloaded syllabi to consult while developing a new course.

The informal session proved to be a very good way to encourage interest in the Internet and electronic information. Another faculty member in the speech communications department heard about *inforM* by word of mouth and looked in the "Women's Studies" subdirectory at a syllabus for a communications class. He learned of a database at Rensselaer Polytechnic Institute that shares syllabi relating to the instruction of communications. He is now using his Internet connection as an active participant in that service.

The "Government" directory of *inforM* has been a valuable source of information for the Augustana library. During the 1992 presidential campaign the Clinton/Gore ticket made use of the Internet as a means of distributing their information. Early on, they made the Democratic National Platform available on the Internet. *inforM* picked up all the documents available from both campaigns and placed them in the "Campaign 92" directory. Our library downloaded the complete text of the Democratic Platform as well as an abstract of the Republican National Platform, all that was available electronically. We placed both documents on a file on our campus network and announced to all campus network users that they could load the documents onto their desktop computers. Ten minutes after the message went out, the college President's secretary called the library and thanked us for making them available.

We have also used the *inforM* system in our relationship with the community beyond our campus. Shortly after the President gave his speech on the state of the union, the local paper planned to run a special feature dealing with how the President's proposed initiatives would impact on our area. The city editor called our library to find an electronic text of the President's speech. He wanted to import whole blocks of text from the speech into articles without having a reporter transcribe them from another printed source. We turned to *inforM* to see if the text was available there. After downloading the file, we converted it into a word processed text that a reporter could use. The episode came to an ironic end when the editor had to drive over to the library for the disk. This local paper, like others across the country, is now looking into access to the Internet.

The final example of how *inforM* has been used on our campus as a reference tool deals directly with student use. We have some sophisticated users of electronic sources of information. After six years of offering CD-ROM indexes the students are becoming proficient searchers. Last January, we introduced Lexis/Nexis to students through an educational subscription. As they become adept at finding information in that database, they realize there is a wealth of information becoming available to them in electronic format. One day, as I was walking through the reference area, a student approached and said with a tinge of urgency that he needed the text of the Bio-diversity agreement that had come out of the UN talks in Rio de Janeiro last summer. He had failed to find it in a search of Lexis/Nexis. I remembered seeing documents from the Rio Conference in *inforM* so I suggested that we might look there. In the "UN" subdirectory, we found the agreement in the "Bio-diversity" file and downloaded it. All this was done within the space of ten minutes.

CONCLUSION

The Internet represents the ability to access a vast source of information that ranges from commercially produced databases like Lexis/Nexis, STN and Dialog to collections of freeware programs that can produce mazes and other designs on your home computer screen. It is a source of information that has the potential to rival the world's greatest libraries. Recent expansion of services for information and data available on the Internet are sprouting like mushrooms on the forest floor after a spring rain. Some are very sophisticated, well-organized databases and others are merely long randomly-ordered lists of data. To think that this type of information will be so easy to use that librarians will have no place in the electronic future is simplistic thinking.

Great strides have been taken in the last few years to make the Internet more "user friendly." Innovations like Gophers, Wide Area Information Servers, Archie servers, and Veronica have made access to information on the Internet much easier. These resources function as card catalogs, reference collections and index tables to the Internet. The Internet will surely become easier for everyone to use, but it is the vast scope of information that calls out for involvement by librarians. Right now sources of electronic information are growing faster than our patrons can keep up with. Our job as reference librarians has always been to connect people with the information they need. If electronic information available on the Internet best fulfills that requirement, we must know where the information is and how to retrieve it. This can often be very challenging in these times of rapid development in the Internet when information can appear, disappear and be reorganized at will. We will probably always live in times where print and electronic sources exist side by side. It is our knowledge of all formats of information that will make us valuable to the people we serve.

REFERENCES

1. Rice, James. "The Golden Age of Reference Service: Is It Really Over?" *Wilson Library Bulletin* 61 (December, 1986): 19.

2. Brody, Roberta. "End-Users in 1993: After a Decade." *Online* 17;3 (May, 1993): 66.

3. Wilson, David L. "Array of New Tools Is Designed to Make It Easier to Find and Retrieve Information on the Internet." *The Chronicle of Higher Education* 39;38 (May 26, 1993): A17-A19.

INTERNET'S IMPACT
ON REFERENCE SERVICES

The Impact of the Internet
on Communication
Among Reference Librarians

Donna E. Cromer
Mary E. Johnson

SUMMARY. The primary purpose of this article is to begin to explore the effects of electronic media and the Internet on communication among reference librarians. We present a brief summary of the literature on communication by librarians, followed by a discussion of electronic media and their effect on human communication. In order to explore these issues in the context of reference librarians, we discuss results of a survey on their communication habits, elec-

Donna E. Cromer is Associate Professor and Coordinator of Reference Services at Centennial Science and Engineering Library, University of New Mexico, Albuquerque, NM 87131-1466 (dcromer@hal.unm.edu). Mary E. Johnson is Assistant Professor and Assistant Director at Parish Memorial Library, University of New Mexico, Albuquerque, NM 87131-1496 (mjohnso@unmb.unm.edu).

[Haworth co-indexing entry note]: "The Impact of the Internet on Communication Among Reference Librarians." Cromer, Donna E. and Mary E. Johnson. Co-published simultaneously in *The Reference Librarian* (The Haworth Press, Inc.) No. 41/42, 1994, pp. 139-157; and: *Librarians on the Internet: Impact on Reference Services* (ed: Robin Kinder) The Haworth Press, Inc., 1994, pp. 139-157. Multiple copies of this article/chapter may be purchased from The Haworth Document Delivery Center [1-800-3-HAWORTH; 9:00 a.m. - 5:00 p.m. (EST)].

tronic and otherwise. In order to see how librarians actually use listservs, the contents of BI-L, LIBREF-L, and PACS-L are categorized by type of message and analyzed in the context of computer-mediated communication. Conclusions are given.

INTRODUCTION

Communication has been defined as "human behavior that facilitates the sharing of meaning and takes place in a particular social context. Any interacting set of social and technical structures which facilitates the sharing of meaning among people is a communication system."[1] The importance of communication among reference librarians–the sharing of techniques, ideas, and resources, old and new–cannot be denied. An interesting question is how this communication is changing in today's electronic environment. The primary purpose of this paper is to begin to explore the effects of electronic media on communication among reference librarians.

First, we present a brief summary of the literature on communication by librarians, followed by a discussion of the electronic media and their effect on human communication. Then, to explore these issues in the context of reference librarians, we discuss results of a survey on their communication habits, including questions about their activity on the Internet using listservs.[2] In order to see how librarians actually use listservs, the contents of three electronic conferences are categorized by type of message and analyzed in the context of the literature on electronic communication. In conclusion, a discussion of the results of the research is given.

PROFESSIONAL COMMUNICATION

Much of the previous work on librarians' professional and scholarly communication has focused on the written literature of librarianship. Communication takes many forms, but it is much easier to study and quantify the permanent written record, rather than trying to discover ways of measuring talk in hallways, conversations at conferences, or discussions in staff meetings. Lyders[3] discusses the role of editors in professional communication. Campana[4] analyzes the written communication among music librarians, Budd[5] discusses the literature of public libraries, and the literature of academic librarians is covered in Budd,[6] Krausse and Sieburth,[7] Swisher,[8] and Watson.[9]

The written literature, however, captures only a fraction of the total communication occurring among librarians. In all the talk, conversation, and discussion, real information is being passed along, problems solved, and innovative programs created. This is a reflection of the 'invisible college'.[10,11] Kadanoff[12] discusses the importance of sharing and talking to colleagues as reasons for attending conferences. In Bunge's[13] informal survey of reference librarians, attending conferences is given as one of the primary strategies for updating professional knowledge. Others are professional and wide-ranging reading, reference staff meetings, and informal discussions. A recent article about special librarians and their use of the Internet comments on the large percentage of Internet use for communication: "The most common reason our respondents use the Internet is to communicate with colleagues and friends, and the value of this activity was stressed over and over again."[14]

COMPUTER-MEDIATED COMMUNICATION (CMC)

Electronic communication is expanding rapidly outside the confines of one's workplace or among known colleagues. Diane Kovacs, a moderator for the LIBREF-L listserv and an editor of the *Directory of Electronic Journals, Newsletters, and Academic Discussion Lists* (ARL) reports in an announcement distributed on May 20, 1993[15] that the third edition of the *Directory* contains entries for 1152 scholarly lists and 240 electronic journals, newsletters, and related titles. This is nearly two and a half times the size of the first edition of July 1991. Librarians share a substantial part of all this electronic communication. Charles W. Bailey, Jr., originator of the Public Access Computer Forum (PACS-L), distributed a list of "Library-Oriented Lists and E-Serials"[16] containing entries for 107 computer conferences and nineteen library-related electronic journals. These cover the spectrum of library activities, including system user groups, subject specialties, and professional affiliations.

Clearly, librarians are active in electronic forms of communication as creators, senders, and receivers. But what do they communicate? And has the medium changed the nature of the communication among librarians?

Communications research has looked at the question of how human communication is altered by electronic media.[17,18,19] For example, electronic mail specifically has been studied in the context of a media richness model. Media richness is defined as a function of the reduction of ambiguity, that is, "the capability of (a) facilitating feedback, (b) communicating multiple cues, (c) presenting individually tailored messages, and (d) using natural language to convey subtleties."[20] The assumption is that the greater the ambiguity of the task or message, the greater the need to use a medium capable of reducing it. "The rank order of media in terms of richness is face-to-face, telephone, electronic mail, personal written text (letters, memos), formal written text (documents, bulletins), and formal numeric text (computer output)."[21] Other rankings place electronic mail below formal written documents on the richness continuum.[22]

Early studies assumed that electronic mail would be used for task oriented work and that discussion of complex, ambiguous topics or group problem-solving requiring nonverbal cues would be reserved for the telephone or face-to-face communication.[23,24] Later researchers argue that the "quality of fixed, impersonal relational communication qualities in CMC may be strictly bounded to initial interaction conditions among previously unacquainted partners and that these effects should dissipate over time."[25] Indeed, one study reports that "experienced computer users rated several text-based media (including e-mail and computer conferencing) 'as rich' or 'richer' than telephone conversations, television, and face-to-face conversations."[26] Walther proposes that the evolution of the group dynamics in electronic conferencing parallels that of groups working face-to-face and only differs in taking longer to achieve effective problem-solving capabilities. He notes "several studies on the progression of small groups through decision-making stages typically describe the first exchanges in group development as heavily task oriented, followed by conflict, then solidarity."[27] He maintains that "CMC messages–as well as those in face-to-face interactions–can be clear, ambiguous, emotional, or factual as communicators use whatever codes are available to accomplish their conversational and relational objectives."[28]

Another interest of communication researchers is the role of status in decision making.[29,30] In face-to-face group communication the high-status member usually dominates discussion and is often a "first advocate." One of the first characteristics noticed about CMC was that social cues regarding status and expertise inequalities are reduced. Reports indicate that "when people use computer-mediated communication, they are less aware of social differences and communicate more across organizational and social boundaries."[31] Although the etiquette of most conferences asks that the sender put his/her full name and paper mailing address at the end of all messages, this does not often include title or indications of place in a hierarchy. As revealed in the survey described below the democratization and equalization of the participants in listservs is one of the qualities most valued.

SURVEY ON PROFESSIONAL COMMUNICATION HABITS OF REFERENCE LIBRARIANS

On April 20, 1993, a survey on the professional communication habits of reference librarians was distributed through LIBREF-L. Only LIBREF-L was selected because we wanted to focus solely on reference librarians. The survey was designed to elicit how reference librarians feel about the importance of communicating with each other about professional issues, how they are doing this, and how much time is spent on all 'professional maintenance' activities. Among the questions asked were: How important is it to you to communicate with other reference librarians? Which journals and/or listservs do you regularly read? How many hours per week do you spend on particular professional maintenance activities? What type of library do you work in? and, How many years have you been a reference librarian? We also asked questions about LIBREF-L itself. Among the questions asked were: How often do you read the list? How often do you post and respond to queries? How important is LIBREF-L to your development as a reference librarian? Do you find important issues covered in LIBREF-L not found elsewhere? and, What do you like best and least about LIBREF-L?

Results

We received 63 replies, 78% via e-mail and 22% via regular mail.[32,33] The majority, 90%, were from academic and college librarians (see Figure 1). Of the respondents, 98% consider it very important or important to communicate with other reference librarians. Some of the more common reasons given are: the need to stay current, the usefulness of knowing what issues/problems other libraries and librarians are facing, and discussion about how problems can be solved. "If you don't communicate, you lose touch with reality."

The question about which journals are read yielded a wide variety of titles. In addition to the seven choices listed in the question, nearly fifty titles in all were mentioned. The top four are *American Libraries, College & Research Libraries, Library Journal,* and *RQ,* read by 78%, 78%, 68%, and 51% of the respondents, respectively. Other journals read by more than 10% of respondents are *Online, The Reference Librarian, Reference Services Review, Research Strategies, Wilson Library Bulletin,* and book review sources such

FIGURE 1. What type of library do you work in?

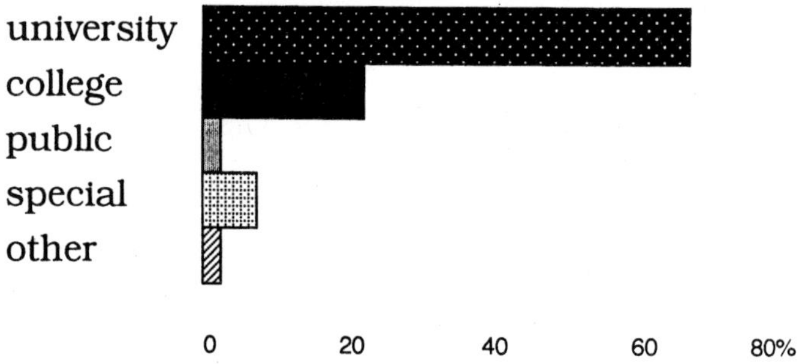

Note: Percentages on 62 replies.

as *Choice*. Nearly all respondents reported reading at least one journal regularly.

The question about which listservs are read also yielded a wide variety of responses. In addition to the six listed in the survey, around forty-five listservs are used. The top three are: LIBREF-L (97%), PACS-L (46%), and BI-L (Bibliographic Instruction Discussion Group) (43%). There is more individuality in people's listserv reading habits, as only one other was read by more than 10% of the respondents–NETTRAIN (13%).

Professional Maintenance Activities

The amount of time spent on various 'professional maintenance' activities per week varies considerably (Figure 2). For ease of reporting, we grouped the answers into seven categories.

LIBREF-L

Reading, Posting, Responding

Ninety-one percent of the respondents read LIBREF-L daily. As for posting a query, only 2% post often, while 32% post sometimes, 56% post rarely, and 8% never post. On the other hand, 10% of respondents respond to queries often, 57% respond sometimes, 29% respond rarely, and 2% never (except they did at least once!).

Importance of LIBREF-L

Respondents clearly consider LIBREF-L important for their development as reference librarians since 29% said it is very important and 65% said it is important. There are many reasons given: "Listservs are my primary professional development tool. I don't have funds or time to run off to conferences . . . "; "It helps to keep me current and gives me a support group,"; and "Another element of knowledge and knowing what is going on in the profession."

Issues Covered in LIBREF-L, Not Found Elsewhere

Seventy-three percent of the respondents said they found issues covered in LIBREF-L that they hadn't seen in other sources, or at

FIGURE 2. Time spent on 'professional maintenance' activities.

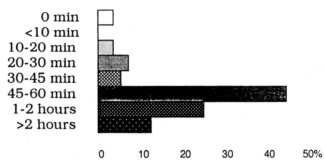

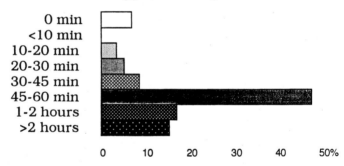

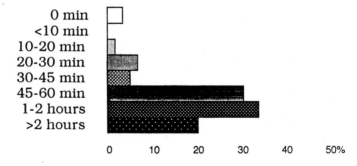

FIGURE 2 (continued)

Reading other Listservs

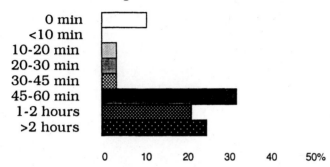

Discussion via telephone

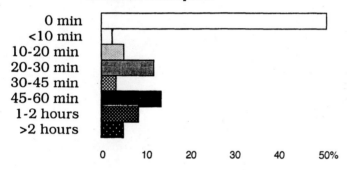

Discussion face-to-face

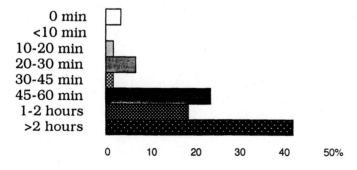

least they discovered them in LIBREF-L before finding them else-where. For example, two of the most frequently mentioned issues "not found elsewhere" were: 'roving' reference librarians and discussions evaluating the latest versions of or newly released CD-ROM products.

What Do People Like Best and Least About LIBREF-L?

Answers to these questions were varied and thoughtful. The most common responses are summarized in the following tables (Figures 3 and 4).

Discussion

The reference librarians who responded to this survey are clearly spending a lot of time communicating with each other in one way or another. Just as clearly, electronic listservs are an important part of this communication. Figure 2 shows that the majority of respondents are spending two or more hours per week reading printed library journals and two or more hours per week reading library listservs. Some reference librarians are spending many more hours on each. Thus, electronic communication is apparently not replacing traditional printed journals, but is being added on top of established professional maintenance activities. Swisher and Smith[34] reported on two surveys of journal reading habits of academic librarians conducted in 1973 and 1978. In both of those surveys, as in this one twenty years later, the top three journals read are *American Libraries, College & Research Libraries,* and *Library Journal.*

Respondents to the survey find LIBREF-L to be an effective means of communicating about issues of importance to reference librarians: "It is good to hear other viewpoints, especially in the controversial areas (some of which I never imagined could be controversial!)" and "I have a sense of security knowing that I can talk to my colleagues around the U.S. with little time and effort." Even though many respondents had common complaints about too much irrelevant and trivial discussion that goes on too long, several

FIGURE 3. What do respondents like best about LIBREF-L?

Variety of topics
Diversity of librarians
Currency/timeliness
Immediacy
Interactiveness
Informality
Other

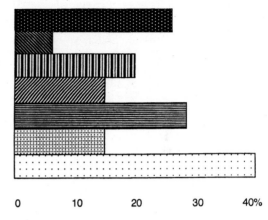

Note: Percentages on 55 replies.

FIGURE 4. What do respondents like least about LIBREF-L?

Inappropriate ref q's
Posting to whole list
Beating subj to death
Inconsistent subjects
Not enough time
Trivial/irrelevant posts
Other

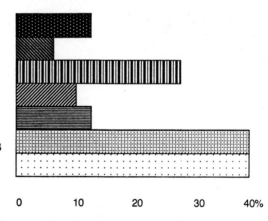

Note: Percentages on 51 replies.

said they would not want to stifle discussion, and simply use the delete key when they are not interested in a message.

One might expect that LIBREF-L and other electronic forms of communication would appeal more to younger reference librarians. As one respondent commented: "It's electronic. Seems to appeal to younger librarians, gives them a forum that otherwise they would not have." But the survey tells a different story (Figure 5). Respondents have been reference librarians for less than a year to more than thirty years. When grouped in six ranges, the spread is relatively even.

LISTSERV ANALYSIS

In order to complement the survey, which provides information about reference librarians' self perceptions regarding their use of listservs, and to ascertain whether library electronic conferences fall into the patterns indicated by communication researchers in other fields, messages for the three listservs claimed to be most frequently read by those responding to the survey were collected and categorized. The three are PACS-L, LIBREF-L, and BI-L.

PACS-L was founded by Charles W. Bailey, Jr. in June 1989 at the University of Houston. It is moderated by Dana Rooks and Jill Hackenberg and, as of May 1993, it had over 6,330 users in fifty-six countries. The provenance of PACS-L is described as " . . . topics such as CD-ROM databases, expert systems, hypertext programs, microcomputer labs, locally mounted databases, network-based information resource, and OPACs."[35]

FIGURE 5. Ranges of years as a reference librarian.

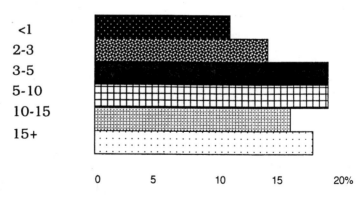

Note: Percentages on 61 replies

LIBREF-L was founded in November 1990[36] by a group of reference librarians at Kent State University. It has 2,744 subscribers in thirty-eight countries. Its moderators describe LIBREF-L as a "roundtable discussion among reference librarians and other interested people that takes place across computer networks."[37]

BI-L was founded by Martin Raish on April 26, 1990, at Binghamton University. It is moderated by Raish and as of April 1993 had 1,427 subscribers in twenty-five countries. BI-L is described "as an international computer conference dedicated to discussing ways of assisting library users in effectively and efficiently exploiting the resources available through the libraries of the 1990s. . . . We examine, explore, critique, appraise, and evaluate strategies, programs, and equipment that we have found to be valuable (or not) in working toward the goal of the self-sufficient library user."[38]

For the analysis, messages covering ten days of activity from April 26 through May 14, 1993 were collected. The messages were then counted and sorted by category. The categories were not predetermined, but emerged from the messages themselves. The categories are:

- Specific queries, defined as a message asking a specific question regarding a fact or a request for information about equipment, addresses, or bibliographic information.
- Responses to queries.
- Summaries of responses.
- Presentation of an issue, defined as a query regarding procedures or policies or a topic such as "what is the virtual library" or "what about gophers and copyright?"
- Discussions, defined as the discussion of topics, policies, or procedures. There tend to be more discussion items tallied than responses to specific queries because the answers to specific questions are usually directed to the person asking the question rather than to the list.
- Announcements, including a general announcement offering information, survey questionnaires, calls for papers, and messages from the moderators about the system.
- Conference announcements.
- Job postings.

Cross-postings were also counted if the message was identified as such. Simple curiosity motivated the count by gender. If the gender could not be determined by the usual association by name then it was placed in the "unknown" category. Names like Chris were categorized as "unknown (Table 1)."

TABLE 1

Category	PACS-L		LIBREF-L		BI-L	
Specific query	27	18%	45	23%	7	12%
Response to query	14	9%	30	15%	2	4%
Summary of responses	0	0%	14	7%	4	7%
	Total: 27%		Total: 45%		Total: 23%	
Presentation of issue	7	5%	13	7%	6	11%
Discussion of issue	47	32%	54	27%	12	21%
	Total: 37%		Total: 34%		Total: 32%	
Announcement	33	22%	23	12%	17	30%
Conference announcement	11	7%	8	4%	3	5%
Job posting	10	7%	13	7%	6	11%
	Total: 36%		Total: 23%		Total: 46%	
Grand Total:	149	100%	200	100%	57	100%*

(* percentages may not equal 100 due to rounding)

	PACS-L		LIBREF-L		BI-L	
Cross-posting	29	19%	28	14%	14	25%
Female participants	41	28%	93	47%	30	53%
Male participants	87	58%	76	38%	22	39%
Unknown gender	21	14%	31	16%	5	9%*

(*percentages may not equal 100 due to rounding)

Discussion

LIBREF-L appears to be the most frequently used when it comes to practical question and answer concerns–45% of the messages on LIBREF-L deal with specific questions and their replies compared to 28% in PACS-L and 23% in BI-L. Discussion about a topic or policy issue accounts for 36% of the messages on PACS-L, 33% in LIBREF-L, and 32% in BI-L. Thus, roughly a third of the messages on all three lists are discussions of topics. In a sense these are problem solving discussions rather than task oriented discussions and indicate a sophistication about the use of the system and its protocol. This is the only category where there is a definite similarity among the lists. Using the lists simply to convey information and post job announcements is also a heavy use of the lists, although the proportions vary. Announcements, conference announcements, and job postings are 22% of the messages in LIBREF-L, 36% in PACS-L, and 46% in BI-L. The amount of cross-posting also indicates the use of the lists simply for disseminating information.

If Walther is correct in his proposition that computer-mediated communication evolves similarly to face-to-face group communication, then it is not surprising that PACS-L contains more discussion oriented messages than task oriented messages since it is the oldest list. However, an explanation may be that there are electronic user groups for online systems such as GEAC, Innopac, NOTIS, RLIN, ALEPH, and DYNIX which can deal with specific system questions, leaving PACS-L to address more general questions or wide ranging issues. Yet, if he is correct, we should see the decline of task oriented messages in LIBREF-L and BI-L and more problem-solving discussions taking place as the participants grow familiar with each other and the medium. A major qualification of this scenario is that in the communication research studies the groups were closed, in that they represented either a select number for the experiment or were groups within organizations, while the listservs studied are open to anyone and the subscribers and active participants may change over time. Therefore, the composition of the group may change and never have a chance to evolve in the way Walther predicts. Another consideration is that as a listserv grows new subscribers adopt the mores of the list and may then bypass the impersonal task stage and plunge right into the discussion, if that is the predominant feature of the list.

Comparing the statements given by our survey respondents to the definition of media richness outlined above, we can see that list-servs facilitate feedback and present individually tailored messages. However, the use of natural language and fulfillment of the fourth criterion of communicating multiple cues is reduced when communicating through computers. The use of codes and employment of computer etiquette compensates for the lack of visual and aural cues. For example, keyboard devices such as ":-)" for representing humor or sarcasm, admonitions against use of capital letters for emphasis, and the advice to keep messages short and to one topic reduce the chances of misunderstanding. The existence of rules of etiquette provided in the moderators' introductions to their conferences indicates a high awareness of the dangers inherent in trying to convey complex and ambiguous messages in such a medium.

The question of irrelevance also arises as information overload impedes the usefulness of the lists. The survey reveals a certain irritation with the "irrelevance" of many of the messages. An assiduous reader of these three listservs in the ten days recorded would have perused and possibly responded to over 400 messages–some, such as conference reports, quite lengthy.

CONCLUSION

The listservs seem to serve the needs and purposes of their users. Our survey indicates that reference librarians turn to the lists in order to reduce their isolation, find out how other libraries do things, keep on top of issues and developments, and review announcements and job ads. The lists function like a newsletter providing a quick, short format for conveying information combined with the opportunity to discuss issues at length over time with the added characteristics of being interactive and immediate. Whether this immediacy and interaction has really changed the nature of the communication is still an open question. Willard McCarty, in his article on the HUMANIST seminar, questions whether e-mail is a new linguistic entity with its own vocabulary, syntax, and pragmatics.[39] He notes the lack of inhibition felt by most participants is due to the lack of visual and audio cues concerning the numbers of people "listening" or reading the communication.[40] Reference librarians value this lack of constraint as indicated by some of their survey comments—"LIBREF-L is a great source for informal discussion," "You can get gut reactions and honesty you never get through a publication process," and "Its wide distribution makes me feel as though one is talking to the profession, not just a clique within it." In an article on writing styles in computer conferences, Spitzer notes that a "computer conference is a unique medium, similar in some of its characteristics to more familiar media but different enough that we need to attend to these differences if we are to use conferencing effectively."[41]

REFERENCES

1. Lievrouw, Leah A. and T. Andrew Finn, "Identifying the Common Dimensions of Communication: The Communication Systems Model," in *Mediation, Information, and Behavior*, edited by Brent D. Ruben and Leah A. Lievrouw (New Brunswick: Transaction Publishers, 1990) p. 37-65, p. 49.

2. Listserv is a software developed for use on Bitnet. The listserv enables messages to be distributed to subscribers and archived as files for search and retrieval. Participants use a listserv much like electronic mail except that the message may be received by thousands of people instead of one or a few known to the sender.

3. Lyders, Josette Anne, "Editing: A Leadership Role in Professional Communication," in *Library Education and Leadership: Essays in Honor of Jane Anne Hannigan*, edited by Sheila S. Intner and Kay E. Vandergrift (Metuchen, NJ: Scarecrow Pr., 1990) p. 99-106.

4. Campana, Deborah, "Information Flow: Written Communication Among Music Librarians," *Notes: Quarterly Journal of the Music Library Association* 47:686-707 (March 1991).

5. Budd, John M., "Professional Communication: The Literature of Public Libraries," *Public Libraries* 31:273-277 (September/October 1992).

6. Budd, John M., "The Literature of Academic Libraries: An Analysis," *College & Research Libraries* 52:290-295 (May 1991).

7. Krausse, Sylvia C. and Janice F. Sieburth, "Patterns of Authorship in Library Journals by Academic Librarians," *The Serials Librarian* 9:127-138 (Spring 1985).

8. Swisher, Robert Dean, *Professional Communication Behavior of Academic Librarians Holding Membership in the American Library Association* (Ph.D. Dissertation, Indiana University, 1975).

9. Watson, Paula D., "Production of Scholarly Articles by Academic Librarians and Library School Faculty," *College & Research Libraries* 46:334-342 (July 1985).

10. Crane, Diana, *Invisible Colleges; Diffusion of Knowledge in Scientific Communities* (Chicago: University of Chicago Pr., 1972).

11. Osburn, Charles B., "The Structuring of the Scholarly Communication System," *College & Research Libraries* 50:277-286 (May 1989) p. 283.

12. Kadanoff, Diane Gordon, "Communication & Cooperation," *Library Journal* 111:58-59 (April 1986).

13. Bunge, Charles A., "Strategies for Updating Knowledge of Reference Resources and Techniques," *RQ* 21:228-232 (Spring 1982).

14. Ladner, Sharyn J. and Hope N. Tillman, "How Special Librarians Really Use the Internet," *Canadian Library Journal* 49:211-215 (June 1992) p. 213.

15. Kovacs, Diane, "ARL Expands 3rd Edition of Directory of Electronic Publications," *PACS-L* (May 20, 1993).

16. Bailey, Charles E., Jr., "Library-Oriented Lists and E-Serials," *PACS-L* (March 25, 1993).

17. Walther, Joseph B., "Interpersonal Effects in Computer-Mediated Interaction: A Relational Perspective," *Communication Research* 19:52-90 (February 1992).

18. Schmitz, Joseph and Janet Fulk, "Organizational Colleagues, Media Richness, and Electronic Mail," *Communication Research* 18:487-523 (August 1991).

19. Ball-Rokeach, S.J. and K.K. Reardon, "Telelogic, Dialogic and Monologic Communication: A Comparison of Forms," *Advancing Communication Science: Merging Mass and Interpersonal Processes,* edited by R.P. Hawkins, J.M. Wiemann, and S. Pingree (Newbury Park, CA: Sage, 1988).

20. Schmitz and Fulk, "Organizational Colleagues, Media Richness, and Electronic Mail," p.488.

21. Schmitz and Fulk, "Organizational Colleagues, Media Richness, and Electronic Mail," p.488.

22. Fulk, Janet and D. Ryu, *Perceiving Electronic Mail Systems: Partial Test of the Social Information Processing Model* (Paper presented to the International Communication Association, Dublin, Ireland, 1990).

23. Rice, Ronald E., *The New Media: Communication, Research, and Technology* (Beverly Hills, CA: Sage, 1984).

24. Trevino, L.K., R.H. Lengel, and R.L. Daft, "Media Symbolism, Media Richness, and Media Choice in Organizations," *Communication Research* 14:553-574 (1987).

25. Walther, "Interpersonal Effects in Computer-Mediated Interaction," p. 54.

26. Foulger, D.A., *Medium as Process: The Structure, Use, and Practice of Computer Conferencing on IBM's IBMPC Computer Conferencing Facility* (Ph.D. Dissertation, Temple University, 1990).

27. Walther, "Interpersonal Effects in Computer-Mediated Interaction," p. 61-62.

28. Walther, "Interpersonal Effects in Computer-Mediated Interaction," p. 82.

29. Dubrovsky, Vitaly J., Sara Kiesler, and Beheruz N. Sethna, "The Equalization Phenomenon: Status Effects in Computer-Mediated and Face-to-Face Decision-Making Groups," *Human Computer Interaction* 6:119-146 (1991).

30. Sproull, L. and S. Kiesler, "Reducing Social Context Cues: Electronic Mail in Organizational Communication," *Management Science* 32:1492-1512 (1988).

31. Dubrovsky, Kiesler, and Sethna, "The Equalization Phenomenon," p. 123.

32. Due to space constraints, we are unable to present complete results and analysis of the entire survey at this time. Only the items of greatest relevance to this article are reported here.

33. Due to the nature of a listserv, it is impossible to determine the response rate of this survey. Considering the potential number of readers of LIBREF-L (over 2,700), the percentage of replies received out of the possible replies is quite small. However, other surveys distributed through several listservs and summarized on LIBREF-L recently, had a similar number of responses. Thus, 63 replies seems like a decent response rate, and we surmise that much of what was reported is representative of reference librarians' views.

34. Swisher, Robert and Peggy C. Smith, "Journals Read by ACRL Academic Librarians, 1973 and 1978," *College & Research Libraries* 43:51-58 (January 1982).

35. "Welcome to PACS-L," *PACS-L* (May 2, 1993).

36. Robinson, Kara and Diane Kovacs, "LibRef-L: Sharing Reference Expertise Over the Academic Networks," *Wilson Library Bulletin* 67:47-50 (January 1993).

37. "LIBREF-L User Memo," *LIBREF-L* (April 13, 1993).

38. "BI-L Overview and Policies," *BI-L* (April 26, 1993).

39. McCarty, Willard, "HUMANIST: Lessons from a Global Electronic Seminar," *Computers and the Humanities* 26:205-222 (1992) p. 213.

40. McCarty, "HUMANIST," p. 214.

41. Spitzer, Michael, "Writing Style in Computer Conferences," *IEEE Transactions on Professional Communication* 29:19-22 (1986) p. 19.

The Internet and Reference Librarians:
A Question of Leadership

Marcos Silva
Glenn F. Cartwright

SUMMARY. This paper examines the efforts of the McGill University Humanities and Social Sciences Library Reference staff to integrate the use of resources found on the Internet with traditional reference duties. It also discusses the Internet instruction workshops designed and implemented by reference staff to help librarians and the university community understand and navigate the Internet. The relationship with McGill's Computing Centre and Department of Educational and Counselling Psychology is examined and a case is made for increased collaboration with other areas concerning Internet instruction and use. Lastly, the proactive role of reference staff concerning the introduction of the Internet to other library staff and to the university community is also discussed.

INTRODUCTION

In the last decade, perhaps no other phenomenon has so significantly affected the provision of reference services as has the In-

Marcos Silva is Computer Services Librarian, McLennan-Redpath Library, McGill University, 3459 McTavish St., Montreal, Canada, H3A 1Y1; ADLC@MUSICA.MCGILL. CA. Glenn F. Cartwright is Associate Professor, Department of Educational and Counselling Psychology, McGill University, 3700 McTavish St., Montreal, Canada, H3A 1Y2; INOO@MUSICB.MCGILL. CA.

[Haworth co-indexing entry note]: "The Internet and Reference Librarians: A Question of Leadership." Silva, Marcos, and Glenn F. Cartwright. Co-published simultaneously in *The Reference Librarian* (The Haworth Press, Inc.) No. 41/42, 1994, pp. 159-172; and: *Librarians on the Internet: Impact on Reference Services* (ed: Robin Kinder) The Haworth Press, Inc., 1994, pp. 159-172. Multiple copies of this article/chapter may be purchased from The Haworth Document Delivery Center [1-800-3-HAWORTH; 9:00 a.m. - 5:00 p.m. (EST)].

ternet. Whereas five years ago there were few articles about the Internet, today a cursory search will retrieve over one hundred articles and many monographs on the subject. And, more importantly, the number of articles devoted specifically to reference services and the Internet has also shown an important increase. Indeed, the advent of the Internet has not gone unnoticed by reference professionals.

Although many articles and monographs discuss implicitly and explicitly the resources of the 'Internet[1] and their potential impact on the provision of reference services,[2] few studies have adequately addressed the issue of how to integrate the resources on the Internet with traditional reference duties. More specifically, few studies have examined how reference librarians can take a leadership role in introducing and promoting use of the Internet to colleagues, library users, and faculty.

The purpose of this paper is to describe the proactive role that McGill University reference librarians played in the introduction and training of Internet protocols to other staff and the university community. It argues that use of the Internet must be effectively integrated in most areas of librarianship and academic research. Also described are the efforts by library staff to seek expertise and advice from other disciplines, university research centres, and most importantly, the Computing Centre. It also examines the obstacles and support faced by staff in their attempts to introduce the Internet.

There are two major themes in this discussion: first is the contention that reference staff are best suited to undertake the introduction and integration of Internet resources to colleagues and the university community. That is to say, reference librarians have the professional responsibility to learn how to navigate the Internet and to promote its uses to the uninitiated. And second, the convergence of telecommunication technology and computers has caused our profession to undergo a powerful paradigm shift affecting the manner by which we access, manipulate, and interpret data.

THE ENVIRONMENT

Computers and telecommunication technology contribute to the creation of a virtual environment where access to information is free of temporal and spatial constraints. The electronic campus allows a researcher to access and manipulate information, often independently from library staff, in vast warehouses of electronic data. Moreover, the dissemination and retrieval of information is both rapid and immediate. With the advent of electronic publishing–there has been a 33% increase in the number of electronic journals during the first two months of 1993[3]–and the scholar's workstation, the impact of electronic technology on research and teaching cannot be overestimated.

In academe, this phenomenon has also caused two contradictory trends: an explosion of information and a fragmentation of knowledge.[4] Fragmentation of knowledge results from the inability to filter, assimilate, and derive meaning from eclectic and diverse information.

This in turn has caused what Gregorian, Hawkins and Taylor[5] see as knowledge–fragmented, specialized communities who are unable to share or communicate their knowledge with others. These overspecialized knowledge communities may unwittingly erect barriers against participation by others holding different views or ideas. In essence, they become unable to synthesize information beyond their own narrow academic confines.

Reference librarians have also experienced a radical shift concerning the provision of reference duties arising from the convergence of computer and telecommunication technology. This shift has arisen out of their attempt to meet the needs of faculty and students who need to locate, filter, and synthesize information pertinent to their research but outside their discipline. Of special interest is the impact of the Internet where information originates from electronic sources or is in an electronic format.

It is not surprising, therefore, to find the term 'reference' being called outmoded and obsolete.[6] According to Campbell,[7] a more appropriate term would be 'access engineers' because it encompasses the new activities demanded from reference librarians: filtering of electronic information so that it may be synthesized into knowledge and creating knowledge maps to allow the uninitiated to navigate in unfamiliar academic areas.

Jennings'[8] response to the same phenomenon has been to suggest that library staff must 'regrow' so as to optimally serve their communities. The regrowing of staff causes administration to recognize the needs arising from a virtual electronic campus, and to plan accordingly. Implicit in the above is that librarians are the best link between the new and evolving electronic technologies and the campus community. Of primary importance is the need for librarians to assume a leadership role concerning instruction and navigation in the new electronic campus. Such was the environment faced by McGill University Computer Services librarians.

THE ADVENT OF THE INTERNET

It has been the advent of the Internet which has focused these issues. Internet protocols make available an incredible array of resources which foretell the power and promise of the scholar's workstation. With telnet, for instance, an Internet standard protocol, researchers are able to access interactively hundreds of online library catalogues and bibliographical databases. Also, using File Transfer Protocol (FTP), users are able to retrieve or send text or binary files from a remote computer, to a host computer.

Although electronic mail was available to faculty and students at McGill for over a decade, access to the Internet has increased the potential for increased communication exponentially. The size and growth of the Internet is staggering; some estimates claim that there are 13 million people presently linked.[9] Moreover, there are hundreds of electronic discussion groups, thousands if USENET (a voluntary worldwide network primarily used to exchange news) is included, giving researchers access to a virtual community of scholars.

It is safe to assume that use of the Internet will continue to grow. Development of Resource Discovery tools such as Archie, gophers, Wide Area Information Servers (WAIS), and World Wide Web (WWW), facilitate the indexing, location, and retrieval of information. In fact, a parallel name for resource discovery tools might be bibliographic information retrieval tools. By exploiting these new software, even novice users are able to make optimum use of the Internet.

MCGILL REFERENCE LIBRARIANS
AND THE INTERNET

McGill University serves approximately twenty thousand full time students, of whom one in four is registered in the Faculty of

Graduate Studies and Research, distributed among twenty faculties and ten schools. Its library system is comprised of seventeen libraries divided among four areas: Humanities and Social Sciences, Law, Physical Sciences and Engineering, and Health Sciences. The Humanities and Social Sciences Library comprises approximately seventy percent of the collection and serves seventy-five percent of the university community.

McGill's link to the Internet is recent; Computing Centre staff gained entry in the late 1980s. Soon afterward, anyone with a VM, TSO, or UNIXcode likewise had access. Still, access was limited and the vast majority of the McGill faculty and student body were excluded. By 1991, the decision was made to extend access to anyone holding a valid MUSIC (Multi User System for Interactive Computing) code, the IBM mainframe operating system used by the majority of the McGill community. Virtually overnight, potential users of the Internet grew by a thousand-fold.

The Humanities and Social Sciences Reference Department is comprised of two other sub-units or departments: Computer Services Reference Unit and Inter-Library Loan. The Computer Services Reference Unit arose out of the need to support and instruct staff and clientele in the use of new technologies such as CD-ROM. In a short time, it assumed responsibility for computer applications, online searching, telecommunications, etc., for the whole of the Humanities and Social Sciences Libraries Area while simultaneously fulfilling their routine reference duties.

Computer Services Reference staff are and remain unequivocally reference librarians. Nevertheless, they view themselves as a reference vanguard and assume that their present duties point to future trends in librarianship. It is not surprising to find among their ranks the enthusiasm and energy necessary to consistently argue and fight for the benefits of automation and networks.

Computer Services Reference librarians are in a unique position: they not only participate in the implementation of new technologies but must also be actively involved in traditional reference duties. This amalgamation of seemingly contradictory duties and responsibilities is in no doubt responsible for the greater insight concerning the possible impact and significance of the Internet.

Computer Services Reference librarians became aware of Internet protocols and resources through subscription to various electronic discussion groups. Although at the time resources were somewhat limited, forty online library catalogues were accessible[10] compared to hundreds today,[11] the implications of the Internet to academic research and librarianship were quickly understood.

Because of the Library Systems' preoccupation with implementation of the Library's new online catalogue, MUSE, guidance and support to library staff concerning Internet protocols was not possible. Still, the decision had been made by Computer Services staff to explore the Internet and gain an understanding of its uses and resources. Limited access to the Internet via VM and UNIX codes, operating systems normally not used by library staff, created a further obstacle. Fortunately, the Computing Centre was sympathetic to the Reference Department's efforts and issued VM codes, normally used by systems operators at McGill, to the Humanities and Social Sciences Computer Services Reference staff. So the first lesson was learned: Computing Centre cooperation was essential for the success of any future plans involving the Internet.

Initial use of the Internet with VM codes was made by the Interlibrary Loan Department (ILL), nominally under Reference supervision. Logon scripts for the telecommunication software Procomm, were written to help staff access the few available online library databases. Of all the accessible services, telneting for bibliographical verification and electronic mail were the most widely used. Soon use of the Internet was quickly incorporated into other reference workflow.

Once access was possible via MUSIC, and because many librarians have MUSIC codes, greater integration and use of Internet resources became possible. Again, Computer Services Reference staff played a proactive role in prodding other reference librarians to become acquainted with Internet protocols and integrate use of Internet resources in their daily duties. Note, however, that the efforts were made to convince other staff members of the benefits of using the Internet.

It should be said that Computer Services received active support from the Head of Reference, who, along with the Health Sciences Library administration, was one of the few supervisors who clearly foresaw the benefits of exploiting the Internet. This support had the effect of averting possible conflicts with more traditionally oriented staff.

Ironically, while the decision had been made to provide the university with open access to the Internet, the Computing Centre made no provision to offer Internet training seminars. Reference Computer Services staff, in conjunction with Library Instruction, quickly decided to offer Internet workshops to McGill students and faculty.

ASSUMING A LEADERSHIP ROLE

In retrospect, three elements make the decision to offer Internet workshops a unique undertaking. First, with the exception of CD-ROM seminars, computer training and instruction were normally under the auspices of the Computing Centre. However, it was felt that because of the increasing integration of computer related technology and bibliographical related research, many seminars had little relevancy to librarians and library users. Because the Internet was understood as being the foundation of the impending virtual library, the workshops emphasized library resources and research.[12]

Second, the decision was made to not only offer support to those familiar the with Internet, but also to pursue aggressively a policy that introduces the Internet to novice users. In other words, scarce resources were devoted to advertising and disseminating information about the Internet. Pamphlets and booklets describing resources found on the Net were printed and distributed. In addition, approximately 65% of the terminals used to search MUSE, McGill's online library catalogue, were modified to give users access to their computer accounts and by extension, to the Internet. And last, a regular column is published in the *McGill Computing Centre Newsletter* ostensibly to inform readers on new developments in the library. The column has quickly become an efficient way to inform the university community on library Internet related services and resources.

The above decision was based on the belief that it is the responsibility of reference librarians to lead the user to the needed information, regardless of its format or location. Reference librarians would be remiss in their duties if use and instruction of the Internet were not incorporated with other traditional reference resources. Indeed, use of the Internet was understood as reinforcing the mandate of McGill reference librarians to offer support to original research and instruct clients in the use of library resources.

Third, similar to the decision to integrate use of the Internet with traditional reference duties, the decision to offer Internet seminars was made by reference librarians in conjunction with library instruction. That such an important decision could be made independently from other non-reference areas, indicates that reference librarians understood the implications and value of the Internet and, at the time, could ably introduce the resources of the Internet to colleagues and the university research community.

Swanson,[13] in his study of computer mediated communication in the workplace, argues that administration or management has lost the ability to control the actions of subordinates in their use of electronic mail. Furthermore, according to Swanson, subordinates claim that computer mediated communication has given them new technical skills that they wish to use during work without interference.

Given McGill's library experience with the Internet, it would be easy to extend Swanson's hypothesis to reference librarians' use and knowledge of the Internet. The autonomy and latitude for action experienced by reference staff will be difficult to relinquish. Indeed, the freedom enjoyed by Computer Services and reference staff, the creativity resulting from it, and the demonstrated leadership, may presage future trends.

CONSEQUENCES

First and foremost, Computer Services Reference staff realized that it is possible to assume leadership in the creation and establishment of innovative programs that enhance the role of the library in the evolution of the electronic campus. Moreover, it is also interesting to note that Computer Services Reference staff have kept their leadership role. The use, promotion, and understanding of Internet protocols is more extensively used by reference staff than by any other area in the library.

Illustrative of the Reference Department's leadership role was its role in the design and implementation of Internet seminars in conjunction with library systems and under the auspices of the Conférence des recteurs et des principaux des universités du Québec, the provincial organization responsible for promoting greater resource sharing among Quebec universities. Four seminars, introductory and practical, have been offered to date to over 125 Quebec academic librarians.

Another significant consequence is the relationship engendered by the Reference Department with other university centres, faculties, schools, most notably the Computing Centre and the Department of Educational and Counselling Psychology. The Computing Centre's reaction to the Reference Department's initiative concerning Internet workshops was imaginative and open to collaboration.

Although not actively offering resources, the Computing Centre gave active encouragement by including information about the workshops with their publications. Furthermore, the Centre also appended workshop information onto the University Campus Wide Information System, InfoMcGill. Barron's *UNT's Accessing On-Line Bibliographic Databases*,[14] Kehoe's *Zen and the Art of the Internet*,[15] and other electronic resources were loaded onto InfoMcGill as requested by Computer Services Reference staff. The willingness of Computing Centre to allow space in their newsletter to promote the Library's use and instruction of the Internet was indicative of their eagerness to support greater cooperation.

As previously mentioned, one of the problems associated with Internet instruction and promotion is that the majority of McGill's computer users must access the mainframe to use the Internet. However, Internet mainframe applications, as opposed to UNIX, MAC or other possible distributed environment applications, are less user friendly and flexible.[16] However, cognizant of the fact that McGill's user community was not making optimum use of Internet resources, the Computing Centre and the McGill MUSIC Product Group created Internet mainframe-based programs that greatly simplify Internet navigation and use.

As a result, novice users are able to quickly use protocols such as FTP and telnet without having to learn arcane commands or experiencing emulation problems. Even more helpful has been the creation of a MUSIC gopher client; optimum use of the Internet by

McGill students is now a very real possibility. Of interest is that these initiatives to create more intuitive interfaces arose out of the need to meet user demands; namely, the request to simplify Internet use. The Library system, therefore, has been exceptionally fortunate; a user friendly mainframe telnet and FTP interface were being created simultaneously with library efforts to promote and increase use of the Internet.

The Computer Services Reference Unit also turned to the Department of Educational and Counselling Psychology for advice and ideas on the philosophy and design of the Internet seminars. Because of the Department's expertise with educational applications of artificial intelligence, computer assisted instruction, and computer conferencing, the library was able to avoid many of the pedagogical errors made during the implementation of new educational programs. The planned content and objectives of the seminars were far more audacious than other computer seminars, including those offered for CD-ROM searching.

Indeed, the humanist approach chosen for the workshops[17] was made after consultation with the Department's faculty and experts. Many of the ideas incorporated into the workshops were taken directly from Professor G. F. Cartwright's graduate courses on Artificial Intelligence in Education (416-660) and Consciousness, Virtual Reality, and Cyberspace (416-609). Emphasis was placed on active participation, a non-threatening environment, and a situated cognitive approach where instruction is personalized and made individually relevant.

In conclusion, the Reference Department's decision to invest aggressively in use and promotion of the Internet has resulted in several tangible benefits: first, recognition of the leadership role of the Reference Department by the university and elsewhere concerning a new resource that is transforming the nature of academic research. Consequently, the Reference Department has increased its influence concerning library policy on automation objectives. At present, most library committees concerned with automation, telecommunications, or networks have reference representation. Furthermore, reference expertise concerning the Internet has engendered closer cooperation and collaboration between library systems and reference. Systems has appreciated our efforts and lends support whenever possible.

Second, the greater cooperation between the Reference Department and Computing Centre has granted the Reference Department the ability to pursue goals that were virtually impossible a few years back. The human and technical resources needed to offer Internet seminars, especially when the seminars are open to the entire university community, should not be underestimated. Although the Computing Centre did not initially offer Internet support, once it became aware of the Reference Department's efforts and program, unrestricted access to its expertise was forthcoming.

In addition, because of the Computing Centre's cooperation, the library was able to reach a far greater audience. Moreover, the workshops gained immediate credibility among many of the science departments because of the Computing Centre's benediction. As a result, they were well attended, allowing the Reference Department to justify its expenditures and to request more resources.

Finally, that the Reference Department was able to seek advice and expertise from the Department of Educational and Counselling Psychology has in no small measure assured the success of the workshops. Moreover, cooperation allowed the Reference Department to have greater insights on how to introduce the Internet to faculty, especially since one of the objectives was to reach faculty with heavy teaching responsibilities. After all, if faculty could be convinced of the benefits of using the Internet, it was assumed that they would incorporate its resources in their instructional methodologies.

Reference also benefited from the said cooperation in its creation of Internet promotional materials and guides.[18] Internet guides are popular with students and faculty. Copies of the guides may also be requested via e-mail and the latest edition will soon be mounted onto InfoMcGill.

CONCLUSIONS

Powerful changes are affecting the way researchers and students manipulate, access, and disseminate information. This has caused libraries to react accordingly; scarce resources have been used to allow libraries to understand and use tools to better exploit new technologies. Of these technologies, it is the creation of high-speed global networks embodied by the Internet that has most significantly changed the ways libraries are able to lead users to information and subsequently, knowledge.

Furthermore, the evolution of the Internet into super networks such as the American National Research and Education Network (NREN) and the Canadian Network for the Advancement of Research, Industry, and Education (CANARIE) will place even more demands on libraries to react in a proactive and innovative manner. The mandate of the library is rapidly changing from offering users a limited warehouse of information to a global gateway containing infinite distributed information resources.

Helping users achieve freedom from information so that they are able to synthesize knowledge into wisdom[19] requires librarians to analyze and filter information. But, most important, it also requires from librarians the ability to show and instruct users how to navigate new electronic highways.

This paper has argued that reference librarians are best suited, ironically because of the contradiction between day-to-day responsibilities and new technologies, to integrate and expand use of Internet resources with traditional library duties. It has also argued that reference librarians should take a leadership role in promoting use of the Internet. To succeed, collaboration with other areas that have needed expertise is essential. In McGill's case, these areas included the Computing Centre and Department of Educational Counselling and Psychology.

For reference librarians to forego leadership and its accompanying responsibilities would be to negate the very essence of our mandate: to guide the user to the needed information. That the means to fulfil our mandate are far different than before is irrelevant; our obligations remain unchanged. This must be understood as an exceptional opportunity; reference librarians have the unique chance to affect the evolution of research and teaching.

REFERENCES

1. Kehoe, Brendan P. (1993). *Zen and the Art of the Internet: A Beginner's Guide.* 2nd ed. Englewood Cliffs, NJ: PTR Prentice Hall; Krol, Ed. (1992). *The Whole Internet: User's Guide & Catalog.* Sebastopol, CA: O'Reilly & Associates; LaQuey, Tracy, & Ryer, Jeanne C. (1993). *The Internet Companion: A Beginner's Guide to Global Networking.* Reading, MA: Addison-Wesley.

2. Kalin, Sally W., & Tennant, Roy. (1991). Beyond OPACs . . .The wealth of information resources on the Internet. *Database*, 14, 28-33; Kovacs, Diane. (In press). A model for planning and providing reference services using Internet resources, in Dennis Brunning & George Machovec (Eds.). *Information Highways*. Oryx Press; Ladner, Sharyn J., & Tillman, Hope N., (1992). How special librarians really use the Internet. *Canadian Library Journal*, 44, 211-215; Ladner, Sharyn J., & Tillman, Hope N. (1993). Using the Internet for Reference. *Online*, 17, 45-49; Raeder, A. W., & Andrews, K. L. (1990). Searching Library Catalogs on the Internet: A Survey. *Database Searcher*, 6, 16-31; Still, Julie, & Alexander, Jan. (1993). Integrating Internet into Reference: Policy Issues. *College & Research Libraries News*, 54, 139-140.

3. Strangelove, Michael. (1993). *Reflections on Developments Draft RFC.* Electronic message posted to Publishing E-Journals: Publishing, Archiving, and Access Discussion list. VPIEJL@VTM1.BITNET, February 15, 1993.

4. Gregorian, Vartan, Hawkins, Brian L., & Taylor, Merrily. (1992a). Integrating Information Technologies: A Research University Perspective. *CAUSE/ EFFECT*, 15, 5-12; Gregorian, Vartan, Hawkins, Brian L., & Taylor, Merrily. (1992b). *What presidents need to know about the integration of information technologies on campus*: (Boulder, CO): HEIRA. [computer file, to retrieve file, send e-mail to HEIRAES@CAUSE.COLORADO.EDU with message GET HEIRA.ES1.BROWN].

5. Ibid.

6. Campbell, Jerry D. (1992). Shaking the conceptual Foundations of Reference: A perspective. *Reference Management, XX*, 29-36.

7. Ibid.

8. Jennings, Lois. (1992). Regrowing Staff: Managerial Priority for the Future of University Libraries. *Public-Access Computer Systems Review*, 3, 4-15. [computer file, to retrieve file, send e-mail to LISTSERV@UHUPVM1 with message GET JENNINGS PRV3N3 F=MAIL].

9. Lottor, Mark. (1993). *Internet Domain Survey*. [Menlo Park, CA]: SRI International. [computer file, sent to various listserv discussion groups by nisc@nisc.sri.com].

10. Raeder, A. W., & Andrews, K. L. (1990).

11. Barron, Billy. (1993). *UNT's Accessing On-Line Bibliographic Databases.* [Denton, TX]: University of North Texas. [computer file, ftp.unt.edu,/library/libraries.txt].

12. Silva, Marcos, & Cartwright, Glenn F. (1993). The Design and Implementation of Internet Seminars for Library Users and Staff at McGill University. *Education for Information, 11(2), 137-146.*

13. Swanson, Douglas J. (1993). Toward a policy for managing the use of computer mediated communication in the workplace. *Interpersonal Computing and Technology: An Electronic Journal for the 21st Century*, 1. [computer file, to retrieve file, send e-mail message to LISTSERV@GUVM with message GET SWANSON IPCTV1N1].

14. Barron, Billy. (1993).

15. Kehoe, Brendan P. (1992). *Zen and the Art of the Internet: A Beginner's Guide to the Internet.* 1st ed. [Chester, PA: s.n.], 1992. [computer file, ftp hydra. uwo.ca,/LIBSOFT/zen.txt].

16. Valauskas, Edward J. (1993). TurboGopher: Internet access with ease on the Macintosh. *Online,* 17, 87-89.

17. Silva, Marcos, & Cartwright, Glenn F. (1993).

18. Silva, Marcos, & Fransiszyn, Marilyn. (1993). *Using the Internet.* [Montreal]: McGill. [Also available as computer file. Send request to ADLC@MUSICA.MCGILL.CA].

19. Cartwright, Glenn F. (1987). Educating for the 21st Century: Special Generalists or General Specialists? Invited Address to the Education for the Twenty-First Century Conference. Cambridge, MA: Cambridge Center for Adult Learning.

MOOving
Towards a Virtual Reference Service

Tona Henderson

SUMMARY. Using the Internet and a software development program called LambdaMOO, it is possible to create a text-based and real-time virtual reality for multiple users. In such a virtual reality, many simultaneous users can logon and communicate with each other, interact with programmed objects, and move around a virtual landscape (generically called a MOO). While, in the past, these kinds of virtual realities have been dominated by dungeons and dragons, some MOOs are now attempting to model more serious work communities for their users. As a result, virtual libraries, in various stages of development, already exist and continue to grow. Accessible through the Internet, these virtual libraries offer the reference librarian an early glimpse at the future of Internet reference services. This article tours the reader through a MOO, examines three virtual libraries, and explains the use of a dictionary. MOO objects, applications, and potential in the virtual library are discussed along with sample logs and explanations for visiting MOO libraries independently.

INTRODUCTION

Using a program freely available on the Internet and an Internet connection, the virtual library is becoming a reality. The program is

---

Tona Henderson is Business Librarian at The Pennsylvania State University, 108H Pattee Library, University Park, PA 16802. Her E-Mail address is tah@psulias.psu.edu. She can be found as tonami_librarian at purple-crayon.media.mit.edu 8888.

[Haworth co-indexing entry note]: "MOOving Towards a Virtual Reference Service." Henderson, Tona. Co-published simultaneously in *The Reference Librarian* (The Haworth Press, Inc.) No. 41/42, 1994, pp. 173-184; and: *Librarians on the Internet: Impact on Reference Services* (ed: Robin Kinder) The Haworth Press, Inc., 1994, pp. 173-184. Multiple copies of this article/chapter may be purchased from The Haworth Document Delivery Center [1-800-3-HAWORTH; 9:00 a.m. - 5:00 p.m. (EST)].

173

LambdaMOO version 1.7. Developed by Pavel Curtis of Xerox, LambdaMOO creates a text-based, multi-user, interactive, and on-line environment called a MOO. Virtual libraries are in various stages of development on three different MOOs discussed in this article. Each one provides an early yet provocative look at the library of the future.

MOO HISTORY

MOOs are based, to some extent, on text-based adventure games called MUDs (multi-user dungeons). Long popular on the Internet, MUDs are often associated with dragons and quests. However, the same techniques that allow players to adventure together and slay dragons allow for more practical applications as well. There are essentially two differences between the MOO and the MUD. First, MOOs are developed using object-oriented source code (hence the MOOs' misleadingly bovine name which actually stands for Multi-user Object Oriented). Second, and more importantly, MOOs are frequently not games at all. Instead, MOOs are most often virtual places capable of supporting customizable environments, objects, and interactions within one consistent electronic location.

MOO DESCRIPTION

A MOO is text-based. The sensation of being somewhere else is conveyed by descriptive paragraphs and words. Thus, unlike expensive immersive virtual realities that require gloves and goggles, the MOO is affordable. Additionally, the text-based MOO is comparatively easy to customize and flexible to adjust for library applications. A MOO is multi-user. Many people can visit and occupy the MOO simultaneously allowing volume to wax and wane as necessary. A MOO is interactive. Participants can communicate with others online and manipulate a variety of programmed objects within the MOO. Because the MOO is an overall encompassing environment, this interaction is standardized for the participant and reduces the need to learn and memorize more than one set of commands for interaction. Finally, a MOO is online. It occupies no physical space save that of the machine on which the program and database are located.

MOO BASICS

Before touring three MOOs and examining their virtual libraries, it is helpful to know some of the MOO basics. For example, MOO themes or structures, movement commands, object use and communication techniques are all necessary to fully explore a MOO and its virtual library.

MOO Themes or Structures

MOOs are customized according to the preference of the MOO designer. This is commonly considered the theme of the MOO. For example, a MOO that focuses on a library (potentially considered a library MOO) would restrict development to library applications. Other themes might focus development of the MOO environment on different applications. To simulate reality, many MOOs build virtual places that reflect rooms or buildings or other geographic details. Each of these rooms or places is filled with programmed objects and other online users. These rooms, objects and users combine to create the unique theme or structure of any given MOO. Regardless of the MOO theme or structure, the ideas of using objects, communicating with other users, and moving around are central to the interactive nature of this virtual reality.

Logging ON

Logging onto a MOO is simply a matter of telnetting to the appropriate address. Logon as a guest by typing the command: connect guest. You can get a name of your choice by registering with the MOO administrators (most entry screens will direct you on how to do this). By popular convention, many librarians choose any name with the suffix _Librarian (i.e., Tonami_Librarian or Ninja_Librarian). On arrival, descriptive information will be displayed to the screen, including where you have arrived, anyone else in the same room with you, and some indication of where specified movement, will take you.

> KEYBOARD: telnet lambda.parc.xerox.com 8888
>
> connect guest
>
> SCREEN DISPLAY: You are in a dark cramped space. There is a door to the north.
> Tonami_Librarian is here.

Movement

Moving around the MOO is necessary because the MOO structure generally reflects rooms or geographic orientation of some kind. MOOs support movement up, down, north, south, west and east. The room description will indicate in which direction to continue to move for specific alternatives. Additionally, many MOOs support teleportation or the ability to relocate immediately using a special command. In the following example, a patron named Dewey would like to move from the library foyer to the periodicals rooms (described on the screen as to the north). Here's how it all looks from the keyboard.

> KEYBOARD: go north
>
> SCREEN DISPLAY: (to everyone in the same room including Dewey): Dewey goes north into the periodicals room.

The teleportation command is handy when movement seems burdensome or complicated. In this example, Dewey would like to go to the library from another location many rooms removed.

> KEYBOARD: @move me to library
>
> SCREEN DISPLAY (to Dewey): You teleport out and arrive in the library.
>
> SCREEN DISPLAY (to everyone else in the room): Dewey teleports out

Moving around the MOO creates the illusion of virtual reality. It also orients the user in spatial layout to prevent confusion. The geographic layout of the MOO anchors the user into an understandable and tangible metaphor.

Using Objects

Everything in a MOO is an object with a name and an object number. It is important to know the object number although sometimes the object name will suffice for use. Objects names are announced to you when you enter a room or location. In this example, Dewey enters the library and the following description is displayed on her screen:

> SCREEN DISPLAY: You are in the library. It is a large place with lots of chairs and shelves. You see a helpdesk and a dictionary here.

The helpdesk and the dictionary are objects in the library that Dewey may use in some way. They are specifically announced to Dewey upon arrival. To see what these objects are, Dewey must interact with the objects. In another example, Dewey looks at the dictionary and tries to use it.

> KEYBOARD: look dictionary

> SCREEN DISPLAY: This is the library's one copy of the dictionary. It is a little frayed but otherwise quite serviceable. Try looking up a word in it.

> KEYBOARD: lookup convention

> SCREEN DISPLAY: I don't understand that.

The key is in the appropriate use of the verb "lookup." Object interaction is based on the correct use of verbs associated with specific objects. There is a command to view the specific verbs used with a specified object.

KEYBOARD: @examine dictionary

A more complete description will appear on the screen including a section called Obvious Verbs. The Obvious Verbs will be conveyed in a certain syntax. Words surrounded by the <xxx> convention indicate this input is variable. All other words must be entered as they are conveyed.

SCREEN DISPLAY: lookup <anything> in dictionary

KEYBOARD: lookup convention in dictionary

And Dewey is rewarded with an on-screen display of the dictionary definition of convention.

The use of objects in a MOO is fundamental. In the previous example, it is apparent that all objects must be identified when they are used. This is necessary so that the MOO program knows exactly which object you would like to use. Because the MOO is essentially a collection of objects, it is important to identify an object in use to avoid confusion. Additionally, there are two levels of object use. First, there is a simple look to view the object and any relevant description. Second, there is an @examine command that further reveals the object's obvious verbs. It is these verbs that supply the basic interaction with any object.

Communication

To communicate in the MOO, there are two essential commands. First, to say anything, precede comments with a quotation mark or the word "say." Your comment will echo to your screen and to the others in the room or location with you accompanied by all the appropriate pronouns. For example, Dewey would like to ask how to get to the library.

KEYBOARD: "Where is the library?"

SCREEN DISPLAY (to Dewey): You say "Where is the library?"

SCREEN DISPLAY (to everyone else in the room): Dewey says "Where is the library?"

Second, to convey thoughts, actions, or feelings, simply precede the description with a colon or the word "emote." For example, Dewey would like to convey a sense of puzzlement.

KEYBOARD: feels puzzled.

SCREEN DISPLAY (to everyone in the room including Dewey): Dewey feels puzzled.

Communication between MOO participants is the heart of the MOOs application. Because a library combines social and resource-based functions, the MOO is especially well suited to address the virtual library as both a place and a process.

Logging OFF

Disconnect at any time by typing @quit.

KEYBOARD: @quit

SCREEN DISPLAY (to everyone in the room including Dewey): Dewey disconnects.

THE MOO LIBRARIES

Virtual libraries exist in the three MOOs discussed in this article. Each one is a little different. The three MOOs visited are LambdaMOO, JaysHouseMOO, and MediaMOO. Addresses and directions to the virtual library, a brief description of the MOO, and sample screens from the library are provided.

LambdaMOO

Address: telnet lambda.parc.xerox.com 8888: connect guest
Library: @go #1670

Description: LambdaMOO is, by far, the oldest and most popular of the MOOs with almost 6,000 registered users. It combines the atmosphere of a carnival funhouse with an otherworld feeling to create a zany world of objects. People here are as frequently bizarre and loathsome as they are helpful. The library is an oasis of calm although strange objects appear with regularity in #1670, as well. Go to LambdaMOO at least once and shoot the breeze with the folks in the living room. You enter through a dark closet. Go OUT to find the living room or, alternatively, just type @GO #1670 to find the library.

Library Information: The library is simply a collection of static text materials arranged in no particular order. Nevertheless, the library is an illuminating place to look around and get an idea of how a library develops. Remember to @examine the books and materials to see the obvious verbs for using them. Figure 1 is a screen capture of the Library description at LambdaMOO.

JaysHouseMOO

Address: telnet jhm.ccs.neu.edu 1709

Library: @go #656

Description: JaysHouseMOO is a small and intimate kind of MOO. Much newer and distinctly calmer than Lambda, JaysHouseMOO contains a number of interesting places including the gopher hole. Folks are friendly but more technically oriented than the average person may desire. Clubby and friendly, JaysHouseMOO is a favorite among MOO programmers. Sitting here and listening, it's easy to pick up on a lot of tips easily. Most people gather in the Living Room here (from the entrance, type GO UP WEST WEST WEST UP UP WEST WEST to get the full flavor of virtual text-based reality). The gopherhole is next to the entrance in the ditch and is worth a side trip. Here, everyone in the gopherhole can see the gopher menus simultaneously.

Library Information: The library here is being built in conjunction with the BioSciences Center. It's pretty bared-boned for now but

Figure 1. The LambdaMOO Library

       The library is built in a style reminiscent of old English
libraries: very stately, walls completely covered in neatly-arranged
books, with a few very comfortable-looking chairs. Each chair
is equipped with a footstool, a small side-table and a reading lamp.
The carpet is very plush and padded. All in all, the room has an old
world kind of charm. You see:

Intrigue	Features Feature Object
Tutorial	yduJ's MOO Lore Pamphlet
SSPC-Help	Ownership Transfer Station
Collections	Generic Hard-Core Porn Rag
Mr. Wanderer	List of Generic Parentables
Address Book	Hierarchy of player classes
Tethys Trilogy	Generic Science Fiction Novel
Dusty Bookshelf	Note on Writing Letters to Moscow
Crash-Test-Dummy	Garin's Index to Popular Literature
Genetic Algorithm	yduJ's Guide to Weird Player Classes
Book of Baby Names	Schmoo-Morphing Do-It-Yourself Manual
Frand's Big Manual	Index to LambdaMOO Reference Materials
Generic Bulletin Board	a stack of Lambda MoosPaper back issues

The MOOTEX Manual, Version 1.0 (beta test)
Answers to Frequently-Asked MOO Programming Questions
a painting hanging on the wall between two of the bookcases
Gary_Severn's Manual With Scratchy Documentation of Variable
Comprehensibility

includes "slates" which are gopher clients. These slates allow the library user to customize a gopher for personal use. Here, there is no standing collection except the biosciences-oriented gopher "slates." Figure 2 provides a snapshot of the Bioscience Center Library and a closer look at the gopher slate.

Figure 2. BiosciencesECC Library

```
This is a large, busy science library. It will be a place where
scientists can gather and use the most modern tools available for
the persuit of research interests. Unfortunately, it is still under
construction. To the north is the quadrangle.
You see the slate dispenser and the bioSLATE here.


BioSLATE
A laptop size computer, with various controls on it.
1. Baylor College of Medicine gopher (menu)
2. Veronica Search (menu)
3. Biology based WAIS databases (menu)
4. Bio-Medical based gophers (menu)
5. Indiana U BioGopher (menu)
6. Steffen's Tumor Gene Database (menu)
```

MediaMOO

Address: telnet purple-crayon.media.mit.edu 8888

Library: @go #1498
Description: MediaMOO is just the kind of community-based MOO
that starts to feel like home immediately. You enter through a Lego
Closet. People here are friendly and helpful. Technicians and
scholars and students mingle freely and events include ongoing
Friday happy hours and special forums attended by international
participants.

Library Information: The infocenter here is created by a librarian
and frequented by librarians from Emory, Woodrow Wilson Institute for Scholars and Penn State University, to name a few. The
electronic shelves are open to any MediaMOO participant and include periodicals, reference materials, government documents, and
electronic texts. The shelves are based on the gopher "slates" mentioned at JaysHouseMOO but, here, contain standing materials to
supplement the individual's own customizable gopher. Figure 3 de-

Figure 3. The Infocenter at MediaMOO

```
This is the Infocenter ... a fledgling library of the future.
You see Periodical Shelf, Book Shelf, Subject Shelf, Index Shelf,
Government Shelf, Reference Shelf, and Infocenter Instructions here.

Reference Shelf
The Reference Shelf creaks under the weight of useful information.
It contains dictionaries, thesauri, etc.
1. Roget's Thesaurus (menu)
2. Webster's Dictionary (search)
3. Oxford Modern Quotations (search)
4. CIA World Factbook (search)
5. American English Dictionary (search)
```

tails what appears on your screen upon entering the Infocenter and looks more closely at the Reference materials.

MOO REFERENCE

Reference services vary at these MOOs from none to sporadic depending on whether anyone is online to assist. However, in a fully operational LibraryMOO, it would be reasonable to expect that a librarian would be available to answer questions and work with patrons to fully and effectively utilize the MOOs' strengths in electronic access. Certainly, a LibraryMOO would need a reference librarian since the amount of sources and kinds of interactions are complex. And, while some standard questions may be addressed with printed help screens, the interaction between the librarian and the patron(s) is a critical component of the MOOs usefulness as a library resource.

The MOO is not without problems. Since there are no visual cues, reference service is more difficult. And, the text-based nature of the MOO will not appeal to everyone. However, MOOs capture some of the best social aspects of the physical library by allowing multiple users to interact simultaneously. And, the MOO does standardize interactive commands consistently throughout the MOO system. Thus, although the MOO is not without difficulty, it does present certain advantages worth exploring in the future of the electronic library and virtual reference services.

CONCLUSION

The most interesting aspect of all MOO libraries is the relative lack of involvement by librarians. The virtual library is now being included and developed on many MOO sites. This is a good sign that the library's functions and services are widely recognized as an important aspect of every reality. However, without a librarian, many MOO libraries are finding it difficult to develop more than a basic shelflist of holdings or a systematic access. In this unsophisticated form, MOO libraries are very basic. Yet, as virtual environments continue to develop and as MOO librarians begin to appear, virtual reference services will form. Virtual collections will develop and electronic patrons will arrive.

The MOO software and an Internet connection can get you started. But, the first step for any aspiring virtual librarian may well be to check out the current situation and get involved. By visiting the various MOO libraries, it's easier to see what the future may hold and how the librarian may interact with a patron in a virtual environment. Most MOOs would be happy to have the assistance of an information professional. And, most MOO participants would welcome the skills and expertise of a librarian to provide collection development and reference services. See you at the MOO.

A New Challenge
for Intermediary-Client Communication:
The Electronic Network

Eileen G. Abels
Peter Liebscher

SUMMARY. Electronic networks provide libraries with new opportunities to deliver services, such as reference services, to users who now find it difficult or inconvenient to visit the library. If remote reference services are to become common, it is necessary for the profession to prepare now by identifying problems and benefits for both clients and reference intermediaries. The library schools at the University of Maryland and at Long Island University are engaged in a cooperative research and teaching project to identify factors that determine success or failure in provision of remote electronic reference services and to develop effective methods to educate and train reference intermediaries to work in this environment.

This is the first of two articles that describe a collaborative project between two library schools to develop tools for electronic reference services and to educate new information professionals in the provision of remote reference services. Part 1 gives the background to the project. Part 2 describes, evaluates, and discusses the results.

Eileen G. Abels is Assistant Professor, College of Library and Information Services, University of Maryland and Peter Liebscher is Associate Professor, Palmer School of Library and Information Science, Long Island University.

[Haworth co-indexing entry note]: "A New Challenge for Intermediary-Client Communication: The Electronic Network." Abels, Eileen G. and Peter Liebscher. Co-published simultaneously in *The Reference Librarian* (The Haworth Press, Inc.) No. 41/42, 1994, pp. 185-196; and: *Librarians on the Internet: Impact on Reference Services* (ed: Robin Kinder) The Haworth Press, Inc., 1994, pp. 185-196. Multiple copies of this article/chapter may be purchased from The Haworth Document Delivery Center [1-800-3-HAWORTH; 9:00 a.m. - 5:00 p.m. (EST)].

INTRODUCTION

The continuing growth in the number of libraries with access to electronic data networks is beginning to impact the way these organizations conduct their business. For library clients, this promises more convenient access to information and to library professionals. Clients will increasingly expect to access information and the services of information professionals through workstations at work and at home. Libraries have new opportunities to deliver services, such as reference services, to users who now find it difficult or inconvenient to visit the library. However, as is evident from attempts to provide reference services through non face-to-face mediums, e.g., telephone reference services[1] and online reference services,[2] the transition will not be easy. If remote reference services are to become common, it is necessary for the information profession to prepare now by identifying both advantages and problems for clients and reference intermediaries alike. Library education's critical role in this process is to ensure that information professionals are adequately prepared to offer remote reference services.

Information professionals have been quick to recognize the value of electronic networks for access to a wealth of information resources, including both people (mostly other information professionals) and databases/archives. The great volume of literature dealing with Internet and Bitnet resources published over the past 2 to 3 years attests to this interest. A search in UnCover using just "Internet or Bitnet" as key words retrieved 197 items. Many information professionals now view the exchange of ideas with distant colleagues as essential to their job performance. Indeed, once the availability of electronic mail and electronic discussion groups becomes ubiquitous, this new form of communication may become an important factor in ending the isolation of many information professionals who provide services in small, even one person libraries. Resource sharing, made easier and less costly through electronic media should also encourage higher standards of library service at even the smallest libraries.

To date most effort has been applied to creating and accessing new information resources, e.g., discussion groups and online catalogs, or to making existing resources more widely available, e.g., electronic journals, etc.[3,4] Some interesting projects have been reported in which libraries have pooled their resources to provide enhanced reference services.[5] However, little has been published on using electronic data communications to provide reference services to remote library clients–those who cannot, or prefer not to, visit the library for reference services. Some exceptions are Ladner and Tillman,[6] who discuss transmitting of requests via a network as oniine reference services, Howards and Jankowski[7] and Weise and Borgendale,[8] who examined reference intermediaries' use of electronic mail to communicate with clients in medical library settings, and Roysdon and Lee Elliott[9] who reported use of an integrated campus network to support question negotiation between library intermediaries and users. Yet adopting such remote services provides great opportunities to reach new clients and to enhance services in a number of ways. For example, the Health Science Library at the University of Maryland uses a menu driven electronic mail system (Electronic Access to Reference Services, EARS) to allow users to request a variety of reference services from their homes or place of work. However, Weise and Borgendale[10] found that where these services are offered, users may be slow to take advantage of them. The EARS service, for example, is used very heavily for requesting photocopy services and very little for requesting reference services such as literature searches (91% of requests were for photocopy services). More recently, an electronic mail survey conducted to determine which institutions offer electronic reference services, indicated that few libraries offer such services. With some exception, those that do appear to attach less importance to these services. For example, almost all respondent libraries report offering only 24 hour turn-around-time for queries. This may not be acceptable to many users and may result in the low usage reported.[11]

THE REFERENCE PROCESS

The reference process begins with an initial contact by a client who has an information need. Typically, the first contact is a face-to-face encounter at the reference desk. Depending on a number of factors including whether the request is a simple request for factual information, or a more complex query, or on library policy, this encounter can be brief or result in a lengthy reference interview during which the client's information need is explored. Often this is followed by a search, not necessarily online, and sometimes by an exchange of feedback information between reference intermediary and client that results in modifying the search. In terms of the librarian-client interaction, there are three elements:

1. the reference interview
2. follow-up interaction, i.e., a feedback loop, and
3. delivery of the final product that addresses the client's information need.

THE REFERENCE INTERVIEW

A vital part of the reference process is the reference interview.[12,13] White made a detailed analysis of the reference interview. She concluded that:

> the reference interview plays a critical role in information retrieval systems. It is an adaptive mechanism, i.e., it allows for adapting the system to the client or vice versa so that a reasonably congruent match between what the client needs and what the system can identify occurs.[14]

White identified a number of points that a good reference interview should include, both in content and in form. White's recommendations are based on her view of the reference process as a process that satisfies user needs rather than concentrating on answering the user's question. White points out that while

> a good interview is neither sufficient nor necessary for good results, the probability of a good end product is enhanced if all relevant factors were identified (by the reference interview).[15]

One problem then in providing reference services over an electronic data network is replacing the face-to-face reference interview, whose interactive nature allows for immediate clarification, with an electronic interaction that is equally effective. As White points out, information flows across several channels, of which verbal communication is but one. Other, non-verbal channels, such as use of inflections and paralinguistic devices are often equally important.[16] Many of these cues are, of course, not present in an electronic interview although, some standardized iconic representations of non-verbal communications are beginning to appear, e.g., :-) indicating humor, etc. However, these are still quite limiting. New and rich protocols for communicating non-verbal signals will no doubt develop to fill the void. In the meantime, while some elements of the face-to-face reference interview, such as interpretation of body language, are difficult to incorporate in an electronic interview, their exclusion may have positive aspects. In some cases, non-verbal behaviors of either librarian or client may hamper an effective exchange of information and at times may be destructive.

Conducting an effective reference interview for a complex information problem is a difficult task. Many factors affect the outcome of the reference interview, for example interpersonal skills, subject expertise, and prior experience. Friendliness, eagerness, kindness, and approachability on the part of the reference intermediary all help to establish a positive rapport. If clients feel comfortable with the process they may be more apt to provide useful information. Where intermediaries are especially knowledgeable in a subject area, they are better able to provide guidance in the clarification of the query, in selecting the best possible keywords for searching, and in proposing the best reference sources. Experienced reference intermediaries are likely to be more adept at ensuring that all important points are covered, that the interaction moves smoothly from area to area, and that the important points are appropriately synthesized and summarized. Clearly the success of the reference interview will vary depending on the reference intermediary, the client, the topic and the nature of the query. However, the process is often aided by adoption of standard protocols, such as reference interview forms that are used in many libraries.

Intermediaries find reference interview forms useful as tools to assist in structuring the reference interview. These forms may be filled out by the client prior to the interview or by the intermediary during the interview. Electronic data communications may make it easier to use such protocols to structure an interview and to ensure that important questions are not omitted. There is evidence that asking clients to consider and write out their requests for information is beneficial to the end result. Even early research in retrieval effectiveness indicated that formal, written requests by users that stated their information problems were important components of a successful reference process. Discussing retrieval performance, Lancaster stated:

> It appears that the best request statements (i.e., those that most clearly reflect the actual area of information need) are those written down by the researcher in his own natural-language narrative terms. When he comes to a librarian or search analyst, and discusses his need orally, a transformation takes place and, unfortunately, the request statement captured by the librarian or searcher is a less perfect mirror of the information need than the one prepared by the requestor himself in his own natural language terms.[17]

While few researchers and information professionals today would suggest that the impact of a "live" reference interview is necessarily negative, Lancaster's findings do show the importance of having clients submit written requests. They suggest that using electronic mail to request reference services may, in fact, be beneficial to the process as it forces users to think about and then state their information needs in formal, written form. There may be definite advantages to using electronic reference templates completed by the user. The impact of conducting reference interviews electronically should, at least in this respect, be positive.

However, clients' responses do not always flow easily from one question to another and real time interaction may be necessary to clarify points. Also, if using an interview form results in an inexorable movement through the form rather than allowing and encouraging the pursuit of new points, important information regarding the client's information need may be lost. Consequently, interactive, real time communications (perhaps using "chat/talk" modes) and/or follow-up contacts (through electronic mail) may also be necessary.

FOLLOW-UP INTERACTIONS

As important as the initial reference interview is, it does not stand alone in the reference librarian-client interaction. Ideally, follow-up interactions take place whenever the need arises. However, in the traditional process–face-to-face interview followed by a search–it is difficult to establish follow-up contact because the client has left the library. Telephone contact is not always possible or satisfactory as both parties have to be engaged simultaneously. Additional visits to the library by the client may not be practical. Follow-up, using electronic communications such as electronic mail, allows one party to send a message when most convenient and the other party to read that message, also when most convenient.

Both parties in the reference interaction require feedback throughout the process. Feedback from reference intermediary to client in the form of intermediate results of a search is common. When a search has retrieved more than a few items, discussions centered on modifying the search strategy are difficult if both parties don't have access to the retrieved items. Intermediate search results can be sent to clients for inspection and comment using electronic mail or file transfer. Such complete feedback is not possible using telephones and is cumbersome using fax. Indeed, while many clients today have convenient access to a computer workstation, fewer have convenient access to a fax machine.

This suggests an additional potential advantage for both reference intermediary and client. Time wasted on fruitless telephone calls or waiting for clients to arrive for interviews is eliminated, allowing the intermediary to devote more time to clients' information needs or to provide services to more clients, or both.

DELIVERY OF THE FINAL PRODUCT

The final interaction between client and information professional entails delivery of the information product that meets the client's information need, followed, possibly, by a post-search interview that assists in evaluating the effectiveness of the reference encounter. As with the feed-back stage, the electronic environment may offer particular advantages as a delivery medium when the search involved was conducted electronically. Discussions have already appeared in the literature regarding both the scholar's and information professional's workstation.[18] For ease of transfer, the workstation used by the information professional should, ideally, be equipped with the tools necessary to search remote online databases and CD-ROM products as well as to communicate with the client. More and more commercial online services are accessible via the Internet, including among others, Dialog Information Services, Lexis/Nexis, BRS and ORBIT. This means that information professionals can already use the same workstation to receive a request, perform an online search, and transfer results to the end-user. Integrating CD-ROM databases to this workstation will increase ease of access and eliminate the need to perform a search on one computer and transfer the results to another.

Transmitting results to a user electronically saves time for the information professional who otherwise has to print the results and mail or fax them to a remotely located client. When the client has access to a printer or wants to utilize the search in electronic form, there are clear advantages to this scenario for both intermediary and client. However, some clients may prefer to receive their search results in print. In that case, the results of the search could be sent directly to a remote fax machine or print server on the client's LAN.

When the search does not involve accessing electronic databases, the intermediary is faced with the problem of transmitting other reference output, such as the content of a telephone inquiry, data from a print source, or a photocopy of a document. Interpersonal and print media do not lend themselves directly to transmittal through electronic channels. Use of a scanner alleviates some problems but not all. It may be that traditional channels of communication such as express mail services will continue to play an important role in information delivery.

THE CHALLENGE

Clearly, there are both potential advantages and disadvantages to providing remote reference services. It may be that combining, in the traditional reference process, both face-to-face interviews with electronic follow-up and feedback will greatly enhance reference services. However, if the library is to expand reference services to clients who now are unable to visit the library, a reliance on the electronic medium is essential. There is little disagreement among reference librarians that a face-to-face reference interview is an important part of the reference process. A decision to provide some reference services remotely implies using a new form of interaction that we know little about. Consequently, a body of experience and research is required to learn how to take full advantage of the new medium to provide the best reference service possible for remote library clients. Ultimately, if current visions of the electronic, virtual library come about, remote reference services will be an integral part of library services to users.

ROLE OF LIBRARY SCHOOLS

Library schools should play an important role in developing instruments for electronic reference interactions and in educating and training information professionals in communicating with clients over electronic channels. Hayes suggests that:

> Library education should begin now to provide the technical tools that librarians need to fulfill their obligations in the world of electronic information.[19]

To the responsibility for developing new tools should be added understanding and mastering the communications process over the new electronic medium. Library schools can conduct research and evaluate various implementations of the electronic reference process. In terms of their function as educators and trainers of library professionals, library schools can apply the results of their research to preparing new reference librarians to understand and operate effectively in this environment. To date this challenge has not, generally, been recognized.

THE PROJECT

The library schools at the University of Maryland and at Long Island University have undertaken a joint project to study the electronic reference interaction. The objectives of this project are:

1. To identify problems encountered by both intermediaries and clients in the remote electronic reference process.
2. To suggest elements that enhance the effectiveness of the remote electronic reference encounter, specifically an electronic request form and follow-up protocols.
3. To suggest approaches to educate and train information professionals to fully utilize electronic media for reference encounters, particularly in communicating with clients.

During the Fall 1993 semester, using electronic mail and interactive "chat/talk" modes, students in an advanced reference course at Maryland will act as remote intermediaries for students in a library networking course at Long Island. Each Long Island student will define a topic for a research paper and will have a student at the University of Maryland conduct a reference interview and a series of literature searches on that topic. The Maryland intermediaries will develop an electronic request form to be used in the initial "reference interview." Both parties are limited to electronic data communications, i.e., they are not permitted to use the telephone, mail, or fax. However, they may use electronic mail and interactive "chat/talk" as they deem most appropriate. The Maryland intermediaries are expected to access all appropriate resources, including online, CD-ROM and print. Each medium is expected to present unique problems for the intermediary-client interaction. To inject a degree of realism, Long Island students are each limited to a "budget" of $300. Maryland intermediaries have charge-out rates of $30 per hour. Charges for online searches will be levied at the commercial rates charged by the database vendors.

Both sets of students will critique the process through questionnaires and through group sessions at each school led by the respective faculty member. While the project examines the entire reference process–from initial contact to delivery of materials–the greatest emphasis is placed on conduct of the remote initial reference interview and follow-ups. Although this is an initial, exploratory study, it is expected that valuable data and knowledge will be gained that will provide the basis for changes in the library school curriculum and for implementing effective remote reference services. It is expected that this cooperative research and training project between the two library schools will continue, thus building a growing corpus of knowledge for both initiating and evaluating remote reference services.

Part 2 of this article will report the results of this project and will discuss the implications of the results for developing effective remote reference services and effective library school instruction in this field.

REFERENCES

1. Riechel, Rosemary. The Telephone patron and the reference interview: the public library experience. *The Reference Librarian. 16* (Winter, 1986): 81-88.

2. Weise, F.O. & Borgendale, M. EARS: Electronic access to reference service. *Bulletin of the Medical Library Association.* 74(4), (1986): 300-304.

3. Kosmin, Linda J. Library reference resources: the Internet challenge. *Online Information 91. Proceedings of the 15th International Online Information Meeting.* London, 10-12 December, 1991.

4. Peterson Holland, M. Real-time searching at the reference desk. *The Reference Librarian. 5/6* (Fall/Winter, 1992): 165-171.

5. Holmer, Susan E. Your best buy: the system reference coordinator. *RQ.* 23(1), (1983): 75-80.

6. Ladner, S.J. & Tillman, H.N. Using the Internet for reference. *Online.* (January, 1993): 45-51.

7. Howards, E.H. & Jankowski, T.A. Reference services via electronic mail. *Bulletin of the Medical Library Association.* 74(1), (1986): 41-44.

8. See note 2.

9. Roysdon, C.M. & Lee Elliott, L. Electronic integration of library services through a campuswide network. *RQ.* 28(1), (1988): 82-93.

10. Flanagan, Daphne. *E-mail reference summary.* Message sent to library discussion group LIBREF-L, 26th May, 1993.

11. See note 2.

12. Dewdney, P. The Effective reference interview. *Canadian Library Journal.* 45(3), (1988): 183-184.

13. White, Marilyn Domas. Evaluation of the reference interview. *RQ.* 25(1), (1985): 76-83.

14. See note 13, p. 76.

15. See note 13, p. 78.

16. White, Marilyn Domas. The Dimensions of the reference interview. *RQ.*(Summer, 1981): 373-381.

17. Lancaster, F.W. *Evaluation of the MEDLARS demand search service.* Washington DC: U.S. Department of Health, Education and Welfare. Public Health Service. 1968, p. 104.

18. Kosmin, Linda J. Electronic reference desk: multimedia integration opportunities. *Proceedings of the 12th National Online Meeting.* New York, 7-9 May, 1991.

19. Hayes, Robert M. The Needs of science and technology. *Science and Technologies Libraries.* 12(4), (1992): p. 32.

Internexus:
A Partnership for Internet Instruction

Sally Kalin
Carol Wright

SUMMARY. A model for Internet instruction has been developed at Penn State by the University Libraries and Computer and Information Systems. The two groups have joined to conduct Internet seminars and workshops for the Penn State community. This team approach has resulted in efficient and effective delivery of both theoretical and practical applications of Internet access, and has maximized the strengths of both organizations in teaching the identification, access, and retrieval of networked information.

INTERNET PARTNERSHIP

Internet technology has significantly altered communication and research patterns in both scholarly and professional work, and has created a collaborative environment in which no individual or group has exclusive authority or expertise. The demand for instruction is expanding; the academic and professional communities are potential students.

Sally Kalin is a member of the Computer-Based Resources and Services Team, Penn State University Libraries, E-6 Pattee, University Park, PA 16802. Carol Wright is Basic Skills Specialist, Penn State University Libraries, E105 Pattee Library, University Park, PA 16802.

[Haworth co-indexing entry note]: "Internexus: A Partnership for Internet Instruction." Kalin, Sally, and Carol Wright. Co-published simultaneously in *The Reference Librarian* (The Haworth Press, Inc.) No. 41/42, 1994, pp. 197-209; and: *Librarians on the Internet: Impact on Reference Services* (ed: Robin Kinder) The Haworth Press, Inc., 1994, pp. 197-209. Multiple copies of this article/chapter may be purchased from The Haworth Document Delivery Center [1-800-3-HAWORTH; 9:00 a.m. - 5:00 p.m. (EST)].

A model for Internet instruction has been developed at Penn State in which the administratively autonomous University Libraries and Computer and Information Systems (C & IS) have formed a team to jointly offer Internet instruction. These autonomous units have enjoyed a continuing positive working relationship. The team approach has resulted in efficient and effective delivery of both theoretical concepts and practical suggestions for application. The title "Internexus" was chosen for the instructional series because the word "Nexus" suggests an interconnection or a connected group, and because the title resembles "Internet."

RATIONALE FOR TEAM MODEL

Several practical factors support the use of a team model. First, a team approach creates a symbiotic relationship. Librarians are routinely involved in teaching the organization and structure of electronic databases and catalogs, while computer professionals routinely work with the communications platforms and software packages that support Internet access. Both libraries and computer centers are user-oriented, offering extensive support services for the University community. Organized, proactive instruction is viewed as both an opportunity and a responsibility. Both groups anticipate significant demands for Internet support from the University community; thus a joint response in times of constrained resources makes budgetary sense. For the attendee, a seamless presentation presents a uniform approach to attendees who will later seek out team members for different kinds of expertise. Last, such library/computer center alliances can form the basis for additional future partnerships.

COMPOSITION OF THE INTERNEXUS TEAM

The initial planning team was composed of ten members: three librarians–the head of Collections and Instructional Services, a member of the Libraries' Computer-Based Resources and Services Team, and a reference librarian who serves as the Libraries' basic skills specialist; an associate director from Computer and Information Systems; three lead research programmers from the Center for Academic Computing; two members from the Office of Administrative Systems; and one member from the Office of Telecommunications. Although not all team members later became instructors, they continue to provide important consultative support. As Internexus expands, more instructors from both the Libraries and C & IS have joined the team, including individuals located throughout the branch campus system. The strength of the team lies in the diversity of assignments and responsibilities of team members. A key example of team diversity is the Associate Director of the Center for Academic Computing, who is also a faculty member in the English Department–thus bridging the technical/academic gap.

THE PLANNING PROCESS

Careful planning is always critical to success, but is especially important in a new team containing individual and unfamiliar styles and approaches, where new technology and information prohibits reliance on previous experience. The Internexus team considered the following in their planning:

- organization of the instructional team
- analysis of the local environment
- development of a syllabus
- selection of delivery mode
- design of evaluation tools
- mechanisms for follow-up
- promotional efforts

Organization of the Instructional Team

- How should the content be divided among instructors? Should they specialize, or should each individual be equally proficient in all areas?
- How many team members are necessary for each presentation?
- How can consistency of presentations be assured?

- How much time is each team member prepared to give to Internexus?

Analysis of the Local Environment

Audience–

- Should instruction be offered broadly to the academic community or targeted to specific disciplines?
- Is interest likely to come more from the faculty or graduate students? Should undergraduates be a target audience?
- What is the audience's level of computer expertise?
- Is the audience located in one geographic area, or are they dispersed, requiring taking the 'show on the road'?

Technical Concerns–

- What is the local level of network 'connectivity'? Are computer 'platforms' consistent across the university, or does instruction need to be generalized to accommodate diverse systems?
- Are demonstration/lecture classrooms and labs suitable for live demonstrations? Are sufficient stations available for hands-on sessions?

Development of a Syllabus

- What are the probable network applications among groups? What is the best 'hook' to use for various audiences and interest levels?
- What should a core curriculum contain? Should all sessions include mail, telnet and ftp? With the availability of finding tools such as Veronica on gopher, WAIS, and WEB increasing, should they be incorporated or scheduled as advanced sessions?
- What is the best sequence of instruction?

Selection of Delivery Mode

- Should initial introductory presentations consist of a demonstration and discussion, or should they also include a lab 'hands-on' component?

- Should demonstrations be 'live', or is it efficient and desirable to develop 'canned' demos with presentation software?
- If more advanced follow-up sessions are required, what should be their focus?
- What is required to take the presentation 'on the road'?
- What is the maximum length for a presentation?
- What handouts and supplemental materials are required?
- Should there be a charge?

Evaluation

- How will the feedback be channeled to the team of instructors and incorporated into future sessions?

Follow-up

- How can attendees receive updated information and continuing assistance?

Promotional Efforts

- Is pre-registration useful, or are walk-ins acceptable?
- What are the most reliable means to advertise upcoming sessions?

INTERNEXUS OBJECTIVES

Analysis of these factors resulted in the following objectives for the Internexus team:

- to introduce the basic concepts of e-mail, ftp and telnet;
- to promote the Internet through a "dim-sum" approach, allowing attendees to see applications to their own fields and to find their own level of comfort and interest;
- to develop an instructional package that can be used with a variety of audiences that have various interests, and at a variety of demonstration sites;

- to establish a base for future referral and user support; and
- to monitor new network applications and audience interest/ proficiency so as to offer more advanced programs as necessary.

Equally important, Internexus sessions did *not* seek:

- to teach specific system-dependent commands for telnet, e-mail, or ftp; to answer specific questions during the session regarding location-specific applications;
- and to make personal recommendations about individual research interests.

ORGANIZING AND DELIVERING INTERNEXUS: LEARNING FROM THE PILOTS

The planning team wrestled with the best way to deliver Internexus. The two most viable options were: traditional lecture coupled with online demonstrations; and a "hands-on" class with exercises.

Both modes of instruction offered advantages. A class consisting of presentations supplemented with live demonstrations was easy to prepare and established the broad networking concepts. Hands-on instruction allowed users to participate actively in the class. It enabled them to build their technological confidence, made abstract concepts more concrete, and stimulated questions that might not arise in a lecture setting.

To determine the more effective format, the planning team sponsored two Internexus pilots that allowed comparisons of the two modes of instruction. The first pilot included brief presentations on each of the three Internet functions–e-mail, telnet, ftp–followed by live demonstrations. The second pilot, a hands-on session, contained the same information and provided participants with the opportunity to: use a group listserv (especially set up for the class); telnet to a pre-selected list of Internet sites; and ftp a file from a popular archive. The audience targeted for both pilots were faculty in the humanities and social sciences because they were considered less likely to be knowledgeable about Internet and therefore most likely to benefit from an orientation.

The pilots were valuable experiences. The first pilot accomplished the goal of "dim-sum" by introducing basic concepts and providing information for further explanation. The second pilot, a hands-on session, was fraught with problems that negatively affected users' satisfaction and created a confusing situation for the instructors. There were four basic problems.

1. It was difficult dealing with the uneven technological sophistication of the audience. Participants ranged from complete novices to those who used the Internet functions routinely (and only wanted a refresher class). Some faculty did not have accounts with the computer center, and therefore were unable to participate as the class went through the exercises. Others were accustomed to accessing the Internet through different means from their offices and were confused by the alternate access offered in the laboratory situation.
2. The hands-on instruction was time-consuming. It was overly ambitious to teach how to use the three internet functions during the course of one three-hour class.
3. The classes were resource-intensive, each requiring not only several instructors to cover all of the Internet navigational tools, but additional personnel to act as "rovers" to assist those doing the exercises.
4. The number of students accommodated in the hands-on class was dictated by the number of available workstations and was fewer than could be taught by the lecture/demonstration method.

Internexus Goes on the Road

The planning team recognized that the nineteen other Penn State campuses were an important potential audience for Internexus because they included nearly half the University's students and faculty. Several regional "road shows" were scheduled to bring Internexus to selected campus locations. This activity was yet another type of pilot, since delivering Internexus to the campuses presented new challenges. For instance, each campus had different backbone connections and staff and faculty varied greatly in their experience levels. Two campus librarians were invited to join the Internexus instructional team. They made valuable contributions to the Internexus sessions because they were cognizant of the special informational needs of the campus clientele.

The pilot "road shows" were well received, and those campuses not included quickly asked to be involved. The planning team concluded that delivering Internexus to the campuses had to be an integral part of the Internexus program.

WHAT THE TEAM LEARNED

Based on the pilot experiences, some general principles emerged regarding effective Internet instruction:

Presentation: Structure and Content

- The core of basic Internexus instruction should be the three Internet navigational tools–e-mail, telnet, ftp. (See Internexus outline, Figure 1.) Internexus participants need a mental model of the logical and physical structure of the Internet.
- The presentation/demonstration mode of instruction better meets the objectives of Internexus than hands-on instruction. The latter is better utilized in smaller, specialized classes that focus on Internet functions in more depth.
- Local developments germane to the Internet should be promoted. Penn State's developing Gopher system became an integral part of the Internexus presentation. Gopher brought the Internet "home" to the Penn State audience because it gave them the assurance that Internet resources could be easily accessed and located.
- The instructors' roles and the time they have been allotted must be clearly defined for each session.
- The audience should be encouraged to ask questions, but at appropriate times so that the questions don't interrupt the flow of the presentation. Instructors should agree in advance on ways to handle or defer inappropriate questions.
- Handouts and tutorials help participants to reinforce classroom lessons. Slides and overheads designed to enhance the technological presentations should be projected on a screen *other* than the one used for the online demonstrations.

- Demonstrations that use unnecessary or illegible screens bore the audience, risk losing some of the drama of the live demonstration, and exclude participants from the total experience.
- Instructors should be prepared with alternatives in case of technical problems.

Personnel

- Each Internexus session requires two instructors–generally one from the Libraries and one from Computing and Information Services–chosen from a broad base of experienced instructors. Rather than always pairing the same two people, it was healthier to change the mix so that the instructors could be exposed to a variety of teaching techniques and approaches.
- Teaching assignments can vary depending on the expertise and interests of the instructors. As the instructors become more comfortable with the Internet, they should be able to teach any segment of Internexus.
- Appropriate libraries, college and campus computing personnel need to be apprised of the Internexus program. If possible, they should receive Internet training so that they are prepared to answer questions and to address rising user expectations.

FIGURE 1. INTERNEXUS Outline (3-hour session)

I. INTRODUCTION (20 minutes)

A. Introduction of speakers
B. Objectives of Internexus
C. Introduction to the Internet: physical and logical structure, history, size/traffic, netiquette

II. FUNCTIONAL ASPECTS OF NETWORKING

A. Messaging (E-MAIL) (35 minutes)

1. What it is
2. How it works

3. Potential uses: conferencing, discussion groups, USENET, etc.
4. Demonstrations
5. How to find out what's available: listservs, etc.

B. Remote Logons (TELNET) (35 minutes)

1. What it is
2. How it works
3. Potential uses: databases, OPACS, CWIS, etc.
4. Demonstrations
5. How to find out what's available

C. File Transfer (FTP) (35 minutes)

1. What it is
2. How it works
3. Potential uses: archives, full-text files, etc.
4. Demonstrations
5. How to find out what's available: archie, etc.

III. CONCLUSION (10 minutes)

A. Present and future developments that affect networking

1. Gopher
2. Sonoma State Internet access program available through online catalog
3. NREN

B. What to do/who to contact if you need more information

IV. EVALUATION (5 minutes)

FOLLOW-UP ACTIVITIES

One of the primary missions of Internexus was to encourage individuals to explore the potential of the Internet. Internexus was an orientation; therefore, subsequent assistance and support was necessary to help participants become independent users. In order to extend Internexus beyond the classroom, the planning team identified appropriate follow-up activities.

* Internexus participants needed access to appropriate Internet reference material.

  Penn State's Center for Academic Computing set up a special electronic file of Internet directories and resources. Internexus participants were told about this file and encouraged to use it. This was particularly important before the development of the Penn State Gopher. The Libraries made a concerted effort to develop the Libraries collections relating to the Internet; subsequent circulation records indicate that Internet materials are in heavy demand. Internexus handouts and tutorials designed to help participants to explore the Internet further were widely distributed.

* Internexus "graduates" stayed involved with Internexus through a listserv discussion group that facilitated a free exchange of ideas. Instructors were also able to inform "graduates" about Internet developments that could be of interest to them.
* Personnel manning the University's technical "help desks" were apprised of Internexus and its curriculum. Monitoring the types of follow-up questions received from Internexus participants allowed the planning team to make adjustments to Internexus content.
* Internexus generated demands for advanced instructional classes on the Internet. Special classes relating to Internet functions and tools–e-mail, telnet, ftp, gopher, WAIS, archie, etc.,–were established. These sessions were taught in a "hands-on" mode and provided the practical instructions that Internexus did not.
* Alternative methods of Internet instruction were explored including online tutorials, drop-in sessions, etc. Those interested in learning more about the Internet, or simply reinforcing what they learned in Internexus, now had several instructional means at their disposal.

ADVICE TO LIBRARIANS PLANNING PARTNERSHIPS

Collaborative efforts require that someone be in charge who will maintain the momentum; otherwise the project will flounder when everyone's desire to be polite overcomes the need to be honest and forthcoming. Planning a joint instructional program requires compromise. In general, the librarians wanted more structure than the personnel from Computing and Information Services, possibly reflecting their background in bibliographic instruction. In contrast, the personnel from the Computing Center advocated an informal instructional environment. Both approaches had benefits, but the planning team had to compromise, incorporating parts of each in order to provide Internexus participants with a quality instructional experience.

Internexus instructors need to be committed. Preparation for Internexus took an extraordinary amount of time, and there was a substantial learning curve for those who did not have Internet expertise. Once an Internet instructional program is established, there is a continuing need to stay apprised of Internet trends and developments. The pool of Internexus instructors can be broadened, but only if the new instructors are given ample time to become comfortable with the program and its subject matter.

The Libraries' role in an Internet training program must be aggressively promoted in order to be recognized by the academic community who may assume that an instructional program in technology is being handled by the Computing Center. Rather than withdrawing from the process once Internexus was established, the Libraries continued to assist in the promotion and continued development of the program.

CONCLUSION

The planning team discovered that Internexus created a symbiotic relationship between the Libraries and Computing and Information Services. Internexus is an excellent example of technology's ability to flatten hierarchies and blur divisional lines. Its success depended upon the team's spirit of cooperation, where territoriality had to be secondary to the larger, common goal.

Internexus has been an especially positive experience for the Libraries. It has garnered much good will, and made the Libraries a more visible presence on campus. The improved working relationship between the Libraries and Computing and Information Services has already demonstrated its benefits: the Libraries have implemented new services, and the University is closer to a true campus-wide information system. Perhaps the greatest benefit is that Internexus forced the librarians to face the technological future. They had to learn more about the Internet and its potential; these skills are essential as the Internet expands and the NREN becomes a reality.

Internet In-Service Training at the University of New Mexico General Library

Nina Stephenson
Deborah J. Willis

SUMMARY. This article summarizes in-service Internet training for reference and bibliographic instruction personnel at the University of New Mexico General Library. The training incorporated hands-on instruction and collaboration with the campus computing center. Sessions included an introduction to the Internet, electronic mail, and FTP; future sessions will cover advanced e-mail, accessing bibliographic and non-bibliographic databases, and the use of the Internet as a reference tool. The authors discuss practical aspects of organizing the training, including logistical and political problems, what we learned from our experiences, and recommendations for future training needs.

INTRODUCTION

Reference and bibliographic instruction librarians have, over the years, developed proficiencies and strategies for assisting their pa-

Nina Stephenson is Assistant Professor of Librarianship, Reference Department, Zimmerman Library, University of New Mexico, Albuquerque, NM 87131. Deborah J. Willis, formerly of the University of New Mexico, is Project Director for Library Technology and Networking, Oklahoma Department of Libraries, 200 NE 18th Street, Oklahoma City, OK 73105.

[Haworth co-indexing entry note]: "Internet In-Service Training at the University of New Mexico General Library." Stephenson, Nina, and Deborah J. Willis. Co-published simultaneously in *The Reference Librarian* (The Haworth Press, Inc.) No. 41/42, 1994, pp. 211-224; and: *Librarians on the Internet: Impact on Reference Services* (ed: Robin Kinder) The Haworth Press, Inc., 1994, pp. 211-224. Multiple copies of this article/chapter may be purchased from The Haworth Document Delivery Center [1-800-3-HAWORTH; 9:00 a.m. - 5:00 p.m. (EST)].

trons with the research process. Traditionally this has involved the use and teaching of print catalogs, indexes, directories, and other reference works. The proliferation of electronic sources, especially OPACs, CD-ROMs, online databases, and other systems, has significantly changed the nature of reference and library instruction. The literature is replete with research and accounts of the challenges involved in training patrons to effectively use the tools of the new automated library. Librarians are increasingly expected to formally and informally teach individuals and groups to search new computer-based systems, often without "attending training classes or having a staff training area."[1]

At the same time that reference librarians are confronted with the task of training patrons to use the tools of the automated library, libraries are shifting from owning material to providing electronic access to materials not held by their library. As Richard De Gennaro pointed out almost a decade ago: "Providing access to information will be the principal goal and activity, and coping with technology and change will be the principal driving force of the emerging information age library."[2] Knowledge about the holdings within one's own library is not enough to quench the information thirst of today's library patron; indeed, it has become "impossible for reference librarians to rely on printed pages (or other information resources) within their own libraries."[3] The reference librarian of the future must be proficient in using the *virtual library,* "a system by which a user may connect transparently to remote libraries and databases using the local library's online catalog or a university or network computer as a gateway."[4] The resources on the Internet serve as the foundation for the virtual library. The use, interpretation, and evaluation of these resources are becoming important responsibilities for today's reference librarians.

The Internet has much to offer libraries and their clientele. Reference by electronic mail, specialized discussion lists, database searching in OPACs and indexes, full-text books and articles, and document delivery are just some of the services and resources available on the Internet.[5] The breadth of these available materials require that "libraries above all need the tools to filter the data, to bring them to a widening circle of users in whatever form they require–and increasingly, to enable users to locate and retrieve the data themselves, easily and transparently."[6]

Identifying, accessing and utilizing materials on the networks can be viewed as logical extensions of the reference librarian's mission. Caroline Arms has written that librarians need to incorporate network resources "by adapting their services and applying their expertise in this new environment."[7] There is an added benefit in librarians learning the resources on the Internet, since these experiences will prepare them to "serve as guides to the emerging infrastructure of machine-readable information just as they do for printed materials."[8] Unfortunately, a resistance to change is often a part of the hesitancy to embrace new electronic sources. Many librarians remain intimidated by the Internet due to a reluctance to learn yet another system or database, and an uncertainty about where to start. Brian Nielsen put it this way: "There is a natural tendency, among those of us who must serve a diverse user community, to cringe every time an announcement is made of a new online system or database."[9] This is one of the first obstacles to overcome in introducing the Internet to a beginning group.

Sheila Creth has written that job training can be a valuable approach to dealing with resistance to change, particularly in terms of automation, and to "begin to build a staff that is flexible and resilient."[10] Although many authors have commented on the need for reference librarians to be conversant with the informational sources available on the Internet, they often say little on how librarians can achieve Internet proficiency. In one article it was noted that learning Internet resources is "often more a matter of 'mucking around' than a structured learning experience with manuals, online tutorials or other instructional tools."[11] Sixty-two of the seventy-five respondents to a recent LIBREF-L[12] survey reported being at least partially self-taught.[13] Thirty-six respondents acknowledged having learned, at least in part, from colleagues while thirty-five respondents reported having used guides as part of their Internet learning experience.[14]

While many people have learned the networks in these informal ways, we believe that formal training is beneficial for many reference and library instruction personnel. This opinion led us to pursue in-service training as a means of offering Internet instruction to University of New Mexico General Library faculty and staff.

UNIVERSITY OF NEW MEXICO GENERAL LIBRARY

The University of New Mexico General Library consists of four branches: Zimmerman Library which houses social sciences, humanities, education, government publications, and special collections; Centennial Science and Engineering Library; the Fine Arts Library; and Parish Library (business and economics). Libraries supporting the law and medical programs are also found on campus, but are administratively separate from the General Library.

All branches offer orientations and instructional sessions for their clientele. Library instruction is decentralized in the sense that outreach and requests for instruction are handled at the branch level; there is no individual coordinating or overseeing library instruction as a whole. A representative from each branch serves on the Library Instruction Committee, a body which makes policy recommendations and shares information regarding instruction in the libraries.

In-Service Training Subcommittee

In 1991, the Library Instruction Committee recognized that its many objectives could not be accomplished by one committee and formed four subcommittees, one of which is the In-Service Training Subcommittee. This Subcommittee[15] established a formal charge and began to prioritize activities. Subcommittee members acknowledged that there were many possible areas for in-service training in the library since staff development and training, like library instruction, is decentralized, but decided to focus on activities that facilitate the training of General Library faculty and staff to enhance library instruction skills and strategies. The assessment of training needs was determined to be an important aspect of the committee's charge. Toward this end, a survey was conducted in June of 1992, which revealed that Internet training was ranked among the highest as a training area for librarians involved in instruction and reference services.

IN-SERVICE INTERNET TRAINING

The Subcommittee began planning for Internet workshops intended for (although not limited to) the needs of reference and library instruction personnel. These sessions would not, however, be open to the campus community at large. Early in the planning process a packet of information containing a variety of materials about the Internet, including journal articles, a copy of *Zen and the Art of the Internet,* and several electronic mail messages and brochures announcing training programs, was circulated among committee members. The purpose of circulating such material was twofold: (1) to supply committee members with more information on the Internet and (2) to provide details on other training programs to help us determine the content of our workshops. Willis offered to prepare a proposal on training program content. The proposal, as accepted by the Subcommittee, consisted of six one-hour sessions covering the Internet: Introduction to Networks and the Internet, E-Mail, OPACs, Non-bibliographic Resources, Transferring Files: FTP and Use-Net, and Using the Internet at the Reference Desk.

We decided that one-hour workshops, delivered as two "mini-series," would be the best format. The first series, scheduled for the fall, 1992, semester, would consist of repeat offerings of the introduction, electronic mail, and ftp sessions. The second mini-series would occur during the spring, 1993, semester and would consist of a repeat of the introduction session, and presentations of the OPACs, non-bibliographic resources, and using the Internet at the reference desk sessions.[16] With the exception of the introductory and reference desk sessions, all workshops would emphasize a hands-on approach. Training would be scheduled in order to avoid conflict with regularly scheduled library meetings. Arrangements were made to use a computer classroom outside of the library. We requested an instructor from the campus computer center; Art St. George, Executive Network Service Officer for Computer and Information Resources and Technology (CIRT, the university's computing center), agreed to conduct the introductory and FTP sessions. Willis volunteered to conduct the fall electronic mail sessions.

To reduce the potential for duplication of effort on the part of other library faculty or staff, and to solicit input regarding the training, the Subcommittee posted frequent announcements out-lining our plans and progress in the library's weekly newsletter. Initial notices requested specific feedback and comments on desired Internet training workshop content and invited readers to contact the workshop coordinator if they were interested in assisting with the training. While we received only a few suggestions as a result of these announcements, we were certain that the faculty and staff were aware of our activities and plans. As soon as the details con-cerning specific trainers, times and locations for the sessions were worked out, a flyer was prepared and included in the newsletter.

All workshops held during the fall semester were well attended and, although formal evaluations were not conducted, many com-mittee members reported receiving very positive comments. Attendees were asked to submit suggestions for advanced or focused training topics.

After the Workshops

An In-Service Training Subcommittee meeting, held after the completion of all the fall workshops, included a debriefing in which we discussed adding workshops on more advanced electronic mail topics as requested by workshop attendees, and general decisions regarding spring offerings. Our experiences taught us that one hour was simply not enough time to cover information and to have hands-on training; therefore, we decided to extend the length of future Internet hands-on workshops to a minimum of ninety min-utes. One of the more animated discussions revolved around the content and form of the planned "Using the Internet at the Refer-ence Desk" session.

The University of New Mexico General Library, like many other public academic libraries in the United States, is in the midst of a period of retrenchment due to budget shortfalls, spiraling journal costs, and mounting automation expenses resulting in a hiring freeze and limited equipment purchases. Although the Internet training sessions were eagerly received, some faculty and staff were understandably wary of adding new services, particularly since some reference points are not equipped to access the Internet, or having to master new skills when they already feel overburdened by their current responsibilities. To address these and other concerns, we submitted a memo to the Library Management Team in December, 1992, clarifying our intent in offering further workshops. We stressed that the workshop addressing Internet as a reference tool would serve as an instructional and information-sharing session, and not as a forum regarding the logistics of initiating Internet use by reference staff. We stated that the workshops on Internet use at reference desks should not be interpreted as making a philosophical statement regarding preferred reference services, or as a recommendation to implement Internet use at reference desks. This approach may seem overly cautious, but in retrospect it was a politically astute move. Since then, an electronic mail reference service pilot project has begun, and a number of people have voiced concern about the additional workload this might bring to reference personnel. One branch library has taken a "wait and see" attitude, deciding not to participate in the pilot project at this time to avoid overburdening staff.

Learning from Experience

From the initial workshops we identified two important areas regarding Internet training: the necessity of a working relationship with the campus computing center, and the need for providing more advanced Internet training along with "training the trainer" instruction for reference and library instruction personnel.

Discussions regarding library and computing center collaboration (or even mergers) are not new,[17] but the emergence of the Internet as a valuable resource for all scholars accentuates the timeliness of this type of mutual cooperation.[18] Clifford Lynch, among others, believes that libraries will not be able to provide the technical support needed to successfully manage Internet access on their own, and advocates close working relationships between the library and campus computing and/or campus networking staff.[19] Our experiences were consistent with Lynch's position since we not only took advantage of CIRT's technical expertise via the participation of their Executive Network Service Officer, but also consulted with their staff during the planning process, and utilized handouts designed for the university's computing community. Further interaction occurred when our Library Instruction Committee and CIRT formed a joint task force to design collaborative instruction programs; Willis was appointed by Subcommittee chair Stephenson to serve on this task force. The advantages of this type of cooperation were readily acknowledged by both sides: CIRT trainers were unfamiliar with the intricacies of searching bibliographic resources accessible on the Internet, while library personnel were frequently confounded by the technical complexities of accessing the Internet and other electronic resources.

Our experiences with the fall semester workshops also indicated the need for training beyond the scope of basic "consciousness raising" training[20] (i.e., "how to do" electronic mail, remote logon, and file transfer protocol). As evidenced at the reference desks of the University of New Mexico General Library, the traditional role of the reference librarian as a "consultant, an information 'filter', and a teacher"[21] is being applied to the Internet. Librarians report receiving questions at the reference desk regarding accessing Internet resources, and are getting requests for bibliographic instruction sessions which may focus specifically on Internet resources or may cover the broad range of materials available regardless of their format. Because of this expansion, individuals providing reference service require training on the practical application skills for working with the new tools, as well as instruction on how to train someone to work with the Internet. In other words, the reference librarian must be able to function not only as an Internet user, but also as an Internet trainer.

Advanced User Training

Advanced user training may take many forms. A few of the possibilities are: workshops focusing on locating information in a single academic discipline; sessions looking in-depth at one or more of the search tools available; or guided exploration using something similar to the Internet Hunt[22] to give participants a broad sense for locating information. For reference librarians, user training must go beyond these types of sessions to include instruction on how to transfer existing skills to working with the Internet, and some training on the technical aspects of working with the network.

Informal observation of workshop participants in basic Internet workshops reveals that public service personnel often fail to recognize that they already possess many of the skills needed to effectively utilize resources available on the Internet. As an example, online searching skills are fundamental to working at today's reference desk. When training reference personnel to work with Internet resources, the trainer must remind participants that they possess these skills and include training on transferring these skills to the Internet. One way would be to point out that use of the library's OPAC, various CD-ROM databases, and vendor-supported indexes available through services such as Dialog or BRS often require familiarity with a variety of search engines. The same applies to searchable Internet databases; therefore, the trainer must design exercises which require participants to determine how search features such as Boolean logic, truncation, and search indexes work within the search engines encountered. Resources such as *Search Sheets for OPACs on the Internet*[23] will aid the trainer in emphasizing how these features are manifested through various search software, and provide the user with practical assistance when working with the OPACs.

A modicum of technical expertise must be included in Internet training. Reference librarians and information specialists need not understand all the technological details of the Internet to make successful use of it, particularly if the computing center can provide appropriate technical support. However, as Lynch pointed out, everyone involved will need "to develop a new, more reactive, troubleshooting-oriented philosophy."[24] This is particularly true since the Internet environment can be extremely volatile, as can be network connections and the local mainframe situation. This state of constant change adds to the excitement and stress of using and teaching the Internet. Internet users must possess some hardware troubleshooting skills and be able to interpret some of the various error messages which might be encountered in the course of attempting to transfer a file from or logon to a remote computer. Without some knowledge of error messages and network protocols, users may not know whether to try again later or contact the computer center because the problem lies at the user's end of the technology chain. A suggested training method would be a presentation on basic troubleshooting skills[25] supplemented by written step-by-step instructions that could be personalized to an individual's own situation. Roy Tennant advocates the use of a cheat sheet including basic commands needed at the various "layers," or operating environments, traversed in an Internet session.[26]

From User to Trainer

As stated earlier, individuals working at the reference desk often find themselves in the position of training a patron to use a particular resource or build a workable search strategy. This will be true with Internet resources as well; therefore, training must be available that will facilitate the transition from user to trainer. The reference librarian turned trainer must possess the knowledge and skills needed to make instructional sessions meaningful to a variety of learners. Because we tend to favor teaching toward our preferred learning style, it is important for the trainer to learn how to design and deliver instruction which takes into account differing learning styles, and to interact with learners in ways that facilitate the learning process.

Learning styles are "fixed patterns for viewing the world."[27] At the individual level, a learning style encompasses the characteristics which determine how a person "perceives, interacts with, and responds emotionally to learning environments."[28] Individuals tend to learn by combining their auditory, visual, and tactile senses into their own learning style;[29] meaningful training provides experiences that incorporate each of these senses. In their study of novice computer users, Maung Sein and Daniel Robey found that "performance in using computer application software . . . can be enhanced by tailoring instructional methods to accommodate individual differences in learning style."[30] Using the four major learning styles (Imaginative Learners, Analytic Learners, Common Sense Learners, and Dynamic Learners,)[31] Bernice McCarthy developed the 4MAT System "to help teachers organize their teaching based on differences in the way people learn."[32] Using this system, the Internet trainer would design instruction that sequentially addresses the learning stages of (1) experience, (2) reflection, (3) practice, and (4) evaluation.[33] Lois Kershner provides some practical suggestions for computer training that can be incorporated in such a model; for example, offering the "why" explanation *following* online task performance.[34] Trainers interacting with students in the computer training environment must take care to provide conditions conducive to a positive learning environment. Fredric Margolis and Chip Bell contribute several tips designed to "enhance the learning potential."[35] These include: "Do not touch a learner's computer," "Train people to think, not just to do or to follow instructions," "Avoid the overuse of jargon," and "Be patient."[36]

Looking Ahead

The vision for University of New Mexico General Library electronic information services involves an expanded and enhanced system emphasizing access *with delivery*.[37] This model presents a comprehensive scheme of "collections and connections" designed to connect users to local, regional, national and international electronic information sources, and to provide delivery of materials identified in their research. The realization of this vision will require considerable staff training beyond what is outlined in this article. Post-training contacts with workshop attendees have indicated that people are now using the Internet in more diverse ways. For example, some library committees have developed electronic distribution lists to facilitate communication among members. Although this is a beginning, staff working in this visionary model will need significantly more advanced skills to function effectively in an electronic information setting.

CONCLUSION

Systematic instruction on the Internet can take place in a number of forums. Library school courses, workshops sponsored by professional organizations or provided by contract trainers, and interactive sessions via the Internet itself, are just some of the ways people have learned the Internet. In-service training, combining the teaching, technical, and research skills of library and computing center employees, is another means of introducing people to the Internet. Such training can benefit people with little or no prior exposure to or knowledge of the Internet, staff who may be uneasy about learning a large and daunting system, employees who have some experience but desire a forum for learning new tricks and sharing their own successes, and reference information specialists who find themselves in the role of using and teaching the Internet.

Knowing how to utilize the Internet also benefits staff other than public services personnel. *Library Resources on the Internet*, for example, lists a number of reasons for searching other libraries' OPACs.[38] Aside from the obvious purposes associated with research and reference needs, systems librarians and administrators, for example, can experiment with different online systems to help them choose the features or particular systems they would like to implement or install locally. Even people who do not have immediate plans to access the Internet can benefit from an introductory overview.

Tennant stated: "It is our responsibility as public service librarians to teach ourselves and others the skills necessary to access these (Internet) resources, as we have for other information formats in years past."[39] As the Internet impacts more professional *and* private lives, and the National Research and Education Network (NREN) moves from a vision to reality, there will be an even greater need for the information specialist to master these skills in order to participate fully in the "developing global web of computer communications networks."[40]

REFERENCES

1. Carol Tenopir and Ralf Neufang, "The Impact of Electronic Reference on Reference Librarians," *Online* 16:3 (May 1992): 55.

2. Richard De Gennaro, "Shifting Gears: Information Technology and the Academic Library," *Library Journal* 109:11 (June 15, 1984): 1205.

3. Clark N. Hallman, "Technology: Trigger for Change in Reference Librarianship," *Journal of Academic Librarianship* 16:4 (Sept. 1990): 205.

4. Laverna M. Saunders, "The Virtual Library Today," *Library Administration and Management* 6:2 (Spring 1992): 66.

5. See Sharyn J. Ladner and Hope N. Tillman, "Using the Internet for Reference," *Online* 17:1 (Jan. 1993): 46. Ladner and Tillman have prepared a list of Internet reference categories. These nineteen categories are divided into three main groups: Work-related Communication, E-mail and Lists; Searching Remote Databases; and File Transfer, Data Exchange.

6. Joan Blair, "The Library in the Information Revolution," *Library Administration and Management* 6:2 (Spring 1992): 72.

7. Caroline R. Arms, "A New Information Infrastructure," *Online* 15:5 (Sept. 1990): 15.

8. Caroline R. Arms, "Using the National Networks: Bitnet and the Internet," *Online* 14:5 (Sept. 1990): 24.

9. Brian Nielsen, "Finding it on the Internet: The Next Challenge for Librarianship," *Database* 13:5 (Oct. 1990): 106.

10. Sheila D. Creth, *Effective on the Job Training: Developing Library Human Resources* (Chicago: American Library Association, 1986), 7.

11. Sally W. Kalin and Roy Tennant, "Beyond OPACs . . . The Wealth of Information Resources on the Internet," *Database* 14:4 (August 1991): 32.

12. LIBREF-L@KENTVM [electronic conference]. [Kent State (OH): Kent State University Libraries.] Available from LISTSERV@KENTVM. This electronic conference, moderated by the reference librarians at Kent State University Libraries, focuses on library reference issues.

13. This tendency may change in the future. In a March, 1993, survey of ALA accredited library schools conducted by Betty Lou Ghidiu, twenty-eight out of forty-three responding deans reported that their graduate programs included credit courses covering networking and the Internet. Betty Lou Ghidiu, letter to the authors, 18 May 1993.

14. Betty Lou Ghidiu. Results of Internet Survey. In: LIBREF-L@KENTVM [electronic conference]. [Kent State (OH): Kent State University Libraries]: 1993 April 28. The following were cited by Ghidiu as the guides most often used: Ed Krol, *The Whole Internet: User's Guide and Catalog* (Sebastopol, CA: O'Reilly and Assoc., 1993); Brendan P. Kehoe, *Zen and the Art of the Internet: A Beginner's Guide* (Englewood Cliffs, NJ: PTR Prentice Hall, 1993); Roy Tennant, John Ober, and Anne Grodzina Lipow, *Crossing the Internet Threshold: An Instructional Handbook* (Berkeley, CA: Library Solutions Press, 1993); and Tracy L. LaQuey and Jeanne C. Ryer, *The Internet Companion: a Beginner's Guide to Global Networking* (Reading, MA: Addison Wesley, 1993).

15. The authors, Stephenson and Willis, were members of the original subcommittee; Stephenson became chair shortly after the committee was formed.

16. The spring series was not held due to other obligations of the individuals involved in the Internet training.

17. See, for example, Richard M. Dougherty, "Libraries and Computing Centers: A Blueprint for Collaboration," *College and Research Libraries* 48:4 (July 1987): 289-296; and Diane J. Cimbala, "The Scholarly Information Center: An Organizational Model," *College and Research Libraries* 48:5 (Sept. 1987): 393-398.

18. See Marilyn J. Martin, "Academic Libraries and Computing Centers: Opportunities for Leadership," *Library Administration and Management* 6:2 (Spring 1992) for a review of the recent literature concerned with the relationship of computing centers and libraries.

19. Clifford A. Lynch, "Linking Library Automation Systems in the Internet: Functional Requirements, Planning, and Policy Issues," *Library Hi Tech* 7:4 (1989): 9.

20. Susan McEnally Jackson, "Reference Education and the New Technology," *The Reference Librarian* 25-26 (1989): 545. Jackson uses the term

"consciousness raising" to distinguish between levels of online searching instruction in library science education.

21. Jackson, "Reference Education," 553.

22. The Internet Hunt [serial online]. Santa Barbara (CA): University of California. Monthly. This electronic "contest," organized by Rick Gates, involves answering a set of ten questions using Internet resources. The current month's Hunt is posted on several LISTSERV discussion groups; previous hunts and answers are archived at several ftp sites.

23. Marcia Klinger Henry, Linda Keenan, and Michael Reagan, *Search Sheets for OPACs on the Internet: A Selective Guide to U.S. OPACs Utilizing VT100 Emulation* (Westport, CT: Meckler Publishing, 1991).

24. Lynch, "Linking Library Automation Systems," 9.

25. See Krol, "Dealing with Problems," in *The Whole Internet,* 261-278. This chapter might prove helpful in preparing such a presentation. In addition, the institution's computer center might provide assistance.

26. Roy Tennant, "Internet Basic Training: Teaching Networking Skills in Higher Education," *Electronic Networking: Research, Applications and Policy* 1:2 (Winter 1991): 40.

27. Adrianne Bonham, "Learning Style Instruments: Let the Buyer Beware," *Lifelong Learning* 11:6 (April 1988): 12-16, as quoted in George M. Piskurich, ed., *The ASTD Handbook of Instructional Technology* (New York: McGraw-Hill, 1993), 23.5.

28. Piskurich, *The ASTD Handbook,* 23.5.

29. Lois M. Kershner, "Training People for New Job Responsibilities: The Lesson Plan," *Library Resources and Technical Services* 34:2 (April 1990): 252.

30. Maung K. Sein and Daniel Robey, "Learning Styles and the Efficacy of Computer Training Methods," *Perceptual and Motor Skills* 72 (1991): 246.

31. Bernice McCarthy, "Using the 4MAT System to Bring Learning Styles to Schools," *Educational Leadership* 48:2 (Oct. 1990): 32.

32. McCarthy, "Using the 4MAT System," 31.

33. See Bernice McCarthy, *The 4MAT System: Teaching to Learning Styles with Right/Left Mode Techniques,* rev. ed. (Barrington, IL: EXCEL, 1987).

34. Kershner, "Training People," 254.

35. Fredric H. Margolis and Chip R. Bell, *Instructing for Results* (San Diego: Pfeiffer & Company; Minneapolis: Lakewood Publications, 1986), 80-82.

36. Margolis and Bell, *Instructing for Results,* 80-82.

37. Stephen Rollins, Associate Dean, University of New Mexico General Library, interview with authors, 6 July 1993.

38. Laine Farley, ed., *Library Resources on the Internet: Strategies for Selection and Use* (Chicago: Reference and Adult Services Division, American Library Association, 1992), 6-7.

39. Tennant, "Internet Basic Training," 45.

40. Clifford A. Lynch, Foreword in *Crossing the Internet Threshold,* Tennant, vii.

The Internet as a Reference and Research Tool: A Model for Educators

Edmund F. SantaVicca

SUMMARY. Reference and research uses of the Internet are discussed through review and comparison of traditional and new criteria for the evaluation of reference and information sources in the context of electronic reference environments. A modular outline for teaching reference uses of the Internet is presented for Internet educators. Also reviewed are typologies of information queries; issues pertinent to public policy, information integration and multi-media environments and contexts; and optional enhancements to the module designed.

INTRODUCTION

One of my favorite passages from Lewis Carroll's *Alice's Adventures in Wonderland* occurs when Alice finds herself lost in the

Edmund F. SantaVicca is Head of Reference Services, Hayden Library, Arizona State University, Tempe, AZ 85287-1006.

[Haworth co-indexing entry note]: "The Internet as a Reference and Research Tool: A Model for Educators." SantaVicca, Edmund F. Co-published simultaneously in *The Reference Librarian* (The Haworth Press, Inc.) No. 41/42, 1994, pp. 225-236; and: *Librarians on the Internet: Impact on Reference Services* (ed: Robin Kinder) The Haworth Press, Inc., 1994, pp. 225-236. Multiple copies of this article/chapter may be purchased from The Haworth Document Delivery Center [1-800-3-HAWORTH; 9:00 a.m. - 5:00 p.m. (EST)].

225

woods, with no idea of how to find her way. She encounters the Cheshire Cat, to whom she explains her plight. When the Cheshire Cat inquires as to where Alice wishes to go, she states that she really does not care, as long as she gets somewhere. To this, the Cheshire Cat replies that it then really does not matter which route Alice might take.

To the novice user of the Internet, perhaps more than to the skilled user, there will appear a parallel between Alice being lost in the woods and the information seeker being lost in the Internet-trying to discern where one is, where one wants to be, and how best to arrive there. Clearly, if one has no idea of where one wants to be, the direction in which one proceeds does not matter. To this end, many of us spend countless hours lost in seemingly vicious nets of cyberspace, perhaps more intrigued and befuddled by where we have arrived than by a clear sense of our destination, unable to discern whether we have reached it or not.

We sail the virtual cyberseas, much like our buccaneer ancestors, searching for undefined yet valuable information booty that we can seize and bring home with glorious and proud satisfaction. In this cruising or browsing mode, we indeed also tend to resemble the traditional bibliophile who browses the shelves of a library or a bookstore for the sake of discovering new areas of knowledge or new information sources: the intellectually hedonistic "information for information's sake" syndrome. This is in stark contrast to the information seeking mode of the individual, similar to Alice, who needs and sets out in search of a specific bit of information, yet has no idea where that information might exist, and who certainly has no idea how to retrieve it: the panicked patron syndrome.

This essay presents a basic conceptual, modular outline for use by the information educator-be that faculty, library in-house instructor, supervisor or manager-in the explication of concepts and precepts of the Internet. To this end, issues regarding information seeking processes in electronic and virtual environments, and implications for what we continue to identify as reference and research services, are included. The following outline, with elements interchangeable according to the goals of the educator, is suggested:

INTERNET FUNCTIONS

As any standard guide to the Internet indicates, there are three primary functions that can be performed on this electronic network of networks: electronic mail, file transfer, and telnet connections to remote locations and/or databases. All three functions require some degree of interactive communication, although in the case of the latter two this is evidenced primarily in the context of logging on and navigating to the intended file or location. That is, we interact (or perhaps interface) in a client/server mode with a computer, not a human being.

It is only the function of electronic mail that evidences continued and ongoing dialogue–dynamic information exchange, if you will–between two or more human beings; and, as such, electronic mail can serve simultaneously as a pseudo-replication of that process which we typically identify as the reference interview, and also as a new conceptual information-bearing environment that in many cases is archived for future consultation and/or perusal. LIST-SERVs, for example, cross over any current virtual boundaries that attempt to distinguish electronic mail from file transfer of LIST-SERV archives.

Conceptually, we might indeed perceive the Internet to be a somewhat large and seemingly comprehensive continuous-revision encyclopedia or almanac of information that resides in an environment identified as cyberspace. Its elements are both static (file transfer, telnet) and dynamic (electronic mail). In the context of reference and information services, our concerns must focus on two basic qualities of cyberspace–and specifically, of the Internet: substance and access.[1]

TYPOLOGY OF TRADITIONAL INFORMATION SOURCES

In one of the standard textbooks on reference sources and services,[2] Bill Katz identifies categories of traditional information sources. These include control-access-directional sources, such as bibliographies of reference sources; library catalogs; general systematic, enumerative bibliographies; indexes and abstracts. In the reference process, these works typically do not aim to present needed information (unless that information should be of an access/directional nature), but rather indicate where the information exists or can be accessed.

A second category of traditional tools are the source type works that do, in fact, present the desired information rather than a path to the information. These include encyclopedias, fact sources, dictionaries, biographical sources, and geographical sources. A third category of government documents remains arbitrarily distinct from all others due to formats, origins and types of information produced by governmental agencies and entities.

Unconventional reference sources comprise Katz' fourth and final category. Here are found community information centers (information and retrieval agencies), vertical files, clearinghouses, and individual experts. It is perhaps by virtue of the inconsistency of quality control of the two key elements mentioned above–substance and access–that sources in this final category are deemed unconventional. This issue will be noted again while examining criteria for evaluation of Internet information sources.

One mode of electronic reference sources once considered nontraditional and necessitating mediated access is that of commercial databases and/or databases deemed specialized by virtue of substance, format or access. These would include a variety of dial-in, remote, magnetic tape, cd-rom, laser disc, system and other databases that demonstrate various levels of user friendliness and search capabilities. To this day, such sources continue to form both an overlay and a transition from traditional print sources to virtual electronic sources, allowing for a variety of information options–so necessary as part of reference and research processes.

TYPOLOGY OF INTERNET INFORMATION SOURCES

All of the categorized information sources discussed above exist on the Internet, in one form or another. In addition, there exists a multitude of control-access-directional sources, direct source types, government documents, and unconventional sources that are in essence variations on an information format theme.

As all information, as well as its sources, falls victim to arbitrary classification, it should come as no surprise to see additional source categories available on the Internet identified with the following labels: lists, quotations, announcements, documentation, lyrics, readme files, articles, drafts, manuals, recommendations, minutes, reports/papers, bills, editorials, monthly reports, requests for comments, newsletters, standards, essays, notes, statements, briefs, fact sheets, poetry, summaries, brochures, policies, surveys, bulletins, press releases, charters, hearings, profiles, testimonies, conferences, humor, proposals, tutorials, weather, journals, publicity, workshops.[3]

Clearly, as we access and experience a virtual world of electronic information sources, contexts and environments, we continually face issues involved with the identification, description and classification of information being sought and processed. These issues have been examined as part of an OCLC Office of Research study that attempted "to provide an empirical analysis of textual information on the Internet, . . . [and] to test the suitability of current cataloging rules and record formats governing the creation of machine-readable cataloging records. . . . " [4] Results of that study are reviewed below.

EVALUATING TRADITIONAL INFORMATION SOURCES

A number of criteria have been used traditionally to evaluate information sources in terms of their role in the context of a reference collection and/or the reference process. Among these are purpose, authority, scope, audience, cost, format, special features, and the existence of reviews which might speak to any or all of the criteria above.[5]

Such criteria as purpose, scope and audience hopefully will be addressed in the preface of the work in question. Authors, compilers and editors will attempt at once to present the user with an explanation of the work, as well as with a statement as to value of the information included. Statements indicating purpose and intended audience generally are perfunctory in the preface to a printed work. Of greater importance to the librarian and the user are scope notes included in the preface.

In examining scope, the reference librarian and/or user will be interested in the extent to which the work in question might duplicate others in the collection. Of equal interest will be the stated (or apparent) scope of the work within the context of a larger subject, discipline, etc. Whether or not the work aims to be selective, comprehensive, universal or exhaustive; whether it is retrospective, current, and/or how frequently it is updated; whether or not it is limited in geographical or chronological scope, are all important and traditional considerations made prior to selection.

The authority of a work has traditionally been related to the perception of an author's credentials, or to the reputation of the publisher. Cost has been easily deduced, and usually weighed within the matrix of a finite acquisitions budget. Physical format is evident from bibliographic description and analytics, publisher's flyers, and/or personal examination.

In addition to scope, and of certain interest to the reference librarian, is the intellectual format or arrangement of the information included–specifically, how effectively the information can be retrieved via classed, alphabetical or any other appropriate arrangement. The presence or absence of necessary indexes is another important criteria of evaluation. Some works, such as annual reviews in lengthy bibliographic essay format, suffer in terms of their reference value when optimal indexing or other effective access approaches are omitted.

Presence or absence of illustrations, their nature, their number and their quality also have been part of the traditional evaluation and selection process of new reference tools. Other criteria have been applied as appropriate by librarians in special or unique settings, or for specialized or idiosyncratic needs; and, in the absence of available information substantial enough to make a selection decision, one might rely on a professional review for the final evaluation and selection decision.

It should be noted that the above criteria also have been used to make selection decisions regarding connectivity to what we might now identify as "traditional" electronic media–such as on-line systems and databases noted above. However, for reasons which no one seems to have addressed formally in the body of professional literature, the above criteria seem not to be applied consistently when one moves outside of categories of print media and into categories of electronic, visual or audio media.

EVALUATING INTERNET INFORMATION SOURCES

"As of November 1992, the Internet comprised 8,561 different networks supporting at least 727,000 host computers in 44 countries communicating via the common TCP/IP protocol. . . . "[6] "More than three million files representing 165 Gbytes of data were available from 1,044 FTP sites. . . . "[7]

Conceptually, these files serve as the virtual library, almanac or encyclopedia of information available through networked cyberspace. During the period of the OCLC study (October 1991-September 1992), the number of FTP sites increased 25%; the number of files, 46%; and the amount of storage, 63%.[8] This comprises a rather large galaxy of data and information within the information universe.

To be sure, traditional criteria used to evaluate printed information sources are, should and can be used to evaluate information experienced and accessed through the Internet–*if* one is able to access and experience that information. Therein lies the rub. Without dwelling on the heroic martyrdom that many of us have experienced in trying to access or locate needed information via the Internet, suffice it to note that the anecdotes of the agony of the hunt have been shared by many reference librarians and patrons.

In a virtual world of Internet information, *access* becomes the *sine qua non* of the universe. If one cannot access the information, one cannot evaluate the information; and certainly, one cannot use the information. Consequently, this single criteria takes precedence over all others. "By every measure, whether you consider the number and types of information objects, the speed of their transmission, or the worldwide breadth of their distribution, computing technologies and high-speed, wide-area networks have changed radically the ways in which information is created, stored, and disseminated."[9] In fact, new criteria to evaluate the process and procedures of access, as regards the contexts and the environments of information, need to be established.

The OCLC Internet Resource project reveals that, once access is achieved, there is scant descriptive information associated with sample FTP files analyzed. "On average, fewer than three (2.47) directory/file names describe any given file. For ancillary informational files such as 'readme' or 'index' files, on average, one readme file exists for every 3.5 directories and one index file for every seven directories."[10]

As regards electronic mail, and the interactive communication between human beings as a process of accessing information, traditional criteria also come into play. However, their conclusions or results cannot be consistently applied or documented as easily as with static FTP files. Those who have exchanged thoughts or sought information via this electronic mode are aware that the universe of respondents influences the quality of application of the criteria (authority, intended audience, etc.); and the information retrieved must be viewed in an information context that differs significantly from the FTP file mode.

One consistent and persistent access flaw shared by electronic mail, telnet and file transfer processes is the inconsistency of adequate descriptive information regarding the source of the retrieved information. "As network access broadens, data storage costs drop, and bandwidth increases, the problems of discovering, accessing and using information on the Internet will likely compound in the absence of additional information management tools and services."[11]

Access entities such as gopher, WAIS, VERONICA and ARCHIE indicate progress in the efficiency of searching and accessing electronic objects and information; but we must remember that their efficiency and effectiveness remain contingent upon adequate analytic or descriptive information pertaining to that electronic object, as well as to the quality of full-text and conceptual indexing of information. In a similar manner, multi-media cyberspace poses additional problems of access and retrieval that will need to be addressed seriously over the next decade.

TYPOLOGY OF INFORMATION QUERIES

Katz[12] presents a variety of taxonomies aimed at creating an information or inquiry matrix. Adapting and synthesizing these into four related categories, we might identify information queries as: (1) directional, typically involving direct data retrieval; (2) ready reference, also involving direct data retrieval; (3) specific-search queries, involving document retrieval, wherein the user either asks for a known item or asks for information without knowledge of a specific source; and (4) research queries, involving document retrieval and the creation and perception of an intellectual relationship connecting the documents retrieved.

Given the current state of scope and accessibility of the Internet, it is unlikely that most libraries or information settings will use the Internet in a service mode to address the first two categories of information query. Simple data retrieval such as population information, moon phases, basic statistics, etc., can be retrieved at present more efficiently and quickly by reaching for a standard printed reference tool. If and when such tools are published only in electronic formats, this perspective likely will change. Clearly, the wealth of information on the Internet will be of value most when it is accessed for the sake of addressing the two latter categories of information query: specific-search queries (including an arbitrarily defined "extended search time"); and research queries, wherein relationships of information contexts and environments must be addressed.

There are two excellent examples of electronic reference processes/services currently available on the Internet. STUMPERS-L, a LISTSERV conceived by Ann Feeney and managed by graduate library school students at Rosary College, is a forum for posing and answering difficult reference questions posed by patrons.[13] The Internet Hunt, created and developed by Rick Gates, University of California at Santa Barbara, is a monthly intellectual exercise for those who enjoy stalking the wild answer to a reference question–that answer existing somewhere in Internet cyberspace.[14] Yet more examples of electronic reference processes/services and information exchange can be evidenced by tapping into the various Freenets around the country. There, both librarians and community users freely exercise their information prowess in supplying answers to information queries.

The developing networks and configurations of electronic objects demand that we begin to create new paradigms of information services and information management, for the sake of optimizing human and electronic resources and processes aimed at user satisfaction. Virtual environments offer new boundaries of perceptions and misconceptions wherein the *trompe l'oeil* of information and the distinction of data vs. document confounds us, while the process of information/knowledge transfer becomes increasingly transparent.

One example of creative research in the overlapping areas of virtual reality and information systems and services is a doctoral project in progress at Syracuse University,[15] wherein the researcher has developed a three-dimensional information system. The project "addresses the constraints inherent in human interaction as an ideal for what a computerized information system user would navigate through (i.e., as the interactive aspect of the interface) to gain access to information and/or data. The system data are organized into the interface according to lexical distance computations, that is, the proximity between content-bearing words in text. These have been analyzed via a principal-components analysis to generate a three-dimensional representation of the words used in the texts that are included in the data base. This configuration is rather arbitrary, but Newby's focus is on navigation as a concept for human-computer interactivity for information retrieval problems. The user then 'flies' through this three-dimensional word space using a VPL Dataglove and 'grabs' words that represent his or her information needs."[16]

ADDITIONAL ISSUES

The authors of *Crossing the Internet Threshold* signal a number of issues regarding the Internet that must be addressed to assure that public policy not lag behind technological development. These issues include: "acceptable uses" of publicly funded networks; copyright issues of Internet accessible or delivered material; commercialization and privatization of the historically public-funded Internet; protection of privacy given increased access to various data; equitable access to information, especially publicly produced information; education and retraining to create or maintain network "literacy"; quality control of networked information; and the integration of network and print tools and industries.[17]

One issue which sorely needs to be addressed in the literature of reference and information services is the future relationship of virtual or electronic and print media within the physical or non-virtual library environment, as this relates to the quality of information delivery. Another issue many large academic and public libraries face is the changing definition, perception, relevance and use of research.

To these might be added issues regarding the changing paradigms of multi-media and virtual environments; the reconceptualization of needs of a service-oriented civilization; and a reexamination of societal values as they relate to the missions of information providers and information gatherers. "Virtual reality technology is being diffused in an environment sensitized to the role of communication media. If anything, VR technology pushes us to reconsider, once again, fundamental issues concerning communication, perception, representation, and the social presence of media."[18]

How and how well the above issues are debated and resolved over the next decade will determine the extent to which those services and resources we traditionally have associated with reference services will change, be enhanced and be diminished through the existence and development of changing electronic entities–such as the Internet and virtual reality technologies–in the next century. With adequate management, access and descriptive control as regards information content, the Internet promises to serve in the future as a key mechanism for information retrieval.

CONCLUSION

This essay presents a basic matrix of intellectual concepts and issues pertinent to information service aspects of the Internet. New electronic information entities will continue to force change in information curricula, and methodologies of effective instruction. Because specifics of technology and connectivity remain idiosyncratic to the physical and virtual environments of both librarian and patron, and to the location and/or mode of instruction, the Internet educator is encouraged to incorporate such specifics within this matrix, as appropriate.

REFERENCES

1. Martin Dillon and others, *Assessing Information on the Internet: Toward Providing Library Services for Computer-Mediated Communication: Results of an OCLC Research Project* (Dublin, OH: OCLC Online Computer Center, Office of Research, 1993), 5. Advance copy.

2. William A. Katz, "The Reference Process," chap. in *Introduction to Reference Work,* vol. 1, *Basic Information Sources,* 6th ed. (New York: McGraw-Hill, 1992), 18-23.

3. Erik Jul, "Project to Analyze Internet Information is Underway: Document Categories," *OCLC Newsletter,* no. 196 (March/April 1992): 14.

4. Dillon, 5.

5. Katz, 23-29.

6. Dillon, 6.

7. Ibid., 4.

8. Ibid.

9. Ibid., 27.

10. Ibid., 4.

11. Ibid., 25.

12. Katz, 11-15.

13. Ann Feeney, "Internet Applications: Stumpers-L," *Computers in Libraries* 13 (May 1993): 40-42.

14. Gord Nickerson, "The Virtual Reference Library," *Computers in Libraries* 13 (May 1993): 37-38, 40.

15. G. B. Newby, "Towards Navigation for Information Retrieval" (Ph.D. diss., Syracuse University, in progress).

16. Michael S. Nilan, "Cognitive Space: Using Virtual Reality for Large Information Resource Management Problems," *Journal of Communication* 42 (Autumn 1992): 118-119.

17. Roy Tennant, John Ober, and Anne G. Lipow, *Crossing the Internet Threshold: An Instructional Handbook,* with a Foreword by Clifford A. Lynch (Berkeley, CA: Library Solutions Press, 1993), 17.

18. Frank Biocca, "Communication Within Virtual Reality: Creating a Space for Research," *Journal of Communication* 42 (Autumn 1992): 6-7.

NREN Update, 1993:
Washington Policy

Carolyn S. Elliott

SUMMARY. This paper focuses on the development of NREN policy and its impact on library network budgets, jobs, and access. It uses papers by and interviews with five leading Washington NREN and library experts.

The interviews provided the answers to several key questions. These answers calmed fears that AT&T would become America's library in 25 years. But they raised fears that user fee rates would challenge equal user access. Opinions varied concerning whether or not librarians were influencing policy decisions. But all agreed that librarians need to be active in developing network access and even network tools. Working with the network will not only ensure survival but enhance library service.

INTRODUCTION

Defining the NREN has been and remains an ongoing challenge. "Ask a dozen people for a definition of the National Research and

---

Carolyn S. Elliot is a graduate student in the Master of Library Science program at The University at Albany, State University of New York, and a Reference Paraprofessional at Miller Library, Keystone Junior College, LaPlume, PA 19440.

The views expressed in Peter Young's interview represent his own view and do not necessarily represent the policies, postitions, or views of the U.S. North Commission on Libraries and Information Sciences or the U.S. Government.

The opinions expressed in Daniel VanBelleghem's interview represent his own view and should not be stated as policy of the National Science Foundation or the U.S. Government in general.

[Haworth co-indexing entry note]: "NREN Update, 1993: Washington Policy." Elliott, Carolyn S. Co-published simultaneously in *The Reference Librarian* (The Haworth Press, Inc.) No. 41/42, 1994, pp. 237-259; and: *Librarians on the Internet: Impact on Reference Services* (ed: Robin Kinder) The Haworth Press, Inc., 1994, pp. 237-259. Multiple copies of this article/chapter may be purchased from The Haworth Document Delivery Center [1-800-3-HAWORTH; 9:00 a.m. - 5:00 p.m. (EST)].

Education Network and you will get a dozen different answers" (Wilson A25).

The NREN has been paired up with many images, "from the highway system to the telephone system, from the national power grid to the agricultural extension system" (*Proceedings* 15). Historical models appropriate for the NREN numbered 13 at an NREN workshop held in September of 1992 (*Proceedings* 10-11).

The most popular image has been chosen by Vice President Al Gore: "When then-Senator Al Gore was garnering support for his visionary National Research and Education Network (NREN) bill, he often pointed to the many benefits of a high-speed, multilane, multilevel data superhighway" (Polly 38). This image can be applied to the varieties of networking experience. "Bottlenecks," "traffic," "entrance ramps," "driveways," and even "tricycles" are familiar images that help people envision the network. The confusion begins when we realize this highway system has not yet been completely built.

What it might be used for does not help define the NREN either: "Some people think it should offer access to a broad variety of people. Others believe it should have a more narrow base of users–primarily those who require extremely high speeds for data transmission" (Wilson A25). Even the most confined use of the network does not identify the NREN clearly. In 1991, Gore wrote it would be used for "aeronautics, meteorology, climatology, astrophysics, biochemistry, geophysics, economics, and dozens of other fields" (Gore 15).

A huge surge in Internet use is adding to the confusion, because the NREN project is being set up on the Internet. User access has exploded, from researchers at universities and the Department of Defense (ARPANET) to K-12 school children and public libraries in 50 states (Henderson), from relatively few "techie" users to potentially millions of "universal" users (Weingarten 27). Network traffic increased fiftyfold over five years to 1992 (*Testimony* 4). The transmission speed is now leaving T-3 and heading for OC3 (155 Mb/s) by spring 1994 (VanBelleghem) and OC-12 (622 Mb/s) later (*National Research* 15). As of March 12, 1992, there were an average of 11 billion packets of information being transmitted per month (*Testimony* 4).

This rate of acceleration and volume of transmissions make the NREN a technological supernova in terms of its impact on Washington network circles. This level of activity opens pre-existing structures and language to chaos. But in spite of its size, there are many people and places the NREN has not yet reached. Outside Washington, it is just beginning to enter the general library community. New, fast moving energy is expanding from an old network core (ARPANET) that no longer exists. As this energy reaches research and education centers such as libraries, these institutions are changing from the impact. What makes a supernova image so useful is that in a supernova the old planets are no longer identifiable, and the new forms have not taken shape yet. This is where the NREN is.

But despite the risks, the Clinton administration is depending strongly on the energy of the NREN and the next network project, the National Information Infrastructure (NII), to play major roles in the federal government's effort to revitalize the American economy (Young, Personal interview, and Lippincott).

Issues

A number of issues are emerging from the chaos of this technology explosion. These issues seem to be stable. There are too many of them to investigate in only a few pages, but some of the more persistently troublesome issues are: protocol compatibility issues (TCP/IP and OSI), Acceptable Use Policy (AUP), Network Information Centers (NICs), "user-hostile" technology (as opposed to user-friendly), funding, equity of access, the role of libraries, and privatization of the network.

These issues are all connected. But the most dominant themes became the focus of five interviews conducted in March and April of 1993. These issues are: current projects, users and access, money, privatization, and libraries. The overarching question of library and librarian survival into the twenty-first century is discussed in the libraries section of this paper. These issues emerged because they begin to bring the role of the library in the network environment into focus.

HISTORY

There are many sources for history of the NREN. One source is an ERIC document which is a bibliography of 255 entries, compiled in 1989 and published in 1990 (Hodson). A second source is a publication of documents and articles from 1990 (Parkhurst). It was recommended by Carol Henderson. A third source is a 170 page book by Charles McClure et al., with 17 appendices, which are official federal documents from 1990 and 1991. A fourth source gives a snapshot of the Internet in 1992 (Lane and Summerhill). These four sources have outstanding authors, contents, and bibliographies. They give most of the history of the NREN project up to 1993.

During a March 24th interview, Carol Henderson, Deputy Director of the American Library Association Washington Office, told the story of ALA involvement in the NREN project:

> The NREN was originally designed to enable scientists to gain distant access to supercomputers and move around large volumes of data for high-end scientific experiments. The network was focused on science, so there was reluctance in some quarters to expand the educational aspect of it.

But universities wanted to put their libraries on the network after they had gotten on it for scientific research purposes. There were previously established library-to-library networks whose existence was threatened by the development of the current network, Internet. But Henderson stresses that this network has great "potential to connect libraries to non-library sources of information. There are also obvious advantages of K-12 use in school library media centers. So that was what occupied our interests for the first couple years."

ALA Involvement

ALA involvement in NREN legislation goes back to the original legislation that established the NREN, the High Performance Computing Act of 1991. The ALA and the Association of Research Libraries (ARL) began working on that effort when then-Senator Gore introduced the first bill (1988). They worked for the support of education as very broadly defined to include all libraries and schools from earliest grades to lifelong learning, in accordance with Gore's vision. Together with other library, education, and research groups, they also jointly recommended certain goals: access for all 50 states, libraries as users, and "involved constituencies having a voice in the running of the network" (Henderson). Joan Lippincott, Assistant Executive Director of the Coalition for Networked Information, commended the strong and early effort of the ALA and the ARL to call attention to the vital role libraries can play in national electronic networking.

Library and Information Science is included in the education and training use of the network in NREN legislation. These broader research and educational uses of the network would have been cut in the legislation, Henderson said, if the ALA and other groups had not made sure it survived. "While the legislation regarding the network has been passed, the funding has not been really sufficient to accomplish the vision that the act actually calls for. So a number of follow-up steps are in place" (Henderson).

There have been frequent and large meetings across the country in the past year. Quite a variety of constituencies are involved. There are differences of opinion, not yet resolved, but there are also some common themes:

> These themes involve the NREN as a program, not a physical network. The federal funding is actually less than 10%, so it is very much a partnership between the government and its agencies and the private sector, research and educational communities, and the library community. It is an example of federal leveraging–a small amount of funding sparking a tremendous amount of activity . . . The Department of Education has been playing a gradually increasing role, though there is still a good way to go.
>
> –Henderson

CURRENT PROJECTS

The information in this section comes almost totally from interviews with the five Washington NREN experts. They described the current projects of the groups they represent.

NCLIS

Peter Young has been Executive Director of the 15 member National Commission on Libraries and Information Sciences (NCLIS) since August 1990. The fifteenth member is the Librarian of Congress. Young said that the purpose of the Commission is to advise the President and Congress, adding that

> President Clinton has created a new federal high level interagency task force on the National Information Infrastructure (NII) as part of the National Economic Council. This shows how closely aligned networking is with economic recovery for this administration.

According to Young, this council will assist industry to develop hardware and software for manufacturing, health care, lifelong learning, and libraries. So some funding for networking projects will come from the Department of Commerce. "If you take an early scan of where the attention of this administration is going, you see an unprecedented emphasis on libraries as places where national networking will revitalize the economy." (Unless otherwise noted, all information from Young is taken from the personal interview.)

Young talked about writing the November 13, 1992, NCLIS report to the White House Office of Science and Technology Policy (OSTP), which is in charge of the NREN project. The origins of this report were a series of meetings and conferences from the summer of 1991 to the summer of 1992 (see *Report*). One open forum produced 95 recommendations from library and information services, organizations, related industries, associations, and institutions. This is typical of the way policy about the NREN is developed.

Young's personal belief is that "electronic networking technology has the potential to transform not simply libraries, but the way people relate to one another." His fear is "that the federal government will view the NREN as simply another federal research and development project." The problem is that federal agencies do not view libraries as federal players, so they may be left out of federal networking plans.

As a result of writing the report for the OSTP, Young realized he had come across an area of the NREN "supernova" that was just becoming visible. He began to see a competition taking place. Three groups are competing for power to influence policy and funding to enact policy: the federal sector, the academic sector, and the private sector.

The Three Sectors

The federal sector includes all the federal agencies whose research branches are involved in the network: DOD, DOE, NIH, NSF, etc. Joan Lippincott of CNI points out that their funding in the NREN is not as big as it seems. In populated areas, the ratio of federal dollars to industry and university dollars is one to six. In rural areas, such as Montana and Alaska, federal funding is one in ten dollars. But Young points out that historically, federal agencies have run America's research networks for the past 20 years–first the Department of Defense (DOD), then the National Science Foundation (NSF), and now the OSTP. So they tend to view the NREN project as their responsibility.

The academic sector is made up of researchers working on a global scale. They need the speed and connectivity of the network to receive and process data on research topics such as global warming or earthquake activity. The "Grand Challenges" part of President Clinton's budget identifies more projects. These projects require fast information from many instruments and laboratories around the world. But universities and academic researchers are often busy and distracted from policy issues, trying to find money to support these glamorous but expensive projects (Young, personal interview).

The private industry sector is the third sector in this competition. These are the businesses already positioning themselves to establish access (and user fees) for every home in America. Young believes they are ahead of the other two sectors, though the outcome of this competition is not yet clear. "The change of libraries from paper to electronic format is directly influenced by who wins this competition," Young warns.

Vision and Advice

In a lecture in November 1992, Young explained his vision of what electronic networking can do for America and the world:

"The distributed linking of intelligent machines on fiber optic networks, provides the potential for radically changing our concepts of community, for redefining learning, and restructuring knowledge" (*Information Network* 4). Librarians are being caught up in "tremendously exciting" technologies, "full of potential for shared creativity, discovery, and innovation in a post-industrial economy" (*Information Network* 5). "Fluid social relationships and dynamic intellectual links" will be replacing the old, isolated way of doing research" (*Information Network* 10). If the academic sector wants to play a major role in network development, it had better organize into teams and get in shape soon, because the private sector is ready for the season to begin.

Young's lecture suggests one way for the academic sector to win the network race. It can team up with libraries as points of presence to provide access to the networks for "the last mile," connecting the network to every home in America. In fact, "libraries must be at the center of this evolutionary process" (*Information Network* 21).

If this does not happen, Young sees only people with money being able to pay high user fees. Only the rich will get to take part in the global knowledge community. This puts Young in the position of a techno-ecologist, arguing, as ecologists do, that the widest range of species possible ought to have access to the global network to ensure survival. With the waters of poverty, overpopulation, illiteracy, and competition rising higher and higher, Young, like Noah, ushers as many people as can possibly fit on to the ark of civilized learning, the global network. To avoid extinction, librarians not only have to get on the boat, they also have to help academia fight for the wheel.

Young identified ongoing involvement in the global network evolutionary process. NCLIS, the ALA Washington office, and CNI are reviewing new White House policy documents on NREN issues and also working on current legislation. Not only has the Windo Bill been reintroduced, but legislation called Gore II has been reintroduced. Gore II (S. 4 and S. 29-37) refers to digital libraries and aims to assure that America leads the world in networking. The Commission and the ALA office follow the rewriting of bills in both the Senate and the House to assure that the goals of their constituencies and those of the new administration are met. Committees in Congress are struggling now over who has jurisdiction over various network aspects like rate fees, video-cable issues, and even trade restrictions on the importation and exportation of information over an international network.

National Science Foundation

Daniel VanBelleghem, of the National Science Foundation, noted that the NSF has provided funding for connectivity for post-secondary academic institutions for several years. They also fund mid-level networks between a number of academic institutions at a multi-campus level, he said.

One big current NSF project is fully funding the InterNIC project (International Network Information Center) to help people find out what is available on the network. AT&T, Network Atomics, and Network Solutions, Inc., are three businesses that will be working to register all non-military networks and data base services in the directory. This represents a big step toward making the Internet more user friendly (VanBelleghem).

The InterNIC will "operate like a reference librarian"; even a novice user can call without charge to find out what is available on the network (VanBelleghem). An announcement about the InterNIC project describes what it is and what it will do: "The InterNIC Directory of Directories will include lists of FTP sites, lists of various types of services available on the Internet, lists of white and yellow page directories, library catalogs, and data archives" (*InterNIC* 1). The access tools are WAIS, Archie, Mail, Telnet, X.500 (in the future), and Gopher (after July 1, 1993). There are no fees for standard entries, no fees for access, and nominal fees for expanded entries. InterNIC Directory Services will be white and yellow pages (*InterNIC* 1-2). Work on this project began on April 1, 1993 (VanBelleghem), and this is private industry, not librarians, here.

Another NSF project is the updating and expansion of the *Internet Resource Guide* (IRG) data base, a catalog of resources on the network that includes libraries, advanced computer devices, remote devices, and software catalogs. Now five to six years old, according to VanBelleghem, the project will be greatly expanded, due to a larger contract. These projects devoted to keeping directories up to date are ongoing, according to VanBelleghem.

Another current information services project that NSF has funded is called The Clearinghouse for Network Information Discovery and Retrieval. It provides information for the software of WAIS, Gopher, and World Wide Web, keeping these somewhat standard and up to date. It is a clearinghouse on the latest developments in information services (VanBelleghem).

VanBelleghem explained the next big NSF project:

> The project everyone has been asking us about is the project solicitation for the new very high-speed backbone for more advanced scientific research. It will be operated at OC-3, or 155 Mb/s. We will have Network Access Points (NAPS) from the lower speed, more production-oriented network. All network service providers (Sprint, MCI, etc.) will hook up to NAPS. We will probably have at least 3 NAPS. They will not have an appropriate use policy attached to them.

VanBelleghem pointed out that the NSF is also involved in many other network projects, but these are the ones currently receiving the most attention.

ALA Washington Office

Carol Henderson at the ALA Washington Office spoke about many projects the ALA is involved in. The Higher Education Act, which Congress must reauthorize every five years, was already well written to allow for technological innovation by libraries, but the ALA and the ARL recommended some changes. In passing this act,

> Congress clearly recognized the move of libraries into the electronic networked environment and into an environment of changing the role of libraries from just providing access to what is within the four walls to making available the resources that users need at the time they need them, no matter where they may be located.

The Library Services and Construction Act (LSCA), due for renewal next year, contains support for public libraries and interlibrary cooperation. The ALA and other library organizations are reviewing LSCA now for ways to include the network (Henderson).

Another current project involves government information dissemination. The ALA is trying to develop legislation

> which would allow the GPO to serve as an Internet gateway to electronic federal databases. The gateway program would be similar to the GPO's printing program, available for free to the federal depository libraries. One version of this type of legislation got approval from committees in both the House and the Senate in late March 1993 as GPO Electronic Access Bills.
>
> –Henderson

She linked the GPO issue to an effort to follow up the High Performance Computing Act (HPC Act) with some NREN applications legislation (Gore II). The ALA is not alone in working to update legislation. Some of the other interested groups are: EDUCOM, FARNET, and the Computer Systems Policy Project (CSPP), which includes the CEOs of Apple and twelve other corporations. "The message of all these groups is that the NREN be developed for more than science. They have recently added government information to their list of applications" (Henderson).

The ALA is looking at federal funding for technology for libraries with depository responsibilities that are not yet on the network. These libraries ought to be ready by the time government information becomes electronic. Some cities where local government information is available could use federal help, too, according to Henderson.

Coalition for Networked Information

The Coalition for Networked Information (CNI) was formed in the spring of 1990. Joan Lippincott is Assistant Executive Director. One-hundred eighty research and educational organizations, institutions, and corporations belonged to its Task Force in March of 1993, but more are expected to join as the NREN develops into the future. The Task Force Membership list includes The Alliance of Network Managers, AT&T, CARL Systems Inc.,

Brown University, Cornell University, Harvard University, Library of Congress, NOTIS Systems, Inc., Princeton University, Smithsonian Institution, Sun Microsystems, and many more. Special funding for CNI comes from Apple Computer, BRS Software Products/Maxwell Online, Digital Equipment Corporation, International Business Machines, and Xerox Corporation (*Proceedings* A-75-A-76).

Paul Evan Peters, Executive Director of CNI, writes that the

> story of CNI's progress . . . is told by the variety of information, service, and technology providers who have joined numerous research and educational institutions and quite a few collaborating professional and scholarly societies in a common program of work devoted to a shared vision of how the nature of information management must change through the end of the twentieth century and into the beginning of the twenty-first. (52)

Lippincott said that the Coalition for Networked Information (CNI) does not have its own legislative strategy because CNI is made up of three sponsoring associations, the ARL, EDUCOM, and CAUSE. "They, particularly ARL and EDUCOM, have their own agendas and CNI works along with them." But CNI sees its task as educating its membership about network developments, for example, in organizing panels of people to discuss how the NREN project is taking shape. A Task Force meeting called "Big Ideas That Make A Difference" was held in March 1993. Part of that meeting was a panel on access to public information:

> CNI feels this issue is very important. It filed a statement calling attention to the fact that the government should disseminate electronic information with the same responsibility as it has had for printed information up to now. Also, CNI stated that government agencies should use the network to disseminate information.
>
> –Lippincott

Paul Peters, master of well-phrased user gripes, is famous for saying that using the Internet is like "trying to drink from a fire hose" (49). (See Lane and Summer-hill for a detailed development of this issue.) Lippincott referred to another of Peters' comments that the information experts on the Internet are in the "Paleoelectronic Era," because it is the era of crude tools. CNI is working to improve these crude tools in a project called Topnode, a Directory of Directories for the experienced network user.

OSTP

According to David Lytel, interviewed on his second day at the Office of Science and Technology Policy (OSTP), current OSTP projects include encouraging funding for NREN access through the National Telecommunications and Information Administration (NTIA). This agency usually funds broadcast-oriented programs. But NTIA could direct some of its 64 million dollar budget for 1993 toward NREN access for K-12 and some libraries. This project is waiting for the federal budget to be passed. Lytel believes it is not clear now where to apply for federal funding for library access to the network. He recommends looking at the *National Journal* at the end of each month for announcements about where funding will be coming from. (A brief article on this topic by Cooke and Henderson appears in the February 26, 1993, issue of *The ALA Washington Newsletter*.)

USERS AND ACCESS

Peter Young does not see the network becoming more user-friendly as a worrisome problem. He is worried about a bigger problem that arises "if I look at an index abstract on CD-ROM, taking home the articles I want without ever even learning about the 15,000 other items that contradict my point of view." He is concerned about what is (or is not) being done to make the user more information critical. Young looks at another view of this issue: How can network users be trained to consider and value points of view different from their own?

Daniel VanBelleghem, at the NSF, partially and coincidentally answered this concern by pointing out that local and regional networks get money from local users of the network. These local and regional networks in turn sponsor workshops. He described a continuing project to "encourage local networks to be evangelical and look for people to sign up and train. The NSF signs up secondary schools, and those schools sign up their libraries."

But Young's concern is that training should be more than just for signing up users. Even for signing up users, there are difficulties:

> There is a very small community, as far as I can understand, that really cares about equal access to NREN. That small community is ill-equipped in terms of the library community's and the education community's lobbying efforts vis a vis the lobbying efforts of the major telecommunications system providers. Congress cares, but you have to be so technologically and policy detailed to know what's really going on that Congressman Boucher [for example] is hard-pressed to explain the electronic village in his district that could be applied nationally for community access to all sorts of things.

For these reasons, the network access available today remains inadequate, Young maintains.

The NSF hopes the Department of Agriculture and the National Institutes of Health will help increase access by signing up rural researchers. The NSF currently has several health projects with rural medical libraries being connected to the Internet (VanBelleghem).

On user access, Henderson said that government emphasis on K-12 and digital libraries has the potential for making the network more user friendly. The use of WAIS and Gopher helps, but librarians with their skills are needed.

Library Involvement

Librarians can also help increase access by training users:

> What we are seeing now are partnerships between mid-level local networks and library networks to provide technological services. For instance CAPCON (Washington, D.C., area) provides technical support in helping libraries pool purchasing power in database searching, and they have an agreement with SURANET to provide affordable dial-up access in this area. They have a computer lab where they provide training on how

to use the Internet for the library staff. That seems a very sensible way of providing access to especially a group of small libraries.

–Henderson

The CNI is trying to help libraries develop strategies to allow everyone to have access to the network through local institutions:

The Coalition is interested in seeing all kinds of libraries play a role in providing network access. But libraries need to feel more responsible for developing political strategies, if they are public libraries. They also need funding strategies.

–Lippincott

Lippincott presents an inspiring point of view: CNI feels librarians need to take some responsibility for getting network access for their communities. But she warns that communities in remote rural places cannot be left to their own devices to gain access to the network. It is much, much more expensive to connect genuinely rural areas than it is to connect in populated areas, and the level of government funding remains uncertain.

For the OSTP, the NREN project is just another way to increase access to the Internet. When there is too much network user access, technology seeks another path. For logjams and bottlenecks on the network, research is developing automatic switches that operate like train switches to send information to the same destination by a different route. This way, the network avoids the problem of too much access (Lytel).

But Lippincott is concerned by a fairly new development. Some people who influence network policy are beginning to envision more than one network operating at a time. VanBelleghem explained that some organizations, like NASA, may need the whole bandwidth occasionally, for example, to work on the Freedom Space Station for several hours. They will have NREN connectivity, but they will also have their own network, which he is calling the NII. CNI, according to Lippincott, "feels this needs more discussion and study, because it does not see having separate networks as providing the best solution to user access issues." She fears that if the widest bandwidth and highest performance network are reserved for advanced scientific research only, it might mean an elementary school teacher's plans to show a multimedia program during peak use time on a network of inferior capacity would not work. Will school children be denied access at times if the network is not state-of-the-art?

MONEY

Young sees the role of the federal government changing as the Clinton administration develops its own policy on the NREN. Policy changes will happen soon in local communities and in aid to libraries. But these new policies do not keep Young from being concerned about network fees in the future. He feels the cost of using the network in the future is directly related to the issue of privatization.

Along with Henderson, Young said that it is time library users realized that all libraries are funded from somewhere. Someone will have to pay for network access. Young wondered

> if the Library of Congress will be the first great major casualty in terms of its 1992-93 LC Funding Act that allows it to charge extra for extra services. Libraries will not be able to survive in this network if they don't recognize that they have to change the funding base of libraries.

On the topic of user fees, VanBelleghem said, "Charging for network use by the packet, like they do in Europe, would be unfair here in the States. The way to make it fair is to charge everyone $5,000 a year as a 'museum rate' where you can pay one fee and stay in the museum for five minutes or all day."

He added that the most advanced researchers, like NASA and the Human Genome Project, are going to be much more expensive to connect. They are in a fee situation that is "not like the rest of us who are seeing user rates drop" from private competition in the open market.

Henderson gave an overview of the NREN evolution process:

As the network either spreads or evolves into the NII, all this is quite fuzzy. I don't think anyone has a really clear picture about how this will evolve. We have a concern that pricing structures [provide] . . . affordable and predictable access for schools and libraries so they can budget for it. There are a variety of proposals on the table now that would help institutions gain access, but it will not even be affordable unless these rate structure issues are resolved.

The government's role here needs to include making access affordable, she says. A large variety of groups in coalitions with the ALA are concerned about keeping network access affordable, because they know they will be very dependent on high capacity telecommunications services in the future. These groups have reason to feel nervous about their obvious vulnerability (Henderson).

Fee, Not Free

Joan Lippincott agrees with Paul Peters that there is a bit of a mythology among people that libraries are free. Libraries are not free. Libraries are funded to provide services without charge, so somebody is going to be paying for the network and for networked information resources, she said, adding,

Decisions need to be made administratively at various levels from the federal government on down to the local library or the local institution about who is going to pay for those fees, whether they will be paid by the government, the institution, or the end user. Part of our role is to get people to start thinking about those things now and to help to feature models of ways it is being done for libraries to choose from.

CNI is working to develop local site license parameters so libraries and institutions won't have to "pay by the drink," as they call being charged for every user. That effort is only for information resources, not for network access. A project CNI is working on through Rights to Electronic Access and Delivery of Information (READI) is focusing on how users should be charged for resource fees (Lippincott).

Echoing the problem of the myth of free libraries, David Lytel of the OSTP said that people need to realize that the Internet was not built for free. It was built by the education and research communities, he said. Somebody paid for it. In the future, with private companies taking over, we may see "sticker shock" in users. But for now, nobody knows what the fees will be.

Here, the paths of private companies, the federal government, and library survival collide–at future fees for network use. Library survival may depend on how much the ALA, ARL, and other library organizations can influence legislation on fees. An image is floating around Washington that private companies involved in the network look at network users as a cocaine dealer looks at customers. The first few doses are free, but once the user gets hooked, the price skyrockets.

PRIVATIZATION

The issue of private companies running the network is not, for example, about the federal government giving the NREN project to AT&T. The issue is about how much private companies will charge the network users. Here is the snake in the network Garden of Eden–the pusher in the playground. Companies are expected to want to make a profit running the network. But the issue everyone but VanBelleghem is concerned with is: how much profit are companies going to want?

Henderson agreed with VanBelleghem that, in essence, privatization of the network has already happened. She means this "in the sense that the federal government is not laying the [fiber-optic] cable, physically building the network for itself. The government is contracting for high speed access, but only funding a small percent of the network." Peter Young said the federal government has agreed that the NREN is an investment, "but they are pushing the major policy issues like privatization off to the side."

The groups joining the ALA in concern about private access fees are "making sure that the current policy ferment underway will protect the abilities of publicly funded institutions to benefit from these technological developments" (Henderson). She regrets that these groups have not yet formed a common expression of where their interests converge.

Daniel VanBelleghem does not see privatization as a problem. He sees it as an opportunity. As long as private companies are allowed to compete in an open market, competition will force prices for access down and quality of service up. No problem.

There is a problem with the popularly held myth that the NREN is a federally funded network, according to Lippincott. "It has been a partnership from the beginning between the private sector, universities, and the federal government." Here she shares Young's view that there are three major sectors involved in network evolution.

Lippincott does not see fees as a privatization problem. Her concerns are about the direction private and federal network management seems to be currently taking, in the separation of networks Vanbelleghem referred to when he spoke about the NII. Lippincott worries that faculty members will have to switch networks when they change the type of information they are sharing. "Also," she adds, "it is simplistic to believe that network use can be easily divided between different aspects such as teaching, research, and training graduate assistants."

She shares Henderson's concerns about the rights of the users of a lower performance network–that a lower performance network might limit use of multimedia technology; for example: "If the network does not have the capacity to support this type of demanding use, then those users need the high performance network."

LIBRARIES

Young said, "The only place libraries have an influence is in the Congress." But things may be changing because of Dr. Michael Nelson, a key Senate staffer on Gore's Senate Committee, who recently joined OSTP. He will now be a key person in terms of whether or not libraries will have an impact. Young does not see the federal government listening to libraries and information services, outside of Nelson's potential influence.

Lippincott sees library impact differently. She feels that, from the beginning of high performance legislation in this country, the ALA Washington Office has, with the ARL, and many other groups, strongly influenced the nature of the NREN and federal thinking about electronic networks:

> The ALA and the ARL have had key roles in getting language concerning library access into the High Performance Computing Act of 1991. They also got language about government information via the NREN into legislation. They had an influence on getting the concept of the network to be for education rather than only for research. . . . They have been doing effective work on the hill.

The ALA's Legislation Committee has recently created an Ad Hoc Telecommunications Subcommittee to ensure it is more visible in its effort to protect library interests (Henderson).

Henderson sees the danger to library survival in fee rates, but beyond that she sees that the NREN greatly enriches the information possibilities for libraries, so it is worth trying to influence its development. Libraries will continue to be important "physical places because of their neighborhood functions as study places for homework and research." Even the economic development of a community can be helped by library information. She sees electronic formats as gateways to a larger world of information and librarians as guides in navigating through electronic formats of all kinds. This implies that the more information the library has access to, the more it can help: "Whether you tap in from remote access or go physically, the public library will remain important."

The network link to other librarians is important in itself. M-Link is an example Henderson cites from Michigan where public libraries can reach the University of Michigan Library on the network for reference expertise. An isolated librarian can ask other librarians questions on the network, bump a reference question, and share problems and solutions.

Peter Young is not so optimistic, but his focus covers a larger picture. He sees libraries as

> a way of encapsulizing human relationships. They are vehicles or conduits for conversations with people who have come before with ideas which are perhaps greater than one individual's thinking. . . . Dealing in an information explosion means

that the caring roles libraries play in facilitating those relationships [need to] function in a very radically different environment in a way that fulfills the pursuit and maintenance of the
values that got these people into the library in the first place.

Providing this environment for communication, as libraries do, may
be lost in the future.

To avoid extinction, libraries need to look at users, he said, and
see how they are using the network. Librarians should go beyond
e-mail and see what can be done to improve navigation and navigation tools on the network. Librarians might ask: How can we help
Americans use this supercapability for something practical in their
lives? Librarians also need to look at what users will want from the
network in the future and set about developing it (Young, Personal
interview). This means librarians could cooperate with engineers
and subject specialists to develop network tools (Henderson). In
addition, Young, Henderson, and Lippincott agree that every library
student ought to take at least one course in networking.

CONCLUSION

This paper presents as directly as possible the way five influen-
tial people in Washington talk about NREN policy. Sometimes their
voices merge, such as on the call to librarians to design networking
tools, and the need for directories and reasonable fee rates. At other
times these voices seem to be coming from different worlds, such as
on the topic of network levels and the NII and on the topic of user
fees. These worlds, at times, can appear remote and isolated viewed
from a library reference desk not connected to the network.

The problems arising from the NREN policy debate in Washington are being constantly resolved by hard study and open discussion. But as the first problems fade into consensus, new problems
arise to take their place. This is how the NREN evolves, diverse
views meeting here and there to form just the beginnings of order in
this explosion of information-sharing that is growing rapidly in our
part of this planet.

That is the cause of the excitement about the NREN. By using the
network, and by discussing policy for the NREN, people from

hugely diverse points of view connect and find an uncommonly harmonious ground–helping each other understand and learn. NREN is a project for sharing something valuable–information. This sharing requires cooperation for a higher cause. But this cause, networking the planet, is going to cost someone a lot of money.

BIBLIOGRAPHY

Cooke, Eileen D., and Carol C. Henderson. "Technology Initiative." *ALA Washington Newsletter.* 26 Feb. 1993: 2.

Gore, Sen. Albert, Jr. "Viewpoint: HPCC Policy Champion Foresees Networked Nation." *Communications of the ACM.* November 1991: 15-16.

Henderson, Carol C. Personal interview. 24 Mar. 1993.

Hodson, James. *The National Research and Education Network (NREN): A Bibliography.* ERIC ED 344 564.

InterNIC. Product announcement. South Plainfield, NJ: AT&T Data Communications Services, 1993.

Lane, Elizabeth, and Craig Summerhill. *Internet Primer for Information Professionals: A Basic Guide to Internet Networking Technology.* Westport: Meckler, 1993.

Lippincott, Joan. Telephone interview. 1 Apr. 1993.

Lytel, David. Telephone interview. 8 Apr. 1993.

McClure, Charles R. et al. *The National Research and Education Network (NREN): Research and Policy Perspectives.* Norwood: Ablex, 1991.

The National Research and Education Network Program: A Report to Congress, Washington: Office of Science and Technology Policy, 1992.

Parkhurst, Carol A., ed. *Library Perspectives on NREN: The National Research and Education Network.* Chicago: Library and Information Technology Association, 1990.

Perspectives on the National Information Infrastructure: CSPP's Vision and Recommendations for Action. Videotape. Computer Systems Policy Project, 1993.

Peters, Paul Evans. "Networked Information Resources and Services: Next Steps." *Computers in Libraries.* Apr. 1992: 46-53.

Polly, Jean Armour. "NREN for ALL: Insurmountable Opportunity." *Library Journal.* 1 Feb. 1993: 38-41.

Proceedings of the NREN Workshop: Monterey, California. 16-18 September. Washington: Interuniversity Communications Council, 1992.

Report to the Office of Science and Technology Policy on Library and Information Services Roles in the National Research and Education Network. Washington: U.S. National Commission on Libraries and Information Science, 1992.

Testimony of Dr. A. Nico Habermann and Dr. Stephen S. Wolff. 12 Mar. 1992. Washington: Committee on Science, Space and Technology Sub-committee on Science, 1992.

VanBelleghem, Daniel. Personal interview. 23 Mar. 1993.

Weingarten, Fred. "Five Steps to NREN Enlightenment." *EDUCOM Review* 26 (Spring 1991): 26-29.

Wilson, David L. "Gigabits Aside, People Can't Seem to Agree on Best Use of Planned High-Speed Network." *Chronicle of Higher Education.* 15 Apr. 1992: A25.

Young, Peter. *Information Network Infrastructure Policy: Towards the Knowledge Community.* 23rd William A. Gillard Lecture. U.S. National Commission on Libraries and Information Science, 1992.

_____. Personal interview. 23 Mar. 1993.

APPENDIX

INTERVIEW QUESTIONS:

1. Current Projects
What NREN issues are you and your organization working on right now?

2. Users and Access
What is being done to make the network more user friendly?
What is happening to assure equal access to NREN?
Is it enough?
Is it too much?

3. Money
Do you think that the Federal Government has the obligation to require or fund access for poor and rural users?
Is there an expected fee range yet for the NREN?
Do you have concerns about fees in the future?

4. Privatization
What are the issues you see emerging from privatization of the NREN?

5. Libraries
How much influence are library organizations having on NREN policy decisions?
Why are they listening to us?
Can libraries survive with this network?
Will NREN help or harm an information democracy?
Can we afford this technology?

Evaluating Physical Science Reference Sources on the Internet

Susan S. Starr

SUMMARY. In the past few years numerous sources of interest to Physical Science reference librarians have become available on the Internet. This article classifies and reviews a representative sample of these sources and suggests criteria for evaluating the role of these new sources in a physical sciences reference setting. Although the focus of the article is on reference sources in the sciences, the evaluation criteria apply to other disciplines as well.

INTRODUCTION

Physical sciences librarians have always prided themselves on their ability to find reference information needed by their clientele, no matter how obscure or esoteric it might be. Phase diagrams of carbon dioxide and acetone, the viscosity of corn syrup, the cost of bulk stainless steel, or the latest articles on building bridges are all within their repertoire. Originally scientific reference sources were in printed formats; in the last fifteen years, with the growth of online services and CD-ROM databases, electronic sources of information have become familiar tools in the physical sciences library. Now, in 1993, the Internet brings a host of new possible

Susan S. Starr is Head, Science and Engineering Library, University of California, San Diego, 9500 Gilman Drive, La Jolla, CA 92093.

[Haworth co-indexing entry note]: "Evaluating Physical Science Reference Sources on the Internet." Starr, Susan S. Co-published simultaneously in *The Reference Librarian* (The Haworth Press, Inc.) No. 41/42, 1994, pp. 261-273; and: *Librarians on the Internet: Impact on Reference Services* (ed: Robin Kinder) The Haworth Press, Inc., 1994, pp. 261-273. Multiple copies of this article/chapter may be purchased from The Haworth Document Delivery Center [1-800-3-HAWORTH; 9:00 a.m. - 5:00 p.m. (EST)].

reference sources to us via the terminal or workstation on our desk. This article attempts to review the kinds of sources currently available to us on the Internet, and to suggest ways to evaluate their use in a physical sciences library. Although the focus of the article is physical sciences–chemistry, physics, mathematics, computer sciences, engineering–much of the content will be relevant to librarians in other disciplines as well.

What is a reference source? Traditionally, a reference work is defined as a work designed by its arrangement, treatment, or content to be consulted for bits of information rather than read in its entirety. Reference materials, meant to be consulted for short periods and for bits of information, are distinctive because of the way in which they are used when compared to most other library materials. Although some texts may find their way into a reference collection (medical libraries commonly include basic medical texts in their reference area, for example), most reference works are organized to provide quick access to either bibliographic or factual information.

Clearly, many of the sources of interest to scientists on the Internet do not meet this definition. Electronic books, government regulations, physics list servers, astronomy usenet groups and electronic journals are designed for "cover to cover" perusal rather than as sources of factual or bibliographic information. An awareness of these sources is important to the reference librarian in the same way as a knowledge of the strengths of other libraries' collections is important; a good reference librarian will want to refer users to the most appropriate source of information, regardless of format. Here, however, we will concentrate only on reference materials, seeking to answer the following questions:

- What kinds of physical science reference information is available through the Internet?
- How might we keep track of reference sources on the Internet?
- When should an Internet reference source be used?

KINDS OF INFORMATION SOURCES

Virtually every major type of printed information source normally found in a reference collection can also be located on the

Internet. Those discussed below were selected both to be representative of this variety and to illustrate the advantages and disadvantages of using the Internet in reference work (Internet addresses and login procedures for the sources below are listed in Table 1).

Bibliographies

Bibliographies on the Internet, like their printed counterparts, can be used for verification and identification or for finding material in a particular subject area. As with their printed counterparts, they vary in completeness; but unlike their printed counterparts, they are generally up-to-date and may even include not yet published material. The Buckyball Database offered by the University of Arizona Library on their online catalog (SABIO), for example, is a bibliography of background material and current citations on the topic of fullerenes and related chemical structures. The bibliography is regularly updated and contains citations to both published articles and those submitted for publication. The SABIO system uses the OPAC interface from Innovated Interface's Innopac, a menu driven system which permits searching by author, title, and keyword in title.

While the Buckyball Database is fairly easy to use, a somewhat more esoteric bibliography, maintained by the National Nuclear Data Center as part of their data service, is perhaps more typical of Internet science reference sources. Nuclear Structure References contains both bibliographic citations and keyword abstracts for publications in low and intermediate energy nuclear physics research from 1910 to the present. Access points for this file have clearly been designed with the scientist in mind; the bibliography can be searched by the nucleus for which the nuclear information is given, the target nucleus, the nuclear reaction, the author, or the nuclear physics topic. Because searching is done by means of multiple menus, it can be quite time consuming. Search topics can be saved for repeated use; still the content and structure of the file limit its appeal to a selected group of users.

TABLE 1. Internet Sources

Academe
Gopher: chronicle.merit.edu

American Mathematical Society's e-Math
Telnet: e-math.ams.com or
    130.44.1.100

Buckyball Database
Telnet: sabio.arizona.edu
Login: sabio
Select: Other databases and
    remote libraries
Select: Buckyball Database

Earthquake Information

Finger:
quake@geophys.washington.edu

Earth Observation Photography Database

Telnet: sseop.jsc.nasa.gov
Username: Photos
Password: Photos

Geographic Name Server

Telnet: 141.212.99.9

LANL Physics Information Service

Gopher: mentor.lanl.gov
select: index to . . . abstracts

Lunar and Planetary Gazetteer
Telnet: 1pi.jsc.nasa.gov
Username: 1pi
Select: Information and Research
Select: Reference files

NASA Extragalactic Database
Telnet: ned.ipac.caltech.edu
Login: ned

National Nuclear Data Center
Telnet: bn1nd2.dne.bnl.gov
Login: nndc
Password: guest

National Science Foundation Awards Abstracts

Gopher: stis.nsf.gov

Netlib

Mail: netlib@research.att.com
Contents of message: send
    index
Pinet

Telnet: pinet.aip.org
Login: new

Statlib

Mail: statlib@stat.cmu.edu
Contents of message: send
    index

Standards and Technology Information System

Telnet: nssdca.gsfc.nasa.gov
Username: nodis
Select: Standards and
    Technology Information
    System
Weather Underground

Telnet:
downwind.sprl.umich.edu 3000

Indexes and Abstracts

Indexes to the contents of scholarly periodicals are probably among the most frequently used tools in any physical sciences reference collection, and more and more often, these are searched online. Unfortunately, as every reference librarian is aware, online searching can be quite expensive. While the Internet does not usually offer free versions of the major online databases available from commercial vendors (although it is, of course, possible to connect to these vendors over the Internet), there are valuable indexing services at low or no cost available that can be very useful in a physical sciences reference collection.

The National Science Foundation maintains the Science and Technology Information System, an NSF gopher which provides, among other resources, access to NSF awards abstracts, from 1989 to date. The awards may be searched by any keyword, including words from the investigator's name, organization, from the grant title, or from the abstract. The file is very current, but unfortunately, Boolean and phrase searching are not currently supported. Using this file, one can find all the grants awarded by NSF to one's institution since 1989, all the grants in that period awarded to a particular author, or locations across the country doing research in a specific area. Some of the information available in this file is available in printed formats, but only the Internet file offers a wide variety of search points and access to such current information.

In some ways, NSF Awards Abstracts is atypical, for like bibliographies, most indexing sources available on the Internet tend to be designed for a specific audience and thus narrower in scope. The Standards and Technology Information System (same name as the NSF system above!) is available through the NASA Science Data Systems Standards Office (NOST). It indexes standards thought to be of interest to NOST users, including those from the computer industry relating to several programming languages such as Fortran and C and standards on magnetic media, data storage, and software applications. ANSI and 1SO standards, as well as standards from IEEE, JPL, and NIST may be found in this file. Standards may be searched by category, organization, or keyword; users retrieve the name of the standard, the issuing agency, an abstract and order information. An even more specialized example, the NASA Extragalactic Database (NED) is a computer based index of published extragalactic data and references covering objects outside the Milky Way. Objects can be searched by name, type, and location; citations include abstracts of published references.

There are also a few instances of more traditional periodical indexes on the Internet. The American Mathematical Society's e-MATH bulletin board provides for author searches of *Mathematical Reviews* from 1985 to date. PINET, a for-fee service from the American Institute of Physics, provides searches of SPIN: abstracts of journal articles and conference proceedings from AIP and AIP member societies. While both these sources partially duplicate commercial services, the search software is not as sophisticated as that found on DIALOG, STN, or the CD version of *Mathematical Reviews* (MathSci), making these sources inadequate substitutes for searches on their more expensive counterparts.

A relatively new kind of periodical index on the Internet are those that index preprints. The LANL Physics Information Service, for example, provides an index to abstracts of preprints in theoretical and high energy physics. The preprints database is maintained at the Los Alamos National Laboratory. Similar preprint databases are available for non-linear sciences, and the astronomy community is beginning to mount preprint files on the Internet as well. While the exact contents of these files vary, they generally include articles to be published, or just submitted for publication. This is an exciting development, since in the past access to preprints depended on being on the correct mailing list. Now these preprints will be publicly available on the Internet.

Handbooks, Manuals and Guides

In a physical science reference collection, handbooks, manuals and guides are essential sources, providing everything from the properties of various chemicals to statistical tables in mathematics. Sources of physical sciences data available over the Internet tend to be very focused, providing in-depth information to small user groups. The Lunar and Planetary Gazetteer is a good example. Available courtesy of the U.S. Geological Survey, the Gazetteer contains information on planetary surface features named and approved by the International Astronomical Union (IAU). Using SearchMagic software, users may loook for items by type, planet name, satellite on which the feature is found, latitude, longitude, etc. This is an excellent source of data for a limited class of inquiries.

Data sources aimed at more general audiences may be peripherally useful in the physical sciences collection. Up-to-date weather and the latest earthquake information is available from the Weather Underground at the University of Michigan. An additional listing of recent earthquakes can be obtained from the National Earthquake Information Center. A useful source for any reference collection is the Geographic Name Server, which allows the user to find any town or city in the United States by name or zipcode and provides population, elevation, latitude and longitude and other data typical of a gazeteer.

A quite different kind of data, job openings, is particularly well represented on the Internet. Both the American Mathematical Society's e-MATH bulletin board, and PINET, from the American Institute of Physics, provide listings of job openings in their fields, while Academe, the *Chronicle of Higher Education's* online service, provides listings from the entire *Chronicle*.

Directories

Two types of physical sciences directories are to be found currently on the Internet, membership directories and "buyer's guides." The first category is best represented by the listings of members on association bulletin boards, such as the AMS e-MATH and Pinet. As with many of the Internet sources mentioned above, the main advantage these sources have over their paper equivalents, is currency. Frequently these sources also allow searches by location; it is possible, for example, to find all AMS members in Peoria, Illinois. More interesting are the "buyer's guides" which list sources of items sought by researchers. By connecting to the Earth Observation Photography Database, users can search for photographs taken during different space shuttle missions; once located they can be ordered from the EROS Data Center or the Technology Applications Center at the University of New Mexico. A quite different set of "buyer's guides" not only locates but actually distributes software to users. Netlib distributes mathematical software in the public domain, including algorithms from the ACM, via electronic mail. Much of it is written in Fortran. Statlib offers a similar service for statistical software. For the user in any of these areas, the Internet is invaluable, providing both listings of software and code in machine readable form at the same time.

TRACKING INTERNET SOURCES

The sources listed above are but a small sample of what can be found on the Internet; tracking Internet reference sources can be a full-time occupation in and of itself. The number of sources keeps growing, as do the tools to find them. A discussion of all the ways to discover information on the Internet is beyond the scope of this paper. In the case of reference sources, however, there are several guides which may be useful:

1. Scott Yanoff, at the University of Washington, maintains a list of Internet sites, including many of interest to physical sciences librarians. To receive a copy of the list, ftp to csd4.csd.uwm.edu, login as anonymous, and locate the file in the Subdirectory pub. The file name is inet.services.txt. The file is updated frequently and contains names, brief descriptions and addresses for a variety of reference sources.

2. Hytelnet is a memory resident listing of Internet resources, including library catalogs. To try the program, telnet to access.usask.ca and login as hytelnet. PC, Unix and VMS versions to mount on your local system are available at this site as well. One of the best ways to stay abreast of new entries on the Internet is to subscribe to the Hytelnet Listserver (send your subscription request to LIST-SERV@KENTVM.BITNET; the contents of message should read Subscribe HYTEL-L [your name]). New sources will appear regularly in your e-mail "mailbox." You can add them to your own copy of Hytelnet or merely file them for future reference.

3. SURAnet Guide to Selected Sources. SURAnet maintains an extensive guide to the Internet, including science sites as well as "how to" instructions for the novice Internet user. To receive the guide, ftp to ftp.sura.net, login as anonymous, and locate the file in the subdirectory pub/nic. The file is named infoguide[version][year].

CHOOSING INTERNET SOURCES

If keeping track of science reference sources on the Internet is difficult, selecting which sources to use is even more problematic. In our excitement over the many new free sources which the Internet has provided, we have sometimes overlooked the obvious; not all sources on the Internet are worth having. Once a librarian locates a printed or CD-ROM reference source of potential value, the next step is normally to determine if it should be added to the reference collection. Generally this calls for an extensive evaluation of the reference source, in part because reference books or CD-ROMs are frequently among the more expensive of library materials. Similarly, once a librarian locates an Internet source, the question becomes, should this source be used to answer reference inquiries? Is this a useful source to add to the other sources already available?

Even though Internet sources may be free, there are several pressing reasons to evaluate them. First, because of the large number of sources on the Internet, it is impractical for the reference librarian to try and remember all of them. Facilities like Hytelnet and campus wide information systems help, but when faced with a reference question, the librarian wants to locate the needed source fairly quickly. That means having determined in advance the utility of the source and noted its location for future reference. Second, if a source overlaps a paper reference source, the librarian must determine whether the paper source should be retained. Such a decision requires an evaluation of the Internet source and comparison to its paper "equivalent." Finally, although there may be no charge for using an Internet source, using it successfully may require an investment of time and energy which are themselves costly.

EVALUATION

What criteria should be used to evaluate sources on the Internet? Katz, in *Introduction to Reference Sources*,[1] lists six criteria which reference librarians should use in evaluating a reference work. One is cost. The others are purpose, authority, scope, audience, and format. These criteria can be used to evaluate Internet sources as well as more traditional reference books, although it may take more effort to apply them to Internet sources than to printed materials.

Purpose

Purpose refers to the intended coverage of the work. In a paper tool, the purpose should be evident from the table of contents, the preface, or the index. On the Internet it is often far more difficult to determine for what purpose a source was designed. Often the introductory screens or help messages will make the purpose clear. For example, the information screen for the Buckyball Database states it is "a bibliography of background material and current citations on the topic of fullerenes and related chemical structures." On the other hand, the Earth Observation Photography Database says it "contains information about photos of the earth taken from space during the Mercury, Gemini, . . . and Shuttle Missions." The reader might easily be misled into thinking that there was actual information about features in the file, when, in fact, it is a tool for locating photos. Even more difficult to evaluate are systems designed originally for in house use and now made available to the Internet community. The NOST Standards and Technology Information System, for example, contains no text which describe its coverage either in the file or in the paper users guide. The purpose of an Internet tool is an essential factor in determining its utility for answering reference inquiries, but it usually requires exploring it thoroughly and may often also involve follow up contact with the information providers.

Authority

Authority refers to the qualifications of the author and to the sources of information used. Many Internet sources are maintained directly by associations or government bodies well known in the scientific community, so that their authority is not questioned. However, as the Internet grows we can expect that lesser known organizations will begin to add sources and that this question will become more relevant.

Scope

Katz[2] states, "the first question of major importance in selecting a reference work is, Will this book be a real addition to our collection and, if so, what exactly will it add?" While Katz lists several points to consider when evaluating scope, breadth of coverage and currency are the two major criteria to apply for Internet sources. In most cases, as we have seen, Internet sources are very narrow in scope. They tend to be much more focused than anything that would be published as a reference work. The NASA Extragalactic Database is a very specific source indeed, and of interest to only selected researchers. For an astronomy library, its scope may make it an important resource; for general collections, referral to an astronomy library or use of an astronomy index may be more practical than remembering this distinctive database. Reference librarians often hesitate to purchase very focused printed reference tools, in part because they tend to be overlooked in a reference collection. By the same token, a very narrowly focused Internet source may be so rarely used that it is more efficient to rely on general sources and make a telephone call to a subject specialist when more detailed information is required.

On the other hand, as we have seen, many Internet physical science reference sources are very current. Frequently they are far more more current than their printed counterparts. This is especially true of bibliographies and handbooks, since publishers rarely issue these materials on an annual basis. The Internet can even be used to find information which changes daily and/or hourly, such as the weather or earthquakes. While breadth of coverage may limit the usefulness of some Internet science reference sources, currency of information can make others invaluable.

Audience

Audience is an essential factor in evaluating any reference source but can be difficult to determine when evaluating those on the Internet. Is this material designed to be used by a general reader? a subject specialist? a scientist? The reference librarian can usually determine the intended audience of a paper source by reviewing the terminology used and the depth of the subject matter. On the Internet, many science sources are designed for a narrow scientific specialty, and it can be difficult to even determine the terminology and depth without an advanced degree! For example, to review the content of the Nuclear Structure Reference bibliography, one must be able to come up with a query in technical terminology. Fortunately, because many sources on the Internet can be searched by author, the librarian can frequently obtain an overview of the content of the material by searching for references authored by common names such as Smith and Jones. Using this technique, it should be possible to determine if an Internet reference tool is actually suitable for use by the library's clientele or if it is better conceived as a source for the research scientist.

Format

Format is the last of Katz'[3] criteria, and a major one to apply in evaluating Internet sources. The ideal reference source is easy to use, but few Internet sources come close to meeting this ideal. In printed reference sources, the reference librarian looks for alphabetical arrangement of material or, if a classification method is used, a consistent and logical one should be employed. In end user online sources, such as those on the Internet, one looks for straightforward menus and easy directions to the novice user. Since Internet sources, as we have seen, tend to be narrow in scope, an easy-to-use format is essential; even the experienced reference librarian is unlikely to use any physical sciences Internet tool on a daily basis. Some Internet sources take advantage of the power of online retrieval to make access far simpler than in paper; a good example would be searching for AMS members on the AMS e-Math Bulletin Board. The user is prompted to "fill in the blanks" to retrieve individuals by name, location, specialty, etc. On the other hand, the Lunar and Planetary Gazeteer uses Search Magic software which is far from intuitive to the average user. The impatient reference librarian may easily conclude that an initial search in more standard reference sources would be better than pursuing this highly specialized file.

Katz concludes his discussion of the evaluation of reference sources with the admonition, "Trust no one."[4] The librarian, he says, must carefully evaluate every reference tool, even from the most reputable publisher. A better maxim for those considering the use of Internet reference sources might be, "There is no such thing as a free lunch." Or, perhaps, "You get what you pay for." Out on the Internet there are bibliographies, indexes, directories, and handbooks available free for use in physical science libraries. Unfortunately, few of these Internet reference sources meet the standards for purpose, authority, audience, scope and format that are normally applied to in print reference tools. It remains the task of the reference librarian to determine if the quality of an Internet reference tool is sufficient to warrant its use in answering reference inquiries.

CONCLUSION

The Internet has clearly enriched our physical sciences reference collections. Virtually all the major kinds of reference sources available in our collections, bibliographies, handbooks, indexes, have counterparts on the Internet. We now have access to sources of scientific data, indexes, bibliographies, job listings, etc., which will make our lives easier as well as those of our users. We also have access to generalized sources on the weather, earthquakes and the like which can broaden the scope of our collections. However, making the most of this access is a time consuming endeavor. Not only must we track the sources on the Internet, but we bear the same responsiblity for evaluating them as we do for any reference source. The Internet has made our jobs easier in some ways, but has created new workloads for us in others.

REFERENCES

1. Katz, William A. *Introduction to Reference Work.* 6th Edition. New York: McGraw-Hill, Inc. 1989.
2. Ibid.
3. Ibid.
4. Ibid.

Developing a Campus-Wide Information System Using the Gopher Protocol: A Study of Collection Development and Classification Issues

Peggy Seiden
Karen A. Nuckolls

SUMMARY. This paper discusses issues relating to the organization of a campus wide information system which is based upon the Gopher protocol. In an effort to develop guidelines for both collection development and classification of Gopher resources, the Library

Peggy Seiden is Associate Professor and College Librarian, Skidmore College, Saratoga Springs, NY 12866. She is Co-Chair of the Coalition for Networked Information's Working Group on Directories and Information Resource Services. Karen A. Nuckolls is Associate Professor and Head of Technical Services, Skidmore College, Saratoga Springs, NY 12866.

[Haworth co-indexing entry note]: "Developing a Campus-Wide Information System Using the Gopher Portocol: A Study of Collection Development and Classification Issues." Seiden, Peggy, and Karen A. Nuckolls. Co-published simultaneously in *The Reference Librarian* (The Haworth Press, Inc.) No. 41/42, 1994, pp. 275-296; and: *Librarians on the Internet: Impact on Reference Services* (ed: Robin Kinder) The Haworth Press, Inc., 1994, pp. 275-296. Multiple copies of this article/chapter may be purchased from The Haworth Document Delivery Center [1-800-3-HAWORTH; 9:00 a.m. - 5:00 p.m. (EST)].

275

undertook a study of, what is popularly known as, Gopherspace. The results of that study provide an overview of various Gopher models and their purpose, the types of resources typically found on campus wide information systems which use the Gophor protocol, and the ways in which Gophers are organized. The paper concludes with recommendations for the development of coherent collection development policies and organizational schemas which reflect the primary user community's needs and interests.

INTRODUCTION

This paper discusses issues relating to the organization of a campus wide information system which is based upon the Gopher protocol. During Spring 1993, Skidmore undertook development of a Campus Wide Information System (CWlS) utilizing the Gopher protocol. The development effort was a joint initiative of the Computing Center and the Library. While the former handled the technical implementation, the latter served as designer of the system. As designer, a natural extension of the Library's role as campus information provider, the Library focused on both collection development issues (what should be included in the Gopher) and cataloging/classification issues (how should the Skidmore Gopher be organized).

In an effort to develop guidelines for both collection development and classification of Gopher resources, the Library undertook a study of, what is popularly known as, Gopherspace. This paper presents the results of that study and recommendations for guidelines for developing Campus Wide information Systems using the Gopher protocol.

WHAT IS GOPHER AND WHAT IS GOPHERSPACE?

As Ed Krol noted in *The Whole Internet.* "Gopher is a lot harder to talk about than to use."[1] The developers of Gopher define it as "software following a simple protocol for burrowing through a TCP/IP Internet."[2] Gopher provides a way of navigating or browsing through resources on the Internet using hierarchical menus. Once a

user locates a resource, Gopher allows her/him to access it or retrieve it without having to know the particular address or file
transfer commands.

Gopher was originally developed at the University of Minnesota
in 1991 as a distributed campus information system. As a client/
server protocol, it permits the client through a single interface to
access multiple distributed servers located at sites remote from the
client. At the University of Minnesota, Gopher was used to access
information on various departmental computers, but because Gopher is based on TCP/IP the information servers it accesses need not
be limited by physical geography, but only by network geography.

Gopher has quickly grown to become one of the primary navigational tools for searching and retrieving information over the Internet.[3] Gopher is not only able to retrieve information from disparate computers, but Gopher clients can access and retrieve, search[4] or
connect to resources in a number of different formats such as individual files, FTP archives, telnet sites, phone numbers from white
pages servers, and gateways to other services such as WAIS databases, World Wide Web, Archie servers, X.500 databases or other
directory servers. To the user it appears as if all of these resources are
available locally, but the pathway that a user follows to a resource
may, in reality, take him/her through several physical locations.

The developers of Gopher modeled the interface on a file system
which presents documents and services arranged in a hierarchy of
items and directories. The user can proceed through levels of the
hierarchy by selecting menu items. Although the primary means for
moving in Gopherspace are through browsing menus, users may
also do keyword searching of Gopherspace using Veronica (Very
Easy Rodent Oriented Netwide Index to Computerized Archives) or
search a single Gopher using Jughead which indexes the local Gopher.

A user may access the Gopher system through a Macintosh, PC,
VMS, Unix, X-windows or other terminal client. The client connects to a "root" Gopher server as the main entry point into the
Gopher system. Once the connection is established the root server
sends back a listing of objects in its top level or root directory. Each
object in the directory has associated with it a number of data
elements which allow the client to identify, locate, and retrieve the

object. These data elements include a name which is displayed to the user, an item type, a unique "selector string" (similar to a pathname) to retrieve the object from the server on which it resides, a server hostname and a port.

Gopher in many ways is a victim of its own success. It was never designed as a solution to locating all network information resources, but as the Internet community awaits the development of other resource discovery tools like Knowbots or distributed catalogs, it has become the ad hoc solution. One reason that Gopher is so successful is that it serves two purposes: as an electronic publication and distribution system for local information and as a way of searching and retrieving other electronic publications.

Because Gopher was and is a grass root effort and it was not intended as an Internet resource guide, there are few guidelines for developing Gophers and no overall organization to Gopherspace. The success a user has with Gopher is generally due to serendipity–while browsing through Gopherspace s/he happens upon a particularly useful item–rather than any systematic way of searching and locating specific resources. Additionally, since Gophers are often primarily local systems, there are no standards of organization from Gopher to Gopher, nor are there standard naming conventions.

At the start of this study, in April 1993, there were some 460 Gophers registered with the root of all Gophers at the University of Minnesota. At the conclusion of the study there were an additional 60 Gophers, a growth of almost 14% in two months. With the growth in the number and depth of the servers, navigating Gopherspace in search of information can be overwhelming. The analysis of Gopherspace and the resultant guidelines for building and organizing Gophers are intended to create a friendlier Gopherspace for all who play therein.

RESEARCH METHODOLOGY

The purpose of the study was to investigate how Gophers are organized and to develop a scheme for organizing Skidmore's Gopher. It was decided that a random sample of known Gophers would form the core of the research study. All known Gophers are listed in "The World" Gopher directory from the University of Minnesota.

At the time the study was begun, there were approximately 460 Gophers listed in this directory. These include Gophers from every continent, except Antarctica, listed in alphabetical order by Gopher name. The study team decided to take a 10% random sample of the World. in addition, the study included notable Gophers, including the ten most popular Gophers, all known Gophers which had some subject organization schema, Gophers to which the team was referred, and many "librarybased" Gophers. In total, the research encompassed nearly 100 Gophers.

The study was designed to answer a number of specific questions on arrangement and selection of resources. The study team wanted to find out the following:

- What types of Gophers exist and for what purpose are Gophers being used?
- What types of local resources are included in Campus Wide Information Systems?
- What types of external resources appear on CWlS Gophers?
- How individual Gophers are organized:
  - What are the most effective arrangements for Campus Wide Information Systems and, in particular, how is locally generated information arranged?
  - What are the most effective schemes for organizing network accessible (external) resources?
- What are the best subject tree arrangements and is one suitable for Skidmore?
- Within a particular Gopher, how much redundancy or see also references are needed?
- How does one arrive at useful names for menu items?

In analyzing each Gopher, the study team tried to limit their investigation to the top levels of each Gopher. It was assumed that the root Gopher in each instance was the critical organizational element, however, in many cases, it was necessary to go four or five levels down in the hierarchy in order to fully understand the organization of a particular Gopher. The general procedure was to go through each item in the root menu and follow the hierarchy down as far as necessary, then go onto the next item in the root menu, etc.

The study group did not investigate any menu items which were clearly external resources, except to note the existence of such items. Each menu was printed so that it would be easier to do cross comparisons. The study group then analyzed the Gophers for resource type and organization.

REVIEW OF THE LITERATURE

There is very little on Gopher in printed publications. A bibliography of various print sources on Gopher is available on the *Gopher-FAQ* or Frequently Asked Questions. A number of Internet user guides include chapters on Gopher. The best of this genre is Ed Krol's *The Whole Internet Users Guide and Catalog*. The chapter, "Tunneling through the Internet: Gopher" describes how to locate a Gopher client for your desktop computer, how Gopher works, and guides the user through using Gopher to look at text files, white pages servers, telnet sources, and FTP. But the rapid growth of Gopher precludes the usefulness of print resources.

The journal literature is even more spartan. A recent article in the *Chronicle of Higher Education* highlighted some of the developments in navigational tools, but most of the other journal articles located during the research were nearly a year old.

The most current and the best sources of information are electronic. Basic information describing Gopher and its features is available using the above mentioned *Gopher-FAQ*. The *Gopher-FAQ* is posted every two weeks and contains about twenty-five questions covering topics like: what is Gopher, how one accesses Gopher, how one adds information to Gopher, as well as more specific questions related to perceived bugs in searching or problems with specific hardware. For technical specifications the most authoritative source is the recently released draft RFC (Request for Comments) on the Gopher protocol.

The best sources for any in-depth discussion of Gopher are the various Gopher discussion groups and mailing lists, *alt.gopher, comp.info.gopher (alt.gopher's* successor*), gopher-news@boombox.micro.umn.edu* and *eurogopher@ebone.net.* Using Gopher's search capabilities, these archives can easily be scanned for information on particular topics of interest.

There was minimal information available concerning the particular focus of this article. There was some discussion of subject classification schemes on the *eurogopher* newsgroup and on *comp.info.gopher*. In the minutes of GopherCon93 which were posted to *gopher-news*, there was a summary of reports given, including a description of the track on resource location and subject classification.

GOPHER MODELS

The Study Team was able to identify the following five models. Their characteristics are described below.

Campus Wide Information Systems (CWIS)

CWIS Gophers serve as mechanisms for distributing college or university academic and administrative information. The responsibility for development of a CWIS usually falls to the Computer Center and many Gophers reflect this origin by including a great deal of computing and networking information. Although there are CWIS which do not use the Gopher protocol, Gopher allowed the scope of the CWIS to expand to include resources from other Gophers at other sites which would be useful to their user community. Examples of well developed CWIS models are Brown University, University of California Santa Cruz's Infoslug and Cornell's CUINFO.

Departmental Information System

These Gophers serve a purpose similar to the CWIS, but are limited in scope. Some departmental information systems are academic (ex., McGill University's MAC Gopher) while others originate from the Computing Center or the Library. The local resources provided by these Gophers relate directly to the function of the Department (e.g., a Computer Center may distribute documentation in this way) and often include selected pointers to highly relevant external resources.

Subject Gophers

These Gophers are discussed in greater depth below. Those which focus on a single subject are sometimes a university departmental Gopher (University of Texas, Health Science Center, Houston or University of California, Santa Barbara Geological Sciences Gopher). Others which try to be more comprehensive are types of virtual libraries (North Carolina State University's Virtual Library).

Non-Academic Institutional Gophers

There are a wide variety of non-academic Gophers. The primary purpose of these Gophers is to serve as an electronic publisher and document delivery server for information which these institutions want to disseminate to the broader Internet community. Many Network Information Centers (NICs) including the InterNIC use Gophers to reach their user community. Other non-academic Gophers originate from corporations (Apple's Higher Education Gopher or O'Reilly publishers), associations (CREN's Gopher), museums (The UC Berkeley Museum of Paleontology), and from state and the national government (National institutes of Health Gopher, National Science Foundation Gopher). These Gophers are often well designed because of their limited scope.

Single Publications

The *Chronicle of Higher Education's* Academe is an example of a very narrowly focused Gopher. As authors and publishers discover Gopher's potential as a publication medium, this type of Gopher will probably grow in number.

SURVEY OF GOPHER COLLECTIONS FOUND IN CAMPUS WIDE INFORMATION SYSTEMS

Most Gopher collections contain both internally developed sources and sources borrowed from other Gophers. Internally developed sources on campus wide information systems include a wide variety of information. In the analysis of campus wide information systems using the Gopher protocol, the study team found typically the following types of information:

- information about teaching and research including descriptions of academic departments, notes about courses, requirements for majors, registration information, grants and other funding opportunities
- descriptions of administrative services such as health services, food services, security
- library and computer center resources including connections to the catalog, bibliographies and user guides, policies, newsletters
- committees and other campus organizations
- student life and activities including study abroad, campus organizations, health related information, residence related information
- policies and regulations including electronically published student and faculty handbooks
- events and schedules including athletic and cultural events, lectures and seminars, exam schedules, academic and administrative calendars
- phone books and directories
- campus newspapers or other news publications

Under Library information in most Gophers, one can find not only local information but other Internet resources. Examples of local information included under library categories are the library catalog, lists of local and remotely accessible databases, indexes and abstracts; scheduled instruction; library guides; library hours; new book lists; periodical lists; interlibrary loan information; and library newsletters. Less frequently one finds things like archives and special collections (University of Iowa); guides to subject specialists (University of Guelph); and bibliographic citation samples (University of Southern Florida).

Library menus frequently cite other resources available at remote sites. Typically these include electronic reference works such as dictionaries and thesauri; electronic journals, newspapers, magazines, and newsletters; on-line books such as those from Project Gutenberg; and, of course, other library catalogs. A few libraries have also taken responsibility for creating virtual or electronic libraries of discipline specific materials. These Gophers are described in more detail below under subject Gophers.

Although the Library usually creates links to other Internet resources, most root Gopher menus include some link to other Gophers or to specific Internet resources. The study team tabulated some of the most frequently referred to Internet Resources. In addition to the sources noted above, some of the most popular are the *Chronicle of Higher Education's* "Academe" (a digest of the weekly printed issue); governmental information including White House and Congressional news and documents, Supreme Court rulings and census data; geographical, environmental and meteorological sources such as the weather, earthquake information, the geographic name server and *CIA World Fact Book*; weather; news (feeds from a commercial service like Clarinet); computing and network information such as FAQ's and RFCs, FTP archives (especially software archives); newsgroups and listservs; various e-mail and telephone directory services; gateways to other information services like WAIS databases or the World Wide Web.

The choice of external resources, like the choice of internal resources often reflects the scope and purpose of the Gopher, although, in many cases, there does not appear to be any focused collection policy behind the selection of items. Clearly some items appear on menus simply because of their uniqueness or entertainment value. It hardly seems likely that many Gopher users plan trips to areas which are considered potentially dangerous by the State Department, but the State Department Travel Advisories were among the most popular of the Gopher resources.

ORGANIZATION OF GOPHERSPACE

Gopherspace, as a whole, is arranged geographically. For example, users can choose to search all Gophers in the world, or particular regions of the world. Countries are listed under regions; the United States is also arranged by state. Special purpose Gophers are also listed separately under General. Within a specific category (e.g., the World or New York) individual Gophers are arranged alphabetically. For the user who wants to begin to explore Gopherspace, but hasn't a clue where to start, there is a list of the most popular Gophers. From this top level there is no easy way to locate Gophers that are either dedicated to a single topic or contain significant resources in a subject area, except by using Veronica. If one can locate a Gopher which uses a subject tree, one can often link to other Gophers or Internet resources on the subject and burrow through hypertext like links.

ORGANIZATION OF INDIVIDUAL GOPHERS

The organization of individual Gophers is no less problematic. Sometimes there seems to be no more of an organizing principle beyond getting as much information as possible into the top level of the hierarchy. The problems of organizing Gophers must be looked at from two perspectives: there are issues related to organizing local resources and there are issues related to organizing all Gopher accessible information in the world, or at least that portion which users will find most relevant. The first problem is akin to arranging a useful student handbook in electronic format. The second problem is akin to arranging a library, a small, but widely distributed library. In analyzing the arrangement of these two types of information, the study team looked at the overall organization of the Gopher, the design of the root menu, and issues related to naming of menu items.

Campus wide information systems have several basic organizational schemes used at the root menu. Information is often arranged by traditional college divisions–the academic, the administrative and the student, or by status of the user (faculty, student and staff) or some combination. The University of California Santa Cruz's Gopher uses the physical campus as a model for its root menu. Menu items include the Classroom, the Computer Center, the Library, the Student Center, the Campus, the Community and the World. Another type of scheme that is used frequently is to arrange information by broad categories such as campus organizations (departments, societies), directories, news or events, and policies and regulations.

Despite the fact that any Gopher hierarchy can be infinitely deep, few Gophers have hierarchies of local information more than four or five layers. Deeper hierarchies allow for shorter individual menus, but a user can easily forget where s/he is in the hierarchy; shallower hierarchies often mean that information is difficult to find on a particular menu. Brown and Cornell are examples of these two different approaches. In Brown's, CWIS menus are kept very brief, but the CWIS uses many subdirectories for organizing information necessitating the user to negotiate through many levels to get to a specific resource. Cornell, on the other hand, uses basically two main levels, but the second level has very large menus wherein the information is only arranged alphabetically.

The key to an easily navigable Gopher is the design of the root or top level menu. Almost all root menus begin with an item which explains the purpose of the Gopher. Sometimes there is information explaining all menu items and information explaining the Gopher protocol. The root menus tend to be very short, frequently including little beyond five or six entries. The default arrangement for all Gopher menus is alphabetical, though non-alphabetic sequences are becoming more common. Non-alphabetic arrangements of root menus may place local information first followed by links to the larger networked world (see Bar-Ilan, Israel), or they may be arranged in some sort of priority order. A root Gopher can also point to other campus Gophers (see McGill, University of Toronto and University of California, Santa Barbara) and serve as a single point for shared information about the university as a whole.

Because a menu-based organization scheme only provides a single access point to a piece of information, many Gophers use redundancy as a type of 'see also' reference. For example, in Cornell's CWIS the academic and administrative calendar is listed under Academic Life, Administration, and Student Life.

One of the most problematic aspects of Gopher organization is the naming of menu items. It is not unusual to find items called "Information" or "Computer Stuff." Some Gophers use a format similar to DOS file names. Gopher allows up to 70 characters in any name, but there is a tendency to create cute but uninformative names. While cryptic names promote exploration, they are increasingly frustrating as an impediment to effective and rapid Gopher navigation. A user should easily be able to determine whether or not a particular menu item is deemed useful. Cleveland State University's Gopher is one example of a better designed interface. It uses single word entries followed by a lengthier explanation (ex., Activities . . . Activities at and around CSU).

THE ORGANIZATION
OF GOPHER ACCESSIBLE NETWORK RESOURCES

Gopher links to other Gophers and network resources are implemented in a variety of ways.[5] Some Gophers may only have a single menu item listed as "Other Gophers and Information Servers." But many Gophers not only point to the "World," but provide listings of specific resources. These listings may be home grown or they may be borrowed from other Gophers. In most cases there will be a single menu item, variously designated as "Internet Resources," "Internet Grab Bag," "Interesting Things I Found on the Internet," "Around the World," "Electronic Information Services," "General Information Services," or "Distributed Information Resources."

This directory of "interesting things" may be a single alphabetical listing. References to other Gophers may include a separate listing for those in the same geographical area. In some cases pointers to external resources may be divided at the root menu according to the type of resource: telnet sites, files and FTP archives, library catalogs, and directories being the most common categories. Mount Holyoke uses the term Document Library to denote files and archives and Internet Services to denote telnet sites. Such headings can be rather confusing to the casual user. Approaches which organize information by format are not unfamiliar to librarians; however, without subject access, such arrangements can quickly become cumbersome.

GOPHER SUBJECT TREES AND SUBJECT GOPHERS

In *The Whole Internet*, Ed Krol laments the fact that the Gopher developers "did not hire highly trained librarians. There's no standard subject list, like the Library of Congress Subject Headings, used on Gophers to organize things. The people who maintain each server took their best shot at organizing the world, or at least their piece of it."[6]

Since Krol wrote those words, there have been some significant attempts to organize Gopher accessible network resources into subject categories. The study team identified approximately twenty-five Gophers which used some type of subject classification arrangement to organize network resources. The Yale University Gopher is attempting to keep track of all efforts to create subject Gophers, although a few are missing from their list.[7] The subject gophers fall into several categories:

- Gophers which attempt to develop general subject trees for all types of information. Some of these Gophers seek to be comprehensive—a national or world bibliography model (ex., Sunet, NYSERNet and Rice). Others seem to be more selective, perhaps targeting resources that are more useful to their immediate community—a local library model (ex., North Carolina State University's Discipline Specific Study Carrels or Michigan's M-Link).

- Gophers which use subject schemes to organize one type of resource. For example, Georgetown's Center for Electronic Text uses a discipline and language scheme to organize its catalog of texts. CICnet has developed a Gopher for electronic journals arranged according to the Library of Congress classification system, and Project Gutenberg (a project to publish e-text versions of major works in the public domain) uses the same scheme to arrange its catalog of books.

- Gophers which only tackle a single subject area, but use very refined subject headings—the index/abstract model. Two such Gophers appear on the Yale list, the Environmental Internet Catalog and the Global Biological Information Servers, but there are numerous law and biomedical focused Gophers, and the University of Texas, El Paso's Department of Geological Sciences has taken responsibility for developing one for geology.

There is no uniform approach to organizing subjects that has been endorsed or adopted by those doing subject Gophers. During Fall 1992, there was extensive discussion on the *eurogopher* mailing list about the best way to arrange subject Gophers.[8] Despite the heated discussion concerning the best subject classification scheme for the Swedish University Network subject tree Gopher, the classification system that was eventually adopted was not a standard system, but one which was developed by those responsible for building the tree. The majority of subject gophers also use in-house classification schemes which rarely include all areas of knowledge. Since subject based Gophers are often run by experts in the field, the organization reflects the user community. Often the process of setting up a subject based Gopher is an iterative process.[9]

Only NYSERNet which uses the Dewey Decimal Classification System and the Australian National University, CICnet and Project Gutenberg which each use the Library of Congress Classification System, use anything approximating a standard classification scheme. Craig Summerhill noted that no single hierarchy will meet everyone's satisfaction and librarians certainly are familiar enough with anomalies in the classification systems we use. In an effort to test the feasibility of a standard classification system, the University of Michigan School of Information and Library Studies is conducting research into the suitability of using Dewey Decimal or Library of Congress classification schedules for designing Gopher Trees.[10]

In most cases, the subject classification scheme is only one hierarchy level deep. In other words, one doesn't typically find Literature broken down into periods or genres or any further subdivision found in most classification schemes. Nevertheless, the subject classes tend to be very broad–equivalent to major areas of knowledge like the Social Sciences or Arts. Most subject lists were able to fit onto a single screen or two, at the most. The largest list of subject headings is found in Texas A&M's Gopher which has 42 subject categories at its top level. Rice's subject tree which is compiled by merging eight other subject Gophers, including Texas A&M's, North Carolina State's and the University of Nevada, Reno's Gopher, has 31 disciplines.

The choice of subject headings in most of the major subject trees also tends to be locally determined. The lack of standardization means that resources relating to the academic discipline of Computer Science may be found under Computing on one Gopher and Computer Science on another Gopher. Nevertheless, despite these problems, the development of these Gophers is a significant step towards creating easier pathways for users looking for discipline-specific resources.

GUIDELINES FOR DEVELOPING
A CAMPUS WIDE INFORMATION SYSTEM

Collection Development

The first decision which any Gopher developer needs to arrive at is the purpose and scope of the Gopher. In the case of a Campus Wide Information System, one needs to determine whether or not the Gopher will include only local information or if the Gopher will also serve as an "electronic library."

At Skidmore, the development team viewed Gopher as an opportunity to easily bring teaching faculty to a certain level of "network literacy." If key resources which would appeal to the faculty researcher were included in the local Gopher, this would obviate the need for the user to spend hours combing through other Gophers for relevant information. Since few faculty have those hours to spend, they tend not to want to venture onto the network at all. The choice to include selected external resources was a choice to remove a barrier to the use of the network.

Local Information

Campus wide information systems closely resemble Information and Referral Files or Community Information sources found in public libraries. They are basically in-house publication systems which not only publish, but organize local information for easy retrieval. In some cases campus wide information systems provide something as informal as a bulletin board listing items for sale or houses for rent or items as formal as faculty handbooks. In between there are many other types of information resources which include computing policies, library pathfinders, course schedules, campus events. The problem is that not all of these resources are easily gettable in electronic format and no single Gopher administrator has the time or opportunity to digitize this information. If the campus culture is already more or less on-line, then developing an on-line information distribution system will be easier than if the culture is paper bound.

Often collection development decisions are driven by what information is readily accessible in electronic format, rather than by specific policy decisions. Getting information is, in part, a problem of getting those who generate the information and the campus administration, in particular, onboard. If the culture does not support this type of information system, it will not only be difficult to build, but it will be impossible to maintain. It is for this reason that one finds many campus wide information systems containing more Computing Center information than anything else, and why there are so many place holders or empty files in CWIS.

The Electronic Reading Room

Although it is time intensive and often frustrating to piece together the local information, the collection development issues are minimal. However, if the Gopher is to be used as a digital library of information resources, collection development policy is very significant. The first question which needs to be addressed is whether or not one needs to create one's own list of external resources, or whether there is already a list which can be adapted. Rice University's subject tree is built using a PERL script which checks other subject trees once a week and merges the trees together. Skidmore has chosen a more selective approach and is creating its own subject tree.

However, this approach again raises a problem concerning who is responsible for updating the external resources. One model, which Skidmore hopes to implement, is to charge subject liaison librarians with the responsibility for "collecting" resources. For those developing new Gophers a certain amount of retrospective collection development needs to take place. This can best be done by combing some of the more comprehensive subject Gophers listed above. To keep current, there are several sources of new Internet Resources. The InterNIC InfoScout's *net-resources* mailing list,[11] a project of the InterNIC, is probably the best one stop source for new resources. By subscribing to this mailing list, a person receives announcements of new resources on a daily basis.

Another question which needs to be addressed, is what constitutes a resource. Should the Gopher point only to other Gophers and collections of information such as On-line Books or Newsletters, or should it point to individual resources or subsets of collections. The decision to include pointers to individual resources, in part, depends upon the overall organization of the Gopher. However, if a resource is further down in the hierarchy of someone else's Gopher there are greater maintenance problems. One also needs to determine the best and most authoritative source for a resource or collection and since there can be multiple sources for any item and it is not apparent from whence a source originates, finding the authoritative source can be very difficult.

In order to build consensus on decisions concerning what is to be included in the Gopher, the development team may want to bring together representatives from diverse constituencies, such as student government, admissions, public relations, the registrar, the faculty, the library and the computing center to design the system and set priorities for collection development. Such a "collection development statement" should outline the scope and purpose and primary audience of the Gopher, the types of resources to be collected, and include specifications about not only the formats or subjects to be collected, but also their level. The statement should also provide guidelines concerning the appropriate use of the local Gopher for contributors. In other words, any issues which are considered in the development of policies for traditional library materials should also be considered in developing electronic library collections. It is no service to your users, to throw anything and everything up on your menus. It only means they must navigate through more screens to retrieve items further on down the menu.

Classification Systems

The dilemma faced by the Gopher designer is to determine the best way to make access to information easy for users without losing them in a maze of menus and listings. There are no published guidelines for Gopher hierarchies, though there are many ideas and models in Gopherspace which can serve as examples. As noted above, developing a logical way of classifying information entails (1) determining an overall scheme for the Gopher as reflected in a root menu, (2) determining the number of levels (do you take one giant step to get to a resource, or lots of little steps), and (3) determining useful names for menu items.

In determining an overall scheme, one approach is to develop a metaphor for the Gopher which can easily become incorporated as a mental model. Metaphors not only provide an overall model, but they can provide a context for deciding upon names. For example, if one chooses to use a campus metaphor, the menu items may be names of buildings. At Skidmore, the development group decided on a metaphor of "electronic reading rooms" based on the college's academic divisions and departments. The team felt that this "community based approach" would be more meaningful and therefore serve as a better model for locating information than any standardized classification system.

The ordering of items on menus will be determined by the way in which information is categorized. However, the first item should always be explanatory and, if possible, include within it a schematic of the overall Gopher. If one is using a campus model, a useful way of organizing the information is to move from the classroom to the campus, to the community, to the world.

There is little data on whether or not a shallower hierarchy with many items is better than a deeper hierarchy with fewer items. User studies of information retrieval systems do show that users will not read whole screens of information and one can assume that menus which go on for several pages are even less successful in catching the reader's attention. Yet, on the other hand, other studies indicate that users quickly become lost if forced to negotiate through many steps or menus to locate a single resource. Finding the balance between these two alternatives often means developing a metaphor which is responsive to the amount of information in any one category. Currently Skidmore's electronic reading rooms are three levels deep (the academic division, ex., Science, the department, Biology, and the resource). As more information is added to the Gopher, it may be necessary to develop a more complete metaphor and classify the information by major divisions in the Biology curricula.

The third critical area in designing an organizational scheme is the assignment of names to items on the Gopher menu. As noted above, the metaphor one chooses may provide relevant names. Names in Gopher serve two objectives: as clear signifiers of what lies beneath and as searchable entries in the overall Gopher index. In the root menu, the first objective is paramount, but as one gets to more specific levels of the hierarchy, achieving the second objective is more important. In naming items at more specific levels in the hierarchy, it would be useful to adopt some controlled vocabulary. As noted above, there has been a significant debate over the best classification schemes for Gophers. Even if there can't be agreement on a general classification scheme, perhaps developers could agree to using the Library of Congress Subject Headings so that users doing keyword searches in Veronica would know what would be the most likely terms for retrieving information.

Some of the Gophers examined furnished other ideas for approaches to one's Gopher. Syracuse University and Cornell have both implemented keyword searching of their local Gopherspace and files within it. Bookmark, an extension to many Gopher clients, allows users to save their favorite Gophers or resources in their own virtual Gopher. If one isn't inclined to build one's own subject tree, including a reference to one in the root or second level of your Gopher may assist users in finding information relevant to their discipline. Redundancy, as mentioned earlier, is another way to insure that potentially useful items will always be apparent to the user at appropriate menus.

CONCLUSION

It is evident from the study that classification/organization and collection development both play critical roles in creating a Gopher which is a highly useful tool for its community. In designing a Gopher, one must bear in mind that its community is both the local and the international network community.

One needs to define the purpose, the audience and the scope of the Gopher. Is this Gopher a campus wide information system for publishing local information; is this Gopher an electronic library? Will the Gopher include both internal and external resources and within each of these categories, what are the kinds of items which the institution should collect? In developing the classification scheme, one needs to decide on the depth of the hierarchy, the overall scheme for classifying resources and naming conventions. More research is needed on how users negotiate the menus. Skidmore planned to do some protocol studies of user search behavior during the Fall 1993.

Through Gopher one can access libraries around the world, research under almost any subject area, investigate colleges one might be interested in attending, look for jobs or funding, check weather reports, or even look for missing children. Whether the original developers of Gopher intended it or not, Gopher has unlocked the door to the vast world of network resources.

Gopherspace currently contains over 10 million resources. If one accounts for redundancy it still contains a staggering 1.5 million resources. At the national level, developers are busy creating extensions that will allow ever better access to Gopher such as the capability of attaching abstracts to Gopher items on servers so that keyword searching is enhanced. At the local level, we, as librarians who are familiar both with the user community and with its information seeking habits, must insure that users can easily tunnel through Gophers to find appropriate information by creating information systems which reflect the community and its information needs.

REFERENCES

1. Ed Krol, *The Whole Internet User's Guide & Catalog* (Sebastopol, CA: O'Reilly & Associates, Inc., 1992), p. 189.

2. Frank Anklesaria et al., "F.Y.I. on the Internet Gopher Protocol" (University of Minnesota, March 1993).

3. In April 1993 Gopher moved into the top ten of most used applications on the Internet.

4. Many *servers* also contain individual resources (search items) which permit keyword searching. The search engines vary with each Gopher implementation. Many clients, particularly UNIX ones, use the WAIS search engine, though certain clients use their own search engine.

5. Although CWIS are primarily used to disseminate local information, the line between local and external resources is difficult to draw. SUNY Potsdam includes both departmental information and Internet resources such as discussion

groups or databases under each academic department and Yale's Gopher takes a similar approach.

6. Krol, p. 191.

7. To access the list of subject Gophers, go to Internet Resources under the Yale University Gopher's root menu. Under that directory there is an item called "Information Organization Attempts by Subject." This menu currently lists 19 different Gophers which utilize some form of subject arrangement.

8. Anders Gillner et al. Various communications on Gopher Subject Trees, eurogopher@sunic.sunet.se (November through December 1992).

9. Tim Kambitsch, "Minutes from GopherCon93,"gopher-news@boombox.micro.msu.edu, April 13, 1993.

10. For information on this project, contact Joseph Janes at the University of Michigan, School of Library and Information Studies (joseph.janes@um.cc.umich.edu).

11. Users can subscribe to the InterNIC InfoScout net-resources mailing list by sending mail to listserv@is.internic.net and in the body of the message type subscribe net-resources firstname lastname.

BIBLIOGRAPHY

Alt.gopher-list.

Anklesaria, Frank et al., "F.Y.I. on the Internet Gopher Protocol, "Draft_Gopher_FYI_RFC.txt. *Request for Comments(RFC)*. Minneapolis, MN: University of Minnesota, March 1993.

Comp.inforsystems.gopher. (Usenet Newsgroup).

Eurogopher@ebone.net.

"Frequently Asked Questions" (Gopher-FAQ list).

Gillner, Anders, Various Communications on Gopher Subject Trees, E-mail on *eurogopher*@sunic.sunet.se, November-December 1992.

Gopher.news@boombox.micro.umn.edu.

Kambitsch, Tim, "Minutes from GopherCon93," on *gopher.news*@boombox.micro.umn.edu.

Krol, Ed. *The Whole Internet User's Guide & Catalog*. Sebastopol, CA: O'Reilly & Associates, 1992.

Wilson, David L., "Array of New Tools is Designed to Make It Easier to Find and Retrieve Information on the Internet," *Chronicle of Higher Education*, 29(38), 26 May 1993, A17-19.

The First Mile Down Internet 1: Development, Training, and Reference Issues in the Use of an X Windows Interface for Internet Access

Jill T. Perkins

SUMMARY. Simpler, faster access to networked information resources is in high demand in today's academic libraries by both librarians and endusers. Generic X Windows technology, which allows multiple sessions on a workstation, is one answer to this need. Binghamton University Libraries Systems staff and public services librarians have developed Internet 1, an X Windows based interface that uses onscreen menus, interactive help, and remote session scripting to provide seamless access to the vast multitude of Internet sources (including client-server applications such as Xgopher). This system runs on SUN workstations with NCD X terminals for user access.

This article discusses how librarians have adjusted to this change in their technological environment, how they have been trained in its

Jill T. Perkins is Assistant Reference Librarian/Bibliographer for Afro-American and African Studies, University Libraries, Binghamton University, P.O. Box 6012, Binghamton, NY 13902. Email: jperkins@bingsuns.cc.binghamton.edu.
Questions about the Internet 1 software may be addressed to the author.

The author would like to take this opportunity to thank Lynn Burns, Andy Perry, Mark Natoli, Shailesh Paranjpe, and the Information and Research Services staff of the Binghamton University Libraries for their help, support, and encouragement.

[Haworth co-indexing entry note]: "The First Mile Down Internet 1: Development, Training, and Reference Issues in the Use of an X Windows Interface for Internet Access." Perkins, Jill T. Co-published simultaneously in *The Reference Librarian* (The Haworth Press, Inc.) No. 41/42, 1994, pp. 297-317; and: *Librarians on the Internet: Impact on Reference Services* (ed: Robin Kinder) The Haworth Press, Inc., 1994, pp. 297-317. Multiple copies of this article/chapter may be purchased from The Haworth Document Delivery Center [1-800-3-HAWORTH; 9:00 a.m. - 5:00 p.m. (EST)].

use, and how Internet 1 has changed the nature of Binghamton University Libraries' reference service.

INTRODUCTION

Librarians are faced with the necessity of providing easy access to the wide variety of networked information sources available through the Internet. Differing online public access catalogs (OPACs), as well as remote file sites with their multiplicity of front-ends and login procedures, require a simpler interface for both the enduser and the reference librarian so that ease of information retrieval is maximized. One solution is to combine the interface or "GUI" (graphical user interface) with the power of an Ethernet connected computer workstation, thus creating a system that can be specifically tailored for the needs of both librarians and endusers. The term "workstation" is used in this article to define an "extended OPAC" that provides value-added access by furnishing expanded entry points, augmented information resources, access to locally mounted and/or remote periodical index databases, and gateway functions to local, regional and national telecommunications networks.[1] Such a workstation would allow both librarians and endusers access to the brave new world of the Internet. This "brave new world," however, requires training for librarians and endusers, adjustment to new technology, and a positive change in the reference environment.

BACKGROUND TO INTERNET 1

In March 1990, the Binghamton University Libraries, in conjunction with the University's Computer Services Department, tackled the problem of producing such a system with the development of what came to be known as the "Librarian's Workbench." The Librarian's Workbench utilized an IBM X terminal, on loan from Computer Services, and the X Window system, an industry-standard software system that allows programmers to develop portable graphical user interfaces.[2] The IBM X terminal was placed on the Main Library's reference desk and the required Ethernet wiring was extended to the reference desk with some difficulty. The installation was primarily designed as a tool for reference librarians to use when assisting clients. The original interface was a series of icons for heavily-used OPACs and databases such as Cornell University and the Research Libraries Information Network (RLIN)[3] (see Figure 1). Other remote hosts such as university mainframes, other library OPACs, etc., were available through Telnet or TN3270[4] icons that prompted the librarian for the remote host's address. Remote host login protocols were not automatically supplied by the system (scripted), because of system limitations, so the librarian was required to enter the proper userid, password, and commands.

The change to a multi-functional environment and the practically day-to-day systems development of the Librarian's Workbench interface constituted an ongoing challenge in the areas of training and documentation. Since I was familiar with the UNIX system, I volunteered to write documentation, conduct "on the spot" training, and function as a troubleshooter/liaison between Computer Services, the Systems office and the Main (Bartle Library) Reference Unit. As systems development proceeded apace, documentation was revised quickly and librarians grew used to working in a multi-tasked environment and coping with an array of login/password procedures.

It soon became apparent to the Libraries' systems and reference staff and computer services personnel that X Windows, because of its multi-tasking and multi-session capabilities, was the key to something bigger and better. The multi-tasking ability of X Windows when added to Ethernet connectivity allows simultaneous access to remote hosts, servers, and file sites, as well as to the University's mainframes and the Libraries' Information System. Librarians were able to run searches through databases such as RLIN and OPACs like Cornell or Harvard as needed for reference queries. Due to the limitations of the system at that time, printing had not been enabled, but cutting and pasting information to a file or into a librarian's e-mail account for later manipulation was possible. The power, flexibility, and ease of use of the X Windows platform prompted the Libraries Systems staff and librarians to examine how to simplify and adapt the software to create a better interface for enduser access. Gradually, the Librarian's Workbench was turning into Internet 1.

FIGURE 1. Librarian's Workbench

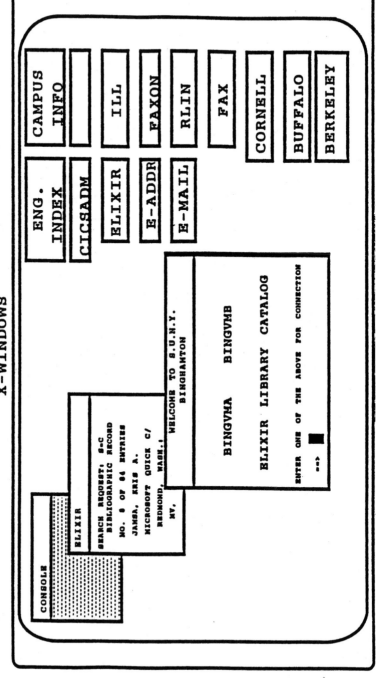

DEVELOPMENT OF THE LIBRARIAN'S WORKBENCH INTO INTERNET 1

Software Development

Because X Windows does not define any particular user interface style,[5] it was the ideal software to adapt for seamless user access to Internet resources. It has the capability for multiple sessions, "point and click" interfaces, and is a good front-end to both X client applications like XWAIS and Xgopher[6] and character-based remote telnet sessions such as OPACs and remote databases.

The initial menu system is an X client and based on the WidgetCreation Library package[7] and Athena Resource Interpreter.[8] This permitted us to create a user-friendly menu that launches the remote session and X clients. The Internet 1 menu comprises three columns: "Online Library Systems," "Utilities" and "Other Internet Resources." The X clients include "xclipboard," "mailer," and "Xgopher" (see Figure 2). The columns are divided into boxes that are sensitized to a mouse click and are highlighted when the cursor is positioned on them. A click on a selection then brings up a pop-up box with basic instructions and two buttons called "click to begin" and "click to quit." The original selection box is "desensitized" and cannot be clicked while the pop-up is displayed. The "quit" button resensitizes the original menu box and eliminates the pop-up. The "begin" button initiates the sessions or launches the X clients while at the same time resensitizing the selection button and eliminating the pop-up. Multiple sessions can be displayed simultaneously (see Figure 3). When items are iconized, the Internet 1 logo is the default icon (see Figure 4).

Underlying all the remote telnet sessions is the Expect language. Expect is a program that "talks" to other interactive programs according to a script. By following the script, Expect knows what can be anticipated from a program and what the correct response should be,[9] thereby navigating the user through to the actual applications. This language is very robust and can handle timeouts and a variety of connection problems. It also can deal with many steps in an interactive process, including logins, passwords, and application identifications.

The one application that needed to be developed by the Li-

FIGURE 2

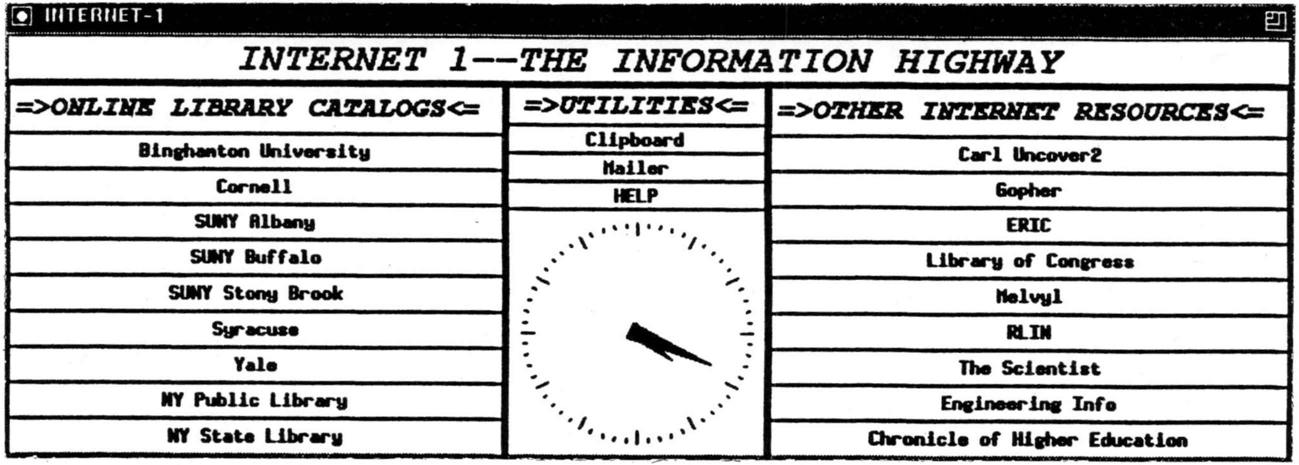
INTERNET-1
INTERNET 1--THE INFORMATION HIGHWAY
=>ONLINE LIBRARY CATALOGS<=
Binghamton University
Cornell
SUNY Albany
SUNY Buffalo
SUNY Stony Brook
Syracuse
Yale
NY Public Library
NY State Library
=>UTILITIES<=
Clipboard
Mailer
HELP
=>OTHER INTERNET RESOURCES<=
Carl Uncover2
Gopher
ERIC
Library of Congress
Melvyl
RLIN
The Scientist
Engineering Info
Chronicle of Higher Education

braries' Systems staff was the mailer tool. It is an X client that allows users to select files they have saved and mail the files to their e-mail accounts. In order not to confuse the enduser, the mailer tool filters out system files and subdirectories from the list of available files. It uses a list "widget" to permit point and click file selection (see Figure 5). Mailing files allows the exporting of data without the added problems associated with handling floppy disks or servicing extra printers. This decision was made based on previous difficulties with the security of our CDROM workstations' hard disks as well as the service, expense, and support related to printers. Since all Binghamton University faculty, staff, and students are able to obtain mainframe accounts from the Computer Services at no charge, there is no additional hardship to the enduser.

The mailer also has a second widget to list all the campus mainframes where users have accounts and again allows point and click selection. The user must enter a userid and click the "sendmail" button. The mail shows up in the user's e-mail account as being from "highway1@library.binghamton.edu" (or highway2, -3, or -4, depending on which account is used) and is easily distinguishable from other mail. Endusers are expected to obtain data by cutting and pasting to the xclipboard or by saving files from Xgopher. Each X terminal is logged into a separate account to prevent concurrent users from saving over each others' files.

The reference staff-use SUNs at the Main and Science reference desks have slightly different screens, with access to functions (such as e-mail) that have been disabled on the public X terminals (see Figure 6). The SUNs also function as "test" workstations for features that may be added later.

Hardware

Internet 1 uses 6 NCD (Network Computing Devices) X terminals on three SUN SparcStation IPC units in three library facilities: the Main Library, the Science Library, and the Systems office. The NCD units met our needs and proved to be less expensive than PC's or Macs. The SUNs are entry-level machines with 8mb RAM and 207mb hard drives and run X11R5 (X Windows software, Version 11, Revision 5). The X terminals have 15 inch black and white

FIGURE 3

304

INTERNET 1—THE INFORMATION HIGHWAY

○ INTERNET-1

=>ONLINE LIBRARY CATALOGS<= =>UTILITIES<= =>OTHER INTERNET RESOURCES<=

ONLINE LIBRARY CATALOGS	UTILITIES	OTHER INTERNET RESOURCES
Binghamton University	Clipboard	Carl Uncover2
Cornell	Mailer	Gopher
SUNY Albany	HELP	ERIC
SUNY Buffalo		Melvyl
SUNY Stony Brook		RLIN
Syracuse		The Scientist
Yale		Engineering Info
NY Public Library		
NY State Library		Chronicle of Higher Education

○ xjgopher

Quit ◆ Other Comma

select ar

Which

» About Using Th
<ldo> Keyword Search
» About Univ. Mi
» News Services
» General Refere
» Humanities Res
» Science Resour
» Social Science
» Library Catalo
» Univ. Michigan Campus Information (GOpherBLUE)
» Other Gophers
» What's New & Featured Resources

ELIXIR   TCP5

BINGHAMTON UNIVERSITY INFORMATION SYSTEMS

Type the **LABEL** to select a database.   Type **NEWS** for current information.
Type **FOR** to see other selections.   Type **STOP** to exit.

DATABASE   (Type **HELP** for online assistance.)

LABEL

Binghamton Library Databases
LXIR   -ELIXIR: Library Catalog
WZRD   -WIZARD: General Periodical Index
ABII   -ABI/Inform: Business/Economics Index
GOVD   -GovDocs: U.S. Federal Documents Index
CRLC   -Center for Research Libraries, Chicago
Binghamton University Databases
UCAL   -University Calendar
UDIR   -University Faculty/Staff Directory
COURSES   -Schedule of Courses

-------------------------------- + Page 1 of 2 --------------
HELP   Select a database label from above   <F8> FORward
        NEWS (Library System News)

Database Selection: ☐

Fetch selection | Info about directory
Remove bookmark
Which libraries
chronicle.merit
bingvmb.cc.bing

305

FIGURE 4. Internet 1 Logo

monitors, 4mb RAM, and run on subnets from the SUN workstations through the use of a second Ethernet card on each SUN.

Security Issues

By completely eliminating access to the file systems and NCD set-up (internal configuration/profile) menus of Internet 1, users cannot get blank windows or do anything beyond what the menu permits. Mainframe account access is limited to mailing files using the mailer tool. We also disabled the finger command which allows outside users to identify the IP addresses to the X terminals because it had the potential to cause annoying system problems.

Each unit is logged into a separate account in the morning and it stays on that account all day. Each account has its own password, with only reference staff being privy to that knowledge. Two librarians function as password "backups" in case of emergencies or fits of forgetfulness. The logoff/exit routine for the X terminals has also been hidden, to ensure that users do not inadvertently exit from their sessions. All hardware has been protected through the use of locking security cables.

SYSTEM DOCUMENTATION AND STAFF TRAINING

No information system functions in a vacuum. It is dependent on proper documentation and trained staff who in turn instruct end-

FIGURE 5

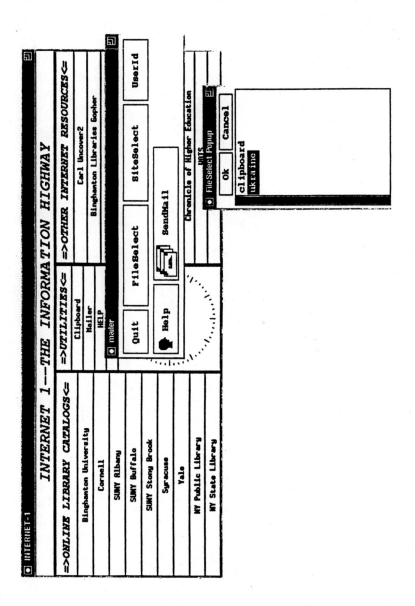

FIGURE 6

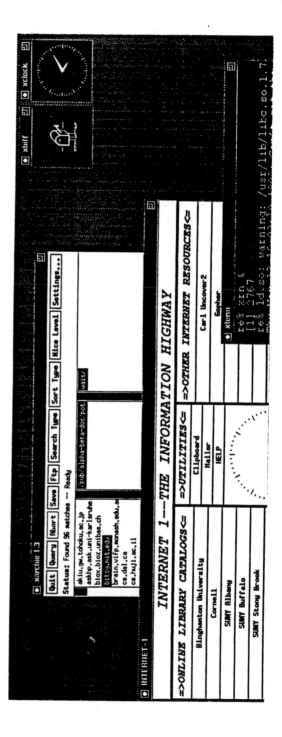

Mailbox is '/usr/spool/mail/jperkins' with 3 messages [ELM 2.3 FL11]

```
   1    May 13  EA06385@BINGVMB.cc  (18)
   2    May 13  craig                (20)
N  3    May 13  Richard Rodgers     (28)    Re: Help with Workshop
```

a)lias, !=pipe, !=shell, ?=help, <n>=set current to n, /=search pattern
C)opy, c)hange folder, d)elete, e)dit, f)orward, g)roup reply, m)ail,
n)ext, o)ptions, p)rint, q)uit, r)eply, s)ave, t)ag, u)ndelete, or e(x)it

Command: □

users. Without this, the most highly-touted user-friendly system becomes unusable. Therefore, not only was it important to have documentation completed before Internet 1 "went public," but staff training had to begin as well.

Due to the Librarian's Workbench project, Reference staff had been introduced to and were fairly comfortable with utilizing a multi-functional environment. They also had experience using different OPACs and databases such as Cornell and RLIN. The change to a SUN workstation in September 1992 and the addition of the Internet 1 menu in March 1993 necessitated further training because of the added applications, such as XWAIS, Xgopher Xarchie, XRN,[10] and additions/changes to system functions and interfaces. Consequently, since I had been responsible for documentation and training for the Librarian's Workbench, I took on the same responsibility for Internet 1, the SUN workstation and the X terminals. To get a handle on the situation, I established two levels of SUN knowledge. The first or "basic" level included startup/exit procedures, a review of familiar OPACs and databases, and introduction to basic UNIX commands.

The second level of training was a more in-depth treatment of the use and usefulness of X client applications, as well as printing, downloading, basic troubleshooting, and a review of any previous sessions. Each 90 minute session was composed of two reference staff members and one trainer, with "one on one" meetings also conducted at the Reference Desk as needed for follow-up. Reference staff were able to individually hone their skills and review documentation either at the Reference Desk SUN or on the Libraries' Systems office SUN which was available by appointment.

Endusers are usually trained on an on-demand basis by reference staff. This arrangement has worked out very well because of the intentional proximity of the public X terminals to the Main and Science Libraries' reference desks. Furthermore, the posted hours of the X terminals usually ensure an available reference staff member. Endusers are encouraged to make an appointment with reference staff in order to obtain more in-depth instruction in using the system. Our experience is that Internet 1 is slightly more complicated than our other systems and endusers need additional training.

Staff Documentation/User Documentation

Staff documentation and user documentation differ in what is presented and how it is presented. Staff documentation contains highly detailed information on operating systems commands, basic troubleshooting and startup/exit procedures as well as "button-by-button" breakdowns of X client applications such as Xgopher. Items are presented as clearly as possible with the idea that they must focus on the users, helping them to overcome their apprehension and resistance to the new and the strange.[11]

User documentation omits why the system works and concentrates on how to make it work. Given that the Internet 1 system is most endusers' first encounter with a windowed environment and mouse operation, it was essential that user instructions be written clearly, avoid jargon whenever possible, provide a glossary, and that it be tested and edited for accuracy.[12] Users are provided with three guides: *The Scholar's Guide to Internet Highway 1; Sources on Internet Highway 1; and Document Delivery with Carl/UnCover 2 and Ei/Page 1.* (Commercially produced RLIN instructions are also provided.) Actual written instructions for non-NOTIS OPACs were deemed unnecessary because most remote OPACs already furnish online help screens.

As with all documentation, ours only works if is read, understood, and used. Many of the problems encountered by endusers stem from an inability to understand or an unwillingness to read any documentation, be it online or printed. The Internet Highway 1 guides are short and to the point, as shown in the following example, taken from *The Scholar's Guide to Internet Highway One* (Figure 7). While many endusers hesitate at first, most are delighted to discover the plethora of sources available and are willing to try different menu items. The most challenging task, however, is getting those endusers who use only one source, such as Cornell or RLIN, or our own library catalog, to try another resource. To encourage experimentation, reference staff try to include applicable Internet resources in their classroom information education sessions, and use Internet resources in other facets of reference service.

FIGURE 7

```
                                        THE SCHOLAR'S GUIDE TO
                                        INTERNET HIGHWAY ONE

SEARCHING A DATABASE
Move the arrow to be within the database window. Follow the
database's instructions for searching.

READING RESULTS
If you do not see the entire document in the window, you can move
within it by using the scrollbar (to the left of the window). Drag
the mouse down the scrollbar while pressing the left button. You
can move forward within the document by dragging the mouse up the
scrollbar.                                              RC93
```

ASSESSMENT OF INTERNET 1'S IMPACT

Reference Service

Internet 1 has altered how reference service is performed at the Binghamton University Libraries. With it, reference staff are able to widen the horizons of traditional reference assistance, to truly become a "library without walls." Librarians now try to include applicable Internet resources in their classroom bibliographic instruction sessions and while providing reference service. Most reference staff are professional librarians with subject-specific collection development responsibilities, so Internet resources are viewed in that light. Librarians attempt to keep track of items useful for their subject area but are not required to become instant expert NetSurfers. This is probably impossible given the almost constant state of NetFlux.

When Internet resources began to be included in reference service, it became clear that reference staff had to adjust to a level of reference ambiguity that many were not comfortable with. In the past, traditional reference service has been based on sources that have the reputation of a publisher, author, or institution and can be verified or, at the very least, someone can be held accountable for the information presented. This is not so with many Internet resources. OPACs and commercial databases or indexes aside, some librarians felt that they had to take much of what they found on the Internet on faith. Trusting to an unknown source somewhere out there in Cyberspace was asking a lot. Questions began to arise such as: How verifiable is the source? What is the site reliability? Does the site update its sources regularly, if needed? Should encouraging endusers to utilize such sources come with a disclaimer, "Searcher beware, use at your own risk"? Or, as one enduser asked, "How do you cite a document from Xgopher when you're not even sure where the information came from, who put it there, or how long it's going to be there?" After much internal debate, it was agreed that reference staff can include Internet resources in all aspects of reference service if they are comfortable with explaining the pitfalls of relying on the whole Internet.

While systems access problems have been alleviated through scripting, connection problems of the "line is busy, please call again" type do sometimes occur. Reference staff are then called on to diagnose problems originating at a site that may be on another continent or predict the flow of Internet traffic at any given time. Typically, when there are connection problems it is because a remote site is having difficulties or there is too much movement on the Internet. Endusers had to realize that these problems are beyond the control of the reference staff and have to be endured. Peak Internet hours can be noted, but since the Libraries do not open at six a. m.; and six a. m. in New York State is probably peak hours for somebody, somewhere, the point is probably moot, anyway.

FUTURE PLANS

Like the Internet itself, Internet 1 is constantly changing. New resources become available almost daily and have to be evaluated for usefulness and applicability to the needs of the enduser. System enhancements are also of primary concern. The design of Internet 1, however, lends itself to the need for modifications. Future plans for changes/additions include:

Downloading

Since the X terminals are not equipped with hard drives, downloading is primarily done from the Main and Science reference desk

SUN workstations on a very limited basis. The downloading process is not interactive and as such requires librarian mediation for optimum success. While the future possibilities of wholesale downloading have not been fully discussed, it does seem probable that downloading from one central hard drive may be possible.

Z39.50/Client-Server Technology

Although Binghamton University's local library system (NOTIS) is still a character-based user interface, the Libraries expected to migrate to the ProPAC Z39.50 X client by the end of 1993. At this time only the MS-Windows version is out–the X version is in development at NOTIS.[13] This would be in preparation towards moving to client-server OPACs. With ProPAC installed in late 1993, we would only have 8-10 X terminals in the Libraries. The long term strategy is to completely replace existing dumb asynchronous terminals with UNIX-based (X or SUN) workstations. This process may take several years.

Printing

Printing was intentionally omitted from Internet 1 for a variety of reasons. It would have increased the already large proportion of time that staff spend servicing printers, created further noise near the reference desk, and it was felt that Internet 1's mailer tool allowed the greatest flexibility of file manipulation for most Binghamton University Libraries users. Printing can easily be added at a later date, however, but will probably be a fee-based service.

Additional Menu Items

Additional menu items are currently being evaluated for public use by a selected group of reference librarians. Issues of content, quality, and ease of use are considered when items are evaluated. Other members of the reference staff participate by testing the new items on the Main or Science SUNs and offering input. After the evaluation process has ended, technical information (addresses, ports, logins, any additional software changes needed, etc.) is collected by the Systems office and the item is added to the menu. Currently, XWAIS, XRN, OCLC/FirstSearch, and several other databases are in the pipeline as possible additions.

CONCLUSION

The response of endusers to the Internet 1 system has been favorable. Those new to GUIs, OPACs, or the Internet are hesitant at first but generally return again and again to further explore the system. Expert Internet/electronic resources users are very vocal in their appreciation of the setup and have helped by suggesting other items for inclusion as well as system enhancements.

Binghamton University Libraries Systems staff and librarians are very enthusiastic about the X windows platform and the Internet 1 system. The system is less expensive than most PC or Mac-based workstations, yet is an equally powerful way to provide Internet access for endusers, and a good computive environment for combining character-based and X client applications.

REFERENCES

1. William Mischo and Timothy Cole, "The Illinois Extended OPAC: Library Information Workstation Design and Development," in *Advances in Online Public Access Catalogs*, ed. Marsha Ra (Westport; London: Meckler, 1992), 38.

2. Douglas A. Young, *The X Window System: Programming and Applications with Xt* (Englewood Cliffs, NJ: Prentice Hall, Inc., 1990), 1.

3. Geraldine MacDonald and Andy Perry, "Information Access: Computing Services and Libraries: A Joint Offensive Team," in *Challenges and Opportunities of Information Technology in the 90s: Proceedings of the 1990 CAUSE National Conference November 27-30, 1990* (Miami Beach, FL: CAUSE, 1990), 399.

4. *Telnet* is the Internet's remote login application. *TN3270* is a special version of telnet that has a 3270 emulator built-in. Ed Krol, *The Whole Internet Users Guide and Catalog* (Sebastopol, CA: O' Reilly and Associates, 1992), 46, 55.

5. Young, 2.

6. *WAIS* is an acronym for Wide Area Information Servers that search indexed material. *Gopher* is a lookup tool that prowls through the Internet by selecting resources from menus. Krol, 189.

7. WCL–a library which allows the complete look and feel of a widget based application and can be used to create and manipulate user interfaces which are

made up of Athena, Cornell, Motif, OpenLook, or any other Xt based widgets. David E. Smyth, *WCL manual pages* (n.p., March 1, 1992), 1.

8. ARI–a tool for developing MIT Athena widget set based user interfaces. David E. Smyth, *ARI manual pages* (n.p., November 2, 1992), 2.

9. Don Libes, *Expect manual pages* (n.p., October 22, 1992), 1.

10. *Archie* is a system that allows searching of indexes of files available on public servers on the Internet. *XRN* is the X client for reading USENET news groups, which are the Internet equivalent of a discussion group or a "bulletin board system" (BBS). Krol, 155, 127.

11. Donna R. Webb, "Writing Effective Manuals: Basic Guidelines and Tips," *Library Hi Tech* 7 (1989): 41.

12. Webb, 43, 46, 47.

13. Z39.50 is an ANSI/National Information standard for information retrieval in a distributed, client-server environment. It provides the mechanism by which one computer system can search for and retrieve information from another computer system on the Internet that is not necessarily manufactured by the same vendor. As such, it provides the basis for the construction of information servers. Mary E. Engle, "Electronic Paths to Resource Sharing: Widening Opportunities through the Internet," *RSR: Reference Services Review* 19 (Winter 1991): 12.

BIBLIOGRAPHY

Adams, Roy. "The Dawson Technology Librarians' Workstation." *Aslib Proceedings* 42 (October 1990): 271-275.

Black, Kirsten. "The Development of IWS–an Integrated Workstation for Librarians." *Program* 24 (January 1990): 49-58.

Brophy, Peter. "Introduction to the Use of Workstations for Library and Information Management." *Aslib Proceedings* 42 (October 1990): 249-250.

Dern, Daniel P. "Applying the Internet." *Byte* (February 1992): 111-118.

Dodd, G. H. "A 'SUNy' Aspect of an Information Centre." *Aslib Proceedings* 42 (Oct. 1990): 251-256.

Engle, Mary E. "Electronic Paths to Resource Sharing: Widening Opportunities through the Internet." *RSR: Reference Services Review* 19 (Winter 1991): 7-12.

Glogoff, Stuart. "Staff Training in the Automated Library Environment: A Symposium." *Library Hi Tech* 7 (1989): 61-83.

Horton, Weldon H. "Microcomputer Workstations as Complements to a Fully Automated Library System." *Computers in Libraries* 10 (January 1990): 20-21.

Krol, Ed. *The Whole Internet Users Guide and Catalog.* Sebastopol, CA: O'Reilly and Associates, 1992.

Ladner, Sharyn J., and Hope N. Tillman. "Using the Internet for Reference." *Online* 17 (January 1993): 45-51.

Libes, Don. *Expect manual pages.* n.p., October 22, 1992.

MacDonald, Geraldine, and Andy Perry. "Information Access–Computing Services and Librarians: A Joint Offensive Team." In *Challenges and Opportunities of Information Technology in the 90s: Proceedings of the 1990 CAUSE National Conference*, November 27-30, 1990. Miami Beach, FL: CAUSE, 1990, 395-402.

McKnight, Cliff. "Workstations for Academic Applications." *Aslib Proceedings* 42 (October 1990): 263-269.

Mischo, William H., and Timothy W. Cole. "The Illinois Extended OPAC: Library Information Workstation Design and Development." In *Advances in Online Public Access Catalogs*, ed. Marsha Ra, 38-57. Westport; London: Meckler, 1992.

Nolte, James. "The Electronic Library Workstation–Today." *Computers in Libraries* 10 (October 1990): 17-20.

Rose, Mike. "The New Information Highway: Computer Networks Make their Mark on Campus Life and Learning." *On Campus*, October 1992, 6-7 and 17.

Smyth, David E. *ARI manual pages*. n.p., November 2, 1992.

_____ . *WCL manual pages*. n.p., March 1, 1992.

Still, Julie, and Jan Alexander. "Integrating Internet into Reference: Policy Issues." *C & R L News* (March 1993): 139-140.

van Brakel, Pieter A. "The Electronic Workstation: Challenges for the Information Specialist." *The Electronic Library* 9 (Aug./Oct. 1991): 211-215.

Webb, Donna R. "Writing Effective User Manuals: Basic Guidelines and Tips." *Library Hi Tech* 7 (1989): 41-48.

Young, Douglas A. *The X Window System: programming and applications with Xt*. Englewood Cliffs, NJ: Prentice Hall, Inc., 1990.

Providing and Accessing Information via the Internet: The Georgetown Catalogue of Projects in Electronic Text

Michael Neuman
Paul Mangiafico

SUMMARY. A study of Georgetown University's Catalogue of Projects in Electronic Text (CPET), while confirming the prediction that access and knowledge management will be major concerns in the library of the future, suggests that the demands of the two desiderata will sometimes clash. This review of CPET charts the tradeoffs between maintenance and access that have marked three successive technological generations of the project, considers the implications of recent data on CPET usage, and speculates upon improvements in maintenance and access that will come with newly emerging utilities on the Internet.

PROJECT BACKGROUND AND BIBLIOGRAPHIC CONTROL

For four years, the Center for Text and Technology at Georgetown University's Academic Computer Center has been compiling

Michael Neuman is Director of the Center for Text and Technology, Academic Computer Center, Georgetown University, Washington, DC 20057 (neuman@guvax.georgetown. edu). Paul Mangiafico, Humanities Computing Specialist at the same address, coordinates the CPET database (pmangiafico@guvax.georgetown.edu).

[Haworth co-indexing entry note]: "Providing and Accessing Information via the Internet: The Georgetown Catalogue of Projects in Electronic Text." Neuman, Michael, and Paul Mangiafico. Co-published simultaneously in *The Reference Librarian* (The Haworth Press, Inc.) No. 41/42, 1994, pp. 319-332; and: *Librarians on the Internet: Impact on Reference Services* (ed: Robin Kinder) The Haworth Press, Inc., 1994, pp. 319-332. Multiple copies of this article/chapter may be purchased from The Haworth Document Delivery Center [1-800-3-HAWORTH; 9:00 a.m. - 5:00 p.m. (EST)].

a world-wide directory of projects that create and disseminate electronic, full-text versions of primary works (masterpieces and linguistic corpora) in the humanities. At present, the CPET directory contains information on approximately 350 projects from 27 countries. For each project, ten categories of information are sought:

- identifying acronym;
- name and affiliation of operation;
- contact person and addresses;
- primary disciplinary interest;
- focus on period, location, individual, genre, or medium;
- languages encoded;
- intended uses;
- formats of production;
- media of access; and
- sources of electronic holdings (including bibliographic).

Excluded from coverage in CPET are bibliographic material and other databases that do not contain full-text material; secondary sources (in the humanist's sense of works about primary texts); electronic dictionaries; computer-assisted instruction (unless, like the Perseus Project at Harvard, full text is included); and image databases (unless, like the international ADMYTE project, the images contain printed or manuscript pages).[1]

CPET staff, like others seeking to impose bibliographic control over electronic text, face the challenges imposed by the flexibility of electronic media they catalogue. "All things flow and nothing abides," wrote Heraclitus, but the initial formats of electronic information are particularly short-lived. Therefore, whether a cataloguing project seeks to gather information about developers of electronic text (as does CPET) or about the bibliographic sources of electronic texts (as does the Center for Electronic Texts in the Humanities), the changing form of the electronic material requires continuous updating of the database. Individual electronic texts, for example, are "versioned": not only emended but also converted to different operating systems, bundled with analytical software, combined with other texts in other electronic media, and subjected to different kinds or different levels of encoding. Similarly, projects in electronic text expand or contract their operations, alter their technologies of production and media of distribution, and change the scope of access to their works on the basis of copyright agreements reached or denied. Each change affects the user's interest, so each change ideally should be catalogued. The National Information Standards Organization (NISO) is expanding the structure of bibliographic records to accommodate the features of electronic products and thereby facilitating the cataloguing process.[2]

The protean nature of electronic text, as well as the burgeoning growth of the medium, imposes on the cataloguer the need not only to expand the scope of coverage but continually to update the information already obtained. Consequently, the process of gathering data and updating the database complicates the tasks of knowledge management and provision of access. In other words, the Internet may have improved communication (for example, by improving the speed of correspondence, streamlining the cataloguer's creation of personalized mass-mailings, and facilitating the respondent's editing of a submission and replying to an inquiry) and thereby hastened the pace of the cataloguer's data gathering, but in so doing it has also hastened the obsolescence of information maintained and accessed on the network.

In the context of this accelerated cycle of data gathering, then, it is instructive to note how different means of disseminating information via the Internet have affected the cataloguer's attempts to balance the demands of data maintenance and user access. The example of the Catalogue of Projects in Electronic Text suggests that while the development of the Internet has brought a steady improvement in access, it has done so at some cost to efficient data maintenance.

THREE FORMS OF INTERNET MANAGEMENT AND DISSEMINATION

Since CPET began in 1989, dissemination of data has improved as network utilities have increased in sophistication (and, of course, as Internet participation has experienced its exponential growth). But thus far, every technological advance has brought new challenges, among them the need to adjust the balance between maintenance of data currency, accuracy, and integrity (on the one hand) and provision of full and easy access (on the other).

Posting to Discussion Groups and Listservs. CPET, from the outset an information service on the Internet, began with a file transmission over the network: Bob Kraft (then Director of the Center for the Computer Analysis of Text at the University of Pennsylvania) forwarded to Georgetown rudimentary files on approximately 90 projects in electronic text. From that starting point, CPET staff emphasized gathering information and expanding the database rather than providing access. Project data–organized geographically and alphabetically by foreign countries and American states–were maintained in word-processor files to facilitate the entry of new data and the searching of current files in order to respond to inquiries. But access was limited: lists of the projects–with titles, contact persons, and addresses–were periodically sent to the listservers of discussion groups such as HUMANIST (the officially sponsored list of the Association of Computers and the Humanities) and to discipline-specific groups such as the Committee on Computer Use of the American Philosophical Association. In addition, the project was announced on numerous discussion groups, inquiries were invited, and responses sent–increasingly by electronic mail–with excerpts from the files. But complete copies of the database were not sent to individuals or posted to the network, in part because the growing size of the file made Internet transmission cumbersome, in part because the acquisition and entry of new data was occurring so frequently as to render any posting obsolescent, and in part because today's generous practice of open dissemination on the Internet had only begun to manifest itself.

As the volume of correspondence increased–from project directors providing data and from users requesting data–CPET staff sought to enhance both the organization of data and users' access to it by creating a relational database and attempting to make it network accessible. INGRES was selected because its SQL (Structured Query Language) had become a de facto standard and because INGRES can run on a microcomputer and then, as the data outgrow available filespace, can be ported to a minicomputer or mainframe. Almost immediately, however, the CPET data were transferred to a VAX host in an attempt to extend access to the Internet community.

Hosting an Online Database. The relational database, designed and programmed by colleagues in the Academic Computer Center, permits project data to be entered in one table and retrieved from many different access points. The key table (Project/Product) contains fields for contact person, source of project information, distribution mechanism, language used, centuries covered, disciplines targeted, analytical programs compatible, and apparatus (or encoding) included. The relational capabilities of the database program enable this project information to be linked to another table (Work) on the text that formed the basis of the electronic version; this table contains fields for the work's title, year of creation, historical period, original language, and author. Projects are then linked to Works by means of an associative table (Project_Work) that contains information on the book that formed the basis for the electronic text, specifically the standard bibliographic details (if known) and the language of the rendering, which in the case of a translation, of course, would be different from the language used by the original author.

For CPET staff and for on-campus users, the database marked a noticeable advance: Project information could be entered in one set of fields and be automatically reproduced in other tables; users would have, by means of the tables and their fields, more than a dozen points of access to the information. For example, a scholar could request data on any project containing works dating from the first century B.C.E. and written in Greek. Such a compound search–not yet possible with the searching capabilities of a word processor or today's Internet utilities–becomes more essential as the number of entries in CPET (and thus the number of "hits" for any given query) continues to grow.

In principle, users who reached the database via their modem connection or telnet utility on the Internet would experience the same benefits. However, because the INGRES database was designed neither for use with the operating systems of all microcomputers nor for Internet access, some remote users experienced problems with keyboard emulation. Several users lacked a keyboard with the function keys needed for basic INGRES operations. Others found that the directional cursor of the database could be moved properly only if their keyboard settings were the opposite of those recommended in the user's manuals; different communications programs linking remote users to the network were generating different responses from the database at Georgetown, and even after free copies of the standard public-domain Kermit software were distributed, not all of the keyboard-emulation problems could be solved. As our computer logs show, some frustrated users abandoned their exploration after two or three minutes of abortive attempts.

Nevertheless, most users continued to experience trouble-free access, as evidenced by logs showing dozens of connections each day. By CPET's third anniversary, over one thousand copies of the CPET User's Manual had been distributed, nearly half sent by electronic mail and the rest, in printed form (with images of sample screens of the database), sent by surface mail. Recipients included the ERIC Clearinghouse on Information Resources and 99 individuals or institutions outside the United States. At the same time, a study of VAX records for six months of CPET use (from August 1991 through February 1992) revealed that 281 different users from 198 institutions had registered a total of 766 sessions. The average time per session was approximately fourteen minutes, and the average time per user over the six-month period was just over 37 minutes.

In many respects, the relational database offers the ideal balance of data management and user access: Developers maintain control over the information, and a single entry of project data yields multiple points of access for the user. Consequently, in order to improve access, CPET staff reviewed correspondence reporting technical problems and conducted a survey of two dozen users identified through VAX logs. On the basis of the new insights, the database was revised to standardize and simplify users' keystrokes (specifically, by creating alternatives to function keys and keys on the extended keyboard), and a new manual was drafted. But implementation was delayed so that a new Internet utility for searching and retrieval could be tested: the Gopher.

Hosting a Gopher Server. Gopher is one of the new RDTs (Research Discovery Tools) to appear on the Internet within the past two years; others include Archie, World Wide Web (W3), and Wide Area Information Servers (WAIS). According to the Library Gopher Report from McGill University, "The Internet Gopher, created at the University of Minnesota and named after its mascot, is now one of the most popular, widely used public domain RDTs. Essentially, a Gopher is a distributed document search and retrieval system that greatly simplifies use of the Internet. . . . Menus eliminate the need to learn computer commands and allow even the novice to access information."[3]

Gopher improved upon earlier utilities such as file transfer protocol (ftp) to such an extent–especially in the ease of searching, browsing, and retrieving–that the CPET data were reorganized for dissemination through this medium. FTP, long available as an Internet utility, has offered the capability for retrieving files from remote computers; anonymous ftp has extended access by permitting the word "anonymous" to be entered as the guest's username in order to gain access to the host computer. But for most researchers on the Internet, using ftp to retrieve a file is like wandering blindfolded through the library stacks to retrieve a book. First one must get explicit directions about the host's directory structure; then, with the copied instructions at hand, one moves haltingly through the host's subdirectories in the hope of finding and retrieving the desired file. Complicating the use of anonymous ftp is the fact that the structure of subdirectories and the names of files on the host computer are likely to have been created incrementally and idiosyncratically at the convenience of the developer and thus to the unfamiliar guest appear anything but logical and intuitive.

By contrast, Gopher servers are designed to facilitate remote access; they provide hierarchical directory structures and descriptive filenames to guide the user's navigation. For example, on a virtual trip across the Internet to the Georgetown University Gopher server and the CPET data, a user would select, from a series of menus on his or her client computer, the following choices: Other Gopher and Information Servers, North America, USA, Washington, DC (in alphabetical order after the state of Washington), Georgetown University, and CPET Projects in Electronic Text. From that point, the structure of subdirectories appears as follows:

1. Information on the CPET Database.
2. How to Access the INGRES On-line Database.

3. Information on the Digests.
4. Digests Organized by Discipline (Directory)/
5. Digests Organized by Language (Directory)/

Within the subdirectory on disciplines, for example, one finds the following lower-level subdirectories that contain the corresponding project information:

1. Cultural Studies (Directory)/
2. Fine Arts (Directory)/
3. Linguistics (Directory)/
4. Literature (Directory)/
5. Other Disciplines (Directory)/
6. Philosophy
7. Religious Studies (Directory)/

From the user's perspective, navigation is easy: The series of menus obviates the need for learning commands, the directories and files are named with enough characters to clarify the content, and utilities for navigating the hierarchical structure and for retrieving files are noted on the screen and explained in online help files. Use of the information gathered from CPET also becomes easier. With the Gopher utility, one can retrieve the ASCII text into one's local mainframe and then download, manipulate, and print it from there. From the developer's perspective, too, Gopher offers clear-cut advantages over a relational database: Data entry is easier to learn, no manual must be written and disseminated to users, project data become part of a larger network of related information resources, and because the retrieval software resides on the user's machine, no degradation of service occurs with an increase in the number of simultaneous users on the host computer.

The Gopher version of CPET–compilations of project entries arranged by discipline and language–was released in February 1993. Announcements were sent to approximately three dozen Internet discussion groups that serve the humanities and library communities. The initial response was striking: From February 14th to February 19th (Sunday to Friday), 474 users–from the United States and twenty-two other countries in North America, Europe, and Asia–performed 2899 transactions, an average of 94.8 users per day, 579.8 transactions per day, and 6.12 transactions per user. Among the factors thought to have influenced this dramatic increase in access to CPET were the novelty and ease of use of the Gopher utility, the growth in Internet participation (at a reported 12-15 percent per month) beyond the previous year, and the developing interest in Internet resources among humanists and research librarians.

Nevertheless, six months of experience have shown that selecting a Gopher server to improve access comes at some sacrifice of efficient maintaining of the data's currency and integrity. One characteristic of the CPET material, for example, is that some projects fit logically under more than one heading: The works of Hegel have been placed both under the discipline heading of philosophy and under the language heading of German. Consequently, while a flat file requires that one enter new data on a project only one time for a single project entry, and a relational database enables one to enter new data in a single table and have it accessible from several related tables, a hierarchical Gopher file structure that allows access to information under different headings requires that the same project data must sometimes be entered two or more times.

A second problem for the developer is that in the current Internet environment, copyright is more honored in the breach than the observance; users tend to assume that information on the Internet is in the public domain. Consequently, to adopt the Gopher utility is to risk giving away one's data. Any file posted on a Gopher server can be retrieved, so the only disincentive to obtaining an entire database of information is the time it takes to select and request each of the many files on the server. While this disincentive can be increased (and retrieval simplified) by limiting files to the size of a single project, this expedient would make file directories too large for efficient browsing and cataloguing.

A related problem for developers of data resources emerges from one of the strengths of the Internet: the increasing reticulation of information nodes on the net. As new Gopher servers emerge, their directors naturally seek to provide information resources for their local sites; their menus, therefore, include "pointers" to other Gopher sites as a way of providing local users with seamless access to remote information. Georgetown's CPET, for example, is currently included on the menus of Gopher servers at more than fifteen other locations, including the Library of Congress. Thus, it has been argued that in the virtual library of the Internet, to catalogue a resource is to accession it. But occasionally such ease of accessioning can cause problems for those who provide the data so widely catalogued. For example, if the pathway supplied as a pointer from the secondary Gopher to the primary data source is not precise, error messages will occur, and local users at the secondary site are likely to attribute them to the primary host.

More problematic still is the case of secondary Gopher site that obtains and reposts data from the primary site. Even if such files are reposted with attribution, the original developer risks losing quality control over the information. The secondary supplier to the Internet will have increasingly obsolescent material as Georgetown staff update CPET data on their own Gopher. Eventually, then, researchers on the Internet will have access to several different versions of the data and unknowingly may retrieve the outdated draft available locally rather than the updated version provided by the project's developers.[4] Loss of quality control over a derivative product in the free-wheeling environment of today's Internet is the reason some publishers cite for their reluctance to permit electronic versions of their printed products, quite aside from posting on the network.

CPET TODAY AND TOMORROW

The computers that serve as hosts for CPET in its two current forms, the online INGRES database and the Gopher server, maintain logs of the transactions by remote users. These logs provide a snapshot of current user activity and raise several questions worthy of further investigation.

The VAX logs for the INGRES database from June 22, 1993 through June 27, 1993 show that there were 114 different logins from 90 different sites in the United States, Canada, and 5 other countries. Connect times and search records are not available.

Meanwhile, the VAX host of the Georgetown Gopher server was logging the date and time of connections, the Internet Protocol (I.P.) number of the computer through which the user received access (but not the name of the user), and the list, sequence, and elapsed time for the files reviewed. For example, one sequence in the log shows that shortly after midnight (EDT), a user in British Columbia contacted the Gopher server, reviewed an introductory file for 1 minute, a second introductory file for 3 minutes, the User's Manual for the INGRES database for 4 minutes, and then two discipline-specific digests for 3-4 minutes apiece.

For the five-day period comparable to the INGRES data above, the Gopher records show 164 logins from 109 different sites in the United States, Canada, and 12 other countries. Of the 251 reviews of files, more than half (136) were for digest files containing the basic information on projects in electronic text, including

13	Biblical studies	7	American studies
12	Philosophy	6	Rhetoric
9	Art	6	Science
8	African studies		
8	English literature		

While the five-day sample is too limited to warrant generalizations about patterns of access, the data of the logs do raise two questions for further study. First, with respect to individual users, to what extent and under what circumstances do they bypass the introductory files and proceed directly to the primary data on projects? Second, with respect to the users' disciplines, to what extent are the retrieval records of the discipline-specific digests a gauge of Internet use and computer analysis within the various fields of the humanities?

Logs of activity in CPET's two forms show surprisingly little overlap in the addresses of the respective users, a fact suggesting that the two utilities provide different advantages or appeal to different preferences of user interaction. But maintaining the data in both forms is difficult, and the utilities by which CPET will be made available in the future are beginning to appear on the horizon of the Internet.

As the net grows and matures, the conflict between ease of access and ease of maintenance continues to diminish. New utilities (in many cases distributed free of charge, like Gopher) become available, and advances are made in the methods of maintenance and distribution of data.

One utility that has recently been gaining in popularity is a client-server program named WAIS (Wide Area Information Server), which allows keyword searching of full-text databases. WAIS servers are generally listed in Gopher menus, and they are very easy to use even for those with minimal computer skills. One simply enters keywords for which to search, and WAIS will present a list of items from the database that contain these words in the full text of their files. The user can then select items of particular interest from the menu and have them sent to his or her local computer. WAIS continues the trend toward ease and flexibility of access for the end-user, while returning to the maintainers of the database a simple and efficient way to store and update the information held in it.

A discussion of the future of CPET may illustrate this point. Plans are underway to reconfigure the database to be WAIS-searchable over the Internet. Each individual project listing will be considered a separate document, yet part of the whole CPET database. When a user initiates a WAIS search of CPET, the WAIS software will provide a list by project title of all the projects that contain the requested keyword. The user can then retrieve these files to a local computer for future reference.

This method of storage and retrieval combines many of the best aspects of both the INGRES version of CPET and the Gopher version. As with the INGRES database, the user has many points of access to the data and is not limited by the predetermined and rigid hierarchical menu structure of Gopher. And even greater searching power is on the way: Future versions of WAIS are expected to permit Boolean searches, allowing users to tailor the results of searches to their particular needs. However, the user still retains the ease of use that Gopher provides, and terminal emulation problems are largely avoided since WAIS clients (as with Gopher) are customized to work with the keyboard layout of the hardware on which they are running.

The maintainers of the database will also note significant benefits from this new configuration. The data are no longer spread out over several files but kept in a unitary database, as with the INGRES version. To update a current listing it is necessary only to change the data in one place, and to add new entries requires only an appending of the new text onto the current database. This procedure will allow for frequent updates, corrections, and additions, and help ensure the accuracy and currency of information being distributed.

In the more distant future, when new Internet protocols permit the user to obtain information from an SQL database regardless of its proprietary database management system (DBMS), the INGRES version of the database may once again provide more advantageous maintenance and access. Already the National Information Standards Organization (NISO), the agency that created the ISBN, has adopted a Linked Systems Protocol (Z39.50) as a standard for system-to-system communication for retrieval of bibliographic information so that a user need not learn the searching conventions of the many host sites. Extensions to Z39.50 will permit the user to retrieve not only bibliographic information but also primary data.[5] The user would have more points of access than Gopher and WAIS can make available, and the developer would be able to maintain greater control over the data and its distribution.

CONCLUSION

For today's networked academic community, this period before privatization may be remembered as the golden age of the Internet: Users have subsidized access to free data and software, and they enjoy an absence of surcharges for connect time or file size of transmission. For developers of data resources, the tension between maintaining the currency, accuracy, and integrity of data (on the one hand) and providing the user with full and easy-to-use access (on the other hand) continues to exist, as shown in this study of Georgetown University's CPET. But networked utilities recently developed or soon to emerge may simultaneously work to the advantage of those who provide electronic information and those who access it over the Internet.

REFERENCES

1. For further background on Georgetown University's Catalogue of Projects in Electronic Text, see Neuman, Michael. "The Very Pulse of the Machine: Three Trends Toward Improvement in the Development of Electronic Versions of Humanities Texts." In *Computers and the Humanities,* Vol. 25 (Spring 1992), 363-75.

2. Cummings, Anthony M., Marcia L. Witte, William G. Bowen, Laura O. Lazarus, and Richard H. Ekman. *University Libraries and Scholarly Communication.* A study prepared for the Andrew W. Mellon Foundation. Washington, DC: Association for Research Libraries for the Andrew W. Mellon Foundation, 1992; accessible from the Gopher server at the University of Virginia.

3. Silva, Marcos, Allan Bell, Darlene Canning, Robert Clarke, Angella Lambrou, Stephen Park, and Sharon Rankin. *A Report on the Need for a Library Based Gopher.* Montreal, Canada: McGill University Libraries, 1993; accessible from the Gopher server at McGill University.

4. For an interesting exchange of views on this topic in relation to electronic journals (specifically, the *Bryn Mawr Classical Review*), see the postings under the heading "Gopher(s) and Copyright" from James O'Donnell (Monday, April 26, 1993), Ann Okerson (Tuesday, April 27, 1993), and Charles Brownson (Tuesday, May 4, 1993) on the *HUMANIST* electronic bulletin board; accessible from the listserv at brownvm.bitnet or brownvm.brown.edu.

The Nevada Academic Libraries Information System: An Application of Internet Services

Carol A. Parkhurst
Myoung-ja L. Kwon

SUMMARY. The libraries of the six campuses of the University and Community College System of Nevada (UCCSN), in collaboration with UCCSN System Computing Services, have developed and implemented a service that provides local and remote networked information resources to faculty, students, and citizens of Nevada through a single point of access. The service, called the Nevada Academic Libraries Information System (NALIS), uses the existing telecommunications infrastructure on the campuses and builds on the library automation programs already present in the libraries. This article explains how the NALIS system evolved through a combination of local circumstances and funding opportunities, describes the components of NALIS, and discusses ongoing issues and future planning related to providing networked information resources.

BACKGROUND

The Computing Environment

The UCCSN libraries have been building a coordinated library automation program for two decades. Beginning with a mainframe-

---

Carol A. Parkhurst is Assistant University Librarian for Systems and Technical Services, University Library, University of Nevada, Reno, NV 89557. Myoung-ja L. Kwon is Associate Dean of Libraries, James R. Dickinson Library, University of Nevada, Las Vegas, NV 89431.

[Haworth co-indexing entry note]: "The Nevada Academic Libraries Information System: An Application of Internet Services." Parkhurst, Carol A. and Myoung-ja L. Kwon. Co-published simultaneously in *The Reference Librarian* (The Haworth Press, Inc.) No. 41/42, 1994, pp. 333-345; and: *Librarians on the Internet: Impact on Reference Services* (ed: Robin Kinder) The Haworth Press, Inc., 1994, pp. 333-345. Multiple copies of this article/chapter may be purchased from The Haworth Document Delivery Center [1-800-3-HAWORTH; 9:00 a.m. - 5:00 p.m. (EST)].

333

based acquisitions system in the early 1970s, the libraries moved through turnkey circulation systems and, in the late 1980s, into full-function, integrated library systems provided by Innovative Interfaces, Inc. One INNOPAC system is located in Reno to serve the University of Nevada, Reno (UNR) Libraries (including four branch libraries and the Medical Library), Truckee Meadows Community College, Western Nevada Community College, Northern Nevada Community College, and the Desert Research Institute. A second system is located in Las Vegas, serving the University of Nevada, Las Vegas (UNLV) Libraries and the Community College of Southern Nevada.

All UCCSN campuses are networked using various combinations of local and wide-area networks. The campuses are connected to NevadaNet, a mid-level regional TCP/IP network that was developed with funding from the National Science Foundation (NSFNet). A variety of computer hosts and end-user devices are used on the campuses. There is no systemwide standardization. The libraries have hundreds of PCs (mostly DOS-based) and asynchronous terminals (primarily Wyse 50). The libraries' local automated systems are UNIX-based, and there is a considerable base of UNIX expertise among staff on the campuses and in System Computing Services.

In 1990, library staff began looking for ways to broaden availability of electronic information services beyond the local catalogs. When System Computing Services decided to replace an aging mainframe computer, the libraries proposed that the new computer be used primarily for mounting electronic databases for shared use by all UCCSN faculty and students. The proposal was accepted by a systemwide computing committee.

Developing the NALIS Plan

The availability of funding for the new computer made it possible for UCCSN to meet the matching contribution required for a College Library Technology and Cooperation Grant (Title II-D: Combination Grant) through the U.S. Department of Education. The libraries proposed to develop a system that would provide, through a single point of access or "gateway," a variety of electronic information resources, some mounted locally and others available remotely via national networks. The system would allow users to access information resources from a terminal or workstation in the library, at home or in the office. The grant was awarded and planning began in earnest in 1991.

The NALIS management team decided to develop a customized front-end "menu engine" to use as the gateway (Figure 1). Staff from System Computing Services developed the system design, built prototypes, and created software for the NALIS menu engines (Figure 2).

NALIS MENU ENGINES: USER SERVICES

The menu engine user interface was designed to be easy to use for all types of patrons. Text is kept to a minimum and most commands require only one keystroke. Patrons who want more information about a service can look at the HELP screens–generally one to five screens of information about each available resource. It is easy to move forward and backward in the user interface, or return to the Main Menu.

There are three types of services currently offered:

1. UCCSN local online catalogs;
2. Databases mounted on a DEC VAX 6000/420 using BRS/Search software;
3. Remote services available through the Internet.

The Local Catalogs

Each menu engine offers the local library catalog as the first choice on the menu. Connecting to the local INNOPAC catalogs posed few challenges. INNOPAC readily accommodates TCP/IP connections and port allocation is already based on groups of users distinguished by login names. NALIS keeps track of how many users are active in each group of INNOPAC ports and issues an "all ports in use . . . " message when needed.

The opening screens on the INNOPAC catalogs were slightly modified for NALIS. Rather than a "Disconnect" message, the

FIGURE 1. How NALIS Works

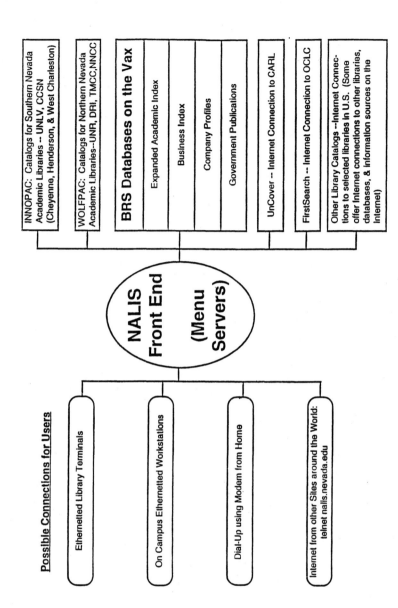

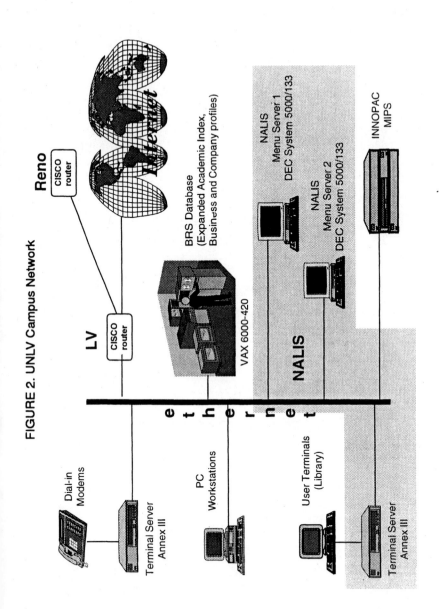

FIGURE 2. UNLV Campus Network

Reno

CISCO router

Internet

LV

CISCO router

BRS Database
(Expanded Academic Index,
Business and Company profiles)

VAX 6000-420

NALIS
Menu Server 1
DEC System 5000/133

NALIS
Menu Server 2
DEC System 5000/133

INNOPAC
MIPS

NALIS

ethernet

Dial-in
Modems

Terminal Server
Annex III

PC
Workstations

User Terminals
(Library)

Terminal Server
Annex III

choice is "Return to NALIS." All public access to the INNOPAC catalogs is through NALIS.

Other Locally Mounted Databases

A portion of the funding received from the Department of Education Title II-D grant was used for acquiring software to mount databases external to the local online catalogs. The libraries chose not to use the INNOPAC systems to mount these databases for several reasons:

1. At the time the analysis was done, the cost for loading each external database on INNOPAC was high (the cost has since come down).
2. The libraries planned to share statewide access to the databases. Loading a database on only one of the INNOPAC systems would potentially overload user ports on that system and require a system upgrade, while licensing and loading two copies of each database would be expensive.
3. While the search features of the INNOPAC catalogs are excellent for library books and serials, library staff prefer access to more advanced search features for article-level and full-text databases.
4. A System Computing Services computer (VAX 6000/400), supported by SCS staff and budget, was made available for systemwide library use for this purpose.

Library and computing center staff selected the BRS/Search software package to be used as the database/search engine on the VAX. After testing various end-user interface options offered by BRS Software Products, the libraries chose the newly developed OnSite user interface. One advantage of using OnSite is that we have been able to modify the interface to meet local requirements and preferences. A senior programming analyst at System Computing Services worked closely with library staff to make the OnSite interface look somewhat like the INNOPAC catalogs, while taking advantage of the sophisticated searching options available with BRS/Search.

Databases currently offered include Expanded Academic Index, Business Index, and Company ProFiles, all from Information Access Corporation. These databases are received in "pre-loaded" form from BRS, so that loading and updating are greatly simplified. Access to the IAC databases is restricted to on-campus users and to those outside users with individual access codes.

The biggest challenge of the locally mounted databases was the GPO Federal Government Documents database, licensed from Marcive, Inc. The GPO records are MARC records that must be "filtered" in order to be loaded into BRS/Search. A software analyst at BRS Software Products developed software to meet our detailed specifications for the MARC filter. Although the problem of searching and displaying diacritics has not been completely solved, the filter program is working well and the GPO database is available through NALIS. The GPO database is available to all NALIS users. Holdings information has been included for UCCSN libraries and for several Nevada public libraries, law libraries, and the Nevada State Library.

Resources Available via the Internet

Currently available through NALIS are UnCover and ERIC (through the Colorado Alliance of Research Libraries), OCLC First-Search, and a selection of online library catalogs around the U.S. The UnCover and ERIC connections are controlled by authorization codes purchased by the libraries to permit a specified number of concurrent users. Printing from UnCover and ERIC is a problem with Wyse 50 terminals. It is possible to do a "screen print," but it has been difficult for patrons to learn the idiosyncracies.

OCLC FirstSearch is offered as a free service by the southern Nevada libraries and as a fee-based service in the north. The patron receives a card with an authorization code valid for ten searches. NALIS logs on to FirstSearch to the "Authorization" prompt, then the user must type an authorization code.

From a user's perspective, the location of an information resource available on NALIS is irrelevant. Users are usually not aware that a resource is located hundreds or thousands of miles away.

THE NALIS MENU ENGINE SOFTWARE

The NALIS menu engine software runs on a series of Digital Equipment Corporation DECsystem 5000/133 computers, each with approximately 1.0 gigabyte of disk and 48 megabytes of memory. The operating system is ULTRIX 4.2. Two Decsystems are running in tandem in Reno and two in Las Vegas. Each menu engine supports approximately 50 NALIS users.

The menu engines support TCP/IP network connections. Xylogics Annex III terminal servers are used to connect the asynchronous terminals in the libraries to the menu engines. Other users connect directly using TCP/IP protocols.

The NALIS menu engine software suite controls the management and display of the character-based user interface. Software for the menu engines was written by Ron Young, a senior software analyst at System Computing Services, using widely available UNIX tools and programs.

The NALIS Resource Manager

The NALIS Resource Manager is used to determine whether a patron can gain access to NALIS and what information services the patron is authorized to use. The Resource Manager also controls access to remote information resources. In this context, "remote" information resources are all resources not mounted directly on the menu engines.

The Resource Manager attempts to identify the terminal emulation being used. If it cannot make an identification, the patron is asked to specify either Wyse 50 or VT100 emulation.

Each patron connecting to the NALIS menu engine is assigned a user category based on the originating network address (IP number and port number). There are four broad categories of users based on origin of connection:

Category 1: Terminals and PCs connected to terminal servers located in the campus libraries

Category 2: TCP/IP-connected workstations at UCCSN locations (i.e., within NevadaNet)

Category 3: Internet-connected workstations located outside NevadaNet

Category 4: Dial-up terminals and workstations at non-UCCSN locations

A limit on the number of concurrent connections may be assigned to each user category. The Resource Manager controls access to services by limiting use of each service to certain user categories. For example, access to locally-mounted licensed commercial databases is generally restricted to users with IP addresses within NevadaNet (i.e., users in the libraries and on the UCCSN campus networks).

The Resource Manager determines how many patrons may concurrently access each resource. It specifies the access information necessary to connect to the resource (e.g., username, password, terminal type), so that the details of connecting are transparent to the user. For example, the Resource Manager allocates specified groups of ports on the local online catalogs based on user category. Users at terminals in the campus libraries experience less contention for online catalog ports than do users at other locations. Some resources are limited to only a few simultaneous connections. The northern campuses have only two UnCover passwords, so when both are in use the menu engine sends a message such as "All ports currently in use; do you wish to queue?" The patron may choose to wait for the next available port, or may choose another service.

Access codes can be assigned to authorized users to allow them to dialup from home or connect from a remote Internet site and use services that are normally restricted to on-campus terminals. A unique set of access codes may be assigned to each remote service.

The Resource Manager can be configured by a library staff member with some technical knowledge. Although most system management tasks may be done while patrons are using NALIS, changes to the Resource Manager must be made when the system is not in use. Since a goal is to make NALIS available 24 hours a day, Resource Manager modifications are made in the early morning hours when system use is light.

The NALIS Display Manager Subsystem

The Display Manager Subsystem controls all screens that are viewed by patrons. It is intended to be configured and run by members of the library staff with little technical knowledge.

The Display Manager Subsystem allows non-programmers to create layered menu screens by writing simple English language phrases into a text file that can be edited with any standard UNIX editor. The phrases (called "directives") are compiled using MENU, a program that takes the input file and translates it into an equivalent C language program. There are several reasons for using a translator instead of developing a custom-written program to handle the menus:

1. By using a menu definition language, the staff needs no specialized computer knowledge in order to make changes to the text of the menus;
2. Since the translator compiles the menu descriptions into a C language program, the engine displays the menus much faster than if the menu descriptions were processed in other ways;
3. The menu language is easy to modify, so features can be added or changed easily;
4. Since the menus are built using standard definitions, the "look and feel" is consistent among menus.

Each menu definitions file contains one or more "screens," each with a unique name, each equivalent to one public screen display. Various directives allow text to be displayed or hidden, allow actions to be taken (e.g., move to another screen, connect to a remote service, initiate help), specify which Resource Manager access table is to be used for a requested service, specify the terminal type required by the remote service, and give commands to the operating system as appropriate.

Expect: Connecting to Remote Services

NALIS uses a package called Expect, a public domain software package developed by Don Libes at the U.S. National Institute of Standards and Technology (NIST).

Expect "talks" to other interactive programs according to a script. Following the script, *expect* knows what dialog to "expect" from a program and what the correct response should be. *Expect* allows the menu engine to have complete control of the data stream between an interactive user and a remote service. To the patron, *expect* acts like a remote system; to a remote system, *expect* acts like an interactive user.

Expect initiates the network connection to the remote service, issues necessary commands and passwords and handles common network errors. *Expect* watches the remote data stream for the text prompts specified, then sends the value of the appropriate variable to the remote system. Once the patron is properly connected, *expect* turns over control of the remote service's data stream to the patron and will exit either when the user presses ^C (control-C) or when the remote service closes the network connection.

The hardest part of writing *expect* scripts is determining the unique text strings that are used by a remote service for user prompts. The best way is to connect to the remote service and look at the data stream.

NALIS Miscellaneous Features

The NALIS "Comments" module allows patrons to type in comments that are sent to library staff and can be posted, along with library staff responses, to be read by NALIS users. New comments are automatically sent to a library staff member's e-mail address. The staff member responds to the comment and mails it back to NALIS to be posted. The ability to place comments and responses into the message base is controlled by a mail_handler.perl script.

The NALIS software constantly gathers statistics. Each menu engine logs every session with a time stamp, the menu engine name, a unique session identifier, and selected information from the menu display program. The menu display program records everything related to menu selection, including both valid and invalid service requests. A separate utility reads the log file and produces a summary report that includes time of day, number of successful and unsuccessful attempts to access each service, average length of sessions, number of active users by time of day, etc.

The "Timeout" directive tells the Display Manager how long to keep an idle connection open waiting for patron input. When the time is exceeded, the system returns to the introductory screen.

FUTURE DIRECTIONS

Now that Phase I of the NALIS project (as defined in the grant proposal) has been completed, library and computing services staff are beginning to discuss future directions. At the same time, new NALIS services are still being added.

The libraries are currently evaluating databases that might be loaded on the BRS/Search system. However, adding locally mounted databases is a costly commitment, requiring database purchase and/or licensing, adequate disk space, programming to customize database loading, alterations to the OnSite user interface, and the continued attention of computing services staff to database updates and system operation. In addition, there are several enhancements to the BRS system that the libraries would like to see:

1. The use of "hot keys" in the OnSite interface rather than requiring a [RETURN] after each command; and
2. Linking library holdings information to the journal citation indexes.

As access to desired information resources becomes available on remote hosts, the libraries will probably choose to purchase access to those services on other systems rather than mount the databases locally. Adding additional remote services is relatively simple with NALIS, although each new service adds complexity for user support. There are several unresolved problems with NALIS access to remote services:

1. Many services have no "timeout" feature, so if a user walks away from a terminal in the library without disconnecting, the next patron is likely to be confused.
2. Methods of printing from terminals are inconsistent and sometimes printing is not possible.
3. The plethora of user interfaces and resources is confusing to many users.
4. *Expect* scripts are expensive to maintain since there needs to be constant monitoring of remote resources to catch frequent changes in login procedures.

The UCCSN libraries' installed base of equipment, particularly the end-user equipment, is aging and needs replacing. For Phase 2 of NALIS, we expect to be using much more sophisticated end-user devices, probably with a Graphical User Interface as an option.

Client-server architecture is being explored in order to make the user interface more consistent among different services.

We have learned that some areas of the project have been easily controlled and others have not, since there are many independent organizations and individuals involved. The hardware/software, telecommunications, and organizational infrastructures are fragmented and complex. In planning for the future of NALIS, it is essential that we improve communications among all the units involved, that we regularly assess the changing needs of our users, that we be flexible in adapting to new technologies, and that we allow room for obsolescence.

REFERENCE

Young, Ronald L. *Draft NALIS Menu Engine Technical Reference Manual.* Las Vegas, NV: System Computing Services, University and Community College System of Nevada, 1993.

MIME and Electronic Reference Services

Christinger Tomer

SUMMARY. Interest in using electronic mail as a basis for reference service has grown considerably in recent years. This paper reviews some of the specific uses reported in the professional literature. In addition, it considers the more sophisticated capabilities of mail systems operating in compliance with the Multipurpose Internet Mail Extensions (MIME) and how systems supporting the interchange of complex, so-called "multimedia" documents may be expected to affect the use of electronic mail for library and information services.

ELECTRONIC MAIL AND REFERENCE SERVICES

In recent years, with the widespread deployment of desktop computers and the rapid growth of access to the Internet, many librarians have begun to use electronic mail as a basis for interacting with colleagues and clients. Today, many librarians regard electronic mail as a basic professional tool. (As Tsai has noted, the interest in and reliance on electronic mail among librarians may be attributed to its flexibility, its economies, both personal and organizational, and its capacity to diminish, if not eliminate problems of time and space.)[1] Witness the following message posted to PUBLIB, the computer-mediated conference for public librarians:

Christinger Tomer is Assistant Professor, Department of Library Science, School of Library and Information Science, University of Pittsburgh, Pittsburgh, PA 15260.

[Haworth co-indexing entry note]: "MIME and Electronic Reference Services." Tomer, Christinger. Co-published simultaneously in *The Reference Librarian* (The Haworth Press, Inc.) No. 41/42, 1994, pp. 347-373; and: *Librarians on the Internet: Impact on Reference Services* (ed: Robin Kinder) The Haworth Press, Inc., 1994, pp. 347-373. Multiple copies of this article/chapter may be purchased from The Haworth Document Delivery Center [1-800-3-HAWORTH; 9:00 a.m. - 5:00 p.m. (EST)].

Date: Tue, 8 Jun 93 00:02:43-0400
To: Multiple recipients of list <publib@nysernet.ORG>
Subject: Internet Success
Sender: plgrp@buffalolib.org

Internet was used for the first time at the Buffalo & Erie County Public Library to fill a reference request. A Foreign Consulate's Office called the Library for 1992 statistics from Construction Review. Unfortunately, we did not receive our issues from the G.P.O.

The librarian dialed into Nysernet, the NYS Regional Network, searched Internet using Veronica, and located the 1992 data in Construction Review on the University of Michigan computer. She logged the requested statistics, printed and faxed the data to the Consulate's Office.

–Mary Anne Casey
Assistant Deputy Dir, Subject Depts

According to reports appearing in the professional literature, communicating with colleagues on a direct basis or through computer-mediated conferences (such as PACS-L or LIBREF-L) has been the foremost use of electronic mail among librarians. However, librarians have tried, with varying degrees of success, to exploit the capabilities of electronic mail in other areas, most notably the area of reference services.

Sometimes, electronic mail service has been linked directly to an online public access catalog (OPAC), so that a user could compose and dispatch a request for service within the framework of a terminal session on the OPAC. (See Figures 1 and 2.) In other instances, libraries have offered an electronic form for patrons, who could download the form, fill it out, and then return it by electronic mail to the reference service.

For example, at the Creighton University Health Sciences Library, librarians have developed a system that uses electronic mail to receive requests for library services (computer search, reference, photocopy, inter-library loan) and allows us to reply via e-mail

---

Figure 1.

InfoTrax: Rensselaer Libraries' Information System
LIBRARY INFORMATION

FILETYPE

```
CATALOG...............................CATalog
ARCHITECTURE SLIDES....................SLIdes
CLASS RESERVE MATERIALS................CLAss
LIBRARY HOURS & INFORMATION............HOUrs
LIBRARY GUIDES & PUBLICATIONS..........PUBlications
REQUEST SERVICES.......................REQuest
To send us a MESSAGE...................MESsage
```

Use RESearch files: CUR, AST and EIP to locate articles in journals.

Type one of the file names from the list above and press RETURN
Press BREAK to return to the MAIN menu

Figure 2.

InfoTrax: Rensselaer Libraries' Information System

REQUEST (or req)

Overview: REQUEST service is a feature of InfoTrax that enables
you to use some library services remotely.

Use to request:
* photocopies of material owned by Rensselaer libraries
    * that material in the libraries be held for you
    * that material on loan be recalled for you
    * extension/renewal of loan due dates
* that material not owned by Rensselaer libraries be
    obtained from another library
* updating of your telephone/address/electronic mail
    information in InfoTrax

To access: * You must be a member of Rensselaer's faculty, staff,
    students or industrial associates.
    * You must have a telecommunications authorization code.
    * Rensselaer's industrial associates must also register
    with the Circulation Department in Folsom Library.
    *
* Press RETURN to continue, enter BREAK, ATTN or press BREAK to quit.

---

when appropriate. To facilitate the process, a user is presented with a menu of reference services. (See Figure 3.) When the user has selected a service, such as "Request a literature search" he or she is provided with a "computer search request" form. (See Figure 4.)[2]

At the National Institute of Environmental Health Sciences, electronic reference services have been offered for several years. Investigators, administrators, and staff interact with the librarians through

Figure 3.

Creighton University Health Sciences Library

```
| * * * INFORMATION SERVICES MENU * * * |
|                                        |
| 1. Request a literature search.        |
|                                        |
| 2. Request Assistance from the Drug Information |
|    Service. (School of Pharmacy & Allied Health) |
|                                        |
| 3. Request Reference Assistance.       |
|                                        |
| 4. Request photocopy or document delivery services. |
|                                        |
| 5. Send a message to someone on the library staff. |
|                                        |
| 6. Other options.                      |
|                                        |
| 7. Pick up your requests/messages.     |
|                                        |
| 8. Quit / Logoff                       |
```

Figure 4.

Creighton University Health Sciences Library

```
| Tab = Next Field                              Ctrl-Q = Quit |
|                    | Computer Search Request |             |
|                    ~~~~~~~~~~~~~~~~~~~~~~~~~               |
| FIRST NAME: Leslie              LAST NAME: Smith           |
| DEPARTMENT: Microbiology        PHONE:  987-6543           |
| STATUS: faculty                 E-MAIL ID: lsmith          |
|                                                            |
| COMPREHENSIVE SEARCH: no        YEARS TO SEARCH: 1985-present |
| ENGLISH LANGUAGE ONLY: yes                                 |
|                                                            |
| DESCRIBE YOUR TOPIC/PROBLEM: _                             |
```

a menu-driven system Institute's VAX.[3] Through this menu, clients are offered the option of using electronic mail to file requests for interlibrary loans, photocopies, and other services. Currently, this service produces about four hundred requests each day. However, although electronic mail is used heavily, it is not a significant factor in requests for reference service, because most users appear to prefer the qualitative advantages of voice communications and verbal exchange with a reference librarian.[4]

Still another approach has been to use bulletin-board systems, not so much for interacting with specific clients but more as a means of a supplemental database of questions and answers. (See Figure 5.) This approach has been used on the Cleveland Free-Net, where the institutional members of the Cleveland Area Metropol-

---

Figure 5.

A Reference Question from Cleveland Free-Net's Reference Service

```
Article #406 (677 is last):
Newsgroups: freenet.lib.questions
From: anonymous@cleveland.Freenet.Edu (Confidential Posting)
Subject: Flowers For Algernon
Date: Mon May  7 16:41:56 1990

I am looking for a copy of the SHORT STORY, Flowers for Algernon, by Daniel Keyes.  Could you
give me the title of the book it's in and its Database Control Number so I can order it through
the online catalog? Thanks.

ANSWERED BY CAMLS LIBRARIES

Here are three books that should contain the short story FLOWERS
FOR ALGERNON:

1. Katz, Harvey A.; Warrick, Patricia, and Greenberg, Martin
   Harry (eds.)
   INTRODUCTORY PSYCHOLOGY THROUGH SCIENCE FICTION
   Rand McNally, 1974

2. Asimov, Isaac (ed.)
   THE HUGO WINNERS
   Doubleday, 1962 (vol. 1)

3. BEST FROM FANTASY AND SCIENCE FICTION (9th Series)
   Doubleday, 1960

All three are found in the Cleveland Public Library Dial-Up Catalog (Control Nos. BDK-1829,
AAI-5403, and AAP-8187, respectively).  HOWEVER, the Katz title seems to be located only at the
Wayne County Public Library.  The other two are specific volumes in series, and you might have
better luck calling Cleveland Public Library by voice (623-2800) to request them.  Remember,
these control numbers only apply to the Cleveland Public Library Dial-Up Catalog.  Area
libraries not using that system (such as Cuyahoga County Public Library)
may also have these titles.

SOURCES:[SHORT STORY INDEX, H.W. Wilson]
        [Cleveland Public Library Dial-Up Catalog]
```

itan Library System (CAMLS) have maintained a collaborative reference service for almost five years.

A variation on the same theme is to use electronic mail as a document delivery service. This approach has been used successfully in conjunction with the University of Minnesota's Gopher system of servers and clients, and by Washington and Lee University, whose Law Library uses electronic mail as a mechanism for responding to requests for documents mounted on a public, network-accessible file server. (See Figure 6.)

More specifically, Ladner and Tillman report that special librarians use Internet mail services for a variety of reasons, among them tasks related to reference services, including electronic reference and technical assistance, requesting and providing ILLs, requesting library materials, and identifying document sources. Still and Campbell point out that intelibrary loan librarians have long been familiar with two forms of electronic mail, the OCLC interlibrary loan subsystem and the National Library of Medicine's DOCLINE system, which allows librarians to communicate and borrow directly from libraries across the country. They note that some vendors communi-

```
                          Figure 6.

                  Washington & Lee Law Library
                           NetLink
                      Second-level menu

   1     ->    changes/notes/new features
   2     ->    leave a message for system operator
   3     -> to Archie
   4     -> to FTP Files
   5     -> to Gopher High-Level Menus (search & link to about 110,000 entries)
   6     -> to Gophers  (around 1,200 Gopher sites)
   7     -> to Hytelnet
   8     -> to Indexes/Databases
   9     -> to Legal Sources
  10     -> to Libraries (U.S.)
  11     -> to Local Files
  12     -> to Netfind
  13     -> to Usenet Newsreaders
  14     -> to WAIS Databases (local menu)
  15     -> to WAIS Databases (SWAIS and Gopher menus)
  16     -> to WWW (WorldWideWeb)
  17     Biocore Facility Chat                                          3   6
  18     Delft University of Technology, Library                        3   6
  19     GrantSource Service (University of North Carolina, Chapel Hill)  3   6
  20     Mining Environment Database, Laurentian University, Library    3   6

1-2613 Search  Move  Next  Last  eXit  Color  Email
      Restrict set        Arrange by name
             &&& escapes interactive connections (Use if no exit instructions)
```

cate with clients via electronic mail, and that Dialog is using Dial-Mail, with a gateway to MCI Mail, as a way of delivery search results to customers. In terms of reference services, Still and Campbell report that the use of electronic mail is increasingly popular, and that there is a growing interest in using electronic mail for delivering data or documents.[5]

How successful have electronic reference services been to date? There is no conclusive data, but the results of a limited survey conducted by Daphne Flanagan, of the University of Windsor, Windsor, Ontario, suggest that usually electronic reference services have been of no more than limited effect on the more general provision of reference services. According to Flanagan:

> The length of time the service was offered varied from 3 years to 3 months. Most replied that they were disappointed with the use of the service. "Business is a little slow, but I expect it will grow"; "No problems and rather light use"; "12-20 questions per month"; "37 times since 1991"; "We are a little disappointed with the number of users of the service, and are looking at ways to increase them"; and "We haven't had the volume we expected."

She notes that the reported impact on service has been minimal, partly because use has been limited, e.g., 1-2 questions a day. In most cases it is a new service, although some have been offering it for 3-4 years. In some cases publicity has specified that questions should require short answers and be relatively straightforward such as facts, addresses, statistics. More detailed questions are referred to subject specialists. It doesn't seem to have impacted telephone reference service yet.[6]

The results of another recent study, in this instance conducted by Betty Lou Ghidiu, a graduate student at the School of Information Science & Policy, the State University of New York at Albany, corroborates Flanagan's findings about how reference services available and transacted by electronic mail are used. According to Ghidiu, only about fifteen percent of the libraries providing reference service via electronic mail receive requests daily.[7]

Why are such reference services used so infrequently? Excluding the variable effects of local factors, it seems that there are at least four basic problems that limit the use of electronic mail for reference services. First, there are today other, less sophisticated forms of reference service that are often more effective and more efficient. For example, in what are presumably the vast majority of instances it remains easier for a remote user to use the telephone to contact a reference librarian and receive some form of reference service. Given the research suggesting that the vast majority of reference questions are answered within the first five minutes, it is not surprising that telephone reference remains a preferred means of interaction for remote users.

The second problem is insufficient interoperability. Simply put, whether the issue is directory services or gateways for exchanging messages between two types of systems, electronic mail is currently limited by the lack of standardization or implementation of standards in several key areas. As Barbara Denton noted in an article about using Dialog's DIALMAIL:

> . . . DIALMAIL could be a much more useful service for searchers if we could send messages from the outside world to a DIALMAIL address and send messages from DIALMAIL to other e-mail systems.[8]

The third problem is the extent to which electronic mail services are available or used. While the Electronic Mail Association estimates that as many as thirty million people and most major organizations are already electronic mail users, the numbers of people and organizations making frequent use of electronic mail are much smaller. So, although it is reasonable to imagine that electronic mail may become a far more general form of communication in the near future, today it serves no more than a small fraction of the population, and presumably no more than a similarly small portion of library users.

Finally, there is the fact that until recently electronic mail systems using the Internet did not have the capability of sending and receiving the complex documents that make up much of a library's resources.

> A consistent complaint about E-mail is that [most systems do not] have the 'richness' of other media. A message read off a computer screen is just words. It lacks the nuance provided by

such nonverbal cues as tone of voice, posture, gestures, eye contact, and facial expressions.[9]

There are potentially significant productivity issues at work regarding each of these problems, but those problems associated with the quality of the documents capable of interchange via electronic mail may be particularly important. It has been suggested that the evolution of the electronic work group will depend largely on developing more subtle, more sophisticated forms of electronic communication, and ones that make access to information more "humanlike." According to at least one commentator, the relationship of the computer "to the user [is changing] from that of an isolated productivity tool to that of an active collaborator in the acquisition, use and creation of information, as well as a facilitator of human interaction."[10] Electronic messaging systems capable of transporting complex documents are often cited as a necessary condition for such developments.

In the realm of electronic library services, it seems almost certain that the same factors will hold true. Many users already complain about the limitations of electronic mail limited to the exchange of ASCII text. They want "multimedia" mail. Besides being able to send ASCII text, they want to be able to transmit and receive documents generated by word processing in their native formats, as well as messages that include binary graphics, digitized facsimiles, and audio clips, and, although it is scattered, there is evidence that these demands extend to library and information services.[11]

Efficiency is another critical, if not always obvious factor in this regard. As Ross Atkinson has noted:

> The primary purpose of information services has always been and will always be to reduce to a minimum the amount of time required by local users to obtain access to that information that they need to do their work. All information service activities are intended ultimately to achieve that single objective. As we move into an increasingly online environment, those service activities will change, but that primary objective will remain the same.[12]

So, it may be argued from this perspective that the success of digital libraries and electronic library services will depend to a significant degree on which digital technologies may be employed to increase the efficiency of the relationship between libraries and their users by enabling users to ask for and receive a full range of information and document delivery services on a remote basis.

The purpose of this paper is to review an important effort to transform Internet mail into an eight-bit system that can support standardized multimedia mail, and to consider how such a system might affect the quality of reference services delivered by means of electronic mail over local and wide area networks. Given its subject, the paper engages, necessarily, in a brief review of the functional underpinnings of electronic mail, before turning to the heart of the matter, that being the Multipurpose Internet Mail Extensions (MIME) and how they enhance the usefulness of electronic mail in a digital library environment.

BASIC ASPECTS OF ELECTRONIC MAIL

Electronic mail is typically a store-and-forward system. In the Unix environment, which is the general frame of reference of this discussion, electronic mail is generally a three-layered scheme. It consists of a user agent that is used to compose outgoing messages and get incoming mail, a routing agent that figures out how to deliver incoming and outgoing mail, and a delivery agent that transfers messages to next routing or delivery agent. As messages are routed across wide-area networks, they may also be passed from one type of network to another by so-called "gateway" services. Typically, three protocols are involved: (1) a messaging protocol used between two user agents; (2) a relaying protocol used between two mail transfer agents; and (3) a delivery protocol used between a mail transfer agent and a user agent.[13]

Examples of user agents in common use today include/bin/mail,/usr/ucb/mail, mailx, elm, pine, and mh. Widely used transfer and routing agents include sendmail, mmdf, and smail. But the heart of most Unix mail systems is sendmail. This program, which purists regard as a "kludge," is a transport agent that mediates relations between user agents and delivery agents. Originally written in 1985 by a student at Berkeley named Eric Allman, this program, which runs as a daemon, controls outgoing mail messages, interprets address of each message's recipient and selects an appropriate delivery agent, rewrites the addresses so that they can be understood by the delivery agent(s), re-formats the headers on the various messages, and passes the messages off to the remote agent for delivery. It also produces error messages and returns messages that are undeliverable. More specific actions of sendmail are determined by the sendmail configuration file. This file is organized in three general sections: (1) definitions of symbols, classes, parameters, and options; (2) rules for rewriting addresses; and (3) definitions for interrelations with users agents and delivery agents, including rules governing how the system will invoke each type of application. The protocol that relays messages from one system to another system in the Internet environment is the Simple Mail Transfer Protocol.[14] SMTP service carries both an electronic envelope and the content of the message. The SMTP envelope consists of the electronic mail address of the originator, one or more recipient addresses, and an indication of the mode of delivery. (Four modes of delivery are possible under SMTP, but today nearly all SMTP transactions are files written to the recipient's mailbox.)

The Structure of Electronic Mail Messages

When an electronic mail message arrives at its destination, it consists of at least two and possibly three parts: the header, the body of the message, and the signature. The header is a record of the message's journey from its source, in which the machines and gateways that have handled the message are identified and the times at which they "touched" the message are noted. In addition, the header includes the subject line, the distribution of the message, in the event that the sender has authorized the distribution of copies to other users, and the status of the message. It may also incorporate information indicative of the content of the message or the system used by the sender, where the system from which the message was sent supports capabilities beyond those of the basic system. (See Figures 7-8.)

A characteristic of more sophisticated electronic mail systems is that they rely on other applications to create, read, or otherwise reproduce various types of presentations. Where such capabilities are at work, the header is not merely a record of where a message has been or how it got where it was supposed to go, but also a set of

Figure 7.

```
From MRAISH@BINGVMB.BITNET   Ukn Sep  1 18:07:20 1992
Received: from VM2.CIS.PITT.EDU by icarus.lis.pitt.edu (4.1/1.34)
        id AA19922; Tue, 1 Sep 92 18:07:17 EDT
Resent-From: BI-L@BINGVMB.BITNET
Received: from vms.cis.pitt.edu by vms.cis.pitt.edu (PMDF #12376) id
 <01GOA2H64V408WWTB5@vms.cis.pitt.edu>; Tue, 1 Sep 1992 18:08 EST
Received: from PSUVM.PSU.EDU (MAILER@PSUVM) by vms.cis.pitt.edu (PMDF #12376)
 id <01GOA2GJFZB48WWUVR@vms.cis.pitt.edu>; Tue, 1 Sep 1992 18:07 EST
Received: by PSUVM (Mailer R2.08) id 1208; Tue, 01 Sep 92 18:06:53 EDT
Resent-Date: Tue, 1 Sep 1992 18:08 EST
Date: Tue, 1 Sep 1992 15:30:12 ECT
From: Martin Raish <MRAISH@BINGVMB.BITNET>
Subject: Hints and Netiquette
Sender: Bibliographic Instruction Discussion Group <BI-L@BINGVMB.BITNET>
Resent-To: CT@lis.pitt.edu
To: Chris Tomer <CTOMER@vms.cis.pitt.edu>,
Reply-To: Bibliographic Instruction Discussion Group <BI-L@BINGVMB.BITNET>
Resent-Message-Id: <01GOA2H64V408WWTB5@vms.cis.pitt.edu>
Message-Id: <01GOA2GJFZB48WWUVR@vms.cis.pitt.edu>
X-Envelope-To: CT@ICARUS.LIS.pitt.edu
X-Vms-To: IN%"CTOMER@vms.cis.pitt.edu" "Chris Tomer",
Comments: Resent-From: Martin Raish <MRAISH@BINGVMB>
Status: RO
X-Status:
```

Figure 8.

RFC 822-specified Fields

bcc	Resent-Date
cc (8)	Resent-From
Comments	Resent-Message-ID
Date (3)	Resent-Reply-To
Encrypted	Resent-Sender
From (4)	Resent-To
In-Reply-To	Return-Path (1)
Keywords	Sender (6)
Message-ID	Subject (5)
Received (2)	To (7)
References	
Reply-To	
Resent-bcc	extension fields
Resent-cc	user defined fields

instructions that causes a user agent to invoke a specific application or set of applications for the purposes of display. For example, a header generated by a system of this type might include a statement in the header indicating that the transmitting system is compatible with the Multipurpose Internet Mail Extensions (MIME), and that there is an encapsulated segment of the message that will require a PostScript previewer for display. If the recipient's system is capable of and has been configured to call a PostScript previewer when presented with such a statement in the header, when the user selects the message, the PostScript previewer will then be called to view the appropriate segments of the message.

INTERNET MAIL

As noted above, Internet mail is based on two standards established in 1982, RFC 821, the Simple Mail Transfer Protocol and RFC 822, the Standard for the Format of ARPA Internet Text Messages.[15-18] These standards limited the transmission of electronic mail to messages that:

- contain only ASCII characters;
- do not include lines longer than 1000 characters;
- do not exceed a length specified locally.

Under SMTP a mail request entails the establishment of a two-way communication channel between the sender and the receiver, where the receiver may be the ultimate destination or an intermediate recipient. An SMTP server listens on TCP port 25 for a client connection. When a client and server have exchanged "greetings," which is essentially an exchange of information concerning the server's mail transfer agent, the client initiates one or more SMTP transactions. (The commands are case-sensitive four-character expressions followed by a single space, argument, and CRLF. The replies are a 3-digit code followed by a space, text, and CRLF. All characters are 7-bit ASCII. The interaction is lock-step: command/reply. In the reply codes, the first digit decides positive or negative status, and whether it is transient or permanent; the second digit decides what type of information follows (syntax, information requests, connection issues, etc.); and the final digit signifies the message format.) When the client is finished delivering its messages, the client and server exchange another set of signals, in this instance releasing the transfer agent from service and closing the TCP connection. (See Figure 9 for an example of feedback generated by Simple Mail Transfer Protocol when mail is used in the verbose mode.)

Figure 9.

```
Connecting to agsm.ucla.edu. via tcpld...
Trying 128.97.74.2... Connected.
220 Welcome to IDA Sendmail 5.65a/IDA-1.2.8 running on agsm.ucla.edu
HELO mic.ucla.edu
250 Hello mic.ucla.edu, pleased to meet you
MAIL From:<wada@mic.ucla.edu>
250 <wada@mic.ucla.edu>... Sender ok
RCPT To:<ggordon@agsm.ucla.edu>
250 <ggordon@agsm.ucla.edu>... Recipient ok
DATA
354 Enter mail, end with "." on a line by itself
.
250 Ok
QUIT
221 agsm.ucla.edu closing connection
```

MIME

MIME is a freely available specification offering a means of interchanging text in languages with different character sets and multi-media mail among the many different computer systems that support the SMTP standard. To be even more specific, MIME represents a way of encoding, in ASCII, a multi-part message structure. A MIME body part is a sequence of bytes with an associated content-type and content-transfer-encoding.

The parts may be nested and may be of seven different types: Text, Audio, Image, Video, Message, Application and Multi-part (nested). The default MIME content-type is text/plain, i.e., a sequence of lines of text.

Provisions are included for encoding binary data in ASCII in a base 64 format similar to uuencode or btoa. (See Figure 4.) In addition, MIME includes support for international character sets, tagging each part of a message with the character set in which it has been written and providing seven bit encoding of eight bit character sets. It also provides a simple "rich text" format for marking text. Finally, there is a mechanism for splitting messages into multiple parts and reassembling them at the receiving end.[19,20]

MIME builds on the established standards for Internet mail by adding new fields for message headers that describe types of content and organization for messages. As a result, Internet mail supported by compliant applications may now contain:

- Multiple objects in a single message
- Text having unlimited line length or overall length
- Character sets other than ASCII
- Multi-font messages
- Binary or application specific files
- Images, Audio, Video and multi-media messages
- Calls to external message body parts

MIME is designed to be compatible with the older Internet mail standards. Nathaniel Borenstein, the principal architect of MIME, has written:

> A major constraint of the working group charged with extending RFC 822 was the imperative that this basic model not be changed. In particular, it was strongly and widely felt that nothing in the new document should cause existing mail systems to break. Not only was the header/body model left unchanged, but so too were the syntax and semantics of all of the standard header fields defined by RFC 822.[21]

As a result, if a MIME-compliant mail agent receives a MIME message, and that message includes encapsulated objects, then it will perform additional processing for the MIME message that it would not perform for non-MIME messages. In order to allow mail reading programs to recognize MIME messages, MIME messages are required to contain a MIME-Version header field. The MIME-Version header field specifies the version of the MIME standard to which the message conforms. (See Figure 10.)

MIME is an extensible mechanism. As a result, it is likely that the set of content-type/subtype pairs and associated parameters will grow with time. Several other MIME fields, such as character set names, are also likely to have new values defined. To guarantee that

Figure 10.

When the user of a non-MIME mailer receives a multipart MIME message, the message will look like this:

```
Date: Tue, 14 Jul 1992 17:55:17 -0700 (PDT)
From: Joe Smith <js@icarus.lis.pitt.edu>
Subject: Test MIME message
To: Richard Cox   <rjc@icarus.lsi.pitt.edu.>

--16820115-1435684063-711161753:#2306
Content-Type: TEXT/PLAIN; charset=US-ASCII
```

The text of the message would go here. What follows is a binary file in base 64 encoding (that has been shortened for this example).

```
--16820115-1435684063-711161753:#2306
Content-Type: APPLICATION/octet-stream; name=login
Content-Transfer-Encoding: BASE64
Content-Description: NeXT login program
```

```
AYAAAABAAAAAQAAAAQAAAL4AAAAAQAAAAEAAAJYAAAAAAAAAAA
AAAAAAAABfsAAADFAAAFswAAAHAAAABwAAAAgAAAAAX190ZXh0
AAAAF9fVEVYVYAAAAAAAAAAAAAAAAAAAAAAQpAAAAxQAAAABAAAA
AAAAAAAAAAAAABfX2Z2bWxpxpY19pbml0MAAAX19URVhhUAAAAAAAA
KQAAAEwAAATuAAAAAIAAAAAAAAAAAAAAAAAAAAAAAAAAAAf9fZnZt
XQxAABfX1RFWFFQAAAAAAAAAAAAAAAAAR1AAAAAAABToAAAAAgAA
AAAAAAAAAAAAAAAX19jc3RyaaW5nAAAAAAAAAf9fVEVYVYVAAAAAAA
BHUAAADQQAAFOgAAAAAAAAAAAAAAAAAAAAACAAAAAAAAABfX2Nv
AAAAAAAX19URVhhUAAAAAAAAAAAAAAAFRgAAACsAAAYLAAAAAIA
AAAAAAAAAAAAAAAAf9fZGF0YTYOYQAAAAAAAAAAAABfX0RBVEEAAAAA
AAVxAAAAQgAABjYAAAAgAAAAAAAAAAAAAAAAAAAAAAAAAAAAAAAAX19i
AAAAAAAAf9fREFUQQQAAAAAAAAAAAAAAAABbMAAAADAAAAAAAAAAAC
AAAAAABAAAAAAAAAAABfX2NvbW1vbjAAAAAAAAAAX19EQVRBAAAA
CAlcwAlZCBMT0dJTiBGQUlMMVVVJFJXMgT04gJXMsICVzAHNlAGxv
Wxsb2Mgb3V0IG9mIG1lbW9yeQoAJXMgdG9pR2xvaWNvbmNNCgAvZXRj
3Vzci9hZG0vd3RtccAAAABAKCMpUFJPR1JJBTTpsb2dpbiAgUFFJP
WRzLTYyICBCERVZFTE9QRVV 6cm9vdCAgQ1VJTFFQ6U3VuIE5vcmlAx
zoyMSBBQU1QgMTk5ZSMoAAAAAAAAAAAAAAAAAAAAAAAAAAAAAAAAAAA
AAAAAAAAAAAAAAAAAAAAAAAAAAAAAAAAAAAAAAAAAAAAAAAAAAAAAA
AAAAAAAAAAAAAAAAAAAAAAAAAAAAAAQCgjKSBDb3B5cmlnaHQgKGMp
DE5ODDcsIDE5ODDqgVGhlIIFJlZ2VudHMgb2YgdGhlIIFVuaXZlcnNp
2FsaWZvcm5pYS4KIEFsbCByaWdodHMgcmVzZXJ2ZWQuCgBAKCMp
wk1LjQwYIChCZXJrZWxleSkgNS85Lzg5AAAAABHUAAAR1f//////
wAAEdQAABHUAAAR1AAAEdQAAAEsAxwREwT/GhkSDxcWAAAB2gAA
AAR5gAAEeoAABHuAAAR8gAAEfYAABH6AAAR/gAAEgIAABIGAAAA
AAB
```

```
--16820115-1435684063-711161753:#2306--
```

the set of defined values develops in an orderly manner, MIME defines a registration process that uses the Internet Assigned Numbers Authority (IANA) as a central registry for such values.

MIME Content Types

Of the properties defined by the first version of MIME, the most important is the Content-Type header field, which specifies the type and subtype of data in the body of a message and the encoding of such data, where encoding has been used. The MIME standard defines seven content-types. Although the authors of the MIME standard say that the set of seven content types is "substantially complete," they expect additional supported types to be accommodated by creation of new subtypes of the seven initial top-level types.

MIME's content types include: (1) a Text Content-Type, which can be used to represent textual information in a number of character sets and formatted text description languages; (2) a Multi-part Content-Type, which can be used to combine several body parts, including parts consisting of different types of data, into a single message; (3) an Application Content-Type, which can be used to transmit application data or binary data; (4) a Message Content-Type, for encapsulating a mail message; (5) an Image Content-Type, for transmitting still image data; (6) an Audio Content-Type, for transmitting audio data; and (7) a Video Content-Type, for transmitting video or moving image data, possibly with audio as part of the composite video data format.

The Content-Type field describes the data contained in the body of the message in detail sufficient to enable the mail reader to select an appropriate mechanism for presentation of the data to the user, or to deal with the data in another, appropriate manner.

The Content-Type header field is used to specify the nature of data in the body or body part, by giving type and subtype identifiers, and by providing parameters that may be needed for certain types. After the type and subtype names, the remainder of the header field is a set of parameters, specified in an attribute/value notation. The set of meaningful parameters differs for different types. In accord with the rules set out by RFC 822, comments placed within parentheses may be placed within structured header fields.

The top-level Content-Type is used to declare the general type of data, while the subtype specifies a specific format for that type of data. For example, a Content-Type of Image/xyz is a message to the mail agent indicating that the data is an image, even if the mail agent is not bound to an application that can be the specific image format xyz. This type of information can also be used to determine whether to display the raw data from an unrecognized subtype. However, as the document outlining MIME suggests, "such an action might be reasonable for unrecognized subtypes of text, but not for unrecognized subtypes of image or audio," because these formats are less standardized. As a result, it is expected that MIME-compliant systems will perform more reliably when registered subtypes of audio, image, text, or video do not contain embedded information of a different type. It is also expected that compound types will be represented by multi-part or application types.

Under MIME, parameters are modifiers of the content-subtype. Although most of MIME's defined parameters function only with certain Content-Types, some of them are "global" in the sense that they might apply to any subtype. For example, the boundary parameter, which is used to show how body parts are separated from one another, is valid only in a multi-part Content-Type, whereas the character set parameter is valid for several Content-Types. The syntax for the content type header field is:

Content-Type := type "/" subtype [";" parameter] . . .

MIME defines four subtypes of the Multi-part Content-Type. The four subtypes are: (1) mixed (which indicates sequential processing); (2) parallel; (3) digest (which shows that each part is an encapsulated mail message); and (4) alternative (which indicates that although multiple body parts are present, each part has identical content, with the part selected for display by the recipient's user agent being a function of that application's interpretative capabilities).

MIME also specifies a Content-Transfer-Encoding header field, which specifies how data may be encoded so that mail transports having data or character set limitations can be used. The classic example is the Simple Mail Transfer Protocol, which restricts mail messages to seven-bit ASCII data with lines no longer than 1000 characters. To overcome this limitation, MIME supports two mechanisms for encoding 8-bit data into a 7-bit short-line format, with the Content-Transfer-Encoding header field indicating that the transformation has been made to represent the part of the message in an acceptable manner for transport and identifying the mechanism used to perform the encoding.

The purpose of the Content Type Message/External-Body is to indicate that the actual body of the message, the data itself, has not been included, but merely referenced. When a body or body part is external, the reference consists of a header, a blank line, and the message header for the encapsulated message. If another blank line appears, this ends the message header for the encapsulated message. Such a reference would look like this:

> Content-type: message/external-body;
> access-type=local-file;
> name=/u/nsb/Me.gif
> Content-type: image/gif

Where this content type is defined, definition of an access type is mandatory, with the definition of other parameters depending on the value of the Access-Type. (The values defined for the Access-Type parameter are ftp, anon-ftp, tftp, afs, local-file, and mail-server. The optional parameters associated with Access-Type are expiration date, size of the file or files, and permission.)

The Significance of MIME

The significance of MIME is three-fold. First, it builds upon the single largest electronic mail system, Internet mail, in a simple, almost elegant manner, facilitating the transmission of complex documents without disrupting service to the installed base of users or requiring any major modifications at the systems level. Under MIME, many users of SMTP-based mail services will be able to send and receive complex documents while continuing to use familiar user agents such as Elm, Pine, or GNU Emacs' rmail facility.

Second, MIME is capable of functional co-existence with both X.400 and at least some of the more important proprietary electronic mail systems, e.g., Microsoft Mail and Lotus's cc:Mail, which means that there should be configurations under which clients effectively have the advantages of not one but a series of standards and systems.[22] Finally, there is the fact that MIME is an open standard–essentially free and public–that should engender rapid evolution and comparatively widespread implementation, and that it can be elaborated by public domain implementation and interfaces.

MIME's shortcomings seem largely "political," rather than technical. Thus far, commercial vendors seem much more interested in X.400. This is largely because as an ISO standard, X.400 seems to afford commercial developers a better documented and presumably more stable base on which to construct both clients and servers. Although a few commercial developers have promised to bring compliant clients to the marketplace, MIME suffers comparatively because none of the major developers have thus far judged it to be in their interests to promote SMTP or its extensions as a mail transport technology. There is, too, the matter of MIME being rooted in the Unix environment, where many major vendors have little or no foothold. By comparison X.400 has the acceptance of the standards communities, a variety of features of potential benefit to users, including the capacity to transport complex documents, substantial and growing deployment in most parts of the world, and the increasing interest of commercial vendors.

Yet, particularly in the absence of significant improvement in the multimedia capabilities of the X.400 Message Handling System, MIME will play a critical role not only on the Internet, but beyond the Internet. There are at least a couple of reasons why this may prove to be so. First, the technologies of the Internet are important by virtue of the Internet's size and continuing growth. Even if low-end Internet services are not "privatized," the scale on which the Internet supports messaging would seem to make it an essential part of any serious effort to standardize the exchange of complex documents at the operational level.

THE POTENTIAL EFFECTS OF MIME ON ELECTRONIC REFERENCE SERVICES

How will MIME-compliant, multimedia mail alter the conduct of reference services? It is hard to know to what extent this medium will change and enhance reference services in the short term, because many librarians view the newer information technologies with fear and loathing, because many libraries are mired in what appears more and more to be a chronic financial crisis, and because the publishing industry has long been seized by the view that without close regulation use of various information technologies is a direct, serious threat to its survival.[23]

Yet, economic constraints notwithstanding, change should be rapid. Today, most Internet users work on what has been labeled the "low-end" Internet. This segment of the Internet is characterized by three basic services: remote login, electronic mail and file transfer services. However, new services are emerging with startling regularity, and the expectation is that in the next decade first the low-end Internet and then the NREN will support a range of new services, including multimedia mail; widely distributed file systems; hypertext-like navigational tools for use on both local and wide area networks with easy-to-learn, easy-to-implement command sequences; hypermedia databases; intelligent agents that can take a natural language string and transform it into a conducted search of distributed digital libraries (the so-called "knowbot"); real-time, multi-media conferencing; interoperable data description protocols; and interactive, online mechanisms for user education and training.[24,25]

Perhaps more to the point, in the long run the ability to exchange messages that consist of or include complex documents is going to add a new dimension to the reference process. Reference librarians will continue to conduct interviews, analyze questions, and plot search strategies, but they will also have the opportunity to take relevant data and files and present them in arrays whose quality and usefulness will depend in significant measure on their creative, compositional talents.

Imagine a user at the University of Washington sending the Institute for Jazz Studies at Rutgers University a request for information concerning Johnny Dodds, the clarinetist from New Orleans who played with Louis Armstrong and Jelly Roll Morton. In return, the user might receive a message from the reference librarian charged with answering the question that includes not only a text message about the conduct of the search, but also bitmaps of select pages of a relevant journal article, a digitized version of a photograph of Dodds, and a series of audio clips presenting representative musical selections as encapsulated segments of the message. So, as a result, the patron will be able to see what Dodds looked like and how he played, in addition to reading about him and his music. (In a related vein, interlibrary requests for copies of articles in journals available in bitmapped editions could be filled via electronic mail. Let's say that the user in Seattle wants to see the complete article about Johnny Dodds. With a request from the libraries at the University of

Washington in hand, the reference librarian at Rutgers could send the appropriate bitmap files to the interlibrary loan account, with an attachment indicating that the enclosed pages had been supplied in response to a specific request.)

Or, imagine a medical librarian in Boston, in response to a question from a local clinician, assembling an array of research papers, digitized medical images, and clinical notes and distributing this material via electronic mail to physicians in, say, Los Angeles, New York, and London in order to support a consultation.

But more traditional forms of reference service will remain firmly in place. No matter how powerful the technologies become, there will be many circumstances under which face-to-face interaction with a reference librarian is preferred. There will also be circumstances under which what we now call telephone reference will be more effective or more efficient than the comparatively more elaborate business of a library patron and a librarian exchanging multimedia mail messages.

ENDNOTES

1. Tsai, Bor-sheng. "The Effectiveness Measurement of Electronic Mail Communications within a Special Professional Community." *Proceedings of the 55th Annual Meeting of the American Society for Information Science*, October 26-29. 1992, Pittsburgh, Pennsylvania, p. 76.

2. As designed by the librarians at Creighton, the reference form may have as many as twenty-five fields, although the scope is limited in this instance to what can fit on a single screen. The description for a form is kept in an ASCII file. Field labels are highlighted and boxes are drawn with graphics characters. Field values may be filled in by default. The user's name, department, phone number, etc., are read in from a file in the user's home directory. The form provides editing features common to most full screen editors.

The FORMS program was written in C to run in a UNIX environment. When a user has submitted a request, another program attempts to send a message to the terminal in the reference area alerting the staff that a request has arrived. In addition, a program was added to the UNIX cron system to monitor several mail boxes and alert the staff if the mail boxes are not empty. As a result reference librarians at Creighton are able to acknowledge and begin processing requests no later than 10 minutes after their delivery.

The FORMS program reads the ASCII file, then sets up the screen. (Different forms have different ASCII files. There is no limit on the number of forms which can be created. A FORM can be changed in a few minutes by modifying its ascii file description.) After the form is filled out and the user verifies that the request is ready to be submitted, information on the form is transferred to an ASCII file, which is then sent via electronic mail to the appropriate library department.

3. The VAX at NIHES offers a network-accessible directory to which all of the workstations on the LAN running WordPerfect may write. This permits a search to be conducted, downloaded converted to WordPerfect file, and saved to the aforementioned directory. Subsequently, the client who requested the search is notified that the results have been posted to this directory. The client then has the option of reading or printing the results of the search, or copying the appropriate file to a directory mounted on their personal desktop system.

4. Wright, Larry. "Re: Electronic Reference." From a message posted on May 28, 1993 to LIBREF-L <libref-l@kentvm.kent.edu>.

5. Still, Julie and Campbell, Frank. "Librarian in a Box: the Use of Electronic Mail for Reference." *Reference Services Review* 21 (Spring 1993): 15.

6. Flanagan, Daphne. "E-mail Reference Summary." From a message posted May 26, 1993 to LIBREF-L <LIBREF-L%KENTVM.BITNET>.

7. Ghidiu, Betty. "Results of Internet Survey." From a message posted April 28, 1993 to LIBREF-L <LIBREF-L%KENTVM.BITNET>.

8. Denton, Barbara. "E-Mail Delivery of Search Results via the Internet." *Online* 16 (March 1992): 53.

9. "Training for E-mail." *Training & Development Journal* 45 (March 1991): 71.

10. Tesler, L. "Networked computing in the 1990s." *Scientific American* 265 (September 1991): 86-93.

11. Elsevier Science Publishing is sponsoring a project that enables participating universities to download and access research journals published by Elsevier via Internet. The project, spanning three years, is called The University Licensing Program (TULIP). It is the first project by a large publishing house involving the systematic release of copyrighted, published material over Internet. It is the view of many observers that the demand for electronic access to journals is already substantial and growing, because decreasing library budgets make it impossible for many libraries to purchase many paper-based publications.

12. Atkinson, Ross. "Networks, Hypertext, and Academic Information Services: Some Longer-range Implications." *College & Research Libraries* 54 (May 1993): 200.

13. Rose, Marshall T. *The Internet Message: Closing the Book with Electronic Mail.* Englewood Cliffs, New Jersey: Prentice-Hall, 1993. pg. 4.

14. Postel, Jonathan B. *Simple Mail Transfer Protocol.* RFC 821. Information Sciences Institute, University of Southern California, 1982.

15. One of the most important issues in the realm of electronic mail is that of standards. Today, almost all of the important issues in the further development of electronic mail systems–integration of the Internet community with the European messaging services, the development of multimedia mail, and using the processing capabilities of personal computers to enhance the electronic mail environment–are likely to be resolved only if the parties concerned agree on some signifi-

cant degree of standardization. As a result, there can be doubt that maintaining an informed view of the development and trends shaping the next generation of computerized messaging services depends largely on understanding standards like the Simple Mail Transfer Protocol, MIME, the Multipurpose Internet Mail Extensions, and some important international standards, particularly X.400 standard for messaging and the X.500 standard for directory services.

16. Crocker, David H. *Standard for the Format of ARPA Internet Text Message. RFC 822.* University of Delaware, 1982.

17. The Internet Activities Board supports the development of documents that define standards for the Internet protocol suite. The IAB has developed these standards in order to coordinate the evolution of the Internet protocols. The majority of Internet protocol development and standardization activity takes place in the working groups of the Internet Engineering Task Force, or IETF. Protocols which are to become standards in the Internet go through a series of steps: proposed standard, draft standard, and standard. Each step in this process involves increasing amounts of scrutiny and experimental testing. At each step, the Internet Engineering Steering Group of the IETF must make a recommendation for advancement of the protocol and the IAB must ratify it for the process to move forward. If a recommendation is not ratified, the protocol is returned to the IETF for review and further development. It is a general practice of the Internet Activities Board that no proposed standard can be promoted to draft standard without at least two independent implementations and the recommendation of the Internet Engineering Steering Group. Promotion from draft standard to standard generally requires operational experience and demonstrated interoperability of two or more implementations, as well as the recommendation of the Internet Engineering Steering Group.

18. An important extension of the electronic mail capabilities embodied by the Simple Mail Transfer Protocol is the Post Office Protocol. The Post Office Protocol enables a UNIX- or VMS-based computer to act as a mail server for microcomputers or workstations (which lack the applications necessary to support mail service). The protocol enables microcomputer clients to communicate with the mail server, sending and receiving electronic mail through the mail transport capabilities of the server. A mail system using the Post Office Protocol as the basis for sending and receiving mail is comparatively simple. It relies primarily on an application called the pop daemon, which is invoked on Unix systems at boot time in the inetd.conf file and usually listens for mail on TCP port 9 or 10. If a user with an account on the system uses a POP client to compose a message, the client application passes the message to the sendmail program running on the host system, with the pop daemon mediating the transaction between the personal computer on which the client is installed and the machine service on which sendmail resides. Once the message is passed to sendmail, it may then be routed to any address on the network and delivered. POP clients use the IP address of the Unix machine as the return address, so the client application must acquire incoming mail to serve as a reader and message processor.

The importance of POP is twofold: first, it means that microcomputers with

Ethernet capability and IP addresses can be fully integrated into electronic mail systems as clients; and, second, POP clients can be outfitted with interfaces and editing capabilities that make composition or management relatively easy. (Some POP clients have been outfitted to communicate with servers over dial-up connections, and some even take advantage of SLIP, the Serial Line Internet Protocol–Northwestern University's NUPop is an example–but these clients work best when they communicate with the mail server via the higher speeds provided by Ethernet connections.)

Because the Post Office Protocol is an open standard, developing more refined versions of the pop daemon and client applications is generally unrestricted. As a result, the software necessary to install a pop daemon is readily available from file servers attached to the Internet, as are the most noteworthy clients. The best of them are NUPop, which is an MS-DOS client in a process of continuous development at Northwestern University, and Eudora, a Macintosh client developed at the University of Illinois and now being transformed into a commercial product.

Also in increasingly widespread use is the Interactive Mail Access Protocol (IMAP) protocol, which is similar to the Post Office Protocol. Like the Post Office Protocol, IMAP is a mail access protocol, as distinguished from a mail transfer protocol such as SMTP. IMAP retains mail on the server and allows the client to retrieve mail as it is read, with the IMAP client catching only the messages requested; because retrieving only the messages specified requested requires less bandwidth, IMAP-based systems are considered desirable in situations where bandwidth is considered a problem. Another feature that differentiates IMAP from POP is that IMAP supports commands sequences between client and server that allows the client to search for messages matching a specified search string and then call the set of messages, if any, from the server to the client-based reader.

19. Borenstein, Nathaniel and Freed, Ned. *MIME (Multipurpose Internet Mail Extensions): Mechanisms for Specifying and Describing the Format of Internet Message Bodies*. Network Working Group, RFC 1341, 1992.

20. An extension of SMTP intended to support eight-bit MIME transport service has been proposed. Under the proposed extension, when a SMTP client requests permission to submit a content body consisting of a MIME message containing eight-bit material, it issues the EHLO command to the SMTP server. If the server responds with code 250 (and the keyboard value 8BITMIME) to the EHLO command, this is an indication that the server supports the extension and will accept MIME messages containing arbitrary octet-aligned material.

21. Borenstein, Nathaniel. *Internet Multimedia Mail with MIME: Emerging Standards for Interoperability*. Unpublished paper, 1992.

22. X.400 is a series of recommendations that define how an electronic mail message may be transported from one system to another and how such messages are addressed. In actual implementation, X.400 also entails a series of related standards, including X.401, which addresses basic intersystem service elements, X.410, which is concerned with defining mail-handling protocols, and X.411, which defines message-handling protocols.

X.400 and its parallel protocol, the Open Systems Interconnection (OSI) Message Handling System (MHS), are the so-called "flagship protocols" in the OSI stack. Many observers view X.400 as a key step toward universal interoperability, where everyone can send and receive electronic messages as part of a worldwide electronic community. Its many critics see X.400 as an unnecessarily complex and underdeveloped system, whose widespread acceptance, they fear, would stifle innovation and impede the progress of the networking community.

The reality is that unto themselves, current implementations of the X.400 MHS do tend to be comparatively too complicated, as well as often too demanding of system resources. They also tend to be unreliable; readers who follow postings to USENET groups such as comp.mail and comp.mail.misc will recall that during 1992 users of MCI Mail claimed bitterly about lost messages, both incoming and outgoing. Moreover, critics such as Marshall Rose have pronounced X.400 addressing "incomprehensible." Even users less critical than Rose find X.400 addressing, with its many variations on the keyword/value pairs, four different allowable configurations, and no official textual syntax, to be too demanding. Usually, X.400 will require more than sixty characters to address a message.

A more serious problem of X.400, given the needs and expectations of many users, is its failure to support the multimedia capabilities that its proponents often cite as one of X.400's most important advantages. According to Marshall Rose:

> [X.400] MHS simply does not specify enough information to allow for reliable exchanges of multi-media contents. In practical terms, this means that MHS does not provide a suitable backbone technology for many messaging environments.

Rose is critical of the fact that X.400 is not suited in its native form to providing transparent gateway services. He is also highly critical of the bulk-mode transfer facility, because the lack of address verification capabilities at this level means that a message transfer agent may accept delivery of a message that it cannot deliver at the user level. He suggests that it is more appropriate "to perform verification optionally followed by transfer."

Yet interest in X.400 is and will remain high, because there is a distinct possibility that it will be enhanced to support the more general exchange of complex documents, because X.400 addressing and related facilities may be used to transcend the numerical limits of the Internet addressing scheme, because it can be bound closely to X.500 directory services (which should tend in the long term to minimize, if not eliminate, most addressing problems), and because, notwithstanding the aforementioned criticism concerning the absence of an explicit gateway methodology, it provides in implementation a basis for integrating incompatible mail systems, e.g., through the facilities of a X.400 mail server, users of IBM PROFS mail, Microsoft Mail, Compuserve Mail, MCI Mail, and Internet mail could exchange messages without loss of information, owing to X.400's ability to re-address messages via its double enveloping capability.

23. It is important to note that not only does MIME-compliant mail not require any major change in the installed technological base for Internet mail, it can be

delivered to end-users without the acquisition of expensive equipment. In fact, many workstations and most Macintosh computers of recent vintage are ideally suited to the task. Intel's 80386 and 80486 computers running Microsoft Windows can also be outfitted without great difficulty to function in this environment.

24. The "low-end" Internet also offers "netnews"; a small but growing number of electronic journals; access to the online catalogs of several hundred research libraries, along with the more extensive library services offered by OCLC, RLIN (Research Libraries Information Network), and CARL (Colorado Alliance of Research Libraries); and a growing array of databases, archives, and services connected to the network by virtue of their location at universities or government-supported research facilities. Commercial traffic on the Internet is growing, too. Advanced Network Services (ANS), the consortium that manages the National Science Foundation backbone, has been authorized to offer commercial services via the Internet. As a result, several commercial database services, including DIALOG and Lexis/Nexis, are now accessible, and several other major services, including MEDLINE, are expected to be connected soon. Some private services, such as AT&T Mail, MCI Mail, and CompuServe Mail, have gateways to the Internet.

25. The notion of "knowbots" is the brainchild of Vinton Cerf, Vice President, Corporation for National Research Initiatives. In Cerf's view of the digital library system of the future, "knowbots" will be small, self-contained programs that move through networks, take up residence in different machines, and carry out algorithms or searches of relevant databases. The knowbots will be capable of communicating with each other, translating requests into specific formats, executing searches, and then, if necessary, incorporating the results of the search into a modified subsequent search.

The Internet and OCLC: Broadening Access to the World's Information

Tom Storey

SUMMARY. The Internet has provided OCLC with another delivery mechanism to support its chartered public purpose of expanding access to the world's information and reducing rising information costs. This network of networks has helped OCLC and its member libraries reach electronically a new audience of end users with new products and new technologies designed especially for them.

OCLC offers three reference products via the Internet: The First-Search Catalog, the EPIC service, and The Online Journal of Current Clinical Trials. All can be accessed using the Internet from an end-user's home, office, dorm room, laboratory, hotel room–or any other location with a modem nearby–as well as from a library.

FirstSearch is a new online information service designed for library patrons, with an end-user interface that allows patrons to move through the online search process in just a few simple steps, without special training or online searching experience.

The EPIC service is an online information service with a command interface designed for the advanced searcher.

Both of these services offer access to a number of databases, including the OCLC Online Union Catalog, an electronic card catalog of 28 million records used by more than 16,000 libraries.

Tom Storey is Marketing Communications Specialist, OCLC Online Computer Library Center, Inc.

Correspondence may be addressed to the author at his business address: OCLC, MC135, 6565 Frantz Road, Dublin, OH 43017-3395 or his Internet address: tom storey@oclc.org.

[Haworth co-indexing entry note]: "The Internet and OCLC: Broadening Access to the World's Information." Storey, Tom. Co-published simultaneously in *The Reference Librarian* (The Haworth Press, Inc.) No. 41/42, 1994, pp. 375-385; and: *Librarians on the Internet: Impact on Reference Services* (ed: Robin Kinder) The Haworth Press, Inc., 1994, pp. 375-385. Multiple copies of this article/chapter may be purchased from The Haworth Document Delivery Center [1-800-3-HAWORTH; 9:00 a.m. - 5:00 p.m. (EST)].

The Online Journal of Current Clinical Trials is the world's first electronic, full-text with graphics, peer-reviewed scientific journal. It combines the rigorous standards of the most prestigious research journals with the immediacy of online technology. This one-year old journal just became available over the Internet.

The fact that more than half of the access to FirstSearch and EPIC is via the Internet is a testament to the success of offering this access option.

INTRODUCTION

OCLC began when the presidents of 54 Ohio colleges and universities wanted their institutions' libraries to work together to reduce costs and improve services. In its Articles of Incorporation, OCLC championed a lofty public purpose:

> The purpose or purposes for which this Corporation is formed are to establish, maintain, and operate a computerized library network and to promote the evolution of library use, of libraries themselves, and of librarianship, and to provide processes and products for the benefit of library users and libraries, including such objectives as increasing availability of library resources to individual library patrons and reducing rate of rise of library per-unit costs, all for the fundamental public purpose of furthering ease of access to and use of the ever-expanding body of worldwide scientific, literary, and educational knowledge and information.[1]

For 20 years, fulfilling that purpose meant building an online computer network and bibliographic database for libraries to use to catalog and share their collections. The results of this library cooperation through the OCLC Online Union Catalog and Shared Cataloging system, forerunner to the PRISM service, are impressive:

- the world's preeminent database of 28 million bibliographic records with 470 million locations for the records
- more than 44 million interlibrary loan requests
- 22 million cataloging and 6 million interlibrary loan transactions annually

- 84 million messages per month–more than 65 per second–sent to the OCLC system

In addition to these impressive results, the impact the OCLC system had on library operations was just as profound: It saved the nation's libraries hundreds of millions of dollars and made their collections accessible to millions of additional students, teachers and researchers.[2]

For the last five years, as libraries have faced new challenges, OCLC's statement of purpose has taken on a broader meaning. To meet new needs, end-user services for online database searching, electronic publishing, and document ordering and delivery have been introduced. This expansion of OCLC's public purpose was driven by libraries and the same forces that brought them together in 1967 to form OCLC: economics, technology and the need to improve services.

For most libraries, the Information Age has brought a relentless rise in reference requests. Today's patrons have more information at their fingertips than at any time in history. And they expect libraries to help them find what they need and deliver it to them, regardless of where the information is.

The surge in information requests and patron service expectations has strained library staff and budget resources. One way libraries have coped, and will continue to cope, with this onslaught is to "help patrons take care of themselves" with end-user services. Affordable, electronic end-user services can help libraries better serve their patrons and reach their service vision of providing information to users when and where they need it.

THE INTERNET AND OCLC'S REFERENCE SERVICES

Paralleling OCLC's expansion into online end-user reference services has been the phenomenal growth of the Internet. The Internet is a largely government funded collection of networks that connects computers in government, university and commercial agencies. It provides users and libraries with electronic mail, access to databases and file transfer capabilities. It is doubling in size every six to 15 months.[3] An estimated 10 million people use the Internet, and many are those that libraries and OCLC serve and are trying to connect with electronically–college and university faculty, graduate students, undergraduates.

Its next phase, the National Research and Education Network (NREN), is envisioned as an enhanced and broadened Internet that eventually will provide "free" telecommunications service to colleges, universities, libraries and individuals connected with those institutions.

OCLC has long recognized the importance of the Internet as a tool for scholarly communication. Electronic mail is the most-used application by Internet users. About one-third of OCLC's staff have Internet accounts through which they communicate directly with librarians, patrons, and researchers, and monitor and participate in lively discussion groups.

However, providing database access is one of the fastest growing aspects of the Internet. It's easy to understand why. The Internet offers reduced telecommunications costs–the phone charges libraries and others pay to get to remote computers that house electronic databases. It also allows libraries/universities to leverage their hardware investment by letting them use the workstations and equipment they've already purchased. And finally, it enables libraries to serve patrons electronically from wherever they are–office, dorm room, laboratory– thereby expanding the reach of library services.

Although OCLC has its own computer network, it began making its reference services accessible via the Internet in November, 1990, for those reasons. The decision was based on OCLC's public purpose:

> The OCLC Network has always been and will remain a means to an end. Before alternatives such as the Internet, it was a necessary means. In terms of availability, reliability, and performance, it will continue to be a highly desirable means. Whether it remains a necessary means will depend on a number of factors over which OCLC has little control. Simply because of the current economics of telecommunications, however, we at OCLC believe that, over time, a transition from the OCLC network to the Internet and the NREN is likely. OCLC's basic objective is to help make this transition

as smooth as possible for its membership. OCLC is committed to increasing access to the world's information and reducing the rate of rise of costs of that information. OCLC is not committed to maintaining a proprietary network, or any other means to those ends, that is not in the membership's best interest . . . The Internet and the NREN offer libraries the tantalizing prospect of greatly reduced telecommunications costs, thereby freeing resources for other uses and easing some of the budgetary strain on collections and services.[4]

OCLC was recognized earlier this year for significant contributions related to the use of the Internet. In March, the Meckler Internet Applications award was presented to OCLC for its broad range of Internet involvement. The award recognized OCLC's efforts in not only providing reference services on the Internet, but also doing research about the Internet, and planning for future use of the Internet.

In January 1993, OCLC released a research report, Assessing Information on the Internet: Toward Providing Library Services for Computer Mediated Communications, which focused on determining the kind of information available on the Internet and the suitability of current library cataloging formats for describing information available.

In addition, OCLC outlined its future use of the Internet with "OCLC's Linking Strategy: Internet and NREN," a three-page white paper on OCLC's policies from 1992 to the year 2000 with respect to linking with the Internet and the NREN.

Despite the many advantages that the Internet offers, there are some disadvantages. For future service links, OCLC must consider the following:

- Reliability. Availability of the Internet varies from network to network and link to link, with some networks being highly reliable and others less so.
- Performance. Service levels and response time vary widely and could affect a library's productivity.
- Security. Open networks, such as the Internet, pose problems for information providers and users concerned with issues of security, proprietary software, and value added services.

- Reach. Not all libraries have access to the Internet.
- Support. Since the Internet has virtually no centralized governance structure, a library having technical difficulties may have to go through several layers of administration and support for problem resolution. OCLC can verify that its systems are operating and that its connection to the Internet is functioning properly. Beyond that, OCLC can only refer the library to the Internet support staff at its institution's computer center.

ACCESSING OCLC REFERENCE SERVICES VIA THE INTERNET

Internet users gain access to OCLC Reference Services using a protocol called Telnet. Telnet allows network users to log on to and communicate with a remote host computer system, such as the OCLC system, as if there were a direct connection between them.

Essentially, there are two ways a library can use Telnet to access OCLC Reference Services via the Internet.

The most common way is using a system-wide local area network (LAN). The library's local system is part of a LAN; the LAN is managed by a computer in a central computing center; this computer is connected to the Internet.

If there is no LAN, a library's local system can directly link to the Internet.

A major advantage of these methods is the ease at which remote as well as in-library access to OCLC Reference Services can be provided. Anyone who is wired to the LAN or to the library's local system, or who can dial into the LAN or the library's local system, can search from terminals in their office or home. Scripts can be written to supply the Telnet connection and the authorization number and password, making logon simple.

The other way a library can access OCLC Reference Services via the Internet is to dial into a third-party telecommunications carrier that is connected to the Internet. The library experiences a direct connect hour telecommunications cost with this method, but it is usually less than the costs of using a private network. The user will have to know the OCLC Reference Services Internet address (telnet epic.prod.oclc.org for FirstSearch and EPIC), the authorization number, and the password.

OCLC REFERENCE SERVICES AVAILABLE VIA THE INTERNET

OCLC offers three reference products via the Internet: The First-Search Catalog, the EPIC service, and The Online Journal of Current Clinical Trials. All can be accessed using the Internet from an end-user's home, office, dorm room, laboratory, hotel room–or any other location with a modem nearby–as well as from the library. There is no change in functionality or the look of any of these services when users access via the Internet versus accessing via another network.

OCLC also is building a number of Internet listservers where users can get online documentation, news articles, searching tips, and be part of a discussion group on electronic publishing.

The FirstSearch Catalog

FirstSearch is a new online information service designed for the library patron, with an end-user interface that allows patrons to move through the online search process in just a few simple steps, without special training or online searching experience. As of August 1993, it provides access to 39 databases, including some exclusive offerings: the OCLC Online Union Catalog, called WorldCat on FirstSearch; two OCLC serials databases, ArticleFirst and ContentsFirst; the MLA Bibliography; Consumers Index; A Matter of Fact. Seventeen H.W. Wilson Company databases are or soon will be mounted on FirstSearch, too.

FirstSearch also provides electronic document ordering, either through a commercial article supplier, Dynamic Information or UMI Article Clearinghouse, or through another library using OCLC's PRISM Interlibrary Loan (ILL) system.

Currently, two FirstSearch databases offer document ordering from commercial vendors; eventually, most will. Users can compare article prices online and select fax, overnight courier, or regular mail as the delivery method.

In addition, three-letter location symbols from more than 5,000 OCLC libraries are linked to records in most FirstSearch databases, enabling users to locate libraries that have needed items. A link to the OCLC PRISM ILL system is available for the OCLC database and ArticleFirst and will be made available for most FirstSearch databases so that users can send interlibrary loan requests for monographs, articles or other materials they want.

FirstSearch is priced by the search or by the year. Libraries can buy searches in blocks of 500; the more they buy the lower the per-search cost. Or they can pay a flat fee for unlimited searching for one year. There are no database connect-hour or record-display charges with FirstSearch. And there is no OCLC telecommunications connect hour charge for accessing FirstSearch via the Internet. Internet access, along with FirstSearch's pricing structure, frees libraries and end-users from having to worry about running up large connect time charges.

FirstSearch is proving to be an effective reference tool for end users, and the Internet is facilitating remote end-user use.

The Ohio State University library offers FirstSearch as an option in a library services menu accessible on the university's Campus Wide Information Service: "Providing such an end-user system in the CWIS environment truly accomplished the task of moving library tools into the campus' working environment."[5]

The University of Hawaii at Hilo concurs. "With the Internet, access to FirstSearch is quick and ubiquitous. Any terminal on campus connected to our Computing Center can quickly log on to FirstSearch. Faculty enjoy the independence of searching in their offices, laboratories or homes through remote dial-up access."[6] Currently, more than 600 libraries subscribe to FirstSearch, and end users are doing an average of 15,000 searches a day. Approximately 70% of the access to FirstSearch each month is via the Internet.

The FIRSTSEARCH-L listserv is a public list maintained by OCLC to provide machine-readable files containing news articles and user documentation for FirstSearch. Users can request files or subscribe to FIRSTSEARCH-L. Users who subscribe automatically receive news stories with searching tips, system features, and database news, OCLC news releases about FirstSearch when they are issued, and announcements of new and revised documentation files.

Less than six months old, FIRSTSEARCH-L already has more than 250 subscribers.

The EPIC Service

EPIC is an online information service with a command interface designed for the professional searcher. As of August 1993, it offers access to 42 databases, most of which are the same databases as FirstSearch, including the OCLC Online Union Catalog and the OCLC serials databases.

Three-letter location symbols from more than 5,000 OCLC libraries also are linked to records in most EPIC databases, to help users locate libraries that have needed items.

EPIC offers users more sophisticated searching features than FirstSearch, such as the Boolean Operator OR, character masking, nested parentheses, and command stacking. The EPIC search language is based on the NISO standard Z39.58.

EPIC is priced like most standard online information systems: database connect-hour and record-display charges. There is no OCLC telecommunications connect-hour charge for accessing EPIC via the Internet.

Use of the Internet reduces a library's overall EPIC costs, since no telecommunications connect time is charged. The savings on a 15 minute search can range from $0.57 to more than $2.50.

Users are doing approximately 5,000 searches a day on EPIC, and about one-quarter of the access each month is via the Internet.

OCLC Electronic Journals Online

OCLC Electronic Journals Online (EJO) is OCLC's new electronic publishing service. The first journal published under EJO is *The Online Journal of Current Clinical Trials (OJCCT)*, the world's first electronic, full-text with graphics, peer-reviewed scientific journal. It combines the rigorous standards of the most prestigious research journals with the immediacy of online technology.

Published by the American Association for the Advancement of Science and distributed electronically by OCLC, OJCCT reports medical findings with unprecedented speed, eliminating the delays that often occur with print journals. Unlike print journals, it is not arranged by issue. Publication is continuous; as soon as an article passes peer review, it is available online within 48 hours. Articles are not shortened or delayed because of space limitations.

Subscribers access the journal using GUIDON, windows-based PC software developed by OCLC that combines intuitive, full-text searching with sophisticated graphical images. GUIDON presents the full text of a journal, including figures, tables, and equations, in a quality that rivals the typeset page. It also allows a large amount of flexibility to readers, who can customize the search and display features to suit their needs.

OJCCT also supports a command driven ASCII interface that runs on a terminal or PC with software emulating a VT100 terminal.

OJCCT is available to libraries and individuals on a subscription basis. There is no OCLC telecommunications connect hour charge for accessing OJCCT via the Internet.

There are more than 1,000 subscribers to OJCCT. About 40% of the access each month is via the Internet. Access via the Internet addresses a very big goal of electronic publishing: to get material available to users directly, obviating a trip to the library.

By the end of 1993, OCLC should have added two more electronic journals that will be available via the Internet.

The *Online Journal of Knowledge Synthesis for Nursing* will provide critical reviews of research literature to guide nursing practice and research. The publisher is Sigma Theta Tau, the International Honor Society of Nursing.

Electronics Letters Online will present the same 1,400 to 1,500 articles per year that appear in the print version of the prestigious biweekly journal of international electronics research, *Electronics Letters*. The publisher is the Institution of Electrical Engineers (IEE). Through links to IEE's INSPEC database, subscribers also will have access to abstracts of references cited in the articles. The INSPEC database is the world's largest and most comprehensive source of reference literature in the field of physics, electrical and control engineering, electronics and computing.

The OCLC-JOURNALS listserv disseminates information about OCLC's new Electronic Journals Online publishing service. Details of new GUIDON software releases and system upgrades are announced via the listserv and subscribers are notified when new articles are published in OJCCT. Descriptive material, pricing and subscription information are retrievable through the listserv. OCLC-JOURNALS has more than 500 subscribers and eventually will become a moderated discussion list.

CONCLUSIONS

The Internet has provided OCLC with another delivery mechanism to support its public purpose of expanding access to the world's information and reducing information costs. It has helped OCLC and its member libraries reach a new audience of end users with new products and new technologies designed especially for them. And it is proving to be a good vehicle to deliver services to end users. The fact that more than one-half the access to OCLC's reference services is via the Internet is a testament to the success of offering this access option.

OCLC is committed to integrating its activities into the emerging, digital, broadband, global community.[7] As part of that strategy, OCLC is committed to linking with the Internet to broaden access to OCLC services while helping libraries leverage investments they've made in terminals, local area networks, and local systems.

REFERENCES

1. OCLC, Amended Articles of Incorporation, as filed December 23, 1977.

2. Smith, K. Wayne, "OCLC: Lifeline in Sea of Information," Business First, September 2, 1991, p. 13, excerpts from a July 29, 1991 speech to the Columbus Rotary Club.

3. Bajak, Frank, "Planet is Being Wired for the Information Age," The Columbus Dispatch, May 30, 1993: p. Bl.

4. OCLC, "OCLC's Linking Strategy: Internet and NREN," August 1992.

5. Snure, Karen R., "The FirstSearch Experience at the Ohio State University, Library Hi Tech, Issue 36–9:4 (1991): p. 31.

6. Roddy, Kevin, "FirstSearch Makes a Splash," PAC-News, Issue 42 (September 1992): p. 3.

7. OCLC, "Journey to the 21st Century, A Summary of OCLC's Strategic Plan," October, 1991: p. 11.

Index

Page numbers in italics indicate figures; page numbers followed by t indicate tables

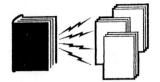

Haworth
DOCUMENT DELIVERY
SERVICE
and Local Photocopying Royalty Payment Form

This new service provides (a) a single-article order form for any article from a Haworth journal and (b) a convenient royalty payment form for local photocopying (not applicable to photocopies intended for resale).

- *Time Saving:* No running around from library to library to find a specific article.
- *Cost Effective:* All costs are kept down to a minimum.
- *Fast Delivery:* Choose from several options, including same-day FAX.
- *No Copyright Hassles:* You will be supplied by the original publisher.
- *Easy Payment:* Choose from several easy payment methods.

Open Accounts Welcome for . . .
- Library Interlibrary Loan Departments
- Library Network/Consortia Wishing to Provide Single-Article Services
- Indexing/Abstracting Services with Single Article Provision Services
- Document Provision Brokers and Freelance Information Service Providers

MAIL or *FAX* THIS ENTIRE ORDER FORM TO:

Attn: **Marianne Arnold**
Haworth Document Delivery Service
The Haworth Press, Inc.
10 Alice Street
Binghamton, NY 13904-1580

or **FAX:** (607) 722-1424
or **CALL:** 1-800-3-HAWORTH
(1-800-342-9678; 9am-5pm EST)

PLEASE SEND ME PHOTOCOPIES OF THE FOLLOWING SINGLE ARTICLES:

1) Journal Title: _____
  Vol/Issue/Year: _____ Starting & Ending Pages: _____
Article Title: _____

2) Journal Title: _____
  Vol/Issue/Year: _____ Starting & Ending Pages: _____
Article Title: _____

3) Journal Title: _____
  Vol/Issue/Year: _____ Starting & Ending Pages: _____
Article Title: _____

4) Journal Title: _____
  Vol/Issue/Year: _____ Starting & Ending Pages: _____
Article Title: _____

(See other side for Costs and Payment Information)

COSTS: Please figure your cost to order quality copies of an article.

1. Set-up charge per article: $8.00
   ($8.00 × number of separate articles) _____

2. Photocopying charge for each article:
   - 1-10 pages: $1.00 _____
   - 11-19 pages: $3.00 _____
   - 20-29 pages: $5.00 _____
   - 30+ pages: $2.00/10 pages _____

3. Flexicover (optional): $2.00/article _____

4. Postage & Handling: US: $1.00 for the first article/
   $.50 each additional article _____
   Federal Express: $25.00 _____
   Outside US: $2.00 for first article/
   $.50 each additional article _____

5. Same-day FAX service: $.35 per page _____

6. Local Photocopying Royalty Payment: should you wish to copy the article yourself. Not intended for photocopies made for resale. $1.50 per article per copy
   (i.e. 10 articles x $1.50 each = $15.00) _____

   GRAND TOTAL: _____

METHOD OF PAYMENT: (please check one)

❏ Check enclosed   ❏ Please ship and bill. PO # _____
(sorry we can ship and bill to bookstores only! All others must pre-pay)

❏ Charge to my credit card: ❏ Visa;   ❏ MasterCard;   ❏ American Express;

Account Number: _____ Expiration date: _____

Signature: X _____ Name: _____

Institution: _____ Address: _____

City: _____ State: _____ Zip: _____

Phone Number: _____ FAX Number: _____

MAIL or *FAX* THIS ENTIRE ORDER FORM TO:

Attn: **Marianne Arnold**
Haworth Document Delivery Service
The Haworth Press, Inc.
10 Alice Street
Binghamton, NY 13904-1580

or FAX: (607) 722-1424
or CALL: 1-800-3-HAWORTH
(1-800-342-9678; 9am-5pm EST)